UNSPEAKABLE Violence

A book in the series
LATIN AMERICA OTHERWISE:
LANGUAGES, EMPIRES, NATIONS

Series editors:
Walter D. Mignolo, Duke University
Irene Silverblatt, Duke University
Sonia Saldívar-Hull, University of Texas, San Antonio

Nicole M. Guidotti-Hernández

UNSPEAKABLE Violence

✳

REMAPPING U.S. AND MEXICAN NATIONAL IMAGINARIES

Duke University Press   Durham and London   2011

© 2011 Duke University Press

All rights reserved

Printed in the United States of America on acid-free paper ∞

Designed by Heather Hensley

Typeset in Minion Pro by Keystone Typesetting, Inc.

Library of Congress Cataloging-in-Publication Data appear
on the last printed page of this book.

To my parents and sister—

thank you for breaking the silence—

and the people whom I write about

in this book, for presenting an

opportunity to counter the silence.

✳ Contents

✳ About the Series

Latin America Otherwise: Languages, Empires, Nations is a critical series. It aims to explore the emergence and consequences of concepts used to define "Latin America" while at the same time exploring the broad interplay of political, economic, and cultural practices that have shaped Latin American worlds. Latin America, at the crossroads of competing imperial designs and local responses, has been construed as a geocultural and geopolitical entity since the nineteenth century. This series provides a starting point to redefine Latin America as a configuration of political, linguistic, cultural, and economic intersections that demands a continuous reappraisal of the role of the Americas in history, and of the ongoing process of globalization and the relocation of people and cultures that have characterized Latin America's experience. Latin America Otherwise: Languages, Empires, Nations is a forum that confronts established geocultural constructions, rethinks area studies and disciplinary boundaries, assesses convictions of the academy and of public policy, and correspondingly demands that the practices through which we produce knowledge and understanding about and from Latin America be subject to rigorous and critical scrutiny.

Unspeakable Violence is an innovative and thoroughly researched book that takes us to archival material, finds it silent about subaltern history, and transitions us to a different articulation of Mexican and American Indian, Mexican American and Chicana/o subjectivities. While mindful of the foundational explorations of mestizaje offered by Anzaldúa and other scholars, Guidotti-Hernández deploys a meticulously historicized and theorized methodology that opens up a counter-nationalist argument against merely celebratory, romanticized visions of identity and resistance and begins to fill in the aporias ignored by the contradictions in a border history and border studies inattentive to Mexican and Mexican American complicity in instances of sexual and racial violence. As with other texts in this series, *Unspeakable Violence* gives voice to the "otherwise" in the Latin Americas: Mexicans, Mexican Americans, American Indians, and Chicana/os.

✳ A Note on Terminology

The terms I use to label persons or groups living in the past and present are as complex as the question of identity itself. In general I use the same terms as the historical documents I rely on in each chapter. In some cases the terminology is blurred, and I attempt to flesh out the meaning of identification by disputing the ways in which certain terms are used. The following are definitions of the identity labels I use in the text:

Chicano/a	A label that arose from the Mexican American civil rights movement during the 1960s to describe an individual who is politically active and aware of the importance of race and class differences
Indian	Term used by the U.S. government and newspapers to describe Natives of North America
Indígena	Mexican Indian
Indigenous	Describes aboriginal or tribal first peoples of the Americas
Latina/o	Term that arose in the late twentieth century to describe peoples of Latin America who have been colonized and dispersed throughout the Americas
Mestiza/o	A person of mixed Spanish, African, and Indian ancestry

Mexican/Mexicana/o	A person born and raised in Mexico in either the nineteenth century or the twentieth
Mexican American	A person of Mexican descent born in the United States, mostly used in the twentieth century
Mestizaje	Used to describe the process of racial and cultural mixing in the Americas as a result of contact with Spanish colonialism. Also an ideology developed by José Vasconcelos as a mode of Mexican nationalism that called for the whitening of the race, that is, breeding out the indigenous and African qualities of the Mexican race.
Native	A North American Indian
North American Indian	A member of any of the tribal peoples native to the continental United States
Texas-Mexican	Term Jovita González uses to describe nineteenth- and twentieth-century Mexicans who inhabited Texas
Transnational	Refers to the circuits of goods, people, capital, ideas, and policies between and among nations
U.S. Mexican/U.S. Mexicana/o	A Mexican in the United States in the nineteenth century who was born in the territories of Mexico prior to annexation of what is now the U.S. Southwest (Texas, Arizona, New Mexico, California) and who remained in the United States after annexation

✳ Acknowledgments

Violence touches all of our lives in some way, shape, or form. I see this book as the beginning of a dialogue rather than an end to a project. It involved years of archival work, tears, frustration, and joy. I am thankful it has become something better than what I imagined at its inception. This could not have happened without the support of many people, including those whose lives I narrate as part of this project's argument. I can only hope I have done justice to the fine-grained stories of so many and would like to express my respect to those whose impassioned histories form the core of this book.

This project began while I was a student at Cornell University. My dissertation chair, Laura Donaldson, stepped forward and was a steady advocate and demanding critic. María Cristina García was an instrumental mentor and dissertation advisor, pushing me to think about the tension between history and literature, always reminding me of the multiple fields with which my work was in dialogue. Mary Pat Brady turned my attention to the centuries-old struggles of Yaqui peoples in the Sonora-Arizona borderlands and greatly helped shape the second half of the book. Collectively, their encouragement to envision the project as more firmly grounded in historical methodologies does not go unrecognized. My core friends from my time in Ithaca, including Leslie Alexander, Susie Lee, Eliza Rodríguez y Gibson, Helena María Viramontes, Pamela Blunt, Nohemy Solorzano, Luivette Resto, Adela Ramos, Peter Choi, Jason DeMera, Michelle Scott, Ángel David Nieves, Angela Cheung, Juan Baharona, Gabriela Sandoval, Jean Kim, Lisa Brooks, and Jose Talavera, created an intellectual community and surrogate family when things were tough.

The staffs at various archives throughout the United States and Mexico were invaluable to the completion of my book. Larraine Daly-Jones of the Arizona Historical Society in Tucson was gracious enough to share materials on the Hughes family and take me into the bowels of the museum collection. The staff in Special Collections at the University of Arizona provided invaluable research support, as did the staff at the Arizona State Museum; Special

Collections at Texas State University, San Marcos; the Bancroft Library at the University of California, Berkeley; the Nettie Lee Benson Collection at the University of Texas, Austin; the California State Library; the Los Angeles Public Library; UCLA Special Collections; Special Collections at San Jose State University; Special Collections at Texas A&M, Corpus Christi; and the Sharlott Hall Museum in Prescott, Arizona. Hugo Martinez fue un guía inapreciable del archivo Genaro Estrada SRE en el Distrito Federal. No hubiera acabado el trabajo sin su ayuda ni sin la ayuda de Monica Toussiant del Instituto Mora. Además, Aracelli Téllez Trejo y sú colega Teresa Matabuena-Peláez, la directora de acervos, y el personal de la Biblioteca de Francisco Xavier Clavigero de la Universidad Iberoamericana fueron tan amables e hicieron los meses de trabajo agradables y productivos. Javier Gámez-Chávez y Enriqueta Lerma generosamente compartieron materiales sobre los Yaquis. Quiero agradecerle a Jonathan Bird, quien sirvió como guía de la cultura del Archivo General de la Nación. También me ayudaron mucho el personal de Galeria 6 y Erika Gutiérrez Mosqueda del centro de referencias del AGN.

The technical aspects of this book formed a major set of tasks along the way. I would like to thank my former research assistants Tina Mendoza, Julia Barajas, Esmeralda Rodríguez, and Florencia Chilavo for their judicious ability to gather materials. I also thank Manuel González Canche, who helped prepare the statistical data for chapters 4 and 5. Paul Lobue at Mapping Specialists was particularly accommodating in producing the maps, graphs, and charts, while Kirsteen Anderson's editing, Patricia Rosas's translation work, and Araceli Esparza's indexing work all helped refine the overall quality of the book. Laura Briggs organized a department-wide seminar that provided the final set of critiques that helped urge the project to its completion.

The project could not have been completed without the financial support of various institutions and foundations. A Five Colleges Minority Dissertation Fellowship at Amherst College allowed me to complete my dissertation and plan the book. A WOSAC faculty fellowship provided crucial release time to work in the archives at the Arizona Historical Society. An SBS Faculty Small Grant from the University of Arizona funded my initial research in Mexico City. The postdoctoral fellowship in the Center for Race, Politics and Culture at the University of Chicago proved invaluable as I was finishing the first half of the book. I would like to especially thank the director of the Center, Waldo Johnson, as well as the staff and friends I made while there: Theresa Mah, Jessica Sparks, Tracye Matthews, Travis Jackson, John Eason, Sheldon Lyke, Jillian Báez, and Dave Ferguson. The workshop provided by the Center afforded me a very helpful critique of the chapter on Camp Grant and also introduced me to Julie Saville, a generous scholar indeed. The J. William Fulbright postdoctoral research fellowship made this book historically accountable. I could not have done justice to the transnational scope of the project without the fellowship support. The staff of COMEXUS, especially Tim Wright, Maggie Hug, and Leticia Becerril, provided the best administrative support one could ask for during my time in the Distrito Federal. Furthermore, my hosts en el Programa de Estudios de Genero en la UNAM fueron increíbles. Doy mil gracias en particular a las directoras, Marisa Belausteguigoitia y Lucía Melgar, y al personal, sobre todo Claudia de Anda y Arelhí Galacia, provedores de mi segunda casa intelectual. A special thank you to Sandra Rosenthal, who guided me through the labyrinth that is the INAH collection and to Benjamín Alonso Rascón, who helped with my work in the AGS. My cadre of friends in Mexico City proved indispensable during the final stages of my work: Chris Fraga, Gabrielle Civil, Angela Herren, Cyntia Barrera, Stephany Slaughter, Noreen Steinke y mi querido y precioso amigo Rodrigo Laguarda. Él me ayudó mucho con las traducciones y con la vida en general. Quiero agradecer a Anita Khashu, mi DF writing partner, with whom I faithfully worked at the Fondo de Cultura Económica en la Condesa during the final stages of writing the book. I could not have finished this book without all of your support, diversión, and friendship in the magical city I love so dearly.

I have been blessed with various mentors and scholars who have taken an interest in my work and professional growth over the years, and I thank them for their support: George Sánchez, Sonia-Saldívar-Hull, Sally Deutsch, Eliana Rivero, María Teresa Vélez, Josie Saldaña-Portillo, Laura Pulido, Norma Cantú, Raquel Rubio-Goldsmith, Montserrat Fontes, Sherm Cochrane, Margo Hendricks, Barry O'Connell, Judy Frank, Andy Parker, Marisa Parham, Karen Sánchez-Eppler, Emma Perez, Abel Valenzuela, Alicia Schmidt-Camacho, Mari Castañeda, Yolanda Broyles-González, KarenMary Davalos, Tiffany Ana López, Eithne Lubheid, Antonia Castañeda, Helena María Viramontes, Susan Gilman, and Michael Cowan.

My book has benefited tremendously from its exposure to various audiences. First, I would like to thank Luis Álvarez and Raúl Ramos of the Mexican American History workshop at the University of Houston for selecting my paper for the seminar in 2003. I faced some tough, nonfeminist criticism there, and the support of these two scholars along with that of George Sánchez was formative in my thinking about making the arguments about Josefa/Juanita's lynching sharp and provocative. Further, audiences at SUNY Buffalo in the Global Gender Studies Department; Gender and Women's Studies at Rutgers University; Latina and Latino Studies at Northwestern University; the department of Spanish, Latin American and Latino Studies at Mt. Holyoke College; and the Center for Race, Politics and Culture at the University of Chicago helped refine many portions of the argument.

Two major groups of people and institutions have largely shaped this project: the Department of Gender and Women's Studies at the University of Arizona and the Tepoztlán Institute for Transnational History of the Americas. Little did I know how instrumental my senior colleague and academic madrina, Laura Briggs, would be in helping the book become what it is today. Briggs encouraged my work from the outset and introduced me to the Tepoztlán collective, one of the most innovative and encouraging environments in which a young scholar can think about transnational history from an interdisciplinary perspective. It is amazing to have such a group of colleagues who care so deeply about reshaping the field, and they have left a lasting impression on my heart and my work. I would especially like to thank David Kazanjian, Pamela Voekel, Elliott Young, Bethany Moreton, Lizbeth Haas, Mikol Siegel, David Sartorious, Yolanda Martínez San Miguel, Freddy Vilches, Jill Lane, Laura Gutiérrez, Maria Elena Martínez, and Josie Saldaña-Portillo for creating such a marvelous intellectual space with Marxist feminist principles as the foundation of the conference ethos. At the Tepoztlán Institute in 2008 and 2009, Renato Rosaldo, Lizbeth Haas, Josie Saldaña-Portillo, David Kazanjian, Lessie Jo Frasier, and Marisa Belausteguigoitia were exceptional readers who pushed me to refine my critiques of violence, nationalism, and indigenous history.

The Department of Gender and Women's Studies and its affiliated faculty have proved indispensable in this process. Several colleagues have read versions of this work, including Eithne Lubheid, Liz Kennedy, Judy Temple, Raquel Rubio-Goldsmith, Carlos Gallegos, Laura Gutiérrez, Julio Cammarota, Maribel Álvarez, Adam Geary, and Caryl Flinn. These colleagues, along with Miranda Joseph, Jennifer Croissant, Sally Stevens, and Sandy Soto, have also contributed to an intellectual environment in which transnational Chicana and Latina studies are taken seriously in a Gender and Women's Studies context. I am particularly grateful to Liz Kennedy and Laura Briggs, who have gone beyond the call of duty to mentor my work. My debt to them both is enduring. My students, past and present, have shaped how I do my work: Tina Mendoza, Natalia de Rook, Shiori Yamamoto, Adrián Flores, Dylan Simosko, Randi Tanglen, Marcela García-Castañón, Julia Barajas, Marc Rivera, Jasmine Kramer, and Michelle Espino. Further, the Women's Studies Advisory Council book group deserves special recognition for providing a space to do a different kind of work, linking community, the empowerment of women, and a love of literature that I cherish.

I could not have completed this book without my friends and family. Elisa López de Nava, Lonnee Apperley, Sobieda Vizcarra, and Belinda Lum have been there from the beginning, and I am blessed to have their emotional support and unconditional friendship. I also want to thank Belinda for serving as an outside reader various times for fellowship applications and talking through the work when I needed direction. There are several people who have read some or all of this manuscript who are dear friends and wonderful colleagues. I would especially like to thank Carlos Decena, David Kazanjian, Felicity Grabiel, Nancy Raquel Mirabal, Wilson Valentín, Maribel Alvárez, Laura Gutiérrez, Cynthia Velásquez-Duarte, Eliza Rodríguez y Gibson, Josie Saldaña-Portillo, and Deb Vargas. Their comments and careful critiques were essential. Carlos deserves special recognition, as we traded manuscripts in Mexico City, one of the most fun and productive meetings of the minds I have ever experienced.

There are a number of people I absolutely adore who have made this process bearable: Gerry Cadava, Jenny Lee, Mako Fitts, Raul Coronado, Stacy Macias, Cynthia Velásquez-Duarte, Jason Ruiz, Lorena Muñoz, Luis Álvarez, Frank Guridy, Deborah Paredez, Ray Hernández-Durán, and Jose Ángel Hernández, who pushed me to think about the work in Mexico from the beginning. My Tucson crew, Adam Geary, Rosa and Damian Baeza, Al McDonald, Alan Osburn, Sandra Morse, Stephanie Ruiz, John Moreno, Patricia Espinosa Artiles, Manuel Muñoz, the Garcia family, Maritza Cardenas, Bram Acosta, and Fred Rodríguez and his entire family have helped make this place tolerable and laughable. I thank all for bringing me back to earth and taking me away from the academy when I needed it most.

While my family may not have always completely understood what I have been doing for the last seven years, they have been supportive in the best way they know how. I am especially appreciative of my sister Kathy, who has been my number one fan from the start. My parents, Richard and Clara Guidotti, along with my late grandfather Joseph Guidotti, nurtured a curious little kid who liked history and allowed her to become a voracious reader and dedicated researcher committed to social justice, sometimes without even knowing it. My parents were especially helpful and compassionate while I was in Mexico City, and I am thankful for it. My immediate families, the Guidotti family, the Hernández family (especially my grandma Valentina), and the LaMacchias deserve my thanks because they have formed an interested and encouraging audience throughout the years. I would especially like to thank my Aunt Susan and cousin Stephanie for their good humor and continual interest.

Finally, I would like to thank the anonymous readers at Duke University Press for their extensive feedback. My editor Reynolds Smith and Sonia Saldívar-Hull deserve special credit for believing in this project from its inception. Duke University Press is the perfect home for this book, and I thank them both for shepherding it through the process. Special thanks to Courtney Berger for seeing it through the final stages of completion. Mil gracias a todos.

An earlier version of chapter 1 appeared as "Reading Violence, Making Chicana Subjectivities" in *Technofuturos: critical interventions in Latina/o studies*, edited by Nancy Raquel Mirabal and Agustín Laó-Montes (Lexington Books, 2007).

A portion of chapter 4 appeared in "National Appropriations: Yaqui Autonomy, the Centennial of the Mexican Revolution and the Bicentennial of the Mexican Nation." *Latin Americanist* 55, issue 1 (March 2011): 69–92.

✳ Introduction

While visiting my parents for Christmas in 2007 I read *Via Magazine*, a publication of the California Automobile Association. Reading it when I am home is a kind of ritual. I always read it with a bit of nostalgia for California, the place I left behind. This issue of the magazine, for September/October 2007, was of particular interest. An article entitled "Downieville: A Former Mining Town in the Sierra Revels in Its Golden Years," chronicled the heyday of this community of 325 people in the Tahoe National Forest. The article describes how the town maintains some of its vintage charm, including "19th century clapboard and brick buildings, narrow lanes and creaky wooden sidewalks, [where] the past feels closer than it does anywhere else in California."[1] As he interviewed locals for the article, some of them in their nineties, the author, Christopher Hall, discovered that "it doesn't take long to realize that folks in Downieville love stories."[2] This love of stories in Downieville, the seat of Sierra County, was born with the influx of up to sixteen thousand prospectors who rushed to the area after gold was discovered in the Downie River in 1848–49. There are still rumors that someone unwittingly found a gold nugget in a pot used to cook river trout. Downieville is a town whose very genesis was tied to a fiercely competitive economic market, where in the mid-nineteenth century people were willing to do anything to strike it rich panning for gold.[3] To this day, tourists can do as the article recommends and visit the Sierra Hardware store, located at 305 Main Street, where they can purchase gear to pan for gold. Yet hidden or buried in this article is the not-so-golden shadow history of Downieville. In a few short sentences Hall makes a cursory allusion to its almost unspeakable past: "You might be nursing a cold one under the watchful gaze of a stuffed bear head at the St. Charles Place Saloon where you overhear two locals debating whether Juanita deserved to get lynched. It may take you a while to figure out . . . the events in question took place more than 150 years ago, not last week. . . . Next to the county courthouse, in a grove of trees you'll come across a restored 1885 gallows. It hasn't been used since the year it was built, and then only once. And well, that's another story."[4]

A reader of this passage might think it comes from a historical document rather than a magazine designed to promote tourism in California. The gallows erected in 1885 to hang convicted people for the crimes they committed in this gold rush community are "another story," as is the lynching of Juanita in 1851 (she is variously referred to in sources as Josefa). These two details are the foundation for basic questions raised in this book. There is something exceedingly disturbing about Josefa/Juanita appearing in a tourist magazine. The banality of evil, the cursory reference to her lynching in the magazine juxtapose death and tourism as the picturesque that renders it minor, grotesque, and yet traumatic. The outrage I experienced at seeing this woman held up as an article of touristic interest is indescribable. Over the past ten years I have collected countless one-sentence references to Downieville and Juanita's lynching because they make me angry. And there is great reason to be angry: through these references the juxtaposition of death, tourism, and lynching becomes quotidian and yet spectacular. These fragments, these utterances seem almost unspeakable; that is, people allude to the event but rarely, if ever, flesh out the details. I call these references utterances because they do something, they posit something, and thus they imply action.[5] Strangely, these utterances are about the flesh, about violence that culminated in the brutal destruction of a woman's body at a time when California's statehood was new and precarious in the 1850s, but they suspend further investigation, preventing the reader from engaging with these narratives of violence on a deeper level.

Such barely noteworthy references to Juanita's lynching can be skipped over, forgotten, or seen as local color, as they typically are; or the lack of detail in their strategic repetition may be understood as a way of instructing us to forget. Precisely because these cursory references say nothing and say everything, I wanted to know why Juanita (Josefa?), a Mexican woman living in the mining town on the banks of the Yuba and Downie rivers, met her brutal, torturous death over their waters. These few lines from an article written for tourists are typical of the way Juanita's lynching has been reported over time and space. There is something grotesque about the fact that the lynching of a woman appears in a tourism article. The grotesqueness of lynching as tourism in these cursory lines evokes the ways in which violence occurred situationally and further how U.S. Mexicanas (female subjects) were and continue to be conceived of in relationship to national history, citizenship, and racialized, sexualized violence.[6]

Josefa/Juanita's story, or lack thereof, said something to me through these shadow utterances that populated the texts I read about California, about the gold rush, about Chicana/o historiography. Josefa/Juanita as a historical subject disappears in these one-line utterances, and all we are left with is fragments of what her life was like. We don't know why she was lynched, how much she suffered when she was hanged, what happened to her body, how she understood her citizenship, how many people were involved in the lynching, or what it meant to be the first Mexican woman lynched in California after statehood. While some might argue that lynching was a common form of punishment in the wild West,[7] what is different and crucial about this one is that women were rarely lynched, and those who were usually were women of color.[8] Given my academic training, I was most concerned with how Josefa/Juanita's racial, gender, and sexual identities played a role in how and why she was lynched and in how the event is narrated.

In this book I investigate the history behind moments such as this one, by arguing that violence is an ongoing social process of differentiation for racialized, sexualized, gendered subjects in the U.S. borderlands in the nineteenth century and early twentieth. I explore the stories of four distinct episodes of borderlands violence: Josefa/Juanita's lynching in 1851, the Camp Grant Indian massacre of 1871, anthropological erasures of racialized and sexualized violence in South Texas in the nineteenth century and early twentieth, and the Yaqui Indian wars of 1880–1910. These diverse events in the U.S.–Mexico borderlands (California, Arizona, Texas, Sonora, and Chihuahua) reveal how regionally situated Aravaipa, Pinal, and Lipan Apache, Anglo emigrants, Chicana/os, Comanche, Mexicans, Papago, Yaqui, U.S. Mexicana/os (that is, Mexicans in the nineteenth century who were geopolitically relocated to the United States as a result of the Treaty of Guadalupe Hidalgo), and their varied relationships to colonialism provide a narrative of systematic patterns of violence as social transformation. Not all Mexicans, Indians, and Anglos are considered equal in this text. Regional identities, government policies, and economic conditions, understood as both U.S. and Mexican colonial residues, drastically affected how one's citizenship, or lack thereof and racial positioning as Anglo, Mexican, or Indian were perceived. Racial positioning, gender, and class alliances were fragile and shifted according to need and economic conditions. Some categories of identity seem to have been more fixed than others.

This book is not a narrative of resistance. The story I tell is not a happy one, yet there is a graciousness to the intervention I'm trying to make. I take up my case studies because they have been or easily could be part of a resistance narrative, the very thing I cautiously try not to reproduce. Hence, I make three basic arguments that unseat and question resistance narratives: first, there is a disjuncture between the celebratory narratives of mestizaje (social, racial, and cultural hybridity as a formation of the Spanish colonial collision with Indians in the Americas) and hybridity that compose Mexican, Chicana/o, and other nationalisms and the literally unspeakable violence that characterized the borderlands in the nineteenth century and the early twentieth. Second, violence is and was the one factor that determined how racial positioning, gender, and class alliances played themselves out in contests over citizenship and resources. Third, the formalistic reporting of these events follows a similar pattern of using repetition as a way of denying violence as a foundation of national history, making these events unspeakable.

The materials I work with convey a sense of immediacy about dealings with dissident populations. As Ranajit Guha, a historian of peasant revolts in India, has shown, official statements are often written either concurrently with or soon after an event. Further, participants in the broad sense, either as actors or as interested onlookers, often wrote accounts.[9] Most important, Guha argues that because the accounts were written after an event as a means of containing an insurgency in the moment of its elaboration, they ultimately produce a prose of counterinsurgency, the desire to stop such uprisings, both discursively and physically. Following Guha's observations, my analysis of what is posited in the contemporary eyewitness reports, military correspondence, and presidential edicts track (critical) glances backward to these discrete moments of violence in the borderlands and the counterinsurgent discourses produced by operative hegemonies. Guha calls this the "intersection of colonialism and historiography," where a doubled sense of movement is "linked at the same time to a system of power and the particular manner of its representation."[10] Drawing attention to the mediated nature of the production of every text, Guha calls attention to the blind spots induced by calling such sources neutral. At some level, the government documents, literature, *testimonios*, and letters in my study presuppose a neutrality that registers silence about some events and complete disclosure of others. In masking culpability for violent acts committed against particular populations in the borderlands that are motivated by racial, sexual, or gender difference, such documents (like the discourse of counterinsurgency) reveal other patterns, elementary repetitions of practice that establish a concrete narrative index in which a document, as Guha reminds us, serves as "more than a mere register of happenings [to] help inscribe it into meaning."[11] Given that these documents were written to shut down insurgency, they both advocate violence as a response to that insurgency and function to silence that violence.

As the anthropologist Fernando Coronil argues, violence is not random;

it is "wielded in the idiom of a society's distinctive history" and therefore produces a logic of disclosure or repression.[12] Methodologically speaking, as Coronil attests, the borderlands communities I analyze have their own specific social context in the production of violence as social practice and must be considered within a transnational framework. Each incident reveals the whole history of violence embedded in the context of the borderlands, most notably through the utterance of that which is almost unspeakable. Both Joseph Roach in *Cities of the Dead* and Diana Taylor in *The Archive and the Repertoire* have argued that selective memory requires public acts of forgetting in order to blur obvious discontinuities, misalliances, and ruptures or to exaggerate them, which mystifies the past in expressive behavior and transmits cultural identity and memory.[13] I tweak their readings of the utterance a bit, arguing that if we read the utterance as the unspeakable, then we are presented with fragments of the very things selective memory bans from individual and national consciousness, the historical traces that are clearly there but not allowed to be heard, seen, or experienced. Roach further argues that the unspeakable may be officially forgotten but that memory retains its consequences: "The unspeakable cannot be forever rendered inexpressible: the most persistent mode of forgetting is memory imperfectly deferred."[14] So it is this sense of deferral that is a series of actions—more precisely defined as memories—that activate the unspeakable. The utterance is reference to that which cannot be spoken fully. Even as the unspeakable nature of violence denies a particular set of histories, it must acknowledge them in order to banish them from memory. My book weaves together the profound meaning found in the unspeakable and the utterance, reminding us that violence forms the foundations of national histories and subjectivity that are often elided.

VIOLENCE, NATIONALISM, AND CITIZENSHIP

Utterances materialize, hail, and deny violence all at once. It is the unspeakable qualities of material and representational violence that are posited in the utterance. I further propose that the utterance and representational violence echo each other as material and historical cognates. Representational violence in fictional texts and journalistic accounts, as in the case of Josefa/Juanita's lynching, echo material violence by repeating the details of an event by effacing her as a subject. At the same time, historical texts echo representational violence in the sense that they also have their own mediated nature in how narratives of violence are told. As the various readings of Josefa/Juanita's lynching unfold, we see the layers of mediation and bias in texts that are read as factual history. Much larger state-sponsored histories of violence in the

U.S.–Mexico borderlands provide the perfect case-study for contemplating, within a transnational context, the movement of goods, people, ideas, capital, and policies between and among nations. I use such terms as *racialized*, *sexualized*, and *gendered subjects* throughout the book to indicate how social processes and social constructions of race, sexuality, and gender inform the citizenship of individuals and communities in the U.S.–Mexico borderlands. As racialized, sexualized, and gendered individuals were and are deprived of control of their bodies through acts of violence, they are also denied access to land, resources, and civil rights. At the same time, those whom we now call people of color in the U.S.–Mexico borderlands were not exclusively victims but often enacted violence upon other racialized, gendered subjects in the name of the state. This is where I make a critical intervention into celebratory discourses about mestizaje, hybridity, and nationalism within the context of Chicano, Latino, and American studies, by teasing out the nuances of how and why multiethnic communities enacted violence against each other. Few scholars are willing to talk about these questions because they pose a direct challenge to nationalist ideologies that celebrate the cultural heritage of Mexico and, in particular, of its indigenous roots.[15] Examining how far people will go to obey national authority, even to the point of inflicting death on another, is part of my project. I also trace how seeing (visual representation) and hearing (discursive representation) challenge claims of not knowing and claims to ignorance, claims on which the success of nationalism depends.[16] In some ways my work is about correcting historiographies, nationalist tracts, and popular lore that have left us with a series of obscured and shortened narratives in which minor descriptions of violated bodies are proof of an unspeakable act. In other words, my book theorizes how and why these unspeakable acts might announce their own disappearance and how those unspeakable acts utter the project of nation formation.

What I have been describing thus far, in regard to Josefa/Juanita's narrative of lynching and other enactments of physical violence in the borderlands, is the erasure of the physical pain these historical subjects felt firsthand, posited in an abbreviated utterance or in complete silence, which leads to a secondary effect of violence as social practice. Elaine Scarry argues that there is an "inaccessible reality of physical pain . . . to anyone not immediately experiencing it."[17] What is lost is the ability to fully understand the physical and psychic pain violence causes individuals and communities. While there is something irretrievable about the experiences of the people who emerge as subjects in the historical record strictly because they are somehow implicated in acts of violence, a kind of social residue polices the behaviors of those who come into contact with that violence through hearing about it, witnessing it, experiencing it, or reading about it. This process highlights the disciplined body in relationship to the nation-state because law, confinement, and punishment inform citizenship.[18] I argue that tracking these processes as they are represented in the historical record and in Chicana/o, Mexican, and U.S. national imaginaries requires that citizen-subjects be theorized in relation to power, pain, and domination.

Then there is another effect, one in which violence manifests itself in the social residues that are sedimented as trauma. Trauma manifests itself in people's behavior, in both the physical body and the psyche. Some who have experienced oppressive treatment do not live to tell their stories. For those who do, the ways violence leaves its traces have been most clearly documented in the numerous accounts of Holocaust survivors, memoirs of sexual abuse survivors, and blues songs that testify to the African American experience of lynching.[19] Violence in any context remains as a social trace in our histories; it affects how we behave, and this is why it is so often an unspoken, underlying social current. Judith Herman argues, "Psychological trauma is an affliction of powerlessness."[20] Writing about trauma is both a formalistic narrative practice and a way to mourn for past violence in order to counteract the sense of powerlessness that histories of colonization evoke. Rereading this archive is a means of responding to atrocities that are often unspeakable. Images of violence against the gendered and racialized body—whether in the form of rape, physical torture, or political disenfranchisement—demonstrate that these forces are normalized, enraging, and extraordinary all at the same time. In attempting to imagine "real" violence and how it was and is experienced by a collective of individuals who are explicit products of histories of colonization, my readings theorize that the pain and suffering that result from violence against the body and the subject are integral to the production of subjectivities. To illuminate the prevailing ideas of domination, violence must be read as both a subject of representation and a historical factor.

All of the histories I recount raise issues about how subjects in these spaces have attempted to enact their citizenship and maintain a sense of bodily and psychic integrity by contesting violations of their person. Citizenship plays a crucial role in the perpetration of violence precisely because national membership, rights, birthrights, and state and local practices were often determined situationally. Following Evelyn Nakano Glenn, I argue that citizenship is based on both universal and exclusionary notions of belonging to the nation-state, conditioning gendered, sexualized, and racialized subjects to police themselves and to understand that their existence is subject to policing by the state.[21] As Akhil Gupta argues, "Citizenship ought to be theorized as one of the multiple subject positions occupied by people as members of diversely spatialized, partially overlapping or non-overlapping collectivities."[22] While Gupta's caveat on split and multiple affinities is an important one, one must remember that racialized, sexualized, and gendered subjects often are not viewed as full members of their respective communities or as full citizens of nations with rights and are more likely to be targets of physical, psychological, or discursive violence. Reconstructing various violent episodes, utilizing a transnational feminist methodology to account for the hegemonic rationales that make these atrocities unspeakable, I theorize the role of the nation-state (a legal and political entity) in forming national imaginaries (discursive formations) that perpetuate dominant narratives of national amnesia. Certainly, I am not alone in this endeavor, as such recent scholars as Leigh Payne, Ned Blackhawk, and Saidya Hartman, among others, have contemplated the role of violence and its repression in historical memory in the formation of nation-states. My project is unique, however, in that I consider how competing understandings of racial projects and models of exchange worked in tandem to produce proper subjects in the borderlands. Chicano nationalist and Chicana feminist scholarship have primarily and to a degree understandably posited Mexican racial and even gendered identification as a refuge from Anglo-American nationalist violence. My historical research demonstrates that this was not always the case, and accordingly I examine how nationalism and individuals collude in sanctioning forgotten violence in the borderlands.

Drawing on archival sources from the United States and Mexico, I further argue that the subjectivities of peoples are refashioned as their connection to space and their civil rights are denied. Mary Pat Brady has argued that space "is a highly social process that has an effect on the formation of subjectivity, identity, sociality, and physicality in myriad ways."[23] Subjugated identities are produced through spatial configurations of power that literally turn a landscape against its inhabitants. The case of American Indians—and, I would add, that of Mexican Indians, the Yaqui population of Sonora in particular— illustrates space as a way of organizing power relations which, according to Ned Blackhawk, "have countered policies aimed at denying Indians access to land and resources."[24]

Through an analysis of space and violent processes of social differentiation, I attempt to gain access to the cultural politics of violence that developed through overlapping colonial systems of the U.S.–Mexico borderlands. When violence leaves its ineffaceable mark, it does not create merely a self–other relationship between violator and violated: rather everyone involved, spectators, enactors of violence, and the recipients of violence, is differentiated through her or his role in these processes.[25] Violence is an underlying social process of differentiation for all involved. The experiencing and enacting of violence are processes that differentiate, and the ultimate form of differentiation is abjection. Julia Kristeva argues that "abjection of self would be the culminating form of that experience of the subject to which it is revealed that all its objects are based merely upon the inaugural loss that laid the foundations of its own being."[26] It is this primary sense of loss, the aftereffects of violence, that creates a sentiment of abjection. The social process of extreme differentiation becomes the foundation for collective residues of violence. The loss is registered in the utterances that refer to differentiation, violence, and abjection. According to the American studies scholars David Eng and David Kazanjian, the utterances are what remain, melancholically materialized in the social, political, and cultural realms, perhaps creating a productive space for reinvigorated histories and politics embodied in loss.[27] While undoubtedly violence is a social process that distances the individual body from the sense of self, individual experiences are irretrievable and this only produces a greater sense of loss. However, a distinction must be made between individual abjection and collective responses to that abjection. I argue two points in relation to abjection, perhaps changing Kristeva's definition. First, for dissident subjects in the borderlands, abjection is a normal state of being in terms of their individual relationship to the state. The moment of recognition of loss is perhaps most vividly articulated in acts of physical violence against the individual. If we examine violence on a case by case basis, the inability to control what is done to one's body shows how state actors vigorously police individuals and represents the moment of differentiation in which violation is the marker of noncitizenship. The abject is the shadow figure that lingers in multiple national imaginaries, signaling an absence of citizenship formed through social processes of differentiation registered upon the bodies and in the psyches of the violated. In other words, in the nineteenth-century history of the U.S.–Mexico borderlands U.S., Mexican, and Chicano nationalism have uncannily relied on the abjection of certain specter bodies—from Josefa/Juanita's body to the Yaqui Indian nation—for the consolidation of their narratives of loss and triumph, of national risk and consolidation.

At the collective level, how this abjection is or is not narrated shows that a great deal of national history is about selective memory and the prioritizing of particular information and events over others. I am not arguing that all the communities involved in these case studies of violence are organized around a collective abjection, but rather that reading these incidents as a collective whole posits abjection as a precondition for registering the impact of violence. Herein lies the reason Josefa/Juanita's lynching gets only one sentence in the mass-market media article instead of a detailed treatment. The inability to articulate subjection, abjection, and the distinct types of violence (physical, psychic, discursive, and epistemic) is located at individual, communal, national, and transnational levels, evading the real reasons why violence "pushes the limits of the permissible."[28]

In the context of Chicano studies, violence in the U.S.–Mexico borderlands in the nineteenth-century has been characterized as a conflict between Anglo and Mexican males over land and citizenship. While this perspective makes important contributions and revisionist corrections to the ways race and class are talked about in the Southwest, generations of scholars have been influenced by how such narratives track a singular idea of Mexican resistance to Anglo hegemony, as if that were the only kind of power struggle that existed.[29] It reflects the narrative emerging from the Chicano power movements of the 1960s, which articulates the Mexican and Mexican American subject fighting the voracious northern neighbor who is attempting to steal Mexican lands (although some scholars have argued that the cession of the Southwest to the United States was a reflection of the administrative disorder of the Mexican nation after independence).[30] Rather than ask the same questions again, I ask, Does the paradigm of resistance to Anglo hegemony always situate an oppositional relationship? or is there a more productive way to ask research questions that uncover the field's strengths? I think there is.

TRANSNATIONAL FEMINIST FRAMEWORKS

Even as I critique the limitations of certain paradigms such as Chicano nationalism, which casts Chicano identity as indigenous and masculinist, I strive to retain the insights these paradigms have yielded in the past, specifically the worthwhile political project of conceiving of Chicana/o studies in a transnational framework. An early attempt at a transnational feminist turn is exemplified by the Mexicana/Chicana Women's History International Symposium held in Santa Monica, California, in March 1982, at which scholars and activists shared research and teaching expertise on the history of Mexican women. Their goal was to enact a "collaboration that underscores the benefits of international exchanges in Chicano studies and in the history of Mexican women on both sides of the border."[31] Eight years later a Chicana graduate student from UCLA, Adelaida R. Del Castillo, a feminist organizer, edited and published an expanded version of the conference proceedings in the transnationally minded anthology *Between Borders: Essays on Mexicana/Chicana*

History.[32] Del Castillo argues that the theoretical and conceptual framework of the book derives from the idea that "Chicana history is the history of Chicano and Mexicano people representative of a transnational labor force in the context of global capital accumulation," and the scholarship it contains focuses on Mexicans on both sides of the U.S.–Mexico border.[33] Del Castillo's anthology not only argues for the consideration of the movement of bodies and peoples through circuits of exchange and labor, but also foregrounds how gender and women's studies have caused epistemological shifts in the study of Mexicana/os. The essays span the period from colonial California under Spanish rule to current debates in Chicana/Mexicana studies (as of 1990). But the distinguishing feature of the work is its publication of essays in Spanish and its focus on the history of the Partido Liberal Mexicano (PLM) during the Mexican Revolution, its exile communities, and the gendering of the revolution's history, from which women have been written out. Del Castillo argues lucidly that "the proximity of the border and the adeptness with which a transborder traffic negotiates movement between the United States and Mexico has historically made possible a cross fertilization of political ideas and organizational activism."[34] While the evidence Del Castillo relies upon comes from the early twentieth century, she nonetheless rejects a Chicano nationalist discourse in favor of a focus on the geographical, political, social, and racial convergences and divergences that PLM historiographies often missed by failing to analyze class and gender oppression. Del Castillo sought to represent a "broad topical diversity, scope, and consciousness on Mexican women's history comprised of an unprecedented collection of interpretive essays and original research on the theory, method, and content of Chicana history," written by an interesting cast of intellectual leaders in the field, including Juan Gómez-Quiñónez, Antonia Castañeda, Raquel Rubio-Goldsmith, Dennis Monroy, and Rosaura Sánchez. The contributors to the anthology pursue not a nationalist agenda but an explicitly transnationalist one.[35]

Sánchez's essay in the anthology, "The History of Chicanas: A Proposal for a Materialist Perspective," critically outlines the kinds of transnational historiographic projects needed to expand the field:

Works tracing Chicana roots in Mexican history need not postulate direct links between us and La Malinche or Sor Juana Inés de la Cruz. References to Aztec goddesses similarly prove absolutely nothing and in fact have been used to idealize the status of Aztec women in pre-Columbian society, both in creative and historical projects, despite documentation which points to the subordinate status of women in pre-Columbian society. In short, Chicana historians need fewer myths and more historical analysis. In all cases, whatever the focus, references to women included in these histories should be accompanied by information on the class status of the historicized figures, for we are often provided information which pertains only to the ruling classes of Mexico.[36]

Shunning the imaginary world and revisionist histories that make Chicanas/os the direct descendents of La Malinche or Coyolxchaulqui, Sánchez provides a refreshing materialist model for writing transnational history, because her analytical focus rests not on the compulsory working-class subject, but on social class in general.[37] In her vision of transnationalized Chicana/o and Latina/o studies, Sánchez urges readers toward a Marxist feminism that acknowledges that sometimes the only extant historical records in both Mexico and the United States are those of upper-class Mexicans, and they say a great deal about power struggles through their discursive absences and presences. Sánchez sees this as an opening to move away from narrow nationalist mythologies toward an analysis of class struggle between and among those who make history.

In a nearly unprecedented move for its time, *Between Borders* consciously includes Mexicana and Chicana historical scholarship by men. J. Jorge Klor de Alva and Gómez-Quiñónez, as Latin Americanists turned Chicana/o studies scholars, demonstrate that it is possible to be a Chicano man and take seriously gender analysis beyond the United States and beyond women. The conclusions in Klor de Alva's essay "Chicana History and Historical Significance: Some Theoretical Considerations" point in a transnational direction. "With regard to Mexican women in the United States," he argues, "not only must they be studied with class and gender categories in mind, but with attention to critical historical variables of ethnicity, race, and international context. Therefore, no single conceptual framework will be able to fully capture the complexity of the Chicana past."[38] He calls for a multilayered, mixed methodology that takes into account international factors as well as issues of race, class, and gender as being central to any study of Mexican women in the United States (and, I would add, Mexican women in the borderlands). Gómez-Quiñónez's "Questions within Women's Historiography" relies on nineteenth- and early twentieth-century Mexico as the basis for his arguments about Mexicana, Chicana, and, more generally, women's history. "In Mexico as elsewhere, male chauvinism and sexism have existed in correspondence to the level of social, economic, and political development," he points out.[39] In discussing the social and gender stratification that affected the lives of all participants in the Spanish conquest, Gómez-Quiñónez notes that "male domination has meant unequal distribution and exploitation along gender lines and the propagation of values and interpretations which sustain this disadvantage among Mexicans."[40] Both Klor de Alva and Gómez-Quiñónez rearticulate the problem of masculinist constructs of history as a field, and both go beyond the United States to view Mexico as a central place from which to theorize problems in epistemology.

But the most overtly transnationalist move of *Between Borders* comes with the publication of several essays in Spanish by Mexican scholars who focus on Mexican women's history in Mexico. The refusal to translate, as well as Carmen Castañeda-García's "Fuentes para la historia de la mujer en los archivos de Guadalajara" the transnationalized study of Mexican women that Del Castillo proposes in the introduction. Castañeda-García invites readers to pursue historical research on Mexican women in Mexico as part of transnationalizing Chicana/o studies. Beginning her catalogue of archival sources in the eighteenth century and continuing through the mid-twentieth century, she illustrates the breadth and scope of the collection, which includes letters, notary records, and government documents. One of the most interesting and compelling portions of Castañeda-García's essay is her presentation of a source from 1856 about Jalisqueña women's relationship to religion. The source elucidated that working-class women's lack of citizenship rights was so complete that the Mexican Congress passed legislation to further delimit the lower-class's heathen, irreligious ways and focus on civilizing the most "ignorant portion of Mexican society" and their rights, who, it was assumed, did not respect moral principles.[41] Most important, Castañeda-García reminds scholars how important it is to examine what the upper class was doing in the period immediately after the signing of the Treaty of Guadalupe Hidalgo because they informed social norms about gender, religion, and propriety for the working classes. Her scholarly preoccupation is not simply with whether class divisions make certain women somehow less or more important to the national project, but rather with how these sources from Guadalajara can contribute to a transnational dialogue on Mexican women's history.

Between Borders shows that transnationalism has been a viable methodology in Chicana/o studies for quite some time and that Chicana feminism is at the forefront of this movement in the field. Chicana feminist scholarship, as the anthology demonstrates, incorporates postcolonial theories of identity that deconstruct and challenge dominant racist, sexist, classist, and heterosexist paradigms to analyze how the effects of colonialism continue to thrive within U.S. borders in new and more complicated forms. Nevertheless, *Be-*

tween Borders relies on a discourse of mestizaje even as it promotes transnational methodologies.

Angie Chabram-Dernersesian similarly argues in "Chicana! Rican? No, 'Chicana, Riqueña!': Refashioning the Transnational Connection" that Chicano/a studies scholarship needs to make good on the claim of transnationality not just in theory but in practice. She marks how rigid nationalist frameworks police her everyday identity struggles as a Chicana-Riqueña. Chabram-Dernersesian chides the belief in authentic Chicana/o identities as she refuses to "engage in the business of putting on a ready-made identity the way nationalists did when they celebrated a glorious Aztec past with questionable relations to the present but neglected to map vital relations to contemporary indígenas or other local underrepresented ethnic groups."[42] She goes on to argue that today's mestizaje is "the age-old political embodiment of the Mexican national who has traditionally occupied this central space and is the subject of contention by many indígenas for whom mestizaje means inequality, a concerted dilution of Indianness and partnership with the Mexican state."[43] Chabram-Dernersesian suggests that evocations of the border and of mestizaje circulate an essentialist discourse, offering a native multiculturalism that is exclusive because of its ethnic absolutism.[44] It seems that the terms *border*, *borderlands*, and *mestizaje* come to stand in for or masquerade as a transnational methodology in Chicana/o studies. We should not dismantle these concepts, but rather consider a different set of questions and methodologies with which to answer them. Stepping out of a U.S. Chicano–based intellectual paradigm with its master narratives of mestizaje, the borderlands, and *lo indio/the Indian* would demonstrate that colonial aggressions are enacted by Chicana/os, Mexicano/as, and U.S. Mexicans as well. Chabram-Dernersesian writes, "Although we live in a period that prizes the multiplicity of identities and charts border crossings with borderless critics, [it is ironic that] there should be such a marked silence around the kinds of divergent ethnic pluralities that cross gender and classed subjects within the semantic orbit of Chicana/o."[45] For Chabram-Dernersesian, the evocation of mestizaje and the border masks inequalities and is essentialist, identifying a single Chicano/a identity that equates with "the" indigenous (Aztec) to the exclusion of all else.

If one maps this transnational alternative theoretical and practical genealogy of the field, the book that most closely exemplifies the happy marriage of feminist critique and transnationalism is María Josefina Saldaña-Portillo's *The Revolutionary Imagination in the Americas and the Age of Development*. In both content and scope, Saldaña-Portillo shows why transnational methodologies matter and what they can produce when scholars expand the parameters of Chicana/o studies, Latina/o studies, and Latin American studies. Exploding multiple nationalisms as she critiques them, Saldaña-Portillo investigates the conjunctures and disjunctures between two narratives of progress—namely, development and revolution—that captured the imagination of three generations of nationalists in the Americas in the second half of the twentieth century.[46] The arguments for taking up the mantle of revolution often mirrored development discourse, the very things rebels sought to liberate themselves from in anti-imperialist struggles. With regard to liberationist struggles in the Americas, Saldaña-Portillo argues that "reading this convergence from the vantage point of postcolonial theory might interpret such revolutionary nationalism as derivative, predicated on a repetition, albeit with a difference, of Western development."[47] What is most revolutionary (pun intended) about Saldaña-Portillo's argument is that she utters something nobody wants to hear: that there are in fact mimetic similarities and collusions with power between Che Guevara's coming to revolutionary consciousness or the Sandinista government in Nicaragua and first world think tanks that promulgate development strategies for the third world. Both Guevara, the embodiment of revolutionary discourse, and the International Monetary Fund render what Saldaña-Portillo calls " 'natural' . . . normative concepts of growth, progress, and modernity."[48] Both discourses, in their continuities and discontinuities between colonial categories of subjectivity and developmental categories of national citizenship, illustrate "how race is revitalized within the domain of cultural attitudes that must be overcome, how gender is allegorized within the domain of active and reactive nationalisms, and how hierarchies and exploitative relations of exchange in a global capitalist system are reorganized into normative levels of productivity that must be achieved."[49] In all of these narratives of progress, the subject is rendered masculine, mobile, ethical, and an agent of his own transformation, regardless of his or her actual gender.

In addition, Saldaña-Portillo critiques the production of the subaltern and subaltern consciousness, which have become the intended beneficiaries of both development and revolutionary discourses in the Americas. Even as the epistemic production of the Sandinista National Liberation Front attempted to privilege proletarian and collective consciousness through state farms and cooperatives, it valued these ideas over those of the smallholding peasantry who made up the majority of Nicaragua's rural population.[50] Avoiding the romance of revolution that is so often produced vis-à-vis liberationist struggles in Central and South America, Saldaña-Portillo stages a respectful critique of the vanguard politics that were originally aimed at helping the peasants, who should be the legitimate subjects of revolution. These small peasant producers later became counterrevolutionaries because their concerns were dismissed by the Sandinista party leadership and conflated their concerns with those of national identity that "necessitated commitment to the revolution, to a particular vision of modernization" and that read peasants and their consciousness as prerevolutionary.[51] In the case of Nicaragua even the most well-intended discourse of revolution could and did primitivize the peasant majority of the country, an utterance nobody wants to hear as a critique of insurgent struggles in the Americas.

Saldaña-Portillo's engagement with the Zapatista movement in Mexico is equally honest in that she shows the movement's democratic and respectful politics without falling into the trap of treating the Zapatistas as unassailable or romanticizing the Central American revolutions of the 1970s and 1980s. What I appreciate about Saldaña-Portillo's methodology is that it leaves no stone unturned; it reminds us "about the many tensions that exist among indigenous peasant groups in and around the Zapatista liberated zones and the Mexican army camps."[52] Admitting that there are tensions among indigenous groups because of language barriers not only saves one from constructing a romanticized, monolithic, universal Indian subject of revolution, but also provides an opportunity to understand the racial and ethnic differences that continue to be reformulated by postcolonial regimes of subjection and that a romanticized discourse of mestizaje ultimately masks. An honest appraisal of the Zapatista movement as a solidarity-based indigenous front built on a foundation of respect for difference makes the romance of mestizaje impossible to sustain.

Finally, and most important for the argument of my book, Saldaña-Portillo suggests that uncritical Chicano nationalism produces romanticized images of a single Indian tribe that later became Chicanos, a system of representation that erases historically accurate indigenous subjectivities. Such nationalist narratives, grounded in biologically based terms of mestizaje and a national romance of a unified indigenous past, do not recognize Indians other than Aztecs as inhabitants of this continent, so that in such narratives, *mestizo* and therefore *Chicano* means *Indian*.[53] Saldaña-Portillo points out that in Chicano studies and Chicano nationalist histories of violence and capitalism, the only venerated Indians are the Aztecs of the past. I build on this argument but take it in a different direction in my examination of the historical record. Late nineteenth- and early twentieth-century archival materials in Mexico and the United States show the complex social and power relationships regarding indigenous communities in the U.S.–Mexico borderlands and proposing an alternative model to that which Chicano studies offers, one that is more relevant to its rich historical context.

THE RESISTANCE TO TRANSNATIONAL FEMINIST METHODOLOGIES WITHIN CHICANO STUDIES

Even though Chicana feminist critical projects have "underscored the 'back and forth' movements of people and ideas within spaces that challenged our notions of discrete domains," these calls in the field most often still go half answered.[54] Norma Alarcón, Sonia Saldívar-Hull, and Chabram-Dernersesian all sounded this transnational call in the late 1990s, but the transformation still seems to be on the verge of happening, not yet quite complete.[55]

Some recent scholarship is highly problematic in that it gives a cursory nod to the transnational, once again using an invocation of the border and mestizaje to stand in for a concrete engagement with transnationalism. One of the main discourses used in studies of the Americas to articulate oppression and resistance is that of mestizaje, which was made famous by Gloria Anzaldúa's now-canonical text *Borderlands/La Frontera: The New Mestiza* (1987). Whereas Anzaldúa's theory was specific to Chicana identity formation within the context of the geopolitics of the U.S.–Mexico borderlands, the new mestiza consciousness she proposes is often taken out of this context and applied to everything and anything that references racial and cultural mixture or borders. In "Miscegenation Now!," a review of recent scholarship on mestizaje, Rafael Pérez-Torres argues that one of the problems with this concept is that scholars focus exclusively on how mestizaje "embodies possibility" and "the emancipatory potential of racial mixture." What is often occluded or oversimplified is the " 'reality' of race in the face of its constructed nature." When racial mixture is evoked as the future, as the harmonizing of disparate identities, it ignores "the more pernicious and hierarchical impulses behind mestizaje in the Americas" and does not complicate the legacy of colonial violence or implicate Chicana/os in the production of racism.[56]

In Chicano studies this discourse privileges indigenismo, or the Indian heritage of Mexicans and Chicanos, as part of a common identity that unites all Chicanos politically.[57] The recent string of books and articles celebrating the literal embodiment of mestizaje in the figure of the native or, more directly, the paradigm of Chicano/as as Indians, "run[s] the risk of representing the [mestizo] body as the realm of 'the real,' " according to Pérez-Torres, superimposing a physical essence on ethnicity.[58] By privileging that "Indian essence," mestizaje fetishizes a residual, abstract, dehistoricized Indian identity that obscures Mexican, Mexican Indian, and American Indian participation in genocide and violence against other American Indians and Mexicans in the U.S.–Mexico borderlands. When we situate these moments of violence in their complex historical matrices, we begin to understand the sexual and gendered dimensions of genocide, which rather than being subsumed under the celebratory gaze of mestizaje deserve to be theorized as transnational moments of violent cultural practices based in fundamental ideas about racial and gender inequality in multiple national contexts.

Ralph Rodriguez, Monika Kaup, José Aranda, and others have argued that we are in a postnationalist moment in Chicana/o studies.[59] Now, Alicia Gaspar de Alba says, "Chicano/a authors can explore the Chicano/a subject in . . . a historically specific ontological space in which Chicana/o identity has been attempting to redefine itself outside of the cultural logic of 'el Movimiento' and its rhetoric of nationalism, essentialism, and carnalismo . . . but now is also estranged from the cultural, linguistic, political, and sexual discourses that structured Chicano and Chicana identity at the time of the Chicano Civil Rights Movement."[60] Yet the excessively recursive figure of "lo Indio/la India" manifests itself in other forms, signaling not a cultural retention but a Chicana/o indigenous reinvention that is not an uninterrupted historical formation.[61]

Kaup argues that "Chicana feminists have achieved this [postnationalist] decentered reconfiguration of their community by rewriting the two major Chicano plots found in male Chicano writing: the indigenous and the immigrant stories. In some cases—the exemplary text here is Anzaldúa's *Borderlands*—the dismantling effect results from playing out these two plots against each other."[62] Even if the combining of indigenous and immigrant stories as one narrative thread in Chicana feminism manages to decenter hegemonic ideas of community, then neonationalism, much like violence, becomes that unspeakable thing that gets remapped as resistance. Neonationalism then becomes the structure of power in the field, shaping the intellectual production and maintaining a particular kind of control over what is venerated as authentically Chicano and what is ignored. Neonationalism is culturally understood as an unspoken ideology or idiom of resistance that most often is articulated as "mestizo equals Indian." So even while scholars like Rodriguez, Kaup, Gaspar de Alba, and Aranda argue that el Movimiento has forged an estrangement from Chicana/o identities, they are talking about representations of the postnational rather than about how both systems of thought (that is, Anzaldúa's mestizaje interpreted as Indian only and neonationalism) are based on resistive agency, a structure that represses and restricts what gets talked about and valued. In the 1970s and 1980s it was gender that was rationalized away by cultural nationalism. Today, gender, for the most part, is included in the analytical framework, but what gets rationalized away now is any sort of critique of indigenismo that does not fit the cultural nationalist script of vindication of "the" Indian subject who is Chicana/o.

This postnationalist reading of *Indian*, detailed in *Borderlands/La Frontera*, reappropriates (misreads?) Vasconcelos's *la raza cósmica* from the 1920s: Anzaldúa theorized a Chicana/o ideological claim to self-determination, dignity, and civil rights through mestizaje instead of reading Vasconcelos for the eugenicist that he was. This move is a response to an aggrieved sense of being wronged.[63] Yet the reclamation of the mestiza/o sharpens the focus on the revolutionary content of any political project that uncritically celebrates this mestiza/o heritage, with a particular focus on an essentialized, dehistoricized indigenous past, most closely paralleled by a "neonationalist" discourse. The common reading of Anzaldúa as taking up the mantle of mestizaje as a theory of Chicana/o liberation in some ways denies the violence, both physical and epistemic, that occurs when the essentialized Indian—who cannot pass for mestizo or cannot celebrate a mestiza/o cultural heritage and is in fact Indian in the eyes of the U.S. and Mexican nations—is eliminated from the conversation. Further, Afro-mestizos and blacks in general form another silent part of racist thought and politics of exclusion in Chicana/o, Mexicana/o, and U.S. national imaginaries. Even though Anzaldúa's *Borderlands/La Frontera* makes a concerted effort to discuss blackness as part of the mestizaje paradigm, we will see these multiple imaginaries gain force by obviating people of African descent. The tremendous feminist influence of *Borderlands/La Frontera* cannot be denied; however, my point is to demonstrate that the politics that center around celebrating or reclaiming mestizaje are highly problematic because of what they elide from the colonial past and nationalist present, especially when Anzaldúa's strategic invocation of the mestiza is unequivocally read as Indian only. One reason mestizaje is so appealing as a discourse is that it deconstructs the totalizing nature of things, cultures, and bodies, liberating Mexicans and Chicanos from the shameful past that has figured them as second-class citizens, a position articulated today as indigenous.[64] Thus, even in this presumably postnationalist Chicana/o culture we have entered, a chain of equivalence still persists: if Chicano, then Mexican; if Mexican, then mestizo; if mestizo, then indigenous; if indigenous, then resistant. So by celebrating mestizaje as a kind of neo-Chicano/a nationalism—an analysis that includes gender constructs but focuses mostly on indigenismo—Chicano cultural studies too often systematically forgets the history of violence embedded in its uncritical narratives of so-called resistance based on homophobic, essentialist, indigenous neonationalisms in an Anglo/Mexican binary. Thus decontextualized evocations of mestizaje, indigenismo, and nationalism eclipse historical moments of violence, meaning, and specificity, just as their complexity is denied because they exclusively address a quasi-proletarian subject.

Further, I examine Mexican ideas about citizenship, nation, and Indians in the late nineteenth century and early twentieth as the *selective* acknowledgments of mestizaje as a strength of the Mexican character. The Mexican documents represent their own kind of selective memory. Mestizaje and positive representations of Indians in Mexico are convenient arguments for nationalism and rarely anything more. One need look only at the daily protests of Oaxacan indigenous communities at el Monumento de la Madre in Mexico City from 2008–2010 to find evidence of the disparity between the convenient Indian of the Mexican national past and the living Indians who must protest in order to be recognized as citizens of their nation. Local, state, and national policy most often disavows Indians and their relationship to Mexico.

For example, Mexican Indian policy dissolved the slightest possibilities of political alliances between Indians and Mexicans in Chihuahua, where the Indian policy of 1849 was still in effect in 1886, demonstrating that the state's position on Indian exclusion did not change for almost half a century and remained exceedingly violent. Félix Francisco Maceyra, the governor of Chihuahua, wrote to Porfirio Díaz in 1886, "You will see that it is a matter of accord in the United States Senate as a decree made in the year 1849 which provides prizes for every Indian killed in action or [made a] prisoner of war. This decree has not been abolished and it has been made to wage the war with some advantage on Indian savages."[65] Díaz responded, "I accept the decree of 1849 as a necessary evil, unless we can find another type of compensation with the same results."[66] The fact that Indian policy had not changed in Chihuahua in thirty years suggests that vigilante violence was standard practice when dealing with supposed savages who broke the law. Maceyra's and Díaz's acceptance of the bounty killing of Indians as a necessary evil tells us two things. First, beheading, torture, and maltreatment of alleged Indian offenders were rewarded with monetary compensation, and cadavers served as the proof of captured criminals. Second, both the U.S. and Mexican states had contracted their labor of killing Indians for monetary compensation to private parties, thus further deregulating Indian policy and making it a matter handled on a case by case basis, outside of the law. People must have literally made a living by bringing in Indian cadavers (which had its own problems because "Mexican" and "Indian" cadavers were not always easily distinguishable) to the Chihuahuan government, thereby conveying a message much like that contained in Andrew Jackson's policy that the only good Indian is a dead Indian—a dead Indian that is clearly not a Mexican or a Mexican citizen. Rather, each Indian cadaver represented what needed to be eradicated to transform Mexico into a modern nation and especially to make its borders safe for capitalism and foreign investment in relationship to U.S. Indian policy.

Furthermore, the same Indian policy can be linked to early twentieth-century, state-sponsored counterinsurgency practice against the Yaquis in the borderlands that is part and parcel of a larger history of empire. Thomas A. Bass has argued that the tactics of counterinsurgency involve "a dominant power forcing its will on a subject people [and] . . . involves a mix of offensive, defensive, and stability operations."[67] Bass refers to the current U.S. intervention in Iraq and offers a way of thinking about the treatment of rebels through a kind of historical continuity. Bass's words on counterinsurgency are directly reflected in Mexican governmental documents from the late nineteenth century and the early twentieth because counterinsurgency was a necessary part of the project of nationhood and the project of Mexico imagining itself as an empire. Mexican governmental documents on the Yaqui Indian wars demonstrate a range of offensive, defensive, and stabilizing operations but in the service of nations imagining themselves, however directly and indirectly, as empires.

The desire to stabilize economic productivity in northern Mexican states like Sonora in the late nineteenth century shows how Díaz's vision of Mexico was one of an empire that dominated its indigenous populations. The vision of Mexico as empire is articulated most concretely in the speeches and biographies of Mexican army generals who directed the counterinsurgency campaigns against the Yaqui in 1880–1910. But even those messages were mixed. Lo indio was invoked as *Lo Azteca*, the precolonial Mexican indigenous, not the contemporary one present within the context of the Yaqui Indian wars. After a decisive victory over Yaqui scouts and the killing of the Yaqui chief Tetabiate at Bacatete in 1901, the government declared the wars over.[68] Gen. Bernardo Reyes, the governor of Nuevo Leon in 1885–1900 and secretary of war in 1901–3, wrote the following treatise in his autobiography evoking the Aztec past as part of Mexican national military glory. Reyes calls on the imperial Aztec past to illuminate the Mexican national present and domination over Yaquis at the battle at Bacatete:

> This race is the Aztec race, and one sees it written down in the Anahuac, on a space covered with lakes and trees; one sees it fighting with the towns-

people and organized in an amazing army: but extraordinary men, and covered with iron, invulnerable to the weapons of the aborigines, and that have the fire of the ray (the harquebus and the cannon), they appear in the East, allied with their countless and already vanquished enemies, and they drown their guerrillas in their blood, and they hold the town subjugated, in a lengthy captivity. . . . How Much Blood and what vitality [they need] to bear the terrible, constant disasters! What an Epoch that of our wars is! The battalions that fight and the remainder that is conquered, or that triumphs, the squadrons impassioned by the vertigo of their office, that fall destroyed; the cannon that thunder and are illuminated sinisterly; the banners floating, running while calling for torches, the fields of friends and enemies, troops spouting blood, that look at each other amidst the fire and the smoke; the shine of weapons, the noise of brass, sounds of bugles, and drums, to burn the conquered or conquering flags, such was the apocalyptic picture of our internal fights.[69]

The pomp and circumstance of an imperialist nostalgia for the destroyed Aztec empire of the past informed Reyes's military present; he strategically evokes the dead Indian past and not the living Yaqui one on purpose. Reyes uses the heroics of Aztec battle, albeit anachronistically, as a way to talk about those fighting for the Mexican nation against the Yaqui. In his time, evoking dead Indians as the symbols and future of the Mexican nation would have completely legitimated the Mexican imperial project in the north that required stamping out the Yaqui in their fight for autonomy. Reyes evokes a more or less strategic kind of mestizaje that included obliterating Yaqui dissent. In other words, the dead Aztec as the foundation of the Mexican nation and ideas about military warriors are used by Reyes to create a complete distinction from the savage Yaqui present. He evokes an uninterrupted continuum of empire as Mexican national history by yoking the "men covered in iron" (the Spanish conquistadores) and "the Aztec race." The two clashing empires are the national narrative and locate the victory of Reyes's troops over the Yaqui at Bacatete within a much larger tradition. Aztec history becomes Mexican history and is defined in the erasure of Yaquis from that story.

Yet this empire has its own narratives of haunting, most closely examined by Claudio Lomnitz in his detailed study of death and nationalism in *Death and the Idea of Mexico*. State, church, local, and cultural practices from the colonial period to the present have made death Mexico's national totem. But relevant to the argument of my book and its critique of national history is Lomnitz's claim that "Mexico is haunted by an entire pantheon of caudillos, who often died at each other's hand."[70] This is crucial to understanding why the Revolution, the Reforma, Independence, the Caste Wars in Yucatán, the French Imperial period, and the end of the Mexican-American war in 1848 are the touchstones of Mexican national imaginaries, whereas Yaqui genocide is actively willed out of the national discourse and history. Focused on such iconic figures as Díaz, Emiliano Zapata, Benito Juárez, Pancho Villa, José María Morelos, Miguel Hidalgo y Costilla, and pre-Columbian heroes like Cuauhtémoc, the national pantheon leaves little room for common Indians like the Yaqui, who existed on the northern periphery of the nation. Yaqui inclusion in the pantheon is not the point; rather, the symbolic power of the pantheon overpowers everything else, like a sponge soaking up the history of violence in the north so completely that it is never seen or heard of again, especially in light of the fact that Yaqui resistance against the Mexican military and government was its own distinct project for national autonomy.

Lomnitz further argues that the national projects around death in Mexico have followed a particular trajectory in the contemporary period, a "syncretism in which the pre-Columbian religion is obsessively tracked in the horizon of 'tradition,' minimalizing the significance of the archaic or outmoded in traditional practices in favor of an exalted affirmation of the historical depth, and in particular, indigenous roots."[71] Because the pantheon of dead heroes leaves little room for critique or recognition of histories of violence, using mestizaje and indigenous roots as the authenticating discourses of national identity lacks historical credence. The current Mexican national infatuation with pre-Columbian religion as the horizon of truth, argues Lomnitz, "is even more exaggerated among Mexicans in the United States."[72] Although some might read this critique of Mexicans in the United States as one more example of calling Mexicans in America *pochos*, or imitation Mexicans, Lomnitz cites the resurgence of the pre-Columbian (lo indio/mestizaje) as a new phase of nationalism that gains strength and fervor from a particular imagined past.

Much as Lomnitz criticizes the discourses of historiography and cultural theories about mestizaje, I question the fixed paradigm of resistance as the only mode of life worthy of study, one often linked to the romanticized Indian and mestizo identities of Mexicans and Mexican Americans. How do researchers account for what is rendered unspeakable when resistance is the primary thing talked about in ethnic studies? If resistance is the only legitimate paradigm, how can we possibly understand what compelled Native Americans, Anglos, and Mexicans to participate in violence against others of their own race in the making of borderlands cultures? What is lost when we relegate intraracial, intracultural, and sexual violence to the periphery of historical narratives in order to focus on interracial violence? Why are we all, no matter who we are, afraid to admit our complicity in extreme physical and sexual violence (whether it occurs in Iraq, in local communities, or in the nineteenth century)? Representations that focus exclusively on resistance potentially lose sight of how Mexicans and indigenous communities were also stakeholders in colonial violence. Perhaps the resistance/victimization dichotomy and that of mestizaje as equal to Indian may not have the same critical purchase in this historical moment as in the past and are perhaps in need of revision. This essentially forms the central argumentative thread of the book.

MAPPING TRANSNATIONAL FEMINIST METHODOLOGIES

Rather than setting nationalism up as a proverbial straw man or suggesting that we live in a uniform, postnationalist moment in Chicana/o studies, I propose that a transnational feminist theoretical approach forces us to pay special attention to the moments when the excessive recursiveness of indigenismo, mestizaje, and nationalism crop up in an institutionalized fashion. The accounts that follow demonstrate that scholars of Chicano studies (myself included) need to be cognizant of how they are mediating voices, often actively forgetting the ethnic, racial, sexual, and gender-specific histories of those individuals whom they are uncritically reclaiming as foremothers, pioneers, and perceived Indians, assigning these groups a privileged identity position in contemporary discourse (even though the subjects did not imagine themselves in that way), and actually displacing or erasing the history of anyone who does not neatly fit the narrative of resistance to Anglo hegemony. Scholars need to be able to discuss critically and respectfully how and why Mexican and indigenous communities colluded in perpetuating violence against each other. I want to account for the long history of racism and elision based on resistance narratives. The four episodes of violence I discuss do not embody the ubiquitous "culture of resistance" that ethnic studies focuses on because the agents in these episodes did not emerge from a place of powerlessness.[73] In fact, I suggest these acts of violence demonstrate moments of complete empowerment. The episodes represented are well-trodden ground for Chicano/a studies scholars for the most part, but those previous accounts celebrate resistance by ignoring key facets of the violence. I describe these misreadings as epistemic violence, a production of knowledge that selectively forgets and remembers some details while forgetting others.[74]

I thereby move to a transnational model that complicates the fixed ways in which race is talked about in the contemporary period. By looking to the past,

I show that alliances (racial and gender categories of socialization) were and continue to be highly malleable, especially where questions of indigenous identity in the borderlands are concerned. Following the lead of works by James Brooks, Juliana Barr, Mary Pat Brady, María Josefina Saldaña-Portillo, Emma Pérez, and Ned Blackhawk and adopting an interdisciplinary approach, I suggest that women, children, American Indians, Mexicans, Mexican Indians, and other migrants were often the power brokers in the conflicts detailed in this book. I thereby try to avoid projecting contemporary ideas about race, gender, and nation onto the past.[75] At the same time, one could view these cycles of violence as a continuation of the social practices of empire that commenced with Spanish colonization of the New World. As Pekka Hämäläinen, James Brooks, and Blackhawk have shown, the Comanche, Apache, Great Basin Ute, and other Native American nations were embroiled in colonial systems of violence and exchange, including trade in captives, livestock, and other forms of property. Brooks tracks ceremonial commemorations as a metaphor for larger enactments of intertwined displays of violence, honor, and gender in systems of exchange in New Mexico.[76] These exchanges created fictive kin networks in which captives were integrated into both Spanish and indigenous communities, often reconstructing families in the wake of violence. Hämäläinen traces similar changes in what eventually became the Comanche Plains empire, especially as it relates to the introduction of horses. Horses made trade and raiding easier and facilitated greater physical mobility.[77] But what distinguishes the Yaqui case is that, unlike the Comanche, Apache, and Ute, they had relatively few native enemies, and horses were never a central part of their economy, except when they used them for food. Unlike the highly nomadic Comanche, Apache, and Ute peoples, the Yaqui did not migrate to the Yaqui Valley. They had remained in the same place ever since the Spaniards made contact with them. Their long-standing land base is essentially what brought them to the attention of the Spanish and later Mexican authorities. Yet the Yaqui quickly became embroiled in what can be called retaliatory cycles of violence that resembled Hämäläinen's, Blackhawk's, and Brooks's characterizations of the exchange systems of the borderlands and plains. In highlighting the Yaquis and their fight for autonomy, I want to make a space for this project in the larger field of borderlands history by showing that the unsubdued Indians who continued to disrupt U.S. and Mexican imperialisms that Brooks, Blackhawk, and Hämäläinen detail with great precision are not simply a phenomenon of the eighteenth and nineteenth centuries. The Yaqui case extends well into the twentieth, up to the 1930's. These social structures of retaliatory violence found their way into the twentieth-century cultural practices of both the Yaqui and the Mexican state. In foregrounding this history, I call into question timeless, unshifting ideas about indigenous peoples as singular and authentic that are evoked as part of romantic U.S., Mexican, and Chicano national pasts.

It is the complicity of groups we have come to call people of color in particular kinds of violence motivated by race or gender because it challenges facile deployments of the discourse of resistance/victimization. A transnational methodology allows one to track the movement of goods, individuals, and ideas in a context in which gender, class, sexuality, and race simultaneously operate to contain and command how these things circulate. Situated both discursively and spatially within the context of overlapping imperialisms— where interracial, intraracial, and intracultural violence were and continue to be the ultimate means of containing even the slightest difference—the punishments I discuss are endemic to nations (imagined and real) that are reconsolidating themselves through the acts of their citizens.

Often the destructive capacity of violence is taken out of its historical context and held up as nothing more than "evidence of minority oppression" within nationalist Chicana/o narratives of resistance.[78] We are often left with historical residues that perpetually cast racialized men and women in the role of victims. My engagement with multiple moments in the history of Mexicans, Indians, and Anglos in the U.S.–Mexico borderlands, in all of their discrete subject positions, corrects this paradigm while nevertheless exposing the inherent contradictions and difficulties in writing historiography of individuals who have been represented as political nonstakeholders and who did not always have the ability to represent themselves in the kinds of historical evidence that most scholars would consider valid. I use the tools of historiography, that is, the tracking of the meaning of how history is told; close textual analysis; and feminist and cultural theory as means of exposing not just the physical and psychic violence that individuals experienced but to also show epistemic violence at work. These interdisciplinary methods allow for the examination of the historiography of the four distinct episodes I identified earlier, namely, Josefa/Juanita's lynching in 1851, the Camp Grant massacre of 1871, racialized violence in South Texas in 1870–1910, and the Yaqui Indian wars of 1880–1910. One might call them case studies of violence against communities in the U.S.–Mexico borderlands. The events are narrated chronologically in order to show the change and continuity in the deployment of violence between 1851 and 1910. I am trying to tell a different kind of story about nation and subjectivity, one that is as attentive to the practices of reading critically as it is to showing how contemporary ideas of the U.S.–Mexico border are divergent. The book moves back and forth between what are separate yet connected geopolitical boundaries, boundaries that are highly contested. As these events attest, the past two hundred years of relations between Mexico and the United States have been marked by violence. In particular, the transnational movement of people, capital, and ideas about difference and power demonstrates that concepts of the nation-state need to be recognized as being mutually dependent. That is, nations like the United States and Mexico need to be defined and historicized in relation to each other. The nation-state is the "historically contingent form of organizing space in the world," and although the United States and Mexico are two distinct nations, the historical subjects that emerge from the zones where the two nations meet experience overlapping colonial histories.[79] As a result, historically extreme violence has been tolerated and in fact legitimated and reinforced by both nations precisely because of their interlocking colonial legacies.

I chose the four episodes because they represent moments in Chicana/o, U.S., Mexican, American Indian, and Latina/o history that are either extremely well known but misrepresented and deserving of reinterpretation or not known at all. On one hand, these moments of violence are not commensurate with each other, and on the other, the physical violence that occurred is incommensurate with the epistemic violence in their historical recording. The violence in all of the cases is racial and to some degree gendered; these moments were instrumental to the foundation of U.S., Mexican, and Chicano nationalism (though, again, not all of these incidents were visible in all three nationalist imaginaries); and these case studies are particularly important for Chicana/o studies because they challenge traditional methodologies and thematic narratives in the field. These moments are historical flashpoints that reflect how violence remade the borderlands for everyone who inhabited it.

I consider the standard narratives of these historical events, provide archival evidence to dispute the record, and try to articulate what has been lost or forgotten in their retelling. What one ends up with when attempting to smooth over violent histories is an empty symbol of disenfranchisement and nothing more. That is, if the history does not show the subject of inquiry resisting some hegemonic Anglo force or it is not about working-class or proletarian peoples, it is somehow rendered unimportant as a subject of study. Constructing narratives of victimization is intrinsic to the ways in which the historical subject is manipulated to reflect the desires of the critic, and to some extent all researchers are implicated in this project. The feminist critic Gayatri Chakravorty Spivak calls such processes "a representational space that exists somewhere amid silence, nonexistence" and "a violent a prioria between subject and object status."[80] It would be too simplistic to portray those subject to violence as a majority of racialized, sexualized women and children. The feminist critic Chandra Mohanty notes that "the writing of history (the discursive and representational) is confused with women as historical actors," and thus women as a group have been represented as being universally duped.[81] Scholars need to recognize that there is a place for studying upper- and middle-class subjects in ethnic studies that are not uniformly proletarian and never were or that gender analysis does not equal studying women alone. A feminist reading can help us avoid such traps. Transnational feminism in particular focuses on the intersections of sexuality, sexual violence, gender, and race as processes of making subjects in multiple national contexts simultaneously. My book is also a methodological proposal in the sense that it demonstrates that transnationalism is not limited to the historical present, nor is it an anachronistic mapping of contemporary concerns onto a historical past. Rather, in the nineteenth century transnationalism was an operative concept, although not named as such, and it was visible enough to be both threatening to and yet enabling of nation-building projects.

My use of the term *transnational* signals a theoretical and historical interest in Spanish and U.S. colonialisms and diasporas, a series of displacements caused by extreme forms of physical and psychic violence; overlapping colonial regimes; and the various ways in which Mexican, Indian, and Anglo peoples colluded in these colonial projects. Although I focus on the U.S.–Mexico border as the site where these violent acts occurred as the result of many communities interacting, the same situation may pertain to the Americas more broadly. I use the methods of transnational feminism not to water down and homogenize the different national groups, classes, and gendered identities of the groups of Apache, Karankawa, Kickapoo, Papago, Kiowa, Comanche, Chicano/as, Anglos, or Mexicans I discuss herein, but rather to reflect how Spanish, Mexican, and U.S. colonialisms had different effects on subjects that were shaped by regional contact or lack thereof, especially as influenced by gender and sexuality. A transnational methodology enables us to see the overlapping historical contingencies that render nations on the same side of a racial divide as well as the *different* histories of racial ideology that lead to the privileging of different kinds of bodies in different nationalisms; and the similarities and differences in the articulation of gender, race, and nation. Such a methodology identifies how we all collude in the selective forgetting of violence against some communities while memorializing and glorifying it against others.

The chapters in this book are unspeakable stories of nation, identity, violence, and citizenship in Mexican, Chicana/o, and U.S. national imaginaries. Because these stories are told in several genres, including historical documents, historical writing, literature, and anthropology, the study requires different modes of analysis. This reveals silences particular to specific disciplines and methods that enact discursive or epistemic violence by selectively forgetting sexual, familial, and racial alliances made through marriage, social practices, and capitalism.[82] Scholarship on the role of violence and the production of subjectivity in a historical perspective focuses on specific types of violence.[83] They have deeply influenced my book; yet I argue that violence is a central category of analysis in and of itself because it is a process of extreme differentiation. Systematic cycles of violence driven by economic anxieties translated into the chronic conflicts of (non)citizen subjects competing for power in overlapping colonial systems. For power, argues David Kazanjian, "understood as subjection, is reiterative and systematic, but it also repeats itself differently or even fails to repeat, allowing the very systematicity of its system to be exposed and troubled. Reiteration, it should be remembered, necessarily exceeds its normative effects and, consequently, the historicity of the norm."[84]

Starting with the intimate details of Josefa/Juanita's lynching in 1851, my book builds upon research on histories of violence that began with the global forces of U.S. colonization of northern Mexico in the nineteenth century. Josefa/Juanita's narrative foregrounds the ways in which economic displacement, transnational industrialization, colonization, and shifting notions of hierarchies of class, race, and gender and their ensuing violence continue to police the bodies and behaviors of racialized subjects in the borderlands. This lynching suggests that disciplining racialized, sexualized women was acceptable at that nineteenth-century historical moment. I isolate the events (her supposed crime occurred on July 4, 1851; the lynching on July 5) and the fact that she was one of fewer than twenty women in the town to make a larger, symbolic commentary about the status of U.S. Mexicana (citizen-)subjects in nineteenth-century California. The contemporary accounts of the hanging express a general sense of discomfort, shock, and horror that people could lynch a woman and also question whether Cannon, the man whom Josefa/Juanita stabbed, may have committed sexual violence against her. Over time the focus has shifted from Josefa/Juanita as a historical subject of her own making to a sensationalized portrayal of the lynching. By examining how critics, historians, and participants have used her story to attain specific political ends, I bring attention to representations of racialized rage, violence, and the body in the context of this lynching and how these representations helped California settlers as liberal citizens of the United States in the nineteenth century and Chicanas/os consolidate their identities as citizens of Aztlán. Tracking how people in that historical moment and the historiography that followed understood disciplinary structures illuminates how capitalist relations of the time were structured around race, class, gender, and sexuality.

Chapter 2 builds on the notions of citizenship, silence, and discipline introduced in the first chapter to consider the joint participation of Mexicans, Papago Indians, and Anglos in the Camp Grant Indian massacre that took place on April 30, 1871, in which 108 Aravaipa and Pinal Apache who had surrendered were slaughtered.[85] I pay special attention to how internalized racism and economic and ethnic alliances influenced subjectivity and concepts of citizenship, for those involved in the massacre. Although a huge body of scholarship in the fields of U.S. and American Indian history focuses on indigenous people's killing of each other in the service of U.S., Mexican, and Spanish colonial powers, there has been little or no discussion of these events in the context of Chicano and Latino studies.[86] The silence surrounding the history of Mexican and Indian participation in genocide against other Indians apparently reflects the power of the resistance paradigm in ethnic studies. The truth is that Mexicans and Indians were not always resisting whites; they often allied with whites against other Indians and Mexicans. This seems to be one reason the history of Camp Grant goes unspoken in Chicano studies.

Chapter 3 analyzes another barely audible history of violence in the Texas-Mexican national imaginary of Jovita González, the first Mexican American woman to earn (in 1930) a master's degree in anthropology at the University of Texas. I theorize González's archive as a site where power and narrative were and are negotiated because many of the materials were not circulated at all or were circulated only posthumously. González's papers and publications grapple with corporal punishment, abjection, and racial, gendered, and sexualized violence enacted upon those who held no power in the Texas-Mexican national project—that is, North American Indians, Mexican Indians, African Americans, and Texas-Mexican women and children—yet rely on a middle-class racist perspective that enacts its own violence, only discursively. Countering a history of narratives about great men of Texas, González's archive mobilizes discourses of gender, race, and class as analytical frameworks to replace a disjointed, skewed past with a more nuanced account of the complex web of violent relations among Anglos, Mexicans, blacks, and Indians in Texas. In the field of Chicana/o studies, González's work has restored historical voice and agency to those she interviewed and those who read her. At the same time, in order to position González as a feminist visionary in the canon, her racism is ignored particularly by feminist scholars, assuming that her racism would be non-feminist. González's oeuvre demonstrates the limits of gender politics, in that lower-class, racialized subjects are portrayed through her own racist lens.

The second half of the book shifts to the Mexican nation-state, specifically to the Arizona–Sonora border region. Chapter 4 explores another unspoken history: the transnational effects of the Yaqui Indian genocide during the Porfiriato (1870–1910). Focusing on the Mexican government's use of violence, sexual force, and deportation as ways of eliminating the alleged Yaqui problem, this chapter examines how U.S. venture capitalists and Mexicanos who had interests in Sonora actively collaborated in a genocidal project of Yaqui extinction. I use little-known archival sources from Mexico to critique how the relationship between indigenous and Mexicano/a and Chicana/o peoples—who were linked through transnational political interests, modes of production, and histories of genocide—has been erased from U.S., Chicano, and Mexican national histories.

Chapter 5 continues the conversation about the Yaqui genocide by contrasting and comparing official Mexican and U.S. government discourses with a literary intervention staged in Montserrat Fuentes's novel *Dreams of the Centaur*. The chapter offers a nuanced, complicated vision of genocide and citizenship as twin transnational projects in the Americas during Mexico's push for modernization in the late nineteenth century and the early twentieth. These evocations and images put Yaqui subjectivity at the center of the picture and alert historians that this violence was abnormal and pathological and needs to be read, as Laura Briggs argues, "for the way it carries traces of very specific histories of violence."[87] These texts collectively comment on discipline and violence enacted against tortured, imprisoned bodies because the public displays of discipline communicate how the Mexican national project of modernity was predicated on Yaqui captivity and lack of citizenship.

The postscript points to the tremendous lessons people can learn from Mexican and U.S. discourses on state and local impunities. Somewhat fittingly, the book begins and ends with discussions of lynching and public displays of violence and the impunity they represent. Although not explicitly situated on U.S. soil, the concept of impunity helps articulate racialized, sexualized, and gendered violence in the contemporary period as part of a larger transnational continuum.

Josefa/Juanita's lynching, the Camp Grant massacre, and the Yaqui genocide were not anticolonial moments of solidarity among Mexicans, Anglos, and various Indian groups. Those whom we would now consider members of colonized, oppressed, and ethnically heterogeneous communities produced inequities by aligning themselves with the states and economies they were a part of. These moments afford vivid examples of temporary Anglo, Mexican, and indigenous enfranchisement through acts of violence and often of genocide. By effectively policing the citizenship of others with violence, eventual marginalized populations were temporarily or symbolically enfranchised. There is a special grammar of violence in each specific instance, and I use it as diagnostic of the grammar of the whole (violent) set of Anglo, Mexican, and indigenous relationships on the border. Each incident reveals the whole history of violence in which it is embedded. Yet we can achieve this reading only through a critical self-reflexivity in which we implicate ourselves in the power dynamics of social and cultural practices. Creating solidarity ultimately requires admitting our mistakes, taking responsibility for them, and moving forward. This transnational turn to deconstruct subjects as being simultaneously of and not of U.S. and Mexican imperial projects of nation and to analyze how these identities are socially produced creates a more nuanced history that is accountable to politics.[88] Such a method avoids co-opting of the historical subjects in this book in the name of nationalism and allows their history to be considered in their own contexts, leading us to contemplate the unspeakable losses and the reasons they are unspeakable.

PART ONE ✳

1 ✳ A Woman with No Names and Many Names

LYNCHING, GENDER, VIOLENCE, AND SUBJECTIVITY

> They could cut each other with knives—these miners—riddle enemy or friend with bullets and smile at it; they could strangle a sluice-box thief, snap the neck of a Chinaman by a twist of his pigtail, whet their appetite for breakfast by the butchery of a ranchería of natives, but injure a child, ill-treat an old man, or do violence to a woman, they could not.
>
> HUBERT HOWE BANCROFT, *POPULAR TRIBUNALS*

> The occurrence, which was published a few days ago, as having taken place at Downieville, proves to be no fiction as several papers supposed. John S. Fowler, Esq., who witnessed the frightful scene, describes the affair as reflecting infinite disgrace upon all engaged in it. The act, for which the victim suffered, was one entirely justifiable under provocation. She stabbed a man who persisted in making a disturbance in her house, and had outraged her rights. The violent proceedings of an indignant and excited mob, led by the enemies of the unfortunate woman, are a blot upon the history of the state. Had she committed a crime of really heinous character, a real American would have revolted at such a course as was pursued towards this friendless and unprotected foreigner. We had hoped that the story was fabricated. As it is the perpetrators of the deed have shamed themselves and their race. The Mexican woman is said to have borne herself with the utmost fortitude and composure through the fearful ordeal, meeting her fate without flinching.
>
> *DAILY ALTA CALIFORNIAN,* "THE HANGING AT DOWNIEVILLE"

The Independence Day celebrations that took place around the newly formed state of California in 1851 marked its one-year anniversary of admission to the Union. The festivities took a violent turn in a small mining community in Yuba County called Downieville. The state senatorial candidate and future

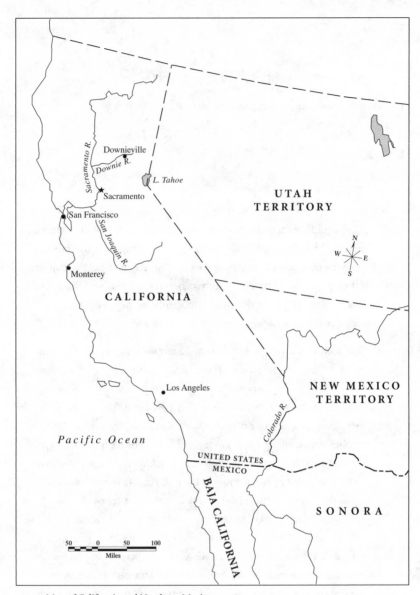

MAP 1 Map of California and Northern Mexico, ca. 1851

governor John B. Weller gave a speech that day.[1] The small town erupted in riotous, drunken celebration that proceeded into the early hours of the morning. Some say that on the night of the Fourth of July, a woman variously identified as Josefa or Juanita, who was alone in her home, was awakened by a rude disturbance. A man named John Cannon had torn the door of her shack from its hinges, trespassing in her home and possibly picking up her scarf from the floor, with the intention of subduing her with it.[2] The drunken, marauding episode apparently enraged Josefa/Juanita, as it was perhaps not the first time Cannon had accosted her.[3] When Cannon returned the next morning to apologize and settle the damages to their home, he and José (Juanita's partner or husband, who is uniformly identified as a gambler) engaged in a verbal argument, and Josefa/Juanita was drawn into the conflict.[4] Apparently they were speaking Spanish to each other, and in the midst of the argument Cannon called Josefa/Juanita a whore. Without hesitating, she picked up a sharp bowie knife and stabbed Cannon in the heart.[5] He died instantly. After the stabbing, José and Josefa/Juanita fled to Craycroft's saloon. There, they were apprehended, and Josefa/Juanita was taken to the town plaza, where a pseudo-trial took place. The mob, which was made up chiefly of Irish immigrants, wanted them both lynched on the spot.[6] Cannon was popular along the Downie River, and nativist sentiments were running high in light of the celebrations the previous day.[7] Two men tried to defend Josefa/Juanita: one was Dr. Aiken, a physician who claimed she was pregnant;[8] the other, named Thayer, protested on the platform. He was ordered by the crowd to look out for his own safety and, like Aiken, was driven from the platform as Josefa/Juanita was sentenced to die.[9] José was run out of town, and Josefa/Juanita was told she would shortly face a lynch mob.[10] Sometime later she was escorted to the Jersey Bridge, where she climbed a scaffold, slipped the noose over her head, and walked out on a plank that was then cut out from under her.[11] The crowd cheered in a scene of ritual male bonding as the plank was hacked off and she dropped. Her body allegedly spun and struggled for a half hour before she was removed.[12] Weller watched the entire event and was accused of pandering to the mob to secure votes because he participated in the lynching as a spectator.[13] Some speculate that Josefa/Juanita and Cannon were initially buried in the same grave but that their remains were later dug up to make room for a new theater.[14]

The contemporary newspaper and eyewitness accounts express a general sense of discomfort over this violent episode as they reveal a metanarrative of Josefa/Juanita's lynching that differs dramatically from the dominant narrative. There are many accounts of what happened to Cannon, why Josefa/

Juanita stabbed him, and why she was lynched. Historians more or less agree on the facts as related above. The narratives that follow express greater ambiguity, shock, horror, and amazement about the lynching and differ on whether or not there was a threat of sexual violence by Cannon. The discursive fight over Josefa/Juanita's body in the historical documents and accounts that follow reflects the ways in which U.S. Mexicana subjects are often constructed throughout dominant histories and dominant literary narratives as having no voice and no agency except when confronted with violence against their person, as static subjects that are whole and transparent, existing outside of language and constructed by racist discourse.[15] If individuals who exercised some agency happened to be recorded in the historical record, it was often because they were subjected to some form of brutal, gendered, and racialized violence. I track the competing discourses surrounding Josefa/Juanita's body as a larger battle over the "truthful" narrative of this woman's brutal death before a mob of some three thousand men.[16] Josefa/Juanita's multiple narratives dispute "the gap between the real and the discursive" and raise a very important historiographic and methodological question: What does it mean for Josefa/Juanita to be inaugurated as a subject through an act of violence?[17] In exploring this question, I analyze the various political agendas that get played out and through Josefa/Juanita's lynched body. I work with a range of primary and critical scholarly sources to show that history, literature, biography, and metanarrative have all used Josefa/Juanita to meet the desires of particular self-serving political agendas.

Maj. William Downie's (the first mayor of Downieville in 1849, and for whom the town was named) memoir has a chapter on Josefa/Juanita called "Lynching a Beauty," a version that remembers some things and intentionally forgets others, such as the Mexican "whose name has been long forgotten [José] . . . who would personally never have been known save for his partner in the clay hut, a woman known as Juanita."[18] Downie suggests that the male subject of this history, José, would not exist without the narrative of his partner, Josefa/Juanita; the roles of gendered privilege and race are shifted as José's masculinity is trumped by Josefa/Juanita's role as a historical actor. We know about Josefa/Juanita and José only because of the violence she enacted against Cannon and the violence of her lynching, but this does not mean she did not exist as a historical subject prior to the lynching. This chapter focuses on questions of desire, rage, agency, and pain as they are represented in narratives about Josefa/Juanita and presupposes that she was a subject constructed through systems of language and not just social forces.[19] Often positioned as ancillary descriptors (rage, desire, agency, and pain), this nexus of power relations reveals the many purposes Josefa/Juanita serves in historical, cultural, and nation-building projects.[20] Further, how her purpose and narratives are rendered and to what end can be quite seductive in the service of the resistance versus assimilation narrative that often grounds ethnic and Chicana/o studies projects. Desire, as it was enacted by Josefa/Juanita and those in her social world, as well as the desires of the critic and historian is a huge, critical piece of the puzzle. As I read the documents, I try to uncover the desires underlying the discourses and silences, for they are strategic in constructing a particular kind of narrative. When scholars desire to repeat the triumphant narrative of Josefa/Juanita's resistance, another layer of silence is created by discursive violence. Rather than being seduced by the resistance narrative that potentially emerges from this history, we need to theorize and historicize Josefa/Juanita's death to reveal how violence was a social practice. Seduction and violence, as we will see, are yoked by both the way in which the stories are told and the fact that their sensationalism, devoid of detail, has a seductive power.

My critique of sensationalism emphasizes how the emotive, extreme, affective, outlandish, and extraordinary aspects of a story such as Josefa/Juanita's draw a reader away from the intentionality behind narrative historical construction and toward an uncritical response. Whereas an uncritical response might take the form of "What an awful story," a critical one might ask, "Why is this story awful, and for whom and to what end?" The uncritical response has the power of sway and is not about truth or fiction but about the psychic and emotive power of a story. In addition, the veracity of the discourse is taken for granted, especially in this case. Working in concert, the assumed transparency of language and sensationalism seduce us into accepting a singular narrative of truth and resistance, one in which we take for granted the emotive power of a singular narrative of the lynching instead of questioning the motives behind it. When numerous Chicana/o studies scholars narrate Josefa/Juanita's utterances on the lynching platform as the narrative of a triumphant survivor who resisted Anglo domination and hegemony by talking back to the lynch mob, they reproduce resistance as the sole narrative account of what her lynching means. Furthermore, the narration of Josefa/Juanita's resistance is often given a sensationalist slant. Sensationalism announces a set of ideas with the intention of displacing or forgetting the contradictory, the gray, and the unappealing, which is why I want to shift the discussion about Josefa/Juanita's lynching away from the seductive and exceedingly appealing resistance narrative of talking back to the colonizer to a discussion of language as radically exterior to the body but part of the processes of subject formation.

Given the triangulation of seduction, sensationalism, and desire to access or control power, I want to focus on the most unspoken, underanalyzed facet of Josefa/Juanita's lynching, namely, how her rage and honor are sensationalized and pathologized in contrast to the portrayal of the lynch mob. Certain things are intentionally unspoken in this story because they unsettle the narrative of victimization and resistance, especially within a Chicano studies and Chicano nationalist context. To sensationalize something is to empty it of meaning, to aim for violently exciting effects calculated to produce a startling but superficial impression. I want to get at the silences underneath the sensationalism, at what is articulated beyond the trivial evocation of Cannon's stabbing and Josefa/Juanita's lynching and at the multidirectional ways in which language is mobilized to cement particular ideas of a racialized subject that exists outside of language. Sensationalism, much like resistance, has a seductive quality. To the African American studies scholar Saidya Hartman, seduction implies a theory of power that demands ultimate submission. Seduction "designate[s] the displacement and euphemization of violence, for seduction epitomizes the discursive alchemy that shrouds direct forms of violence under the veil of 'enchanted relations.' "[21] The theoretical insights of Hartman's analysis of sexual and physical violence against slaves address the insistent masquerade of "enchanted relations"—that Josefa/Juanita and Cannon were lovers and were buried in the same grave—built into depictions of Josefa/Juanita's sexuality and rage. Miscalculations of these "enchanted relations" account for a rage so hostile and so deeply experienced in the flesh that the myth of reciprocity is replaced with an act of murder, an act to defend bodily integrity. By linking articulations of rage, honor, seduction, desire, and pain, we may better understand how radical subjectivities are produced.

A WOMAN OF NO NAMES AND MANY NAMES

Josefa/Juanita's name is unclear in the historical record, which points to a larger problem of identifying marginal subjects in traditional archival sources. Her multiple names, her multiple racial identities, and the multiple narratives about her death exemplify how subjects existing at the interstices of multiple colonial regimes are consistently transformed into racialized objects that have several names at once.[22] Having no names and many names also signifies how we can reinterpret the narrative of Josefa/Juanita's lynching as a complex, contradictory moment in a larger discussion of subject formation and historiography. These signifiers shift us away from a solely race-based or ego-based understanding of arrangements of power and force us to focus on how language functions "like an alien body that grafts itself onto the order of the body and of nature."[23] Something that seems easily dismissed as a transparently racist gesture of misidentification, the name of Josefa or Juanita or both in the historical record is actually something quite complex, showing how language is what makes the subject and the body.

The local historian of central California William Seacrest suggests that Josefa/Juanita's name has been adulterated. Because of a lack of interest in her story "she has gone down in history simply as Juanita—Juanita of Downieville."[24] Nothing is known of her prior to her lynching; it is as if she did not exist as a subject prior to that day. To further confound historians, "Just how the name 'Juanita' became associated with the woman is hard to say, but the early newspapers and eyewitness accounts . . . refer to her as Josefa. I see no reason why this shouldn't be assumed to be her real name."[25] Yet Seacrest still titles his piece "Juanita," perhaps to mark her popular name. In most sources written by Anglo-Americans she is referred to as Juanita. Josefa/Juanita's name is the focus of a tale by the California folklorist Cora Older entitled "Juanita of Downieville, 1851" as well.[26] Older writes, "At Downieville among the pines and cedars of the towering Sierras, there was Juanita. What was her last name? *Quién sabe*? [Who knows?] No one in the boisterous mining camp knew or cared."[27] Older is one of the few narrators who dares even to suggest that Josefa/Juanita might have had a last name. However, in the same breath in which she raises that important question, she undermines the importance of Josefa/Juanita's last name with the Spanish interjection "*Quién sabe*," implying "and really, who cares or cared." Here, a last name marks status in the community as well as status as a citizen. At this time white women were addressed by their surnames as Mrs. or Miss _____; calling them by first name would have been a sign of disrespect, a usage reserved for the intimacy among family and friends. In the context of a mining camp, however, a presumably unmarried woman of color who remained in such a place was often assumed to be a prostitute.[28] Calling Josefa/Juanita by her first name only, then, is an indication that U.S. Mexicanas were not afforded the same status as white women and were automatically assumed to be less than "ladies" and that the structuring of femininity was racialized. In addition, the use of her first name only further feminizes her because a last name would identify her with a male subject (a father or husband).[29] Marta Cotera, one of the founding scholars of Chicana feminist thought, states that Josefa/Juanita's last name was Segovia, while Rodolfo Acuña, the author of one of the first canonical Chicano history texts, suggests that it was Vasquez.[30] The multiple names offered by Chicano scholars stages the contradiction between her popular name and her actual legacy in Chicana/o intellectual circles and in the broader history of the gold rush. Both Cotera and Acuña signal another issue: that desire to recuperate the full names and lives of violated U.S. Mexicana/o subjects in a Chicana/o studies context is one way of attempting to mourn a loss by declaring a truth, a truth about something that is simply irrecoverable. The desire to name Josefa/Juanita expresses a desire to fix her in history, to make her a part of the history of nation (in both U.S. and Chicana/o history), to make her story significant as a plotted moment of Chicana/o oppression. There are several benefits to fixing Josefa/Juanita's place in history, the first being that she can be claimed as a resistant foremother of Chicano liberation politics. The second benefit is to make a legitimate claim to U.S. citizenship for Mexicana/os in the nineteenth century by substantiating their presence within the geographic boundaries of the nation. At the same time, Chicano nationalism and the field of Chicano studies need a hero/heroine, someone to hinge an identity on, a single point of reference that translates the goals of the movement and the field deep into the historical past in the shorthand that is her last name. Last, fixing Josefa/Juanita as a named historical subject secures the footing of both Chicano studies and to some degree Chicana feminism as fields of intellectual value because they are called upon to provide a different kind of knowledge about her in place of the Anglocentric history that contains the primary narratives of her life and death. On the opposite side, the unfixed nature of Josefa/Juanita's name suggests that U.S. Mexicanas are unimportant in the dominant historical record because they were and are racialized and sexualized as different—so unimportant that no one knew for sure what their name was.

Exposing my own desires as a critic and historian, I intentionally refer to this woman as Josefa/Juanita to express the unfixed nature of her identity in the numerous accounts of her lynching. Recent evidence has emerged that José María Loiaza, Josefa's husband, filed an unsuccessful claim with the U.S. and Mexico Claims Commission during the convention between the two nations held on July 4, 1868. The claim proves that Josefa was not Juanita, that she had a last name, and that she was married. Still, I think it is of critical importance to invoke all of her names because they constitute the multiple ways she has been historicized in the record.[31] Use of all the names together evokes fragments of cultural memory,[32] an attempt to reconstruct what fragments of her experience we have rather than to seek a unified, whole truth; for I would argue that there isn't one. At the same time, the use of both names acknowledges the ambiguous nature of her story and the ambiguity with which the story is retold. Using both names points to the fact that the society that reported her lynching did not care enough about her as a human being even to get her name right or to cite her last name. They were uninterested in affording her the markers of a respected citizen-subject. The shift in names also indicates the presence of her narrative in oral culture, folk tales, and larger narratives of California in the era of the gold rush. The story appears and reappears as a folk tale in which the transgressions of one U.S. Mexicana and the lynch mob who hanged her are repeated, to reinforce that such a horror should not and will not occur again. With each retelling the name is skewed: sometimes she is Josefa, sometimes she is Juanita, and sometimes she is simply "the Mexican woman." Other times she is referred to as the "Spanish American woman,"[33] and she is also often called "the greaser."[34]

The violence, both epistemic and material, manifested in having no name and many names returns us to the objectification of Josefa/Juanita's body in a historical context. The potential for the nameless, racialized, sexualized, gendered body to betray itself resonates in Josefa/Juanita's names and points not only to an explicit, time-honored Anglo tradition of misnaming, renaming, and forgetting names of the racialized bodies attached to them, but also to a Chicana/o project of reclaiming them. As I argued in an essay about epistemic violence, my project is not about recovering these stories from the dustbins of history, but rather about becoming a listener capable of hearing all the nuances in a narrative, even if they don't accord with masculinist or cultural nationalist projects.[35] Through the continuous naming and renaming of Josefa/Juanita's body, we experience it as a historical text, a text that has been written over by dominant historical narratives that embody the practices of racism, sexism, nationalism, and nativism, all carried out in language.[36] By calling attention to all of Josefa/Juanita's names, we defy the practice of making her nameless and problematize the question of truth in historical scholarship.

To examine the narratives that define Josefa/Juanita's subjectivity is to think about her as a subject cut by language, often overdetermined by discourse. It is to recognize that the historiography of the event reveals much more about the tellers of her narrative (white men mostly) who witnessed the event.[37] Although I have sought to understand Josefa/Juanita's story, I have found it almost impossible to find any substantive information about her in historical records.[38] Even when we attempt to seek out individuals and histories to try to correct the dominant discourses of erasure, the silence says so much. Lack of attention to the details of the lynching, the conflicting accounts about it, and a larger analysis of the role of gender and sexuality are critical to understanding how and why Josefa/Juanita met her brutal death. As the historian H. H. Bancroft argues, "No one thought of her" until the stabbing and the lynching.[39] Had she not been lynched, we might well never have known she existed. The competing narratives that begin with the discrepancy about Josefa/Juanita's name and racial identity demonstrate how those who wrote eyewitness accounts of the lynching were implicated in the production of its larger meaning.

THE COMPETING NARRATIVES OVER JOSEFA/JUANITA'S BODY

David Pierce-Barstow's "Statement of Recollections of 1849–51 in California" is one of the few eyewitness accounts of Josefa/Juanita and her lynching. He described her as "a very comely, quiet, gentle creature apparently, and behaved herself with a great deal of propriety" (7). Inscribing her with Victorian ideals of womanhood, Pierce-Barstow understands Josefa/Juanita as a harmless person, a woman who conducted herself within traditional gender constraints of feminine virtue. This seems to be one reason the lynching is questioned by the reporters of the *Daily Alta Californian*, who are forced to interrogate the exceedingly contradictory nature of what it means to be an American citizen in the context of her lynching.[40] Even while the editors of the *Daily Alta* bring Josefa/Juanita's citizenship into question by referring to her as a foreigner, the writer sides with her by calling the perpetrators un-American: "Had she committed a crime of really heinous character, a real American would have revolted at such a course as was pursued towards this friendless and unprotected foreigner."[41] The gendered apprehension is staged quite succinctly in the tension between universal ideals embodied in the figure of the citizen, which are supposed to have a broader reach in the United States. Even if she had been guilty of a heinous crime (recognizing possible extenuating circumstances in this case), Josefa/Juanita should have been afforded the rights of citizenship, including due process and trial by jury in a court of law whether or not she was a foreigner.[42] In assuming Josefa/Juanita to be a rights-bearing subject, citing democratic ideals, and expressing sympathy for her as a woman and foreigner, the article expresses honest discomfort over the fact that the victim of the lynch mob was a woman. Yet the writer reads Josefa/Juanita as a foreigner, not as a U.S. Mexicana, on the assumption that Mexicans are not Americans (even though the lynching occurred after Mexican California became a part of the United States through the Treaty of Guadalupe Hidalgo); framing the lynch mob as un-American underscores the friction inherent in what constitutes a real American. Apparently Josefa/Juanita does not represent a real American, but neither does the lynch mob, who "shamed themselves and their race."[43] Neither represents U.S. democratic principles in their idealized state. Women like Josefa/Juanita pose the ultimate challenge to American democratic beliefs and Victorian notions of womanhood and the people who claim to uphold them. She existed between what it meant to be a lady and something else, creating contradictions that ultimately were worked out in the violence against her body.[44] This violent incident attests that Americans in 1851 were still unable to reconcile the inconsistencies in relation to skin color and citizenship rights. The lynch mob did not view Josefa/Juanita as an American citizen, and this subtle difference facilitated the violence, while challenging the mob to think about citizenship rights in a racial manner. Ironically, in their effort to defend Josefa/Juanita's action as something outside of a "crime of a really heinous character," the *Daily Alta Californian* reinscribes that she is always already un-American. Yet hysteria around the foreign body is quieted as the writer imposes "racial shame" upon an unlikely object for that historical moment: the Anglo-Irish lynch mob. Moreover, the article is most concerned with portraying a sympathetic image of the "unprotected foreigner" to create a countercultural narrative of a highly contested scene of violence.

This editor saw the lynching as an outrage against democracy, which elucidates how the violence became an alibi for why California needed to be incorporated into the United States. In other words, the lynching was proof of the need for more U.S. law. Josefa's body literally swings both ways: evidence of the lack of justice becomes a call for more justice. Alternatively, her lynching provides incorporation of the Irish immigrants into the state in contradistinction to the Mexicans, under the rubric that Mexicans were not white like the Irish. While not all Mexican territories became states following the Mexican-American War in 1848, California did become a member of the Union in 1850. According to articles VII and IX of the Treaty of Guadalupe Hidalgo, former Mexican citizens and their property were to be incorporated politically into the United States. The treaty affected some one hundred thousand Mexicans in the newly acquired territories, which included large numbers of Hispanicized and nomadic Indians in New Mexico and California.[45] However, at the time of the treaty Mexicans were legally considered white in the U.S. census even though the matter was disputed in the courts.[46] The anthropologist Martha Menchaca argues that Mexicans who wanted to keep their lands in California and hold the citizenship rights hammered out in the state constitutional convention insisted on their whiteness.[47] Some even went to trial to prove it. This conflict arose because of the colonizing impulse implicit in the policies of territorial expansion, which later became known as

Manifest Destiny.[48] Such policies called for the rescuing of lands from the racially and mentally inferior Indians and Mexicans of the Southwestern territories.[49] Since it was believed that Mexicans were not prepared to govern themselves and their land, it was an act of divine providence that justified the taking of ill-marked properties within the newly acquired territories. Racial difference and doctrines of inferiority stood in direct contrast to the treaty's marking Mexicans as white. Josefa/Juanita's whiteness and femaleness, under the law, did not work in her favor. Instead, her foreignness and linguistic difference justified the lynching as an act of enfranchisement for the Irish and other white foreign miners who made up the lynch mob.

The writer of the article "Woman Hung at Downieville," printed in the *Daily Alta Californian* on July 9, 1851, recognizes, contextualizes, and legitimates the rage that led Josefa/Juanita to stab Cannon; by contrast, other accounts attribute her rage to biologically determined stereotypes linked to racism.[50] The editorial states,

> We are informed by Deputy Sheriff Gray, that on Saturday afternoon a Spanish woman was hung for stabbing to the heart a man by the name of Cannan, killing him instantly. Mr. Gray informed us that the deceased, in the company with some others, had the night previously entered the house of the woman and created a *riot and disturbance*, which *so outraged her*, that when he presented himself the next morning to apologize for his behavior, he was met at the door by the female, who had in her hand a large Bowie knife, which she instantly drove into his heart (emphasis added).

Using the language of injury, assault, and violent disorder, the article highlights the invasive nature of Cannon's presence in Josefa/Juanita's home. Cannon's entrance is presented here as a crime of outrage, a disturbance and violation inflicted upon Josefa/Juanita's living space and her body. This account is not transparent in meaning because the article sympathizes with Josefa/Juanita and not the lynch mob, describing her outrage as justified. Had she not been Spanish, her act of self-defense might have been permissible. Here, a Spanish racial identity is not linked to European or Anglo-Saxon identity; it is racialized as an other identity. Standing in for Mexico and Spain, two fallen empires in the Americas, with a racially confusing ancestry, she is hailed as either loving or, in this case, hating the conqueror. Even though the editors of the *Daily Alta* were anxious about the lynching of a woman as an amoral act, those who actively participated in the lynching used their involvement as a means to transcend their personal anxieties about the tenuous nature of citizenship in mining communities and in California at that particular historical moment. Their participation as spectators was a means to act out legal and extralegal control as a part of the process by which the former Mexican territories and their citizens were subsumed into the U.S. nation-state. When we compare and contrast the anxieties staged in Josefa/Juanita's lynching—the amoral crime of lynching a woman, fear of the foreign body, citizenship concerns for foreign Caucasian miners, and racialized claims to citizenship—we see a sense of the competing ideologies surrounding lynching as a cultural practice. For the larger processes by which subjects are constituted through violence is an example of how extreme physical violence was a means of creating social order around race and gender ideologies.

Still, many historians, including Seacrest, the author of *Juanita of Downieville*, whom we could consider to be a California local color historian from the mid-twentieth century, make the excuse that there were too few women in California during the gold rush to justify violence against them. Subscribing to a Victorian middle-class notion of womanhood, he writes, "Women were venerated and cherished, because they represented homes and families that had been left behind."[51] Seacrest reflects the idea that women embodied civilizing influences. Given that he argues there were too few women in the mining communities to justify their killing or, more accurately, their lynching, the fact that Josefa/Juanita was brutally hung, in his account, suggests that in the logic of Victorian femininity her racialized female body did not constitute womanhood. Narrative histories of Downieville report a shortage of women in the town in 1850 and well into 1851. Cora Older claims that in 1851 there were fewer than eight Mexican women along the Yuba River and that "most decent women kept away from Downieville and other camps."[52] Other accounts state there were fewer than a dozen white and Spanish women in the town.[53] The census records of 1850 for Yuba County show that Josefa/Juanita's name was nowhere to be found. Most of the women recorded in the census were white (there were 181).[54] Four women were black. Mexican women were not specifically identified by racial identity in the census unless by place of birth or surname.[55] Their occupations were innkeeper, 10; storekeeper, 8; assistant, 5; and cook, 1.[56]

The shortage of women also suggests that Josefa/Juanita's lynching had spatial implications. A group of women entered Durgan Flat, a mining area outside of Downieville, in 1851. They were coming to work in the town and find potential mates who had made their fortune in the gold diggings. When they were spotted, a mob of men approached them, terrifying one of the women: "As they neared town it grew dark, and the miners crowded in from up and down the river, cheering and yelling up the crowded main street, till they landed at the Gem Saloon. One of the women was so frightened when she entered that she fainted, fearing that they were going to be lynched, as the Spanish woman had been hung by a mob on the 5th of July that same year."[57] Downieville, as a place, is associated with a lynched Spanish woman's body (notice here Josefa/Juanita is not Mexican and not of the Americas or Mexico). The Chicana studies scholar Mary Pat Brady argues that "the regulation of space reinforces the regulation of desire and pleasure, as well as the extent to which social reality, in all its minutiae, is spatialized."[58] Even an Anglo woman who journeys to the mining town to seek a husband faints in horror when she is confronted by the spatial memories attached to Downieville. Here, the bodies of the two women are linked, as the white woman's body and trauma recall Josefa/Juanita's body and trauma, producing an emotive and physical response to this history. What seems like an anecdotal line actually reveals a cultural narrative that exposes how any woman who came to Downieville in the 1850s after Josefa/Juanita's lynching could identify with the peril of violation of the female body. Just as memory haunts the women entering Durgan Flat, Josefa/Juanita's Spanish or Mexican heritage (again, note that her ethnic identity is as unstable as her name) disappears in the way the white woman registers her own fear. Josefa/Juanita thereby becomes a (racially) universal gendered subject that represents the potential for violence that women had to contend with in mining towns and has an immediate disciplining effect: the women remember. Women scarcely occupied the space. According to Downie, "Many had come there to stay, but the place was isolated, far from the center of law, order and protection, and so the people took the law into their own hands, when the occasion demanded it."[59] Josefa/Juanita's lynching defined the space and place of women in the community.

These disputes about gender and the body demonstrate the inflexible attitudes of patriarchy toward lynching and crime in general. Such attitudes are nowhere more evident than in Josefa/Juanita's trial. The kangaroo court was perhaps not so unauthorized after all. It "formed . . . in the plaza, occupying the same platform from which Wells had spoken the day before,[60] and a lawyer by the name of William Spears, who was afterwards killed in the Washoe Indian war, acted as a public prosecutor, and a jury of 12 men was selected from the crowd, and the whole day was given to the trial of the woman, Wells sitting on the stand while the trial was foreclosing. Towards night they found the woman guilty and sentenced her to be hung at sundown."[61] In this moment, the law was a performance of patriarchy, precisely because the jury and mob were entirely composed of Anglo men who were not Josefa/Juanita's peers. The serving of justice was not a process that was racially or gender neutral, and the most detailed accounts of the court proceedings reflect this.

A reporter from the *Steamer Pacific Star* acted as the court reporter for the trial, detailing the names of the judge, jury, and witnesses but not that of the defendant: John Rose, Esq., of Rose's Ranch, judge; E. Hyde, L. Williams, A. S. McMillian, F. A. McCamly, G. Underhill, E. Bleeker, A. L. Brown, A. R. Burr, C. F. Mattison, E. D. Ferrin, W. B. Reed, and Albert Woodruff, jurors. After the court was organized, the reporter stated, "I was invited to take a seat upon the stand for the purpose of hearing and reporting the testimony."[62] Two things can be said about a newspaperman serving as a court reporter: either it was a sincere effort to make Josefa/Juanita's trial as close to the real thing as possible outside of an actual court of law, or the detailed report serves merely to put a veneer of justice on a predetermined outcome. An ironic sense of justice is inherent in the statement "Judge Lynch was about to ascend the judgment seat," which suggests that a lynching was about to take place. But was the metaphorical, symbolic seating of Judge Lynch at the trial proceedings something that was declared before the trial took place? or was it something the reporter used to describe the proceedings after Josefa/Juanita was lynched? Posed differently, if the name *Judge Lynch* was invoked by the jury, the judge, and the bystanders at the trial, prior to its taking place, then from that moment onward justice is undermined by sensationalism, which set the tone for everything that followed. If not, then perhaps the kangaroo court was not so disorderly and false after all. But according to the reporter, "Previous to the organization of the tribunal, there was a considerable impatience manifested, and cries of 'Hang them,' 'Give them a fair trial and hang them!'" were frequently heard. The excitement, however, subsided to a great extent, when it was known that the examination was commenced."[63]

"Wm. S. Spear, Esq. undertook the prosecution for the people. Once the prisoners [Josefa and José] being brought to the stand, the question was put, shall the prisoners be allowed counsel, which was decided in the affirmative, and Messrs. Pickett (formerly from our city) and Brocklebank were appointed." This description is evidence of some sort of judicial process, but one reflected more in the court of public opinion than in written law.[64] Roughly two pages of testimony by witnesses to Cannon's stabbing and the events leading up to it were recorded, whereas Josefa's and José's testimonies are recorded in roughly three short paragraphs.

The most revealing testimony came from Cannon's mining partner, a Mr. Knowles, and another miner, Richard H. Martin. Knowles stated,

Deceased was my partner; we had come down to the Forks for provisions; was looking for him in the morning; when I found him talking with the Spaniard Jose, who appeared to be angry; deceased seemed in perfect good humor; Jose put his hand to his bosom as if to draw a weapon, when Mr. Lawson said to him, if you draw a weapon I will knock you D____d head off; deceased seemed desirous of making up the difficulty; the two prisoners now present retired into the house together, when the deceased walked up to the door; a moment after he saw the blow struck; saw the hand that inflicted the blow, but not the body of the person; the woman on going to the house looked very angry and determined; on receiving the blow, deceased turned round and exclaimed 'see she has stabbed me.' The prisoner, Josefa, is the woman."[65]

Note that the reports at the beginning of the article state that Cannon came to José to offer reparation, which suggests that José confronted Cannon. Most of the testimony focused as much around confirming that Josefa/Juanita was the killer as corroborating the actual events. By adopting a formal tone ("the deceased" and "the prisoners"), Knowles uses legal rhetoric to give credence and validity to his testimony as lawful and objective. Formality provides a kind of objective distance in the linguistic expression, making the testimony seem truer and more accurate. José's and Josefa/Juanita's anger contrasts with what Knowles describes as Cannon's "perfect good humor," a denial that he caused emotional disturbance or became hostile or angry toward the defendants, casting them as hotheaded, racially inferior subjects with no just cause for violence. Indirectly, Knowles's testimony implies that the Spanish language is what paints these racialized, gendered individuals as overly emotional and unreasonable. Speaking Spanish, in this context, does not signal California nativeness but foreignness and racialized difference.

The witness Richard H. Martin was a neighbor of Josefa/Juanita and José: "My room was adjoining that of the Spaniard's. After the company left in the morning, overheard the two prisoners in conversation. The conversation was in the Spanish language but I understood some portion of it. *Here the witness explained what the conversation was, which it is unnecessary to repeat, as it was obscene.* He knew the meaning of the language used, he said, from having been informed by the prisoner Josefa. On his explanation, in broad language, the prisoner seemed highly delighted and laughed heartily."[66] Through this reference, Martin destabilzes the national origin and ethnicity of the couple while fixing José in the trial's public performance and larger civic imaginary as foreign. José and Josefa/Juanita are further made to seem other by both their conversation in Spanish and the fact that it was too profane to repeat in front of the crowd and jury. This silence, or omission of testimony, does four things. First, important evidence is omitted, and that omission *becomes* the evidence or testimony. Second, José and Josefa/Juanita are automatically labeled as immoral for engaging in profanity following their encounter with Cannon over the broken door. Third, the silence about the violence of the language and the event itself, as I argue throughout the book, is an utterance that posits action. Failing to disclose what Josefa/Juanita and José said fuels their culpability, places morality within the realm of the Anglo miners testifying on behalf of the defense, and does not acknowledge anger or rage as a valid emotional response to physical threats. Instead, the unspeakable profanity is called upon to stand in for the supposed fact of testimony. It also posits that an omission of evidence on the basis of morality performed by an Anglo man had more weight than what the defendants said and did. Fourth, and most important, the reason for the profanity is not revealed; the witness remarks that "the prisoner seemed highly delighted and laughed heartily" after using profane language in reference to Cannon.[67] Somewhat pathological in tone, this particular testimony suggests that Cannon's murder was premeditated and that Josefa/Juanita took pleasure in planning the murder. The social pathology of the criminal woman, the Mexican-Spanish murderess, acted to justify the decision that followed the conclusion of the testimony: "The jury finds that the woman, Josefa, is guilty of the murder of—Cannan, and that she will suffer death in two hours. Amos L. Brown, Foreman. The man, Jose, is found not guilty, but the jury earnestly requests that Judge Rose advise him to leave the town in twenty four hours. Amos L. Brown, Foreman."[68] Notice that the verdict does not state how Josefa/Juanita will "suffer death," leaving open the possibility for multiple modes of capital punishment.

The testimony of José and Josefa/Juanita is also recorded in a formalist lexicon but contrasts greatly in length and content. Following the gendered order of the time, José spoke first:

Deceased in company with several others, broke down the door to my room. On meeting the deceased in the morning, and asking him for payment, he used insulting language, called me a liar and a s— of a b— [son of a bitch]. He then drew back his fist as if to strike me, when I stated to him that I did not wish to fight; he was large and I a small man. At this time the woman, Josefa, came forward and told him to strike her. She also was insulted. He called her dear, and then after that a w—r [whore]. She went into the house at my solicitation. When in, she took a knife from the table, and as the deceased was about to enter, still calling her bad names, both in English and in Spanish, she stabbed him. Only one hinge of the door was broken, the top one had been previously broken. The door was fastened with two staples, one of which was pulled out when forcibly entered.[69]

Several things about this testimony are noteworthy, including the fact that José and Josefa/Juanita were apparently both fluent in English and that Cannon spoke some Spanish. The conflict, according to this testimony, was not originally about Josefa/Juanita being raped, as many of the other narratives of the events would have us believe, but about José's seeking monetary compensation for his door being broken down. Cannon's denial of financial responsibility for reparations unleashes a whole different set of hostilities toward José, as Cannon questions his honor (calling him a liar and a son of a bitch) and physically threatens him. Instead of playing into nineteenth-century stereotypes of the bloodthirsty Mexican ready for a fight at a moment's notice, José appealed for peace, realizing that his small stature was a mismatch for Cannon's large frame in a physical fight. Josefa/Juanita, according to her husband's testimony, provoked Cannon, daring him to hit her because an insult to her husband was an insult to her person as well. Cannon's lack of respect and informal language (calling her dear and then a whore) no doubt provoked her to anger, yet her obedience to her husband's command that she return to the house shows a respect for traditional gender roles but with a twist. When Cannon breeches her space, she promptly responds by stabbing him in the heart.

These were not the only legal claims José made, and they fell on deaf ears. As I mentioned above, José filed a claim in 1868 with U.S. and Mexico Claims Commission, a transnational body established in 1851 following the discovery of gold in California to determine the validity of Spanish land grants and settle losses of citizens from both nations incurred in the United States after the Treaty of Guadalupe Hidalgo. José sought three hundred thousand dollars for "the lynching of his wife and banishment of himself by a mob."[70] Although filed in 1868, the claim was not decided by the commission until June 11, 1875, twenty-five years after Josefa/Juanita's lynching. This claim was number 904 of 998, the majority of which were filed by Mexicans against the United States for a number of losses, most notably for Indian depredations. Of these claims against the United States 831 were denied. Those that were paid out, 167 in total, totaled $150,498.41. Of these, 131 came from an incident in Piedras Negras on October 6, 1855,[71] in which volunteers in service to the state of Texas, under Captains Callahan and Henry, took property and destroyed the town.[72]

José's recorded testimony lacks details, preserving another kind of unspeakable code of silence about gender, sexuality, and honor. Josefa/Juanita is recorded as giving only one sentence of evidence on the witness stand that differs from that given by her husband: "I took the knife to defend myself; I had been told that some of the boys wanted to get into my room and sleep with me; a Mexican boy told me so and it frightened me so that I used to fasten the door and take a knife with me to bed; I told the deceased that was no place to call me bad names, come in and call me so, and as he was coming in I stabbed him."[73] For José to admit that the conflict between him and Cannon was based on sexual competition over the body of his wife would have provoked far too much *vergüenza* (shame). To admit that a sexual competition over Josefa/Juanita's body existed would have suggested that José could not control his woman or control what others thought about his woman within the context of a highly patriarchal community. Instead, José abides by the code of honor that preserves his masculinity by making the conflict a monetary dispute that erupted into violence that was sexual in nature when the word *whore* enters the exchange. It is Josefa/Jasefa/Juanita who admits that some of the "boys" (a diminutive way to describe the miners like Cannon, in terms of both masculinity and maturity) wanted to get into her room and sleep with her, which explains why she slept with a knife beside her.[74]

But if Josefa/Juanita was afraid of Cannon and the threat of sexual violence, why did she invite him into her home? Wouldn't logic suggest that if one is afraid of someone, the last thing one would do is invite him into one's home? Further, why dishonor your husband by inviting the man who physically threatened the two of you into your home? The answer could be that Josefa/Juanita acted out her rage and frustration in a premeditated murder, trumping all the systems of gendered honor and behavior through enacting a retributive physical violence of her own. However, given the multiple interpretations of what was said between Cannon and Josefa/Juanita, perhaps this was a mistranscripton of something like "how dare you come in [to my home] and call me so."

In the record of the proceedings, all of the witnesses except for José and Josefa/Juanita are referred to by their full names. José and Josefa/Juanita are familiar, completely knowable individuals and thus referred to by their first names, just as their testimony is shortened in length. All of the witnesses' testimony was highly mediated, so there is no guarantee that any statements are complete, word-for-word testimony, rather than being interpreted through the lens of the reporter. The trial could be described either as a mockery of the justice system or an imitation of justice. But it could also be read as a mockery of democracy and the idea of blind justice because, according to the *Steamer Pacific Star* reporter, it took place within the presence of a "crowd, so far as I was able to judge, [that] numbered about six hundred, but I might as well here remark that the numbers rapidly increased, so that at the close of the tragedy, there could not have been less than two thousand souls on the ground . . . previous to the organization of the tribunal."[75] It seems that maintaining order among a crowd of two thousand would be virtually impossible; the presence of such a large number of people transforms the proceedings into a spectacle or entertainment rather than a forum of justice. At this moment law was practiced as a system of racial distinction as the scene of racialized justice was turned into a spectacle that stood in for due process. A fair trial involves deliberation, discussion, the weighing of information, and the careful considering of evidence. The foreshortened process of the kangaroo court not only undermines the liberal values of time, evidence, and deliberation, but also trumps law as it transforms a system of protection into an arbitrary set of codes that solidifies racial difference. The act is literally performed as a farce, perhaps funny to some, tragic to others, seducing the mob and literally setting the stage for violence against Josefa/Juanita's body. I use the word *body* here and not *person* because in this pseudo-legal realm she is a body rather than a rights-bearing subject. In co-opting the legal realm the farce substitutes for real law and legitimates any actions that follow the legal decision. Here, the gendered Mexican body becomes the performative ground of justice. The violence was condoned and legitimated through the participation of then Senatorial candidate Weller, who presided over the events on the platform.

Other members of the crowd interpret the scene of pseudo-justice by linking it to the bodies of wives and daughters as a means to quell the hungry mob. Pierce-Barstow says he witnessed the following: "During the trial of the woman, [illegible] had to be brought into requisition to keep the mob back; they would once in a while make a rush for her, and the —— [contenders?] of the prosecution would have to appeal to them, calling on them to remember their wives and daughters, to give this woman a fair trial, and in that way they were kept quiet until the woman was executed."[76] Once again, spatial memory links Josefa/Juanita's body to the bodies of other women outside of this event. As the prosecutor calls on them to remember the bodies of their wives and daughters, women's bodies that they know intimately, bodies that they themselves, one hopes, would never defile, the link between womanhood as a representation of civilization and purity and Josefa/Juanita's body is the only thing that temporarily saves her from being dismembered. Men's own sense of honor and masculinity are invoked to allow the trial to take place, displacing other kinds of desires. Sexual desires to ravage and destroy Josefa/Juanita's body are mediated by evoking wives and daughters in a clear-cut moral reference to incest, physical violence, and rape, acts no self-respecting man would want to commit. Temporary circumvention of sexually charged forms of violence spare the woman who is simultaneously an object of desire and disgust. Wives and daughters are people; Josefa/Juanita is an object. The temporary reprieve grants her subject status so that the alleged criminal trial can take place and make evident her lack of status as a rights-bearing subject. Yet it seems clear that the lynching would have taken place with or without the pseudo-court or the evocation of familial intimacy, showing that sentiments about race and crime weighed more heavily than discourses of (racialized) women's scarcity, and their social and intimate value in this male-dominated community. Ultimately, the trial alleviates any sense of guilt about the lynching because Josefa/Juanita's crime was judged prosecutable by a group of her peers (if a group of Anglo-American men can be regarded as the peers of a nineteenth-century U.S. Mexicana) and the guilty conviction justifies the punishment.

The simultaneous expression of desire and disgust over Josefa/Juanita's body makes it a focus within the context of the trial and her altercation with Cannon. Downie's description of her straddles a line between desirability and repulsion: "Her figure was richly developed and in strict proportions; her features delicate, and her olive complexion lent them a pleasing softness. Her black hair was neatly done up on state occasions, and the luster in her eyes shone in various degrees, from the soft dove-like expression of a love-sick maiden, to the fierce scowl of an infuriated lioness, according to her temper, which was the only thing not well balanced about her."[77]

Downie attempts to present a "balanced" account of Josefa/Juanita but convicts himself through his own words. His romanticism about a brutally defiled body before its destruction reveals her tremendous beauty and his conviction that he felt it needed to be disciplined. This was a body that needed to be controlled and, at the same time, a body that made men unable to control themselves. His sentiments exemplify the historian Antonia Castañeda's arguments about the typical portrayals of nineteenth-century U.S. Mexicanas in travel journals written for white settlers: descriptions of the racialized, gendered body, assumed sexual deviance, and prostitution. These women, she argues, are represented as "purely sexual creatures. . . . [W]omen of easy virtue and latent infidelity easily led to the stereotype of the Mexicana as a prostitute in the literature of the gold rush."[78] With the exception of the historian Leonard Pitt and Cannon himself, who calls her a whore, most of the accounts surrounding Josefa/Juanita's lynching do not overtly state that she was a prostitute, but the language they use evokes transgression of sexual propriety along racial and class lines.[79] In line with the tradition of highly sexualized accounts of Mexican women on the frontier that Castañeda cites, Bancroft, Downie, the newspapers, and Seacrest allude to Josefa/Juanita's beauty and her petite, feminine frame. Describing Cannon's murderer, Bancroft states, "It was a little woman; young too—only twenty-four. Scarcely five feet in height, with a slender symmetrical figure, agile and extremely graceful in her movements. With soft skin of olive hue, long black hair, and dark, deep, lustrous eyes, opening like a window to the fagot-flames which kindled with love or hate, shone brightly from within. Mexico was her country; her blood Spanish, diluted with the aboriginal American. Her name was Juanita."[80]

First, her ethnic and national origins constantly shift in various accounts. She was a Mexican citizen of Spanish blood mixed with Indian blood, meaning she was a mestiza. In the vein of nineteenth-century scientific racism, to which Bancroft was no stranger, perhaps the Indian blood is what contributed to her need for discipline and her "craziness." But was she a Mexican citizen or a naturalized U.S. citizen by virtue of residing in the territory annexed by the United States when the Treaty of Guadalupe Hidalgo was signed? Either way, her unstable national and ethnic identities in the historical record make it difficult to identify her as a citizen subject.

It is assumed that the violence in her nature ("the fagot-flames kindled with love or hate") makes Josefa/Juanita prone to sudden, disobedient, episodic outbreaks of rage and passion. This characterization is consistent with the preoccupation of Mexican mid-nineteenth-century reformers, who claimed that Mexico and Mexicans were obsessed with blood lust and indifference to death, a charge they leveled at the supposedly barbarous lower classes.[81] Here, blood lust is invoked to diminish any claim to propriety Josefa/Juanita might have and to deflect all culpability away from white men and onto the U.S. Mexicana body.

At the same time Josefa/Juanita is desirable and beautiful. Yet her blood is the product of racial mestizaje, and Bancroft deploys the discourse of scientific racism to fixate on the idea that her nature makes her predisposed to acting with extreme and uncontrollable passion. Although she is portrayed as a tempting Mexican seductress, the fact that Josefa/Juanita killed Cannon suggests she did not desire him or desire to seduce him for money or pleasure. Here *passion* is a code word that pathologizes her anger, misreading her desire to be free of harassment as the actions of an amoral, uncontrollable sexual being. In these descriptions, she becomes a colonial subject of sexual fantasy.[82] Here the violence is mystified by mythologies of enchanted sexual and social relations between Josefa/Juanita and Cannon, instead of being explained in a straightforward manner that would account for the resulting violence.

What if Josefa/Juanita had been a prostitute, as Pitt argues in *The Decline of the Californios*?[83] How would that change the perceptions of her narrative and the violence enacted upon her body? Would that fact influence the desire and disgust expressed by Cannon and the Anglo male lynch mob? Would that have been all the more reason to lynch her? I pose these questions to show the chain of utterances that follow Cannon's own utterance of "whore," unleashing connected signifiers about racialized sexuality and gender. As the Chicana feminist critic Irene Blea argues about Josefa/Juanita's historical moment, "Women were categorized according to whether their sexual activity was sanctioned and unsanctioned."[84] The claims that she may have been a prostitute render Josefa/Juanita's sexual actions morally unsanctioned but possibly economically sanctioned. If Cannon was seeking sex in exchange for money, was Josefa/Juanita supposed to consent in such an economic transaction? As the historian Nancy Cott argues, prostitutes and prostitution represented the "coercive, and the more that prostitution could be shown to be coercive, the more marriage could be assumed not to be."[85] Coercion represented not a relationship based on love or mutual respect, as marriage was supposed to be, but an amoral social relationship of exchange in which the body is imagined in gendered terms of criminalization and social deviance. On the other hand, Pierce-Barstow describes Cannon's entry into Josefa/Juanita's home as

> one man whose name I don't remember, on a frolic on the night of the 4th, and he, with some companions, after running all night, strolled along to this house where this woman lived, and knocked for admission. At [his] knocking at the door, either by accident or design, the door, which was hung on wooden hinges, fell in. The woman was in that room in bed, and on a sudden call of that character, the door of the house pushed in, in broad daylight, the woman sprang from out of her bed, and seized the knife which lay on the table closely, and as this man who pushed the door in, in his drunken condition, reached out his hand to apologize for pushing the door in.[86]

Describing what are usually discussed as separate events, Pierce-Barstow suggests that Cannon was drunk at the time the set of events transpired and that he intentionally went to Josefa/Juanita's house in broad daylight. Was it because she was a prostitute that he sought her house directly? Or was she an attractive wife who had rejected his advances, and, in a drunken state, he let go of his inhibitions and acted on his sexual desire, using the word *whore* to justify his actions?

Four assumptions operate here if Josefa/Juanita was a prostitute and was treated as such. First is the assumption that she was not capable of love or mutual respect outside of her work activities, relegating her relationship with José to the margins of the narrative. Second is a fundamental assumption about Cannon's privilege as a man with money, which would have made him feel entitled to Josefa/Juanita's body and her services. If she was a prostitute, she would have no right to refuse his money and deny him her services, in defiance of his male privilege. Her status would have made her, not Cannon, the coercive element in the exchange (a reading contradicted by the violence against Cannon, which suggests he was the one who used coercive behavior). Third, condemnatory discourses surrounding prostitution would suggest that a prostitute exchanges sex for money and therefore cannot be raped. Last, identifying Josefa/Juanita as a whore puts her in a fixed identity category as a nonsubmissive woman engaged in an occupation and social position that are viewed as highly desirable economically but as a crime against morality.

Given that the number of women in this mining town was estimated to be fewer than twelve, to commit physical violence against a prostitute, or any woman for that matter, regardless of her racial identity, would have been a bad move economically. This is where the narrative of the fallen woman comes into play. In this case it takes on a particularly racialized dimension. In a review of scholarship on prostitution, the historian Timothy Gilfoyle argues that "prostitutes were ordinary young females, confronting limited possibilities and making rational and sometimes desperate choices" and were often symbols of disorder, excess, pleasure, and improvidence.[87] As a national or racial outsider (she was described as a foreigner by the *Daily Alta Californian*), Josefa/Juanita already symbolized disorder and excess within the U.S. body politic simply by virtue of living in the Downieville mining community. Had she been a prostitute, living outside of a legitimate family structure recognized by Americans (that is, a marriage), she would have constituted a further threat to the nation and sexual order based on individual responsibility.[88] And while José's claim of 1868 established she was his common-law wife, this was not part of the public record in 1851 when the lynching took place, demonstrating why the discourses about Josefa/Juanita migrated so easily into a discourse of prostitution as time went on. In the discourse of the fallen woman, the prostitute, Josefa/Juanita's status as an outsider, both racially and possibly professionally, would have furthered the social process of differentiation that occurred through her violent lynching. All accounts concur that women were scarce in Downieville, and hence so was the possibility for sexual encounters between men and women, whether paid or otherwise. Perhaps her being perceived as a prostitute was overdetermined by the disparity of male-female relations. In other words, this disparity would cast a kind of suspicion on all women because of the dearth of their presence there.

Whether or not she was a prostitute does not negate that Josefa/Juanita felt violated and acted from this position. Being a prostitute does not make one less of a person or less of a citizen, although in this historical moment Cannon's calling her a whore marked a class claim that subordinated her body and rights to his. The discourse that casts Josefa/Juanita as prostitute uses social constructs of racial and sexual normalcy as a means of justifying the control of her allegedly deviant body. Her lynching was the enactment of ultimate control over her social deviance, a deviance understood by her representation as a prostitute.

The discursive construction of Josefa/Juanita as a prostitute allows José, her Mexican common-law husband, to be written out of the narrative, for why else would he matter? He is represented as a speaking subject only in the first published newspaper account in the *Steamer Pacific Star* and is not mentioned in the other newspaper accounts. He is, however, mentioned by other narrators in order to direct the discussion of her body and morality: "Some of the miners stared hungrily at the young Mexican girl, but whatever her moral standards were, she seemed to be content with her José. Josefa was attractive by all accounts, and a contemporary described her as rather low in stature, stout built, with raven tresses that flowed freely over her neck and shoulders—black eyes, teeth regular and of pearly white. She might be called pretty, so far as the style of swarthy Mexican Beauty is so considered. She dressed with considerable attention to taste."[89]

If this narrative is to be believed, the lynching can perhaps be linked to a larger sense of animosity toward Josefa/Juanita because she did not accede to the sexual desires of any of the miners in the camp, preferring "her José." Seacrest's account also suggests she was chaste and monogamous. Perhaps the lynching was a way to release the miners' sexual frustration and larger animosity toward the sexual object they could never fully own. In other words, either despite her racial identity or because of her racial identity, she was in fact sexually desirable. Destruction of her beauty through an act of violent physical disfigurement stands in complete contrast to the accounts that speak of her beauty, grace, gentility, and attention to taste, even though she was Mexican.[90]

One utterance, Cannon's calling Josefa/Juanita a whore, triggered the discourses about her appearance and race that led some to believe she was a prostitute. The effects of language on the speaking organism (either via utterances by the subject or those filtered through the voices of others) are what inaugurate prostitute as a potential identity for Josefa/Juanita because in this case it is a fixed, static, transparent, gendered, ethnic-racialized identity, all based on Cannon's primary utterance "whore" at the scene of the crime. The miners' desire to destroy Josefa/Juanita's physical beauty through lynching perhaps reflected their need, based on a cultural logic about race and the gold rush economy, to regard all Mexican women as prostitutes. But Josefa/Juanita was not a prostitute, so the violence between her and Cannon may have occurred as a means to make her conform to the assumption of sexual deviance. Because Josefa/Juanita was not a prostitute, she was not available to the miners as a Mexican woman should have been, and this is what most likely caused the series of disagreements.

The conflicting stories about Josefa/Juanita's sexual and racial identities are further complicated by Older's work, which uses highly racist language in identifying Cannon's murderer: "Cannon spoke Spanish. In that language passersby heard him say to Juanita, 'What's the matter with you—you whore'—. Juanita plunged the knife into Cannon's heart. With José she fled up the street to Craycroft's saloon. . . . To the farthest camp up and down the Yuba, sped the words, 'A greaser woman killed Jack Cannon!' leaving picks and pans, miners hurried into Downieville. The bitter feud that had begun with the conquest of 1846 flared up anew between Mexicans and Americans. 'Clean out the greasers! Lynch the greasers!' The Mexicans fled."[91]

Ironically, Older's telling of the "Juanita of Downieville" story appears in a volume entitled *Love Stories of California*. One can't help asking, What could possibly be "romantic," as the author calls it, about a Mexican woman being lynched?[92] Her body being tortured? This is a clear example of the euphemization of violence and the seductive quality of sensationalism.[93] Sensationalism turns a historical occurrence into fiction and romance. This extraordinary, almost unbelievable quality is the very thing critics and historians have focused on. One eyewitness, Franklin S. Buck, stated, "It takes time and distance to soften these things down. The story of the Spanish girl 'Josepha,' whom I saw hanged by a mob in Downieville could be worked up into a good novel now."[94] While advocating historical distance between Josefa/Juanita's lynching and its potential for good fiction, Buck articulates how fiction and sensationalism can displace the historical event and the individuals involved, euphemizing violence.

The pieces of evidence, in all of their contradictions, bring together the terms of feuding races, imperialism, racial slurs, and gendered vigilante violence within a sensationalized framework. The ultimate focus settles upon the nativist thought of that period. The idea that the mob in Downieville expressed a uniform, nativist Anglo-American rage through Josefa/Juanita's lynching is problematic, however, because Pierce-Barstow's eyewitness account states that the mob was "of all sorts, as good men as anyone among them, a large foreign mixture, chiefly Irish, and much of the randyism came from that element."[95] Pierce-Barstow's testimony about the Irish being foreign members of the mining community presents us with the fact that there was a heightened need for violence as a social process of differentiation that would allow foreign miners like the "randy" Irish (another example of racism) and other recent European immigrant groups to differentiate their bodies from the truly foreign body of Josefa/Juanita through the performance of lynching. Pierce-Barstow's appeal to the idea that the Irish were responsible for public disorder, poverty, and the use of systematic violence exemplifies how they were often discursively marked as premodern people.[96] Putting the blame on the Irish solidifies the mythology of Anglo-American civility and immigrant inferiority, disrupting the idea that whiteness is uniform and without its own race and class hierarchies. Still, the participants performed an American kind of whiteness in a ritual of social cohesion and solidarity through the lynching of the racialized, sexually deviant foreign body.[97] The violence against Josefa/Juanita was necessary to erase the racial and class divides among white men through the eradication of trespassing "greaser" bodies like hers.

Further tension vis-à-vis the bodies of cultural transgressors arises when Pierce-Barstow later states, "There was considerable bad feeling towards Mexican gamblers and women generally, and there was no other way but to hang her."[98] Racial conflict demonstrates how the categories of identification as Mexican gambler (José)[99] and Mexican woman (Josefa/Juanita) collapse into a single symbolic meaning (social deviance). Collapsing two signifiers, two types of racialized bodies, reveals a discursive representation of the desire to eliminate such cultural transgressors. Here the politics of misogyny and xenophobia structure the social practice of violence. Pierce-Barstow does not suggest that Josefa/Juanita was a prostitute, but he does link gambling with Mexican womanhood. Slippage in meaning causes gambling and Mexicana womanhood to be linked as social deviance, "driving people beyond the recognized limit of their humanity" through the act of lynching itself.[100]

I want to shift from the archival materials and contemporary accounts of the lynching to the ways in which Chicana/o narratives use Josefa/Juanita's body to accomplish specific discursive tasks. The one thing both sets of evidence and discourse have in common is that they engage in ventriloquizing her, even when they may appear to recuperate her agency. Chicano critics and historians frequently evoke Josefa/Juanita's lynched body but do not supply much detail. Acuña's *Occupied America* and the essay "Millennial Anxieties: Borders, Violence, and the Struggle for Chicana and Chicano Subjectivity" by the cultural critic Arturo Aldama evoke the brutalized, dead body of Josefa/Juanita in a disturbing way. Both writers rely upon the same sources as Seacrest to conclude that Josefa/Juanita's lynching "evokes a brutal and tragic moment."[101] The Chicano cultural studies critic and creative nonfiction writer Alejandro Murguía brings new sources into play in his analysis of the lynching, yet he overidentifies with her in what he calls a "highly subjective" history of Josefa/Juanita when he anachronistically labels her a Chicana. In addition, Chicana feminist accounts like that of Maythee Rojas attempt to vindicate Josefa/Juanita through a feminist reading. All of these accounts of the lynching raise questions about epistemic violence and the appropriation of the narratives for specific nationalist purposes in Chicano/a studies.

Acuña provides a four-paragraph account of the event in *Occupied America*. As a means of telling the larger story of how California was lost to Anglo-Americans and their colonization of the territory, Josefa/Juanita's story documents that some losses were greater than others. Citing California's entrance into the international economic market, Acuña argues that the Anglo conquest of California was a direct result of this newly burgeoning economy, most deeply reflected through the discovery of gold in 1848. He cites Anglo-American resentment of successful Mexican peddlers in the gold camps. But Acuña calls Josefa/Juanita's lynching "the most flagrant act of vigilantism."[102] Rejecting the idea that she was a prostitute, Acuña claims that Josefa/Juanita's killing of Cannon was an act of "stand[ing] up to years of abuse in which Mexicans, especially women, were fair game for arrogant bullies."[103] Suggesting that Cannon's killing was justified by years of unwarranted violence, displacement, and harassment, most notably in this region, where the foreign miner's tax drove many Mexican, Chinese, and Chilean men out of mining and into the service economy that emerged in the gold rush era in California,

Acuña plots her lynching as an injustice toward all Mexicans and Chicanos as a way to justify Josefa/Juanita's violence against Cannon.

After describing the events leading up to Josefa/Juanita's lynching, Acuña writes, "Lynching became commonplace and Mexicans came to know Anglo-America democracy as 'Lynchocracia.' "[104] Here Acuña deploys the same sensationalist tactics as later scholars, especially in his claim that "Josefa was pregnant and . . . they would [have] been killing two people."[105] The pregnancy raises a whole other set of issues around sensationalism that I will address shortly. Masquerading as a quest for one truth about what happened to Josefa/Juanita, such sensationalized readings blur the ability to recognize the complexity of the event and how Josefa/Juanita is constructed in history. Sensationalism cues the reader to feel outraged and sympathetic; however, the discussion needs to move beyond outrage and sympathy to investigate the gray areas where sex, race, gender, and culture came to bear on this lynched woman's body. This entails also moving beyond a narrative history of resistance: far from restoring Josefa/Juanita's voice or history, Acuña's political intentions in using her narrative are entirely to place her story at the service of the larger, more important nationalist history.

Similarly, Aldama's essay is a survey of violence and Chicana/o subject formation. Moving very quickly between the contemporary and the historical, the survey glosses many events in Chicano history in which violence is the root cause of how we have come to understand Chicana/os in relation to the nation-state. In Aldama's reading, Josefa/Juanita's lynching is little more than a "brutal and tragic moment" in Chicana history.[106]

Relying on Acuña's words and sources and using similar tactics of sensationalism and outrage, Aldama treats Josefa/Juanita's lynching in one paragraph. His text raises several questions about what counts as valid evidence. He claims she was pregnant at the time of her lynching and that Cannon raped her, even though none of the major newspaper accounts or eyewitness accounts suggests either.[107] While we cannot factually substantiate whether or not Josefa/Juanita was raped or was pregnant, there is more than factual accuracy at stake in Aldama's (and by extension Acuña's) portrayal of Josefa/Juanita as a pregnant, raped, lynched subject. Aldama needs her to be raped and pregnant not only to position her as the ultimate victim, to excite moral outrage, and to substantiate his critique of violence as cultural practice, but also, more important, to solidify what Rosa Linda Fregoso has called "political familialism," a defense of the Chicano family against colonialist images of pathology, machismo, and poverty.[108] Through a close reading of Gregory

Nava's film *Mi Familia* (1995) Fregoso concludes that the construction of the Chicano family relies on heteronormativity and uncritically mirrors the dominant culture's nostalgia for family values, one of which is that women are static guardians of tradition, but within the context of a Chicano nationalist script. Following Fregoso, I suggest that Aldama and Acuña need Josefa/Juanita to be raped and pregnant because that calls for their defense of the moral parameters of the family and its importance in displacing social pathologies that construct Chicana/o bodies. So in replacing the figure of the "antisocial prostitute" with that of a raped and pregnant Josefa/Juanita, Aldama appeals to morality staked in heteronormativity and nostalgia for the family.[109] He transforms destruction and defilement of Josefa/Juanita's body into a literal destruction of tradition—the death of a foremother, if you will—that deploys a static gendered object to stake claims for the family and thus the historiography of resistance of the imagined Chicano nation.

Acuña and Aldama also need Josefa/Juanita to be pregnant in order for her lynching to double as the metaphorical lynching of the contemporary Chicano national family. Evoking the hanging in the contemporary period carries out the symbolic destruction of Chicano familial mythology. But the source material published a week after the lynching took place contains a very different account of the pregnancy.[110] According to the detailed testimonies, a Dr. Aiken stated that he

> believed the prisoner to be *enciente*, thought she was three months gone. Here a consultation was called and Drs. Chamberlin, Hunter, and Hardy of Marysville, with Dr Aiken, proceeded to a private room with the prisoner for the purpose of an examination. At this period, the crowd, which had, before been orderly became perfectly infuriated, and cries of bring her out! hang her! resounded with every portion of the dense throng. Epithets not very complimentary to Dr. Aiken were freely indulged in, and by many it was considered extremely doubtful whether this person would be safe. The crowd rushed to the stand, and were about, as was supposed, to commit violence, when it was rumored that the committee of doctors failed to agree, or at least those last called in did not agree with Dr. Aiken, whereupon the jury retired.[111]

Whether Aiken was lying to save Josefa/Juanita or whether she was in fact pregnant and the other doctors were lying, the French word *enciente* describes the state of being with child. Nonetheless, pregnancy was used as a moral argument to escape corporeal punishment and it was the close scrutiny of her that brought great pain upon Josefa/Juanita.

Although it continues the trope of "political familialism," *Medicine of Memory* (2002) by Murguía at least gets to an analysis of race, class, and gender as he chronicles his own journey to Downieville, beginning with the proclamation that "Josefa's is the [story] that matters most to me, the one I choose to recover from the dustbins of history."[112] Openly flaunting his power to recover this history, he falls into the proleptic irony of using her story to tell his own. Shifting between his experience driving to Downieville to take in the scene of the lynching and his interpretation of the lynching itself, he effaces the story through disclosure.[113] He writes, "But her courage in the face of an angry mob of forty-niners is the stuff of legend, in the same league with Joan of Arc or whatever woman warrior you want to compare her to."[114] Instead of considering Josefa/Juanita's lynching in its context, Murguía elevates it to sainthood on a par with a French Catholic icon of war and salvation. This parallel is no coincidence. What is interesting about this analogy is that Joan of Arc was a virgin martyr who heard the voices of Saint Michael, Saint Catherine, and Saint Margaret telling her to recover her French homelands from English colonial domination. When she entered the failing French war against the British at the Battle of Orleans, the tide of the war completely changed. Joan was captured by the British and put on trial for heresy, her testimony was nullified or altered, and she was executed by burning on May 30, 1412. The parallels between the two women's histories are quite obvious. Casting Josefa/Juanita as a figure perhaps inspired by divine providence to defend her Mexican/Chicano homeland and her body (a metaphor for the homeland) from Anglo-American colonialism, Murguía canonizes Josefa/Juanita in his own pantheon of resistance, making her into the highly visible and celebrated figure of the woman warrior. The comparison with Joan of Arc makes Josefa/Juanita a parallel virginal political martyr. Sexuality and sexual purity bring us back to the heteronormative family romance, positioning Josefa/Juanita as a pure body, an exemplary member of her race, who died for a political cause. Having established that link between the two virginal political martyrs, Murguía continues, "Josefa knew there was no man or law that would defend her if she was raped or even killed. It was just herself. Perhaps you can explain why Josefa did what she did."[115] Setting up a discussion of honor and self-determination, this narrative unabashedly centers Murguía's specific actions as an author as an attempt to reclaim a historical subject in order to save her and claim her as part of his "Mexica clan."[116] Although he situates her within a Chicano nationalist paradigm of resistance, he does so via a paternalistic gesture to save her because she could not save herself.

When Murguía finally comes face to face with the latest version of the

Jersey Bridge where her lynching took place, he says, "I stand on the bridge and look over the railing, and I can almost see her face in the water, surrounded by her long hair. I want to do the most natural thing and give her a last name, my last name, make her part of my clan, so her spirit will always have a home. But she deserves the honor of her single name, because she represents all the nameless ones who lived and died here and never made it rich."[117] Instead of seeing his own reflection in the water, Murguía sees his Chicana foremother, registering the generative nature of his personal feelings of loss. Still, the naturalizing paternalistic impulses of the Mexica/Chicano family are one way in which Murguía replaces the story of violation and loss with a desire to claim Josefa/Juanita as symbolic kin. While such a critical move is clearly a part of a Chicano nationalist project of forging a racial, cultural, and political mestizo family heritage, Murguía is guilty of epistemic violence by locating Josefa/Juanita's actions in the discourses of heroism instead of as part of an overarching history of violence as social practice. The paternalism embodied in literally renaming her by wanting to give his own name to Josefa/Juanita is not a nice gesture at all. This is a classic example of the tendency of brown men and their respective nationalist movements to want to save brown women from white men. Murguía is fighting an Anglo-American masculine history of Josefa/Juanita's lynching, but in some ways his desire to give her his Mexica, brown man's name shows he is fighting other brown men and even women over the right to claim her body as his own. Her identity as subject is once again fully dependent upon the social constructions Murguía imagines and is enacted by "saving" her from the "dustbins of history" and giving her agency through his historical recovery rather than assuming that we all are and always have been agents.

Some Chicana feminist scholarship pursues the same mode of inquiry, enacting the same kind of hero/heroine trope in the methodology and actual analysis of Josefa/Juanita's lynching. When we uncover new information about a historical event, what happens when we ask people to completely change the official record based on archival discoveries? Are we enacting epistemic violence by taking earlier accounts out of context, even if they are perceived as being incorrect? Do not such attempts to fix Josefa/Juanita in history by stabilizing her name attempt to canonize her in that same nationalist pantheon of heroes and resistance? Perhaps we should not obsess on a single truth about Josefa/Juanita as a historical subject but instead, following Spivak's model, should examine narratives of power relations and discursive power that could help us construct a more complex vision of the violent events that made her visible as a subject.

Rojas's works, including "Re-membering Josefa," are the closest things we have to a Chicana feminist reading of the event, but they have their problems as well, especially with regard to the triumphant discourses of nationalism and feminist resistance. Rojas provides a different reading of the narrative of Josefa/Juanita, including a detailed social analysis of how travel narratives and contemporary journalism on mining and social relations of the gold diggings around Downieville may have influenced how the hanging took place.[118] I find it interesting that she does not use the term *lynching*; perhaps her choice of words is a means of dissolving the sensationalism around the case or perhaps it enables her to look at the violence as an isolated event rather than as part of a larger system.

Rojas argues that the accounts of Josefa/Juanita's crime and her subsequent lynching reflect a conflict between her gendered identity as a desirable woman and her racial identity as a Mexican. Curiously, Rojas turns to the Native critic Rayna Green's theoretical construct of the "Pocahontas Perplex" to talk about the virgin/whore dichotomy in explaining these conflicting desires. The Guadalupe/La Llorona/La Malinche complex, which comes from Mexican, Mexican American, Chicano, and Chicana feminist cultural contexts, would seem more apt.[119] Quoting Green, Rojas argues that the perplex "illustrates the symbolical role that Indian women have played within the American imaginary."[120] Josefa, however, was always identified as Mexican, Spanish, or foreign, never as Indian. This slippage in ethnic applications of theory—Rojas's turn to an American Indian studies model instead of a Chicana feminist one—is no accident. As I argued earlier, it is the discourse of mestizaje that allows for the conflation of a Mexican identity with an Indian one. As a stand-in for the Indian princess figure most closely embodied in Pocahontas, Josefa/Juanita represents the good and noble princess whose "overt and realized sexuality converts the image from positive to negative," thus reducing the "princess" to a clearly racialized and inferior squaw status.[121] This slippage between Indian and Mexican, princess and squaw, as a mechanism for reading the virgin/whore dichotomy as a justification for Josefa/Juanita's lynching subconsciously follows the argumentative line of Chicano nationalism in which Mexican *is* Indian. So even in a feminist attempt to recuperate and vindicate Josefa/Juanita, vindication is achieved only through a nationalist subtext that subsumes realities of indigenousness into Chicana/o victimization.

Much like Aldama, Acuña, and Murguía, Rojas attempts to recover and vindicate Josefa/Juanita as a part of her critical project, following the trajectory of the Chicano family romance, heteronormative historicism, and heroism. The anthropologist David Scott's work on C. R. L. James's construction of Toussaint L'Ouverture as hero of the Haitian revolution is most helpful in explaining the critical move to vindicate and romanticize the hero/heroine figure. In *Conscripts of Modernity* Scott argues that the construct of the hero is grounded in a self-conscious moral attitude in which the measure of all worth is lodged in a kind of heroic, "great hearted simplicity."[122]

The portrayal of Josefa/Juanita by both Chicano studies critics and the contemporary observers follows the convention of heroism. Rojas cites an editorial by J. J. McClosky that appeared in the *San Jose Pioneer* on November 12, 1881, as an example of how "the memory of Josefa gets displaced in favor of the men responsible for her death" but still within the confines of her own vindicationist narrative.[123] McClosky wrote, "My information came from one who knew Juanita well, and she described her as a heroine in every sense of the word. She killed a ruffian at her door step, who had attempted violence to herself the night before, and who had vowed vengeance on her."[124] McClosky's description of her sincerity and simplicity as a "woman defending her honor" and a "character above the average of camp women of these days," according to Rojas, conveys that she was the calm bearer of the truth of her people, an exemplar in both life and death, the stuff of which heroines are made.[125]

I want to return to Scott for a minute because of how he reads the figure of the hero as part of a discourse of vindicationism, the discursive thread that holds Rojas's argument together. Scott argues that vindicationism "is not merely a response to a sense of oppression or exploitation but an aggrieved sense of being wronged or slandered."[126] Scott's work focuses on the interdependent relationship between Black nationalism and vindicationism, and he raises important points about how histories that try to respond to a sense of historical and ethnic injustice often end up creating a romantic image of the hero that is far removed from who the person actually was and that further problematize how history is socially constructed. Similarly, when any of these Chicana/o critics—and in particular Rojas through her feminist critical methodology—attempts to, in Rojas's words, "vindicate an unjustly executed woman" or call Josefa/Juanita an "unsung woman of history" or claim to "undo her objectification and grant her recognition," we are sucked into that familial romance where the first woman lynched in California is elevated to a pantheon of national heroes. This glosses over the historian's power in the work of historical recovery and the fact that history is like a palimpsest, with layers upon layers of meaning.[127] This is not an unmediated process. "Granting her [Josefa/Juanita] recognition," even within a Chicana feminist context, denies Josefa/Juanita agency in the retelling of her story because the intent is to paint her as a victim, not as someone who murdered a miner, even if she is figured as a historical actor.[128] I am not justifying Josefa/Juanita's lynching, the treatment of her body, or her misrecognition in history; rather, I want to convey how problematic the discourses of heroism, Chicano family romance, victimization, and vindicationism are, precisely because they do not interrogate the ruses of power both in the historical moment of the event and in how scholars reinterpret and retell these without interrogating our own power as narrators.

While Rojas is cognizant of not evoking Josefa/Juanita's brutalized body uncritically to show a pattern of resistance and victimization, Chicano scholars routinely rely on the romance of the brutalized woman to cement the position of nationalism and the narrative of familialism. Josefa/Juanita's experience is offered up as evidence of collective oppression in order to solidify the heteronormative tradition of the family and morality and to counter the social pathologies constructed in colonial discourses. All of these examples demonstrate the discursive fight over Josefa/Juanita's body, her subjectivity, and her history, reminding us of the seductive nature of sensationalized information that obscures meaning and the figure of the (non)citizen subject as historical actor in order to secure a place for Chicano nationalism, Chicano studies, and even, to some degree, Chicana feminism.

"I WOULD DO IT AGAIN": HONOR, RAGE, AND SUBJECTIVITY

Why have no scholars theorized the place of rage in Josefa/Juanita's motives? Most historians and literary critics have read her murder of Cannon as an act of self-defense and resistance, a function of their need to identify a heroine from which to launch into heteronormative nationalism. By thinking about Josefa/Juanita's murder of Cannon as an act fueled by rage and the social constraints of being a desirable U.S. Mexicana in a predominately white, predominately male community, perhaps we can move away from celebratory resistance narratives and examine the situation as one in which U.S. Mexicano/a conceptions of gendered honor were at play. This type of rage is best defined as what the black feminist scholar bell hooks calls, in her book *Killing Rage*, an anger ascribed to the relay of discrimination along gendered and racial lines that imparts to a person a feeling of animosity that exceeds the parameters of normalized emotional responses to a given situation.[129]

As hooks puts it, "White rage is acceptable" whereas brown or black rage is not.[130] She details the range of emotions she experienced after dealing with a series of racist incidents at an airport, culminating in a confrontation with a white man who refused to move from the seat he occupied even though hooks's traveling companion was assigned the seat. hooks writes, "I wanted to stab him softly, to shoot him with the gun I wished I had in my purse. And as I watched his pain, I would say to him tenderly 'racism hurts.' With no outlet, my rage turned to overwhelming grief and I began to weep, covering my face with my hands."[131] hooks articulates the hypervisibility and invisibility she experiences as a woman of color. When she asks for fair treatment and the recognition of her rights as a person, she is invisible. When she sobs in her seat, however, she becomes hypervisible, almost pathological in her emotional response to racism. The dichotomy of invisibility/hypervisibility does not acknowledge the oppressive nature of everyday confrontations for women of color. hooks is in a public space surveiled by others and subject to laws preventing her from enacting the violent scene she has imagined. When hooks says, "racism hurts," she acknowledges the inaugural loss of the subject in language and a body cut by the language of race. Instead of accepting racism as a condition of everyday life, hooks expresses her loss through anger and rage and finally, most aptly, in crying, the ultimate physical sign of mourning. But in this context mourning is figured as pathological rather than a sign of powerlessness. For hooks the conversion of rage into crying is a "potentially healing response to oppression and exploitation" and "a passion for justice."[132]

Perhaps killing rage is what motivated Josefa/Juanita to gain power over her white male tormentor, a rage provoked by the desires of her assailant, Cannon. Such rage can be contextualized as a way of negotiating the loss involved in realizing the position one occupies in a community. Perhaps Josefa/Juanita's stabbing of Cannon was an attempt to position herself as an honorable woman, while knowing that such a status was irretrievable even as she enacted violence in self-defense. In reading this moment as an instance of finding an outlet for rage in a society that did not allow U.S. Mexicana women to express such a feeling, we move beyond what Priscilla Wald calls official histories that generate "authority [as] they command, articulated, as they are, in relation to the rights and privileges of individuals" to focus on the social systems that informed the history.[133]

At this historical moment in formerly Mexican California, rage and honor were twin social practices that allow us to understand the role of the physical body in defining citizenship and subjectivity because dress, actions, demeanor, and status determined communal perceptions. In describing Cannon's stabbing, Bancroft states "that little arm must indeed have been tempered by most murderous passion."[134] There was an unspeakable quality to the rage Josefa/Juanita experienced and enacted. Describing the murder as fueled by so much passion that it could propel a "little" woman's arm to violence allows Bancroft to locate the reader within a "crime of passion."[135] *Black's Law Dictionary* describes a crime of passion as "a crime committed in the heat of an emotionally charged moment, with no opportunity to reflect on what is happening."[136] Heat of passion seems to come closest to a likely reason why Josefa/Juanita killed Cannon: "rage, terror, or furious hatred, suddenly aroused by some immediate provocation, usually another person's words or actions."[137] In this context, of rage over an immediate provocation, Josefa/Juanita may very well have acted without premeditation. She could have decided in an instant that she would no longer tolerate Cannon's advances, and his destroying her home and calling her a whore (a term that claims a particular deviant sexuality for her and a kind of class superiority for Cannon) drove her to such rage that she could respond only by plunging a knife into his heart.

When hooks argues that to maintain the dominant social order "the sound of rage . . . must always remain repressed, contained, trapped in the realm of the unspeakable," she suggests that the silence is used to secure the rights, pleasure, and desires of everyone except the person experiencing the rage.[138] And conversely desires to repress the emotional content of Josefa/Juanita's motive for murder are self-serving and reify structures of power. Instead of silencing Josefa/Juanita's rage, Pierce-Barstow states, "the hanging of the woman was murder. No jury in the world, on any principle of self-defense or protection of life and property, would ever have convicted a woman. She was raised from her sleep in the early morning, by some ruffian pushing in her door, and in an instant it was in his heart, without time for reflection or thought. No jury in law or Christendom would have held the woman guilty of murder."[139] Yet those miners, while not viewing Cannon's trespass into her home as a crime, did not hesitate to punish her. Josefa/Juanita's behavior is a response to the destructive, pervasive racism that systematically made her actions a crime.

Whereas hooks addresses the emotional content of rage and its necessary silencing, the legal studies scholar Judd Sneirson connects criminality and rage. He discusses a case from 1846 in which a court ruled a black man insane and therefore not responsible for his crime as a result of the brutality he faced as a free black man in upstate New York. Sneirson outlines the criticism and support in legal circles for the "black rage thesis," the idea that black people's language and actions embody a kind of constant racial stress.[140] The "black rage thesis" of social pathology, which emerged in the courts just five years prior to Josefa/Juanita's alleged crime and lynching, seems to have some currency in reading these events as well. Arguing for a legal precedent of "political legitimatization of aggressive responses to racial oppression," Sneirson shows that rage is codified in law and in the courts as a plausible defense.[141] In the kangaroo court proceedings that preceded Josefa/Juanita's lynching, however, the veneer of law pathologizes her rage, reinscribing the image of the uncontrollable, insane brown woman. But the whole reason for pathologizing the rage of people of color, Sneirson argues, is white fear and guilt.[142] Josefa/Juanita's rage does not enable her to escape criminal responsibility for her act; rather, it stages her acceptance of her crime and punishment. Josefa/Juanita's behavior should not exclusively position her as that of either a victim or a resistive agent; it is merely that rage opens up an entirely new avenue for analysis of the events and discourses that make up her history in the sense that emotive response is an articulation of desire. And, as we read this articulation of desire in her rage, it is individual; it is not Josefa/Juanita literally operating as a resistive political actor for the Chicana/o peoples, as she so often is read, but rather a complex expression of self. We could also read it as an enactment of subjectivity for a woman who is denied subject status in her death and in each historical retelling that uses her to articulate the desires of others.

Perhaps her killing of Cannon had more to do with rage provoked by a desire for honor and fortitude than with resistance. The historian of the Southwest Ramón Gutiérrez defines the ideology of honor as twofold: honor was "society's measure of social standing. . . . The second dimension of honor was a constellation of virtue ideals. . . . Females possessed the moral and ethical equivalent of honor . . . if they were timid, shy, feminine, virginal before marriage and afterwards faithful to their husband, discreet in the presence of men, and concerned for their reputation. Infractions of the rules of conduct dishonored men."[143] Honor fundamentally defined the gender roles of women of all classes in Spanish America. To participate in this code of honor and have the desire to emulate it, even if one did not belong to the upper classes, reflects a set of cultural beliefs that no doubt still exists in some form today.[144]

Readers can hypothesize that Josefa/Juanita's desire to be honorable and not disgrace herself in effect was enacted through the vehicle of rage, leading her to stab Cannon. If we ascribe to the discourses of honor, we have to be cognizant of the fact that it comes from a patriarchal order of being in the world. Perhaps Josefa/Juanita was acting under the Catholic religious tenets of her day that demanded she defend her body and home from men other than her common-law husband. The anthropologist Ana María Alonso argues that transactions of honor are negotiated through discourses focusing on the body: "Insults of honor, whether verbal or physical, transgress the boundaries of the body."[145] Because personhood is about property and personhood is gendered, the only property women like Josefa/Juanita possessed was their bodies. Therefore, the insult against Josefa/Juanita's person (calling her a whore and entering her home) became a contest over her property, her body. The breach of spatial and corporal boundaries is what caused Josefa/Juanita to act to maintain her bodily integrity by physically enacting her rage. Hence, the stabbing evinces her desire to assert herself as a self-governing, independent individual. What distinguishes my readings of honor codes as codes of patriarchy from those of Murguía, Rojas, Aldama, and Acuña is that there is no uncritical claiming of her body in the name of Chicana/o nationalism and as an example of collective victimization. Rather, I stress the contradictions of the patriarchal system of honor and religion that circulated in mid-nineteenth-century Mexican communities, which perhaps shaped Josefa/Juanita's emotive and physical responses, a kind of body speech in lieu of any recording of her words in the written record. Instead of putting words in her mouth or claiming her as a Chicana nationalist foremother, I want to read other signifiers of meaning she left us with in the historical records and critical texts that do something very different. Many scholarly observers assume what the set of texts already mean within multiple mobilizations of nationalism and thus advocating for a close re-ereading yields a different set of issues.

In this light the speculation that Josefa/Juanita and Cannon were buried in the same grave until they were disinterred to make room for a new theater seems to implicate a different kind of nationalism, an American one that rewrites this tale as a love story. In truth, however, there were no "enchanted relations" here, as far as I can see, no lover's quarrel. Josefa/Juanita's response was not abnormal in a Spanish American cultural framework. She wasn't a spurned lover or a rejected prostitute, because insults were often responded to with violence during this period, and her interaction with Cannon was not an enchanted relationship, mystified by love and affection, but an expression of hatred and rage.[146]

Complicating these notions of honor even further are the numerous accounts suggesting that Cannon reappeared at her home the following morning to apologize for breaking down her door the previous night.[147] The apology defines Cannon's behavior as genteel and appropriate. In other words, oddly, the apology suggests that Cannon recognized he had wronged a woman and trespassed against her home and body. Yet, if the apology was actually given, something happened between the previous night's activities, the apology, and the stabbing that created "a disturbance in her house and outraged her rights."[148] If Cannon's intent really was to apologize, Josefa/Juanita's actions seem all the more irrational because the attempted apology represents him as a gentleman. That fine distinction between an accepted apology and his death can be explained only by Cannon's possible utterance of the word "whore/ puta," a clear claim of entitlement and citizenship on his part and devaluation of her humanity and rights as a gendered citizen subject. Ultimately, Josefa/ Juanita's code of honor has little meaning outside of her own frame of reference because the miners who lynched her did not operate within or care about her cultural and social beliefs. Because she was living in a community that was almost entirely made up of European American men (they were immigrants from different nations), the lynching reflects different gendered codes of honor.

Within a patriarchal Spanish American code of honor, the stabbing oddly emasculates José because in carrying out the stabbing she defends herself rather than letting him defend her.[149] As Alonso argues, "Masculine reputation is central to almost every aspect of everyday life, to be bested in a conflict of honor is to be emasculated and disempowered."[150] The record says little about José other than that he was "a quiet, inoffensive sort of man, if his appearance was a good indication of his character," and Cannon "then drew back his fist as if to strike me, when I stated to him that I did not wish to fight; he was large and I a small man."[151] José's failure to defend Josefa/Juanita's honor and her agency place his masculinity in question. Possibly forced from his previous occupation as a miner, José may simply have been an example of nineteenth-century stereotypes of Mexican men as small, physically weak, and cowardly.[152]

Given these notions of honor, we must question Bancroft's version of Josefa/Juanita's reaction on hearing the verdict against her: "Juanita gave a quiet little laugh, as if to say, 'How droll!' "[153] Although Bancroft obviously is putting words in her mouth, a sense of purpose and intention, not irrationality, pervades all his descriptions of her leading up to her lynching. For example, Bancroft further states,

> Juanita made her will verbally, gave her few effects away. During it all her heroism carried her far beyond the usual stolid fortitude of her race. At a time when men tremble and pray, she was her natural self, neither gay nor

sad. She was as far from looking lightly upon the matter as giving way to senseless sorrow. . . . With a light elastic step, surrounded by her friends, chatting with them quietly along the way, Juanita walked down to the bridge. She shook hands with them all, but not a tear, not a tremor was visible. By means of a step-ladder she mounted to a scantling which had been tied for her to stand on between the uprights underneath the beam, took off her head a man's hat, which had been kindly placed there by a friend, shied it with unerring accuracy to its owner, meanwhile smiling her thanks, then with quick dexterity she twisted up her long black tresses, smoothed her dress, placed the noose over her head and arranged the rope in a proper manner, and finally, lifting her hands, which she refused to have tied, exclaimed, Adios, señores! And the fatal signal was given.[154]

If Josefa/Juanita killed Cannon in a rage, Bancroft paints her as devoid of affect or emotion in the moments leading up to her death. He situates her within a community of friends at the moment of her execution, suggesting that she was not a complete racial and cultural outsider and that the Mexican race inherently operates with fortitude. The presence of her own community at the lynching would account for Josefa/Juanita's attending to her own body as she prepared to die in front of them.

The historian Alberto Hurtado also affirms that Josefa/Juanita met her death with dignity, "ascending the makeshift scaffold without assistance and adjusting the noose so that it did not tangle her hair."[155] Hurtado highlights her domesticated behavior in the face of the undomesticated mobs. Through her small acts of bodily preservation (attending to her hair), Josefa/Juanita makes her death into a ritual with meaning for herself and her community. She performs her death in front of the crowd during the march out onto the platform. This is an example of a public enactment of subjectivity in a situation where her citizenship was completely denied. Thus, we can view the stabbing as a function of rage and Josefa/Juanita's calm reserve before her lynching as a complex display of conflicting gender and cultural relations.

According to the eyewitness accounts of the lynching, "this woman walked up the ladder, unsupported, and stood on the scathing, under the rope. . . . The woman adjusted the rope around her neck, pulling her braids of hair."[156] If indeed she killed Cannon in a rage, it is extremely problematic to argue that she was not forced onto the platform but rather climbed it of her own accord as a kind of defiance. I nonetheless want to venture into these dangerous waters because it allows us to understand the full weight of her acknowledgment that she was being punished for murdering Cannon. The attentiveness to her body is yet another act of self-preservation in a moment when the mob is simply not willing to recognize her as a rational, thinking human being. From the moment of the stabbing onward, Josefa/Juanita seems to accept the fate that awaits her. Even as she complies with the mob's demand for capital punishment, there is a sense of intentionality in her behavior. The descriptions of her gestures and calmness of mind portray a woman who faced her impending death as the consequence of her actions, not a woman who was pathologically maniacal or hysterical. She does not express emotional excess; on the contrary, the mob does. This optimistic reading challenges a "simple construction of [her] agency as either a powerless victim or a triumphalist survivor" and interprets her actions instead as situational enactments of subjectivity.[157] Hence, it is important to recognize that Josefa/Juanita may have been operating within a set of Mexican cultural standards about honor that allowed for the expression of rage, rather than imposing on her a Chicano nationalist mindset in which political familialism and heroism become the only reading of her experiences.

Josefa/Juanita's cultural worldview suggests that she understood that because she was violated, whatever form that took, Cannon must die. But would she also believe that taking a life would justify her punishment by death in return? Older writes,

> When the guards asked her for her last words she looked into their eyes one by one and slowly replied, "I would do it again. That man insulted me." Juanita herself adjusted the hard thing about her young throat as if it were pearls from Loreto. She smoothed down her blue-black tresses over the rope. What was it—only a bit of hemp. Men envied her calm as with unshaken hands she put back the long braids. Juanita's guards tied her small brave hands behind her back and placed a white handkerchief over her eyes. "Adios senores!" spoke Juanita. . . . There was no word from Juanita. Axes glistened. One stopped. Another blow and the rope holding the plank was hacked off. The board fell. Like a ghastly top Juanita's body twisted round and round for half an hour hung in mid-air. On July 5, 1851, three thousand men stood watching her dangling from a rope.[158]

Josefa/Juanita enacts her own type of mourning to remedy the loss that ultimately leads to her death and thus shapes history. The scene of the body twisting in death does not deny the psychic content of violence and lynching. Instead of inscribing her body with meaning merely through the language and actions of those standing on the plank, the scene confirms several self-generated acts of meaning. What also becomes evident in this scene is that her

body was not burned, dragged, or dismembered after she was lynched, perhaps reflecting the sexual politics of lynching as a social practice. No one took
home her hair or her bones or attempted to collect pieces of her body as
souvenirs of their participation in the lynching, nor were her genitals exposed
and mutilated, as were those of numerous male African American lynching
victims in the late nineteenth century and early twentieth.[159]

Bancroft and Older ascribe the flippant words "Adios, señores" to Josefa/
Juanita immediately before she drops to her death. This phrase locates us in a
Spanish linguistic lexicon and links to the larger space of Mexican and Spanish identities and modes of communication. Whether or not she said those
words is not the point; several accounts state that she did speak, which gives
meaning to the utterance and focuses us upon the act of speech itself. The
Daily Alta Californian recorded a similar defiance on Josefa/Juanita's part:
"On being asked if she had anything to say, she replied, 'Nothing; but I would
do the same again if I was so provoked,'—and that she wished her remains to
be decently taken care of."[160] If the goal of vigilante violence is to map the law
upon the body of the sufferer, then the utterance prior to the actual death
demarcates that through lynching "the body [is] emphatically, crushingly
present by destroying it, and [makes] the other, the voice absent while destroying it."[161] The tension between voice and silence becomes apparent in the
moment of destruction of the subject. The utterance transforms how we read
this history. Perhaps we can read the utterance as one way that women can
and do speak from the colonial archive through moments of rupture.[162] The
utterance is a mark of subjectivity and, once more, it identifies how an extralegal practice governs the bodies of transgressors, at once making them highly
visible and invisible through their destruction. Her utterance "I would do it
again if provoked" serves the lynch mob's desire to disavow the illegality of the
act because it brings her intent into the public realm. By making such a claim
in public, Josefa/Juanita gave verbal evidence that she was aware that killing
Cannon had legal, life-and-death repercussions, providing the justification
and anger the miners required in order to lynch her.

In contemplating the spectacle of the body twisting in the air, we cannot
know that "one aspect of great pain, as acknowledged by those who have
suffered . . . that it is to the individual experiencing it overwhelmingly present,
more emphatically real than any other human experience, and yet is almost
invisible to anyone else, unfelt and unknown."[163] One cannot comprehend
such pain through the recreation of the moment in narrative. The image of
her body twisting round and round for half an hour presses against the
reader's conscience but "convey[s] only a limited dimension of the sufferer's

experience."[164] Although the reader confronts the act of taking life from the body, their experience is limited. In narrative we are unable to access Josefa/Juanita's interiority and desires. The inability to comprehend being put to death by the hanging weight of one's own body distances us from the destruction of the subject. The subject suffers great pain because of the weight of her own body. Hence, the body is turned against itself. This lynching was about maintaining socioeconomic control, displaying power through the graphic mutilation of a brown, sexualized, gendered body.[165] Even if her demeanor and utterances from the platform tell a different story of Josefa/Juanita's sense of self and subjectivity, the mob created its own law in lynching; it is clear that mere jail time was not a sufficient sentence for women of color who allegedly violated such rules.

CONCLUSION

Competing discourses—primary documents, newspapers, critical and historical texts—literally position Josefa/Juanita's history and body which are used to serve various political agendas. The narratives about her in their many incarnations show a continuum of violence as a mechanism of socialization. But they also show a crisis in meaning where lynching's violence has the potential to sensationalize or serve Chicano/a nationalist agendas centered around political familialism, morality, and heteronormativity.

Texts on Josefa/Juanita's life and lynching are not uniform precisely because her story has been deployed for different purposes by different critics and historians. Although it is highly problematic that Josefa/Juanita does not become a subject in the historical record until inhumane public violence is inflicted upon her body (her property), I have shown throughout this chapter that racialized, sexualized subjects are often visible as subjects only because they were the targets of state-sanctioned violence. Her only property, her body, becomes the crux of a more complex feminist rendering of subjectivity in a borderlands context because, as a subject of her own making, we don't have to make her story conform to a resistance or vindicationist narrative in the name of nationalisms.

As the brutal treatment of Josefa/Juanita's body confirms, the Treaty of Guadalupe Hidalgo, which admitted California to the Union failed in its promise to extend full citizenship to U.S. Mexicana/os because of the intersection of color and gender hierarchies. The Irish and other European immigrants who made up the lynch mob could enact justice in the name of the nation and purchase political enfranchisement through participation while Josefa/Juanita was completely denied her rights to protection as a citizen.

Instead of extending the possibility of citizenship, the nation-state, through the actions of the kangaroo court and the lynch mob, disciplined and created docile bodies, actually opening up the gendered brown body to further violence. Josefa/Juanita's "texts" collectively recall a history of disciplining the body in which violence intimately shaped and continues to shape personhood or the process of being inaugurated as subject, adhering to the assumption of a static, ethnic-racialized subject that exists outside of language. For it is only through her murder of Cannon and the lynching itself that Josefa/Juanita becomes an identifiable historical subject. Cannon's behavior was not considered a crime by the jury, while Josefa/Juanita's stabbing of him was. It is these two crimes, her rage and the lynching, that make her visible in the historical record.

Josefa/Juanita's stories provide a complex point of entry into transnational feminist critical discussions of subjectivity in the Americas as well. While she very rarely speaks for herself in archival records, her actions speak to us as utterances that remind of the need for a multidirectional critique that interrogates the intentions and desires behind the resistant and vindicationist construction of her narratives. In the discourses reporting Josefa/Juanita's lynching, physical and epistemic violence can be read as an undoing of subjectivity in the sense that they presume a transparent, psychically whole subject that is fractured only through extreme injury of the body, whether physical or psychological.[166] It is the multiple utterances about her character—Cannon calling her a prostitute, the actual crime preceding the stabbing (that is, Cannon tearing down the door to José's home), Cannon calling José a son of a bitch, the unspeakable Spanish language exchanges between José and Josefa and among Josefa and Cannon and José—that posit a chain of action around details and words that remain unspeakable in the historical record. This unspeakable quality about the violence of erasure and elision and the actual physical violence carried out against Josefa/Juanita's body remind us that the logic of silence is a thick veil not easily penetrated. The power of law, race, gender, and sexual inequality gain their force through the silence, omission, and strategic articulation of particular details that led to this lynching in various kinds of political agendas, whether nationalist or racial. And even when José made a claim for justice before the binational commission, the case is its own utterance: one line stating simply that the claims to retribution by an aggrieved Mexican man for the lynching of his wife were denied.[167]

Yet in Josefa/Juanita's case the lynching ended her life in a ritualistic, public, extremely grotesque fashion, but how the narrative is told and to what end are the matters we should focus on. Her attempt to exert agency over her body (for a reason we cannot definitively determine) reinforces the notion that U.S. Mexicanas' bodies constituted their property and claim to citizenship. Her lynched body functions as a sign of the transformation of governance in California. Thus, reading the inconsistencies in the historical record of Josefa/Juanita's lynching offers a useful model for understanding the pitfalls of the writing of history. Although we sometimes can do no more than speculate, we must not reproduce histories or narratives that buttress constructs such as Chicano nationalism and Chicano familialism and put words in the historical figures' mouths. Larger cultural and symbolic meanings complicate the facile deployment of the term *resistance* and allow us to look more deeply into the complex changes in citizenship that continue to affect borderlands subjects.

2 ✳ Webs of Violence

THE CAMP GRANT INDIAN MASSACRE,
NATION, AND GENOCIDAL ALLIANCES

> In view of all of these facts, I call on all Arizonans to answer their
> conscience: can you call the killing of the Apaches at Camp Grant on
> the morning of April 30th 1871 a massacre?
>
> W. S. OURY, TUCSON, ARIZONA, APRIL 8, 1885

> It was the most cowardly murder that ever occurred, as they knew the
> Indians had no arms.
>
> ANDREW HAYS CARGILL, CLERK FOR THE CALIFORNIA OFFICE OF
> THE ATTORNEY GENERAL

The story of the Camp Grant Indian Massacre of 1871 has important implications for narratives that were unspeakable for multiple nations, the identities
they forged through violence, and questions of citizenship. Here is a typical
narrative of the massacre: "Don Jesús María [Elías] and his friend William
Oury masterminded an even larger assault upon the hated Aravaipas, who
were camped under the protection of the U.S. military near Camp Grant on
the San Pedro River. Known as the Camp Grant massacre, this expedition
turned into a frenzy of violence in which more than one hundred Apaches, all
but eight of whom were women and children, were slaughtered."[1]

This two-sentence account does not indicate the number of people who
perpetrated the massacre or their ethnic makeup. Further, the voices of the
indigenous people who participated in the massacre are erased. The superficial content and lack of detail are representative of the ways the history of
this massacre is told at a basic level.

Seventy miles northwest of Tucson, roughly 108 Aravaipa and Pinal Apache
who had earlier surrendered were slaughtered just outside of the military
fort where they had made peace with the U.S. government via the post

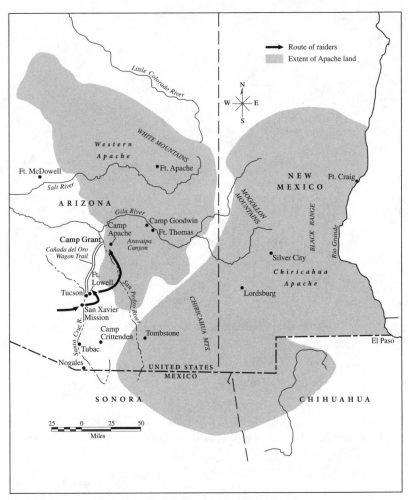

MAP 2 Map of Camp Grant Indian Massacre and surrounding area, ca. 1871

commander, Lt. Royal Whitman, in January 1871. The number of participants in the massacre and the death count are disputed in the historical record, as these sources are highly politicized. The averages suggest that about 48 Mexicans, 6 Americans, and 94 San Xavier Papagos (148 people total) carried out the actual massacre.[2] Sidney R. De Long, the primary defendant tried for the murders, stated that there were 46 Papagos, 50 Mexicans, and 5 Anglos.[3] The number killed was approximately 106 women and children; one old man and a boy of some fourteen years of age were the only males found dead, making the body count 108.[4] Chief Eskeminzin was near the camp when the raiding party attacked and managed to escape with his young daughter.[5] The rest of his immediate family (his wives and children) were killed. The attack was "so swift and fierce that within a half hour the work was ended and not an adult Indian left to tell the tale"; some 28 to 30 "papooses," or babies, were spared and brought to Tucson as Indian captives, six of whom remained with Tucson's prominent Mexican families while the rest were sold into slavery in Sonora.[6]

The Aravaipa and Pinal bands had originally settled along a tributary of the San Pedro River that they called Little Running Water (Aravaipa Creek), which is where their creation story was based. This was one reason they surrendered at Camp Grant: to be close to their homelands. The night before the massacre, according to the Aravaipa tribal member Sherman Curley, there was a great dance to celebrate their coming to Camp Grant. Curley further stated that many of the people were shot while they were dancing.[7] When the Apache men returned from hunting to the camp later in the day, they found the bodies of their kin. Lieutenant Whitman convinced the scattered survivors of the massacre to come in and camp within one mile of the fort for protection. They were relocated to the San Carlos Apache Reservation in late 1871, eventually sharing it with Chiricahua, Coyotero, Mimbreño, Mogollon, Pinaleno, San Carlos, and Tonto Apache. When the Aravaipa were attacked again in 1874, Eskeminzin and his followers went on the warpath, eventually surrendering and returning to the San Carlos reservation six months later.[8]

There was a long history of retaliatory violence and exchange among Anglos, Mexicans, and indigenous inhabitants of southern Arizona and the U.S.– Mexico borderlands in general. Spilling the blood of Aravaipa and Pinal Apache women and children aligned Anglos, Mexicanos, and Tohono O'odham (San Xavier and Pan Tak Papago)[9] with the territorial government of Arizona in an act of ritualized, state-sanctioned violence. The historian Juliana Barr has argued with regard to the eighteenth-century culture of indigenous exchange and warfare in Texas that "vengeance and recovery of lost family members was required" as a mechanism of survival, garnering and maintaining social, cultural, and economic power.[10] The historians James Brooks and Pekka Hämäläinen suggest that during the eighteenth century and the nineteenth the New Mexico–Rio Grande basin area and the Texas Comanchería were places where Native policies toward colonial power were driven by more than simple survival. Rather, both convincingly argue that Indians waged war, exchanged goods, made treaties, and absorbed peoples in order to expand, extort, manipulate, and dominate, just as their Spanish, Mexican, French, and Anglo-American colonial contemporaries did.[11] At the same time, the historian Karl Jacoby informs us that within this history of violence and exchange, the way the history is told and by whom (in this case, by the Anglo-Americans, who had the means to create a historical society and official history) ultimately "supplanted not only the accounts of the Nnee survivors of the massacre, but those of the attack's Mexican-American and Tohono O'odham participants" at Camp Grant.[12] Given the complexity of the historical relationships among numerous Apache groups, Tohono O'odham, Anglos, and Mexicans in southern Arizona, all of whom were jockeying for power, and given that such relations were often negotiated through violence, the fact that Mexicans and Native Americans participated in the Camp Grant Indian Massacre was not unusual: it took place within a larger pattern of exchange that was a part of everyday life. Arizona has a distinct history of *indios bárbaros* that goes back to occupation of the territory by the Spanish and Mexicans, both soldiers and the Jesuits, a fact that clearly influenced how the Apache were seen and how Mexican and Tohono O'odham peoples saw themselves as existing outside of those discourses of barbarism. This event has a distinctly transnational history because both Spanish and Mexican rule reinforced the idea of the Apache as indios bárbaros, and in an effort to make their own claims to power within the multiple national contexts that make up Arizona's colonial past, Tucsonenses (Mexicans) and O'odham peoples repeatedly sought to disassociate themselves from them. This was more a project of whitening Arizona than of westernizing it.[13]

Although issues of interracial and intraracial violence have long been a topic of analysis in the field of history, very few studies of Chicano/a and indigenous communities conducted within the field of Chicano studies acknowledge this history of Mexican Americans as Indian fighters.[14] But given my investment in a critique of contemporary debates on mestizaje in Chicano studies that equate Mexican/Chicano with Indian, my reading of this massacre seeks to interrupt the recent returns to indigenismo in Chicano studies and demonstrate that these contemporary notions of identity have grounding in the history of places such as nineteenth-century southern Arizona. In exploring why nonwhites participated in the slaughter of Apaches, most of whom were women and children, I examine notions of citizenship, silence, violence, and discipline by revisiting this history with a critical eye that challenges monolithic representations of Chicano identity as essentially indigenous. I suggest that perhaps we should abandon celebratory, uncritical discourses of mestizaje and indigenousness altogether and concentrate more on the socially constructed nature of gender relations as they produced racialized systems of power and capital.

Most brief accounts of the Camp Grant massacre present the conflict as

Anglo versus Apache in nature. However, the participation of Anglos, Mexicans, and Papagos in the massacre complicates the picture of what constitutes resistance and mestizaje as topics of analysis in Chicano studies. In this chapter, I examine standard narratives of the event and why some writers insisted on calling it a raid rather than a massacre: the portrayal of the event depended upon whom the writer was related to, how he viewed his racial identity, and how he understood his citizenship (the contemporary writers were all men). This massacre or raid, which took on an extremely sexualized dimension, exemplified a social contract of sorts, a negotiation of power, especially in relationship to captivity, race, gender, and sexuality. The attack against Aravaipa and Pinal Apache problematizes the facile deployments of indigenous-Mexican ethnic cultural similarities that some scholars have proposed.[15] Issues of Chicano nationalist-based paradigms of indigenous identity become much more complicated when we analyze the fact that Mexicans and San Xavier Papago Indians constituted the bulk of the corps who killed the Apache women and children while they slept; at this moment Mexicans certainly did not imagine themselves as Indian and the San Xavier Papago did not see themselves in alliance with the Aravaipa and Pinal Apache.[16] I demonstrate how race, class, gender, and sexuality are being negotiated and brokered throughout history, not just by the participants in that historical moment but also by historians through their reinterpretations of social memory. By reviewing the varied trajectories of events that led to the Camp Grant Indian massacre, the archival documents that discuss these events, and the perpetrators' gendered, sexual, and intimate motivations (in particular, excessive masculinity and criminal femininity as social constructs), I examine how and why Tucsonenses and San Xavier Papago colluded in perpetrating violence against Indian groups like the Apache as part of a larger structure of power and exchange. That structure is most concretely represented in the ritualized practice of attack and counterattack among dominant tribes and other ethnic groups in the area. Interracial alliances among Anglos, Mexicans, and non-Apache Indians shaped identities, some producing instances of violence against the bodies of gendered, racialized, and sexualized individuals in nineteenth-century southern Arizona for the purpose of gaining power and domination. Nineteenth-century discourses surrounding Tucson Mexican, O'odham, and Apache identities, which were often generically reduced to one monolithic group, and their roles in producing subjectivity and self-concepts of citizenship suggest that Mexican and Indian participation in genocidal practices against fellow Mexicans and Indians is situated in a profound silence and is constructed through methods that enact epistemic violence by selectively forgetting sexual, familial, racial, and profit-driven alliances made through marriage and capitalist ventures, as well as the power differentials they create. The Papago, Anglo, and Mexican raiders at Camp Grant, the 108 Pinal and Aravaipa women and children (2 males) who were slaughtered, and the 28–30 children who were sold into captivity suggest that the history of the Camp Grant massacre leaves little documentation of an alternate history in which women are anything but victims of patriarchy because the sexual violence against the women is eliminated from the majority of the narratives. They are described as casualties of war waged between and among men. Revisiting the evidence, I arrive at a different set of conclusions, conclusions that are contradictory yet more representative.

The narratives about the Camp Grant massacre are colored by the prejudices of their tellers. The historical documents and accounts that follow reflect the fact that Tucson Mexican and Arizona indigenous voices are mediated throughout by dominant Anglo histories. Their narratives need to be acutely understood as social and cultural exchanges within the context of male power, privilege, and honor, whether Mexican, Anglo, Apache, or Tohono O'odham.[17] One of the highly problematic features of the historical documents about the massacre is that the names of the slaughtered Apache, of a large portion of the Mexican participants, and of almost all the O'odham raiders are omitted, suggesting that they were not citizen subjects worthy of acknowledgment in the historical record. Yet, unlike the Apache, all who participated in the massacre temporarily secured the right of citizenship. For Mexicans and Anglos the massacre secured the right to own property and trade in formal economies. The Papagos were able to enact revenge and gain reparations against the Apache, who had recently raided their mission lands, stealing their wives, children, and cattle. The Papagos were said to have performed the bulk of the physical violence, yet they were not citizens of the United States until 1924 and did not have voting rights until the 1950s. The historical reasons for the Mexicans' and Papagos' participation in the raid had nothing to do with Anglos because both groups had suffered losses such as lives, cattle, crops, and ammunition at the hands of Apache raiders. Yet Anglos and Mexicans were the ones who organized the event, so one cannot rule out the possibility that the Anglos and Mexicans thought they were using the Papagos' labor as instruments of state-sanctioned violence, even though the Indians clearly had the agency to decide how to participate and to what ends. On the other hand, the Papago could have been using the Anglos and Mexicans to mobilize a counterattack on the Camp Grant Apache to avenge depredations and losses they had recently suffered. Ultimately, all of the groups involved in the Camp Grant massacre were contesting notions of territory and property through the logics of ritualized attack and counterattack that governed the lives of tribal and nontribal peoples alike at this historical moment. I explore the linkages forged through spatial, historical, social, and economic alliances among Anglo, Mexican, and indigenous peoples as well as the formation of a particular class of people in the larger Arizona–Sonora borderlands. Space and spatial transformation shaped responses to such alliances, their products, and thus scholarly ability to understand the political consequences of economic and communal desires.

One of the debates in the historical record is the very representation of the Camp Grant attack itself. Those who acknowledge the Apache perspective, including officials of the Bureau of Indian Affairs (BIA), call it a massacre. Those writing on the side of the Anglos, Papago, and Mexicans call it a raid. This framing of the event exemplifies how "perceptual, somatic and emotional events occur; thus, between the two extremes can be mapped the whole terrain of the human psyche," according to Elaine Scarry, a scholar who has studied pain and violence.[18] Calling the attack a raid entails a conscious choice to represent the violent acts as one's civic duty and to absolve from guilt those who participated in the violence. A raid implies economic necessity and exchange. Women and children were often captured and exchanged in raids, as were durable goods and ammunition, but they were not always the targets of violence, bloodshed, and death.

In the Camp Grant massacre, women and children were unmistakably the targets of ritualized violence, which suggests the perpetrators had a different set of objectives, including Apache pacification. Thus the choice of words has huge semantic implications, in that to call something a massacre is to acknowledge the extreme force and violence of the act and perhaps even to recognize it as genocide. Use of the word *raid* minimizes the sexual and physical violence and implies that the attack was a justified response to previous Apache raids to steal cattle and provisions at both San Xavier and Tucson. A raid does not have the implication of physical or sexual violence carried out to rectify short-term imbalances in goods and power. *Massacre*, on the other hand, implies premeditated violence and recognizes the Apache's status as prisoners of war in that they had surrendered to the U.S. Army at Camp Grant. De Long calls the attack "an interview": "Americans, Mexicans and some friendly Papago Indians, in a body started for old Camp Grant, where these murderous Indians were camped for the purpose of interviewing them. The interview so ably described by Ex. President Wm. S. Oury, I am happy to state had the desired effect. So much so, Southern Arizona enjoyed peace for a while."[19] To call what happened an interview is a gross misrepresentation of physical violence and indeed seems to hint at irritation on the part of the author. Denying the existence of the pained body by characterizing the event as a site of civil exchange or locating the acts in discourse (an interview) rather than in the physical realm is a complete and utter denial of Apache subjectivity and a confirmation that the Apache who were killed at Camp Grant lacked citizenship status. As Scarry argues, "To acknowledge the radical subjectivity of pain is to acknowledge the simple and absolute incompatibility of pain and the world."[20] Locating the physical violence and torture experienced by the Apache slaughtered outside Camp Grant in the physical realm would acknowledge that they were rational, thinking human beings, an attitude incompatible with De Long's worldview. Political power entails the control of self-description, and there is no power greater than to deny violence that was designed to wipe out a population.[21]

NO LOVE FOR THE APACHES

The buildup to the massacre was lengthy and showed a kind of national, regional, and ethnic complicity in the violence. As De Long stated, "The great scourge of Arizona from at least 1861 up to 1872 was the Apache Indians," not just for Anglos, but for Mexican settlers and Papago Indians alike.[22] Just eight days before the Camp Grant Indian massacre, the *Weekly Arizonan* published a long investigative piece focusing on the virtues of the Papago, praising their peaceful agricultural and sedentary ways. In both the Tucson public imaginary and in relations between Anglos and Mexicans, the Papago were cast in opposition to the Apache in public discourse. This was not a new perspective. It started with the Spanish fighting the Apache indios bárbaros with Papago support as early as the seventeenth century in Arizona.[23] At their trials, the defendants in the Camp Grant case recounted a long history of hostilities between numerous Apache groups and the Papago. For example, the defendant Jose Maria Yesques said, "I understand the relation of the Apaches with the Papagoes, from conversations with them. The Apaches understand that they are always at war with the Papagoes and want no peace with them. The Apaches under no circumstance would agree to any peace with the Papagoes."[24] While it might have appeared exceedingly strategic to mark Apache hatred and hostility toward the Papago in order to justify the attack against them, both Mexicans and Anglos in the Arizona Territory knew of this longstanding history of violence between the two indigenous groups. The Papago are said to have performed the bulk of the physical violence against the Apache of Camp Grant, even though they were uniformly classified as peaceful Indians. "It is mortifying to observe the sad neglect, by the government, of these good, industrious people, on the one hand, and the pampering of the accursed Apache on the other," stated an editorial, reflecting common sentiments.[25] The Tucson community relied heavily on the labor force at San Xavier and found the Papago to be trustworthy. Unlike the Apache, "these Indians, with the best opportunities to rob and steal, have never been known to unlawfully appropriate one single dollar's worth of property belonging to any settler."[26] Polarized discourses of good and bad Indians are often predicated upon the uses that could be made of their labor. Here, we are brought back to the question of economics. The Papago facilitated the economic success of the settlers by working on the ranches surrounding Tucson. In stark contrast to the ways in which the Apache were seen to disrupt the economic order and productivity, the San Xavier Papago were portrayed as helping to create it.

In fact, one of the factors motivating the San Xavier Papago to participate in the massacre had to do with a long history of Apache depredations of their property and of mutual violence and hatred. On January 21, 1871, the *Weekly Arizonan* reported, "a band of Apaches, on Thursday last, swooped down upon a herd of fifty horses belonging to the Papagos, and dashed off with the booty towards the mountains." As a result, 150 Papago braves saddled up "with every implement of destruction from the newest style rifle to the veritable war club." Even though it was illegal for Indians to possess or purchase firearms, the editorial staff of the newspaper clearly knew the Papago had guns and supported their use to recover the stolen horses from the Apache. As we can see, the retaliatory tactics were often about the recovery of property, or what Hämäläinen has called "a means of rectifying a short term imbalance."[27] Such antagonisms and competition over resources erased any possibility for peace and escalated hostilities between the Apache and Papago, which the Arizona press supported.

Hatred of the Apache peaked in early 1871. Southern Arizonans were frustrated over the lack of success of military efforts to subdue them and the subsequent turn to peacemaking as an alternative. The national government's new policy was seen as hollow, unproductive, and costly: "Again, making peace with Apaches, and furnishing them with gifts, is the veriest bosh that ever emanated from an addled pate. The whole system was contrived for the benefit of the white trader and agent."[28] The *Weekly Arizonan* accused those Anglo-Americans who had U.S. government contracts to provide rations to the Apaches (at highly inflated prices) of being race traitors. The truth of the matter, however, is that many local Tucson merchants benefited from such contracts, including Sam Hughes, Hiram Stevens, and the firm of Tully, Ochoa and DeLong, a freighting company. These merchants profited from what was in many ways a wartime economy and were complicit in the massacre by provisioning both the Apaches and the raiders. Yet much to the dismay of Oury direct Anglo participation in the massacre was very small: "In view of the fact that 82 Americans had solemnly pledged themselves to be ready at any moment for the campaign and only six finally showed up, was at the least rather humiliating."[29] Although most Anglos did not physically participate in the massacre, they donated guns, food, bullets, and horses to those who did.

The massacre is often inaccurately portrayed as an Indian–Anglo conflict, yet the Mexican and Papago participants in the massacre outnumbered the Anglos by as much as seven to one, reflecting the politics of capitalism and citizenship. Tucsonenses and Anglos alike scoffed at Gen. George Stoneman's report to Congress and President Ulysses S. Grant, in which he suggested that the Apache posed no threat to the Arizona Territory. Stoneman's testimony was politically motivated, as the U.S. government was strapped with post–Civil War reconstruction costs. The same year (1869), Governor Anson P. K. Safford of Arizona appointed a committee to investigate the losses sustained through Indian depredations, most likely to prove General Stoneman wrong:

> To the people of Arizona, Gen. Stoneman has done a grave and serious wrong—to express his action in the mildest possible terms . . . it is necessary that a strong military force be stationed in Arizona; for it should be considered that the southern boundary line of the territory is also the boundary of a foreign State. True, we are at peace with Mexico, as a government, but locally we are not at peace with her criminal classes. All countries and communities have their law-evading ghouls that prey upon the industry of others, and Mexico has hers. In organized bands they invade our frontier, murder our settlers and carry off their property—and then take refuge in their own country.[30]

Sounding suspiciously like descriptions of Apache raiders carrying their plunder from the United States into Mexico, Safford's account lumps together Mexican desperadoes and Apache raiders. These were conflicts between citizens and nations: Mexican, U.S., and Apache nations and Mexican and U.S. citizens, with the figure of the Indian as a noncitizen suspended in the middle of the dialogue. Safford's call for a military presence to contain Mexico's wayward citizens casts Mexico as a deterrent rather than a partner in the development of border industrial capitalism, namely, the development of ranching and the construction of a railroad, the accomplishment of which necessitated the pacification of Indians. Furthermore, Safford was probably making a calculated play on the feelings of xenophobes in Washington to gain support for military interventions in the borderlands. Mexico and its citizens, like the wayward Apache, were a hindrance to the accumulation of private property and establishment of settled life. He was also most likely making a calculated play to justify continued military action, given that the economic and human cost of Apache raids was minuscule in comparison to that of the Civil War. As the economist Robert Higgs argues, private property rights are the foundation of successful market systems.[31] Therefore, it only makes sense that the Papago and Tucson Mexicans chose to ally themselves with the territorial and local governments against the Apache, even though, or precisely because, they were to some extent conflated with the sinister character of the Apache.[32]

In January 1871 Clint Thompson of Florence, Arizona, sent an Anglo, and two Papago Indians out on his wagon, pulled by four mules, to collect hay. Seven Indians attacked them, stealing the animals, destroying the harness, and burning the wagon. Fifteen men pursued the Indians. In a letter to the editor, a Florentine states, "It seems that Angel González, an estimable young man and well known at Tucson, got ahead of the party by some means or other, and the men who were riding the trail discovering what they supposed to be an Indian, fired on him, inflicting a wound which must certainly prove fatal. They immediately returned, procured an ambulance and brought the wounded man to Adamsville where he now lies."[33] People like Angel González demonstrated, in both life and death, how fragile the line was between being Mexican and being Apache. One misrecognition might bring unwarranted death. The fact that González was mistakenly identified and shot as a result suggests one possible motivation for Mexican participation in the Camp Grant massacre: it was perhaps a political move to decisively mark themselves as non-Apache. The only way to achieve such a distinction racially, socially, and nationally was to participate in state-sanctioned genocide against the very people one is compared to and to claim the rights of citizenship by defending small-scale private property, "the petit bourgeois basis for the reproduction of capitalist relations" according to María Josefina Saldaña-Portillo.[34]

In the massacre, the Stevens, Oury, and Hughes families and the San Xavier Papago bands blurred the line between government action and personal action. That is, they embodied the state's right to use violent means as they attempted to exterminate the Aravaipa and Pinal Apache at Camp Grant. Through violence they guaranteed themselves state protection and authority over other individuals. Fighting the Indians who potentially threatened their livelihood was a way of defending their social and cultural legacy as well as the economic stability they derived from ranching and agriculture. Developing cross-cultural communities cemented through violent physical and sexual relationships, the Mexican, Anglo, and Papago participants in the massacre defined their citizenship and ideas of community in opposition to the Aravaipa and Pinal Apache, who were deemed savage and undeserving of protection from the nation-state. These sexual and political alliances challenge Chicano/a studies paradigms of mestizaje, family romance, and violence as simple resistance. In these borderlands, there was a long history of attempts by the Spanish and Mexicans to "civilize" Indians by teaching them the value of property and sedentary agriculture, a project that was never completely accomplished with groups like the Apache because it meant converting them to a different set of economic and religious beliefs.[35] But it also would have made those Indians into subjects recognizable to the nation and granted them citizenship, land rights, and a way of life that would make them rights-bearing individuals. The O'odham were able to accomplish this to some extent in their relationships with both the United States and Mexico, but the Apache unquestionably were a target of extermination in both Mexico and the United States.[36] Through violence, Mexicans marked themselves as non-Indian and the Papago differentiated themselves from the warlike Apaches and thus brokered a temporary place for themselves within local hierarchies of power. The narrative of citizenship and capitalist preservation takes precedence in the historical record as the dominant line of memory. In some ways, the call for citizen vigilantes was an appeal to constitutional values, the protection of private property, and the right to bear arms.

Newspapers from as far away as New York, Washington, Chicago, San Francisco, and San Diego covered the events in Arizona with great fervor. The Camp Grant Apache, as they were known, had agreed to peace in January 1871, under much protest from southern Arizona residents. The *Daily Alta California* was particularly sympathetic to the so-called innocent pioneers suffering from Apache hostilities. As early as January 9, 1871, newspapers like the *Daily Alta California* and the *Arizona Weekly* had taken to reporting on events in Arizona at least three times a week. In articles entitled "A Carnival of Blood" (February 4, 1871), "The Indian Question" (January 18, 1871), and "Apache Outrages" (February 7, 1871), the regional press favored the position of Anglo pioneers, Mexican Indian fighters, and Indians aligned with capitalism and the territorial government. Mining, ranching, and agriculture were of the utmost importance to national development. The "Indian question" was never mentioned without a discussion of its role in impeding commerce. An example is an article in the *Daily Alta California*, "Mining in Arizona": "The evils to which we have referred are but temporary in their nature, and are already beginning to disappear. The Indian question is the most pressing. . . . Whatever may be said about keeping peace with the tribes of other regions, all parties agreed that the only thing to be done with the Apache is to fight them." Venture capitalists were afraid of the Apache mostly because they disrupted capitalist expansion. The U.S. census for 1870 recorded only two to six inhabitants per square mile in Arizona, which explains why the settlers were so vulnerable to Apache attacks.[37] The problem was not one of lack of population per se but of citizenship, territorial control, and capitalist development, including ranching, farming, and the coming of the railroad. Not surprisingly, people thought that "if this is to be done vigorously, there can be but one result. They [the Apache] will be thoroughly exterminated."[38] The Camp Grant Apache were pursued for interrupting the daily lives and livelihoods of pioneers in and around Tucson through their raiding practices, and, as we can see from the *Daily Alta California*'s position, mining and development were just two of the reasons it was socially and politically acceptable to exterminate the Apache. In this aspect, the national discourse supported the local one and justified extreme physical violence on a local level, marking a shift from the highly localized economies and markets of the pre–Civil War era to the post–Civil War desire for larger-scale markets that extended beyond U.S. national borders.

Such national sentiment is what kept U.S. Army troops in the Arizona Territory fighting hostile Indians. In 1871 there was much anxiety about protecting citizens and their property as the government was diverting its financial and military resources to pay for Reconstruction: "Great alarm prevails in consequence of a report that the troops are to be removed from southern Arizona, much of which country is infested by hostile Indians, who commit frequent depredations."[39] The anxiety was reflected in the Sixth Legislative Assembly of the Arizona Territory, which met on January 16, 1871. It advocated a policy of extermination against the Apache and "the placing on reservations of the Pinals and Tontos [Western Apache tribal groups]; recommends that volunteers raised in the country, inured to the climate, acquainted with all the habits of the Indians of the country and fighting for their homes, as being more efficient than soldiers, and in the end more economical for the government than regular troops."[40]

While the Camp Grant massacre is often historicized as a local reaction to a lack of federal interest in protecting capitalism in southern Arizona, the Sixth Territorial Legislature proceedings demonstrate that Indian genocide was legislated by the nascent territorial government. The series of economic depressions that hit the borderlands ultimately influenced Indian policy in the 1870s. A depression in Sonora in the late 1860s no doubt affected the Tucson economy, fueling Indian tensions.[41] The local logic of settlers familiar with the Indians was based in their own nativism, and Indians became scapegoats for local and national economic problems alike.

The desire to locate the Southern Pacific Railroad in southern Arizona to help counteract the economic downturn also fueled the fervor to eliminate the Apache.[42] With the Indian problem deterring the building of a rail line, southern Arizona continued to be "[a] vast fertile and auriferous country lying waste."[43] Ultimately, the railroad was also seen as a solution to the Indian problem: "If the passage of this railroad bill does not wipe out the Apache and bring the millennium to Arizona, as well as to ourselves, we know of no other measure that will hasten that grand event, or condition—or whatever it may be."[44] The desire for economic shift demonstrates that the goal of subjugating the Apache was not necessarily to take away what they made or produced but to force them to make or produce something different, to harness their labor for the linking of Arizona's local economy to a national one.[45]

Reports in Tucson about Indian hostilities were linked to development discourses of enlightenment and capital accumulation. Around March 11, 1871, members of the Tucson community were traveling between the town and the so-called Camp Grant reservation (an informal reservation never federally ratified), attempting to track the numbers of Aravaipa and Pinal Apache who had surrendered. There was little public support for reservations because they were viewed as "a source of evil, from the fact that [they] give . . . protection and support to squaws, and old, useless men, while the warriors are out stealing live stock and murdering citizens."[46] The *Weekly Arizonan* reported that one Sam Drachman arrived back from Camp Grant to report that there were about ninety Indians there but "that number is expected to swell to 200 within a few days" as a result of a treaty made between Lieutenant Whitman and Chief Eskeminzin in late January–early February 1871. In response to the treaty and to an increase in depredations carried out by unknown perpetrators, that spring, "at a mass meeting H. S. Stevens, chairman, H. S. Hinds, Samuel Hughes and D. A. Bennett were elected a committee to superintend the work of raising a volunteer force to carry on a 3-months campaign against the Apaches."[47] The assault appears to have been at least premeditated, if not practically legislated.

Apache became the catchword for all hostile Indians in Arizona, even though the government knew there were many independent bands of Aravaipa and multiple Apache groups carrying out raids. Francis A. Walker, the commissioner of the BIA, argued in his report for 1872 that "many of the bands of the tribe (if it can be called a tribe—habits, physical structure and language all pointing to a great diversity in origin among several bands) are seemingly incorrigible."[48] Even when other groups, like the Pima, were suspected of plundering, the attention always focused on the Apache: "The Pima have the reputation of 'good Indians,' and if we consider them in connection with the Apaches they are, certainly, comparatively 'good.' . . . The Pimas are shrewd enough to observe with what impunity the Apaches may depredate upon the settlers, and it is hardly a matter to occasion surprise—savages as they are and secure in their strength—they should endeavor to take advantage of this license."[49] Therefore, despite the fact that there were twenty discrete Indian tribal groups either living in or migrating through Arizona at this time, the Apache, no matter what band they were from, were consistently blamed for Indian depredations. A wire article reprinted from the *San Diego Union Tribune* calls the proposal for an Apache reservation by the New Mexico Indian agent

an insane idea. . . . The Indian Agent afore-said should be accommodated with first class apartments in a Lunatic Asylum. For more than two hundred years the Apaches have been the same race of murderers, kidnappers and robbers they are to-day; the history of ancient Spanish settlements in New Mexico and Arizona presents just such a dreadful record of murder, pillage and devastation, as we find in the newspapers of those Territories. While the Pimas, Papagos, Maricopas, and other Indians of that part of the country have learned to cultivate the arts of peace, to till the soil and live in harmony with the civilization around them, the Apaches wander in predatory bands, carrying desolation in every direction.[50]

Indian affairs in Arizona in the early 1870s lurched back and forth between peace and war. Each new round of Indian hostilities brought increasing conflict between the settlers, seminomadic Indians, and the soldiers, leading Gen. E. O. C. Ord to declare that war was the foundation of the Arizona economy and that civilians demanded more troops because they wanted profit, not peace. Westerners generally favored exterminating the Indians.

In "A Suggestion to the People," an editorial of January 21, 1871, the *Weekly*

Arizonan excoriates General Stoneman, the military official in charge of Arizona at that time, for his lax, uninformed policies toward the Apache during his recent visit to Arizona. Stoneman's report to President Grant states the following: "The Apache nation in this region, compared with what I knew of it more than twenty years ago, is nearly harmless. . . . In conclusion it gives me pleasure to be able to express the opinion that the Indian, as well as other affairs in the department, are in as satisfactory a condition as can be reasonably expected." The editorialist responds to this with a staunch critique: "We do not propose to question the veracity of Gen. Stoneman, whose stay in the Territory has been insufficient to enable him to speak from personal observation, but it is evident that his report was compiled without any knowledge of facts—perhaps entirely from the representations of others . . . we have no hesitancy in declaring a series of the *grossest misrepresentations* . . . we know, and every citizen of Arizona knows, that the last three years constitute the bloodiest page in the history of Arizona."

In the eyes of the federal government and the residents of Tucson the withdrawal of military posts and troops from Arizona was an economic question. The federal government, coping, as noted, with the excessive costs of Reconstruction and Civil War reparations, was now less inclined than before to fund frontier defense. Soldiering had transformed the economy of southern Arizona,[51] and the merchants of Tucson earned their livelihoods through government contracts to feed, clothe, and supply these soldiers and their outposts. Profits were easy, and there was little incentive to develop new markets: "Many of the inhabitants of southern Arizona, it is true, have amassed considerable wealth in this limited field, but the sameness and routine character of business thus conducted have shed an apathy upon the general business character of the country, that is now becoming painfully evident."[52] In the post–Civil War economic depression, the transformation of southern Arizona into a site of capital production was not inhibited by the Apache. In fact, war with the Apache facilitated the economy. In 1871–72 merchants in Tucson and the San Xavier Papago lost a small number of horses and cattle to Apache raiders, but in that same year the military was ordering as many as two thousand head of beef and one thousand of mutton to supply the U.S. Army in the Southwest, orders the contractors were unable to meet.[53] As Tucsonans found out, a poor and unstable economy was the result of the final subduing of the Apache because in the 1860s and 1870s military contracts and a constant state of warfare, what many have called the Apache wars, made many a resident wealthy. There were several visions of territory and spatial transformation at this time: local merchants and ranchers saw opportunities to continue amassing wealth, the Apache saw an opportunity to defend their spatial claims to land and livelihood, the Mexicans were attempting to maintain the political power and property they had, and the Papago sought to maintain their way of life. Competition among these groups over land and capital was the ultimate source of the struggle, especially given the depressed economy, a reminder of why so many members of an ethnically diverse community had no love for the Apaches.

VIOLENCE, CAPITALISM, AND GENDER: WHY CAMP GRANT?

According to Elizabeth Grosz, people "play a part in various structures of violence."[54] Capitalism and development operate as social forces, which were common motivators for violence, including state-sanctioned genocide. The historical moment at which the Camp Grant massacre occurred was extremely chaotic: real estate prices in Arizona were plummeting, the Territorial Legislature had published a pamphlet documenting Apache depredations in 1869–70, and President Grant was threatening to withdraw all troops from the territory and eliminate federal support for Indian fighting in Arizona and New Mexico. Soldiers and officers were known to barter with the Indians, exchanging cartridges and ammunition for game, which suggests that government officials were indirectly assisting Indian depredations.[55] In the face of all these complex social changes, the Camp Grant massacre was a means of preserving the honor, power, and decency of the dominant populations involved in traditional formal capitalism (Anglos, Mexicans, and Papago) at the expense of nomadic bands (Aravaipa and Pinal Apache) because maintaining a foothold in this shifting wartime economy required as much.

The anthropologist Chip Colwell-Chanthophonh points out that the accounts of the massacre differ in their descriptions of the racial composition and size of the attacking force and that the accounts were written almost exclusively by the Anglos who participated in the attack, even though only five or six were actually present. Colwell-Chanthophonh argues that none of the accounts of the massacre is accurate in all respects, and that the discrepancies in the record give new insight into the history of violence against indigenous people.[56] While I use a synthesis of the materials to tell the basic story of the Camp Grant massacre, we must remember that none of these sources is transparent. In keeping with Colwell-Chanthophonh's assertion, the Camp Grant massacre needs to be critically situated among the complex social relations existing in Tucson's wartime economy, where Anglo, Papago, Apache, and Mexican men and women defined and contested questions of citizenship and belonging through acts of extreme physical violence and the protection of private property.

Many of Tucson's prominent Mexican, Anglo, and Indian families were major players in the raid. There were the Santa Cruz sisters, Petra and Atanacia, native Tucsonenses whose mother was a Pima Indian and whose father was a Spanish settler of the presidio. They had married the prominent Anglo immigrants Hiram Stevens and Samuel Hughes, respectively.[57] The Elías brothers, Jesús and Juan María, considered themselves gentrified Spaniards and were born and raised in Tubac presidio. Others were Bill Oury and his wife, Inez, born in Durango, Mexico; and the Papago warriors Chief Francisco Galerita of the San Xavier Papago, his kinsmen, and men from the village of Pan Tak, for example. The massacre was planned in the Hughes house and in meetings between Jesús Elías and Oury in saloons and in Oury's home near Tubac.[58] Family networks, economics, and kinship were central in bringing about the Camp Grant massacre. The collaboration in the massacre (from strategic planning, supplying arms, and making bullets to serving as raiders) suggests the intimate nature of Arizona's territorial history of violence against indigenous communities. The imagined capitalist future of the state once it was rid of the Apache and the political practices of the Arizona Territory literally passed through the homes and social networks of these families.

The participation of Atanacia Santa Cruz de Hughes, a woman of Spanish and Pima descent, in state-sanctioned violence reflected the ambivalence and instability of racial politics. Based on an ethnographic interview conducted for the Arizona Pioneers Society in 1926, Edith Kitt states, "Mrs. Hughes does not attempt to tell about the massacre of the Indians in the little settlement of Camp Grant," thereby evading the political consequences of being responsible for genocide and instead representing the event as a moment of pride and civic duty.[59] This is a common theme in the press coverage and in participants' memories of both the massacre and the events that precipitated it. In this *testimonio*, Santa Cruz de Hughes stated that most of the planning for the massacre was done in the Hughes home, but on many occasions "civilians and army officers all came there for advice." In the words of Sam Hughes, " 'I had a spoon in every soup,' and it seems as if Mrs. Atanacia Hughes had her husband's complete confidence and quite a share in the 'soup.' "[60] In fact, Atanacia seems quite proud of her participation in the planning and carrying out of the raid to eliminate the Camp Grant Indians who had been stealing from citizens. She states, "I don't know how many Americans went but I am sure there were more than six. . . . No, Mr. Hughes did not go to Camp Grant but he furnished the means to go. He approved the plan and gave the ammunition and arms—yes, they were given out from this very room we are sitting in and I helped to make the bullets. Our own wagon was loaded with the supplies, the arms, the grub and the ammunition."[61] Santa Cruz de Hughes understands her participation in the massacre in terms of a citizen's call to defense, one that was rooted in the Spanish–Mexican heritage of Tucsonense Indian fighters of the region. That is, the U.S. Army stationed in the territory would not protect the property and lives of U.S. citizens, so vigilante citizens took care of the problem for them. In this testimonio we can see a complete disconnect between Santa Cruz de Hughes's identity as a Mexican indigenous woman and her attitude toward the Camp Grant Apaches, whom she saw as less than human and fit to be exterminated. Santa Cruz de Hughes had a socially privileged position in Tucson as a *descendiente*, a native Tucsonense and a descendant of Spanish conquistadors who built the presidio.[62] This is the identity she embraced and that informed her perspective on the Indian question for people in the region. For Tucsonenses like Santa Cruz de Hughes, attempting to convert Indians like the Apache into civilized people was a project that had been tried in Mexico and had failed long before the 1854 Treaty of Mesilla.[63] Rather than whitening the indigenous populations through the project of mestizaje or making them into Mexicans (or even into Americans), extermination was thought to be the only viable option, even by those who might be classified as indigenous themselves. Marriages and cultural practices ultimately demonstrate the "totalizing grasp of the disciplinary forces exerted by civil institutions and social groups" that made racialized women identify with a particular kind of exclusionary economic politics.[64]

Santa Cruz de Hughes appears in many of the chronicles of the massacre, including Don Schellie's novel *Vast Domain of Blood*. Like many hegemonic, Anglo-centered, male historians, Schellie, in order to compensate for a lack of source material on Samuel Hughes, uses Santa Cruz de Hughes as a representational vessel to talk about her husband's role in the massacre. Santa Cruz de Hughes, by contrast, saw herself as part of the history of the Camp Grant massacre and spoke regularly on the subject. The fact that the means of war and violence were prepared in her home suggests that the frequently argued dichotomy between public and private spaces and gendered identities is historically false. That Santa Cruz de Hughes made bullets in her own home demonstrates the tremendous interplay between family, nation, and genocide, irrespective of one's own ethnocultural identity. Furthermore, her participation suggests that the mobilization was supported not just by men but by women as well. Nineteenth-century women like Santa Cruz de Hughes had a political position on the Indian question that was directly opposed to the sympathetic, reformist attitudes of, for example, Helen Hunt Jackson and Lydia Maria Child.[65] Rather, Santa Cruz de Hughes exemplifies what the gender studies scholars Sidonie Smith and Julia Watson call, within an auto-biographical framework, "the processes of self-decolonization [that] may get bogged down as the autobiographical subject reframes herself through neo-colonizing metaphors."[66] Santa Cruz de Hughes was a woman who did not imagine herself as being indigenous or colonized and therefore took up the neocolonial project by making bullets and politically supporting the massacre of the Apache at Camp Grant. If anything, her position on the Camp Grant massacre was informed by the Spanish and Mexican discourse of indios bár-baros, grounded in the belief that such Indians were inherently barbarous and incapable of conversion or assimilation. It also seems that capitalist citizen-ship took precedence over any other forms of alliance, especially in this case. The Hughes family had become wealthy by dealing in beef, grains, and real estate, lending money, ranching, mining, and fulfilling government contracts, most of which activities require secure landownership and free movement across the territory, to which the Apache were the major impediments.[67]

Samuel Hughes served at the time as the territory's adjutant general, re-sponsible for coordinating territory-wide efforts to protect and defend the interests of the community, state, and nation. In his court testimony, Hughes described his responsibility as receiving, marking, and reissuing guns to those who needed them. He stated he "never issued any guns to the Apaches and there was no other way for them to get arms but from murdered citizens."[68] Hughes believed he acted in good faith and within the authority of his office to protect the territory in handing over government-owned weapons to the Anglos and Mexicans in the raiding party.[69] But Andrew Cargill, clerk for the attorney general during the trial of the Camp Grant massacre defendants, went so far as to say that "the adjutant general [Hughes] furnished a wagon-load of arms and ammunition for the Papago Indians."[70] The Hughes family also contributed their own private capital in the form of wagons and food for the use of the state and its agents. On March 9, 1871, Apaches had attacked a wagon train of government freight, and on March 18 a band of Apaches "put in an appearance on the farm of Mr. Hughes, near Camp Crittenden."[71] Hughes's foreman Cook was killed a short distance from the Hughes home and his horses taken and the house pillaged for useful items (three guns and ammunition); all other items were destroyed and left behind.[72] Hughes and his wife, like many other Tucson ranchers, had experienced economic and property losses that influenced their participation in the massacre.

Along with Hughes, William S. Oury, the property recorder for the city, was one of the primary organizers of the raid. Oury and his wife had a special hatred for the Apache because their only son died during an Apache raid on their rancho in 1864. Oury's Mexican wife reflected a set of values about indios bárbaros similar to Santa Cruz de Hughes's, but in her case as the daughter of an elite Durangense family. Moreover, the Oury family had repeatedly lost money on their ranching and cattle ventures, especially in the years leading up to the economic depression of the 1870s, one of the most severe after the Civil War.[73] As Union troops were withdrawn from the territory in the 1860s to fight in the Civil War, Apache raids and, consequently, settler losses increased. Evidently Oury blamed the Apache for his financial hardships, although his later correspondence shows the Camp Grant massacre did not improve his situation. In a personal letter to his daughter Lola Oury Smith dated December 24, 1885, Oury writes, "The winter is now half over and we have as yet had very little rain and unless it does come down and plenty of it before April next the Stock interest of Arizona will be almost entirely destroyed which means for us poverty because nearly all of us have an interest in that line, as for the piles of adobes we have in Tucson they count for very little as real estate has depressed so much within the last two years."[74] Similarly, in a letter dated September 8, 1884, Oury expressed his desire to attend a reunion of Mexican War veterans in St. Louis but couldn't afford it because of drought and the failing cattle industry.[75] This correspondence demonstrates that Apaches were scapegoats for the failure of businesses and the falling price of real estate in Tucson during the 1870s. Overgrazing, prolonged drought, and an economic recession that lasted roughly thirteen years after the Camp Grant incident were at least equally important. The Camp Grant massacre, in theory, should have stimulated the local economy because it opened up space for transnational capital flows. That it did not reminds us that the voracious appetite for capital accumulation was not aided through the obliteration of indigenous bodies and that the Arizona economy was dependent instead on a continuing state of war against those indigenous bodies.

Jesús Elías was believed to be the main organizer of the massacre. The Elías family had also lost a huge amount of capital in Tubac because they were unable to defend their stock and ranching businesses from Apache raids. The family had originally settled a Spanish land grant in Alamos, Sonora, in the 1720s and had acquired land grants as far north as Tubac when it was a Mexican presidio. But because of their specific history with the Apache, they had no interest in any policy of assimilation and colonization. The Elías brothers also supported all-out extermination because Apaches had killed their brothers, Cornelio and Ramón, after which the two surviving brothers were forced to abandon their land in Tubac and move to Tucson in 1849. Moving to Tucson was an act of surrender and a dishonor, but it also meant that the Elías family could maintain social power because of their distinguished Spanish name. The men's sense of honor and their masculinity were under threat as long as the family was struggling to recover their cattle ranch in Tubac. From that point on, Jesús became known as an Indian fighter, avenging the deaths of his brothers and his property losses. As Jacoby has shown, Mexican men in Arizona fashioned their identities as Indian fighters, a direct signaling that their public enactments of subjectivity were manifest in violence against indigenous peoples, regardless of their gender.[76] Jesús Elías and people like him began to seek out conflicts with Apaches to regain their sense of honor, their masculinity, and their property.

As late as January 1871 Apaches were said to be making raids on Tubac, killing one man and carrying off several thousand dollars' worth of plunder, pushing settlers like the Elías family to leave the valley.[77] The family's troubles continued as well. On February 4, 1871, it was reported that Indians had stolen fourteen head of Juan Elías's cattle from his ranch, which was only a few miles from Tucson's city center. In view of their losses, Mexican ranchers and landholders like the Elías brothers had every reason to be motivated to participate in and orchestrate the Camp Grant massacre in order to recover economic and psychic losses.[78]

Chief Galerita and the band of San Xavier and Pan Tak Papagos that made up the majority of the attackers were part of a continuum of Pima bands that were separated from their southern kinsmen following the Gadsden Purchase in 1853. Many of the Papago spoke Spanish because of Spanish missionization efforts in New Spain. The Papago were also very familiar with being the frontline fighters for dominant groups. In 1748 they fought on foot to remove the Seri from coastal Sonora and Tiburón Island for the Spaniards, who could not fight on horseback in such arid terrain.[79] Although the Papago did not recognize themselves as a tribe, the various Papago bands were united through bonds of extended kinship, which were often publicly expressed in alliances for planting, harvesting, hunting, and, for centuries, fighting the Apache as well as in their alliances with the Spanish, Mexicans, and Anglos in fighting the Apache (the O'odham name for the Apache means "enemy"). Local bands formed alliances to defend themselves against the Apache and sometimes even mounted preemptive attacks to prevent future raids. It was commonly believed that the Apache were not interested in settling on land, as the Anglos and Mexicans were, but simply wanted food, goods, women, and children to make up for the constant losses they suffered in their nomadic lives.[80]

The Papago concentrated around the mission San Xavier del Bac were a seminomadic population who maintained a land and cultural base where they built semipermanent structures, farmed, and raised cattle. That they were viewed by Anglos as good Indians compared with the Apache is clear from BIA reports describing them as the "well intentioned Papagoes of Arizona, [who] contrast just as strongly with the dealings of the Government by their traditional enemies, the treacherous and vindictive Apache";[81] in fact, the U.S. government classified the Papago as "semi-civilized Indians." Because "these Indians [had] no treaty relations with the U.S."[82] they were not legally obligated to enlist in local militias, so their participation in the Camp Grant massacre was entirely voluntary—and perhaps the lack of government oversight even facilitated their involvement. Still, the Papago desire for safety, economic stability, and autonomy from the Apache coincided with Anglo and Mexican desires to eradicate the Apache. As late as April 1871, according to Oury, a letter carrier from San Xavier brought "the sad intelligence that the Indians had just made a descent upon that place and had driven off a large number of cattle and horses," showing a long trajectory of Papago losses to Apache raiders.[83] In his court testimony in the case of *United States vs. Sidney R. De Long* Rais Mendoza stated that the people who followed these cattle thieves from San Xavier were himself, Juan Elías, Jesús Mangia, Tomás Elías, Refugio Pacheco, William Zeckendorf, and Ramón Pacheco. Following the trail for eighteen leagues, they found it led in the direction of Aravaipa Canyon.[84] When they finally caught up with the Indians, they killed one and recovered five horses and twenty-five head of cattle. The horses belonged to Francisco Carrillo. This example shows how Anglos, Mexicans, and Papagos had a common interest in eliminating the Apache threat. In addition, the U.S. Army had a history of encouraging hostilities between Indians of different tribes, including the Papago and Apache, as a means of deterring intertribal alliances.[85]

Traditional songs recorded and translated by Ruth Underhill in the 1920s suggest a long-standing Papago oral memory of hostilities against the Apache. María Chona, in an interview with Underhill, sang this song: "Kill the Apache, kill the Apache! / Dry the skin, dry the skin! / Soften it, soften it! / Hang it up, hang it up! A-a-a-a-ah! / There are still some Apaches left."[86] Men who killed Apaches were given the honored title of Enemy Slayer and accorded an exalted status within the community.[87] Participating in war against the Apaches was a true honor, a way to prove one's masculinity through public acts of revenge and violence. Underhill stated that the O'odham did not really like to go to war, but "fierce Apaches who lived in the mountains near them often attacked their villages and carried off horses, women and children."[88] Knowing this history and being aware of the recent raid whose perpetrators had headed toward Aravaipa Canyon, the leaders of the Camp Grant massacre met with Chief Francisco to solicit his help in organizing a posse.[89]

The court documents in the ensuing trial of De Long included Papago testimony attesting to the long-standing violence between the two groups. However, the Papago who appeared in court were given fictitious names in the record. While they may have not admitted to the crime because the stakes of loss were higher, Indians rarely testified in courts of law, and Anglos and Mexicans were rarely punished and in fact were encouraged to kill Indians. We can also read the inability to identify the Papagos as legal subjects within the context of the Camp Grant trial as an example of Anglo mediation of their subjectivity.[90] Apaches were not called as witnesses to testify at the trial because they were viewed as rightless. A witness who identified himself as Asencio stated,

> I am a Papago Indian. I am a Captain. The Papagoes are at war with the Apaches, have been so since I was born. The condition between the Papagoes and the Apaches is the same now as ever. Never [has there] been any peace between them. If I was alone among the Apaches they would kill me. They would do so with any of my tribe we would look for nothing else. . . . The Apaches are now and have been always in the habit of stealing stock from us. When stock has been stolen from us by the Apache, we follow on the trail and try to recover the stock. The Papagoes usually follow until they find either stock or Apaches. When we follow sometimes we recover stock and sometimes not.[91]

Asencio's testimony does not relate specifically to what happened at Camp Grant, but historically does contextualize why the Papago and Apache have such a violent history. The involvement of Papago family- and kinship-based groups illustrates how raiding and trading drove cultural and economic exchange and patterns of violence.

The family histories of the Papago (Chief Galerita's and Ascencio's testimonies), Mexican (Santa Cruz de Hughes and the Elías brothers), and Anglo (William Oury and Sidney DeLong) participants in the massacre contradict some of the facile claims of Chicano studies scholars. We cannot continue to assume that Mexicans were always indigenous; certainly they did not view themselves as such, especially in nineteenth-century southern Arizona, even if they were products of mestizaje. Moreover, the long-standing conflict between the San Xavier Papago and the Aravaipa and Pinal Apache complicates monolithic portrayals of indigenous identity, forcing us to recognize indigenous communities and histories as plural, regional, social, and complex. The Apache were far from unified either, consisting of several independent bands. Yet in the last half of the nineteenth century the press and the communities fighting them, in suggesting that they were without exception a savage race, indios bárbaros deserving of "social extinction," intentionally homogenized them.[92] It did not matter which Apache bands were raiding around Tucson— or even if the raiders were Apache at all—the settled population of southern Arizona automatically assumed that it was the Apache who were disrupting their daily existence, formal economy, and livelihood. The Camp Grant Apaches were nearby, their location was known, and they were believed to have been the men who had recently raided the Papago, so they became a logical target.

The Anglo, Mexican, and Papago raiding party carried out this act of extreme violence as a means of maintaining power and exhibiting control. As Brooks points out, "To see this borderlands violence only in terms of its debilitating effect . . . overlooks the fact that one people's loss was another people's gain."[93] The Camp Grant massacre, in all its gruesome complexity, was a moral contract carried out by the raiders: Tucson businessmen had lost huge amounts of livestock as a result of raiding; O'odham communities had lost stock and women at the hands of the Apache; and Mexicans, who had lost land, stock, and power on multiple levels, were defending their identities as economic contributors in the region. These factors in the context of a failing economy ushered in a scenario in which such alliances are not all that surprising.

The territorial and U.S. governments had set up conditions that inevitably would encourage such a massacre.[94] The BIA *Report of the Commissioner of Indian Affairs* in 1870 stated, "No appreciable progress has been made in taming or conciliating the wild and warlike Apaches of Arizona. Their thirst for rapine and blood seems unquenchable and unconquerable."[95] Prior to the Camp Grant massacre, the citizens of Arizona had applied to the secretary of war for arms and ammunition to defend themselves. The request had been granted, so the people were well armed.[96] Attempts to pacify the Apache were at a standstill and depredations continued. *Memorial and Affidavits Showing Outrages Perpetrated by the Apache Indians in the Territory of Arizona during the Years of 1869 and 1870*, a report issued by the territorial government in 1871, illustrates that private citizens' acts of revenge against the Apache were encouraged. Recording the testimony of some ninety-nine individuals, the report sought to prove (with more than a little hyperbole) the extent to which "the subtile Apaches have been so constant in their depredations and destructive of life, that nearly all of the early pioneers have already fallen by their hands, and every industry and enterprise has been paralyzed."[97] Documenting 178 murders and 3,768 animals lost was a way to publicize Apache depredations and goad legislative action, in addition to justifying the armed campaign against the Camp Grant Apache. The publication of the memorial was an attempt to turn a regional and territorial issue into an issue of national and international security, for the writers of the memorial "desire[d] immigration and capital."[98] These sworn testimonies were taken from merchants, property owners, and army officers and included some of the ninety-five men named in the trial affidavit following the massacre.[99] Further, the memorial was a way of creating a sense of connection to the nation for a territory that was marginalized in the national imaginary, which explains why it was sent to San Francisco to be printed and distributed. At this historical moment there were competing visions of nation as the Apache challenged the stability of the nation-state in formation.

The testimonies reflect a desire to protect private property, development, and individual livelihood, all in the service of preserving a particular landholding class of people. The chief complaints regard the theft of cattle. For example, in the two-year period 1869–70, Fredrick Marsh, who had a stockraising business eighteen miles from Tucson, reported that he had lost forty head of cattle and four horses, incurring losses totaling approximately $1,250. Marsh further stated that "depredations are more frequent than two years ago, and the roads are unsafe for small parties."[100] This attitude was not exclusive to Anglo venture capitalists, for the Mexicano testimonies reflect similar sentiments and losses: Guillermo Telles, "a native of Arizona; occupation, farmer; [who] owns a farm, three miles south of Tucson and has lived there for sixty years; [testifies] that in the month of September 1869, the Apache Indians stole from him seven cows, and in November of 1870, eleven head of cattle—total value of all being $900; that he has never known the Indians so hostile and so dangerous as at the present time; that there is no security for life and property in the territory."[101] In addition, army officers and government employees complained that high-ranking officers issued arms to the Indians for hunting, so that the government could reduce its expenses for Indian rations. The Indians then used those arms in raids, as reported by employees of Tully, Ochoa and DeLong Freighting Company, whose total losses were said to be $18,000 over the two-year period.

FIGURE 1 Untitled painting by Edward Zinns, ca. 1869–70. Attack on Tully and Ochoa wagon train at Cañon del Oro, Arizona. Arizona History Museum, Tucson.

A painting by Edward Zinns, a mining man from Colorado, depicted his experience as a participant in a three-day standoff between a Tully, Ochoa and DeLong wagon train and Apache Indians along the Cañada del Oro trail on May 11, 1869. The work, one of the few visual representations we have of such events, shows the wagons virtually surrounded by Apaches on all sides, with a large flank of what appear to be about forty Apaches waiting in the background.[102] The painting's depiction of the helplessness of pioneer capitalists in the face of Indian oppression cannot be denied. In the left middle ground the cavalry from Camp Grant ride to the rescue, suggesting that the U.S. military was stationed in the Arizona Territory so that capitalism could thrive. Symbolically, it is as if the Apaches are killing capitalism, embodied in the flailing defeat of the pioneer merchants commanding the wagon train. The painting stays true to the historicity of the moment, as in the lower left-hand corner two Apaches are "roasting" a Papago member of the wagon train, a man who most likely worked for the firm.[103] The local press coverage of the event shares an equal sense of mourning the temporary death of capitalism in the attack on the wagon train:

> The train of Messrs. Tully and Ochoa, consisting of nine wagons and some eighty mules, left here on Monday last laden with government freight for Camp Grant. On Tuesday morning they discovered a large party of Indians at a short distance, and evidently preparing to make attack. The wagon master, who bears a very high reputation as a skillful Indian-fighter, immediately [had] his wagons hauled around so as to form a circle and then

turning the mules within this enclosure, entered with the entire party some fourteen men and awaited the approach of the Indians. These cunning individuals[,] well aware that they could obtain their prey only after an obstinate resistance which must be fatal to many of them, sent forward one of their party who, addressing the wagon master by name, (Santa Cruz) told him in Spanish that the Indians did not wish to injure him or his party; that they were strong enough to take the train by force and advised him to leave everything and they would permit the whole party to go unharmed. The wagon master briefly responded, that they could have the train when he could no longer hold it. No sooner had the Indian translated to his fellow warriors the wagon master's reply than the fight commenced. The little party was surrounded by about 200 Indians who kept pouring vollies of arrows and bullets. After having maintained the struggle for about ten hours, the wagon master discovered his stock of ammunition was about exhausted and three of his men lay dead. . . . seven cavalry men coming from Camp Grant to Tucson showed up on the scene . . . the wagon master agreed to leave everything . . . Messrs. Tully & Ochoa have lost in this raid property to the amount of about $12,000, and the loss to the government and to the parties at Camp Grant, when added, will make a total loss of hardly less than $20,000.[104]

Interestingly, the article describes, first, a set of rules of engagement, a logic preceding the violence, in which Apaches spoke Spanish and asked for what they wanted, and, second, that a Mexican Indian fighter named Santa Cruz was the most desirable choice to lead a wagon train for a joint Anglo-Mexican business venture operating out of Tucson. Even though the *Weekly Arizonan* labeled the attack an "Indian Outrage," they meant not an actual outrage over the violence but an outrage over the capitalist losses to the tune of an over-inflated figure of $20,000. The Apaches wanted to avoid bloodshed and tried to negotiate a peaceful solution prior to the attack. But, as we see, the wagon master Santa Cruz and his men defended their capital-for-exchange until they could no longer do so, even with the help of the seven cavalry members from Camp Grant, for whom the shipment of goods was intended. While there would be no painting commemorating the losses suffered in the Camp Grant massacre, Zinns's depiction, in immortalizing the event, mourns both the massacre of capitalist exchange at Cañada del Oro and the Anglo and Mexican pioneers' economic catastrophe.

While the painting is a kind of documentation that differs from the testimonies in the memorial affidavit, taken together these documents deeply reflect the differences in how various peoples understood capital and private property. The Apache and other Indian bands that raided had a vision of economic exchange that diverged completely from that of the pioneers. Having been pushed westward off the plains by the Comanche, they sought to support themselves and continue their traditional way of life with the resources they saw around them: cattle, horses, and oxen that the victims of their raids considered private property. The Apache seasonally planted corn and harvested and roasted mescal roots for food to supplement their raiding, but they needed additional means of subsistence.

That some of those who gave affidavits in the territorial government's memorial later participated in the Camp Grant attack puts in relief the connections between capital losses, government power, and the desire to retain citizenship that were driving forces in the action against the Camp Grant Apache. While the memorialists did not specifically cite the Camp Grant Apache as perpetrators of raids, they did use Camps Grant, Crittenden, McDowell, and Goodwin as landmarks to spatially locate the Indian raiders in relationship to their land bases: "In June 1870 [Samuel Hughes] with twenty-five others were attacked, twenty-two miles from Camp Grant, by about fifty Indians; Newton Israel and Hugh Kennedy were killed; two wagons loaded with merchandise, and seven mules were taken at the same time."[105] The same incident was reported by Lt. John C. Bourke, later a noted Indian fighter in Texas, as he "went in relief of a train that was attacked by Indians on the Camp Grant road, twenty-two miles from Camp Grant; found the burning ruins of two wagons, the dead body of a man named Israel, also a man named Kennedy mortally wounded. Three weeks afterwards a party of prospectors were attacked fifteen miles from Camp Grant, by about sixty Indians, capturing horses, wagon, provisions and all they had, wounding three men."[106] These testimonies regarding raids in the vicinity of Camp Grant provided circumstantial evidence that the Camp Grant Apaches were either participants or complicit in the raids. Moreover, three Papago Indians hired by the U.S. Army to follow the trail of the depredators found that the signs all led to Aravaipa Canyon near Camp Grant.[107] This was the evidence that incriminated them.

The Aravaipa were camped about three miles below the fort at a place close to the site of their creation myth, the Little Running Water. There was plenty of shade and water there, and they received one-half ration per day. Lt. Andrew Cargill, who worked at the fort at the time of the raid, stated that only fourteen soldiers were stationed there. "[The Apache] surrendered as prisoners of war," Cargill stated.[108] There was an Apache ceremony in which the prisoners disarmed by turning in their guns; they retained only their knives and bows for hunting. No one was allowed to leave, and Lieutenant Whitman and his men counted them all regularly. Cargill writes,

> Matters went on very smoothly until the first day of May 1871. I was again at the post and we had not yet finished our morning coffee when Maria Jilda came and said he thought there was something wrong as he had not seen any Indian nor smoke from their camp. We mounted at once and rode and found 86 women and children and one very old man killed. No live Indians were about. We knew at once that it had been by parties from Tucson. We brought all the men we had down and buried the bodies. The Indians sent up another smoke that afternoon, saying they would come and talk.[109]

Judging from Cargill's testimony, the U.S. military immediately knew that Tucsonans were the perpetrators of the attack. Cargill doesn't express surprise that it occurred, and the clinical tone of his report reflects as much. The establishment of the Camp Grant reserve demonstrates increasing economic interdependency between Indians and the government that was resented by the greater borderlands community centered in and around Tucson. Cargill's description suggests a cordial and reciprocal relationship between the surrendered Apache community and the soldiers at Camp Grant—a relationship Tucsonans resented. Although it did not directly encourage such an attack, the U.S. Army did nothing to protect the unarmed Apache camped at Camp Grant, leaving them open to physical attack precisely because of the perceptions about interdependency and justice.

CHILD CAPTIVES ARE NOT APACHE WOMEN

The fact that the majority of the Camp Grant victims were women and children and that the children who were not killed were sold, enslaved, or adopted by prominent Tucson Mexican families shows how settlers' conflicts with indigenous communities have always embodied familial and economic politics simultaneously. A clear distinction must be made between the treatment of Apache child captives as "salvageable," that is, suitable for proper socialization and servility in Mexican households on both sides of the U.S.–Mexico border and the murdered women who were marked in death as "irredeemable." Brooks argues that in the Southwest in the late nineteenth century the practice of taking women and children captive was a means of creating kinship, labor, and social networks, an example of how exchange and ransom of sacred symbols "allowed mundane, and latently shameful economic transfers to occur as a subtext of a narrative of men's contests over honor."[110] But the position of the child captives from the Camp Grant massacre represents another kind of violence that requires a different theoretical framework. Family, violence, and captivity could not exist independently of one another, and this is most evident in the aftermath of the Camp Grant massacre in that no adult women were taken captive or integrated into Tucsonense families; they were killed, perhaps in part because after the federal ban of 1868 on the Indian slave trade in the Southwest, and the ways in which children were considered genderless and thus were not considered adults capable of insurrection. Stressing the different politics of the Camp Grant massacre, this violent incident facilitated a trade in children because they could not fight back, and the people who traded them would not be held accountable. The rhetoric of family and kinship espoused by the state to justify their captivity deceptively euphemizes the violence of the children being taken from their families and ultimately shifts the emphasis toward the notion that the children were better off in their new Mexican families or in servitude in Sonora than among their Apache families. What is more, the rhetoric of parental benevolence was deployed to support two forms of patriarchy and civilization: Tucsonense Mexican families on the one hand and the U.S. project of empire on the other. The comforting rhetoric of civilized Mexican families cloaks the harsh aspects of captivity, for example, the fact that the children witnessed the slaughter of their kin by the very people with whom they were now living through kinship ties.

Ironically, the majority of the captured children either ended up with prominent Tucson Mexican families or were sold into slavery in Mexico, further cementing the fact that Tucsonense Mexicans were not Indians and were therefore publicly thought of as civilized. The smaller number of children who ended up with the Papago were integrated into the tribe to replace women and children kidnapped by the Apache.[111] These captives, like the men who killed the sleeping Apache women and children, were subjects socialized by an economy of pain and retribution. That is, the massacre, like all economically motivated attacks against indigenous communities during this epoch of Arizona history, was a response to conflict. The exchange of captives created a "shadow kinship" that was seldom acknowledged and that created permanent ties to the Apache even as massacres like the one at Camp Grant attempted to eradicate them.[112] Everyone knew who the child captives were but did not speak of their capitivity, except, as I show in the following passages, when the courts or the state demanded it.

The silence surrounding the fate of the Apache captives in the historical scholarship is countered by a two-year debate about them in BIA reports and in local correspondence. In 1871 and 1872, the Camp Grant Apache appealed for the return of the captive children, and six were returned in 1872. The Camp Grant agent stressed the "wishes of the Camp Grant Indians" to have the captive children returned. "Six of those have been returned to Camp Grant, and are in the custody of Mr. E. C. Jacobs, your agent, but are not yet delivered to the Indians; the rest, twenty-one in number, are reported to be in Sonora Mexico. It should be remembered that their captors sold these children. I believe that no act of the Government could so much attach these people [the Apache] to it as the return of these captured children."[113] Here we see an ambiguous set of state politics about Apache rights to their children and a shifting of responsibility away from the state (both the U.S. and Mexican states), for it seems, judging by the language, that the twenty-one children in Sonora would be impossible to recover because they had been purchased through capitalist exchange.

Still, the territorial governor, A. K. P. Safford, and the district attorney promised cooperation in returning the children who were living in Tucson. Yet the Indian agent O. O. Howard stated the following:

When we came to find them in the families of Mexicans who had purchased them from their captors, the case was embarrassed. One excellent family had a little girl to whom they were all attached; the head of the family was a leading citizen, much respected. He pled for the child with tears; asked if there were no parents, if he might keep the little girl. I said substantially that he would have to take the child to Camp Grant, or others would follow his example; that undoubtedly, I could arrange with the Indians, in such a case if there were no parents, for the little girl to remain where she was so well cared for. In this I was simply mistaken. I failed to make the arrangement.[114]

What made it acceptable for Howard to actively neglect to arrange for the little girl to be returned to her people was an issue of civility, care, and socialization. Here Western notions of civilization trumped family and communal ties, especially those of indios bárbaros, and it was the socialization of these children in Mexican families that made it nearly impossible to return to their Apache families. The request of a man from a leading Mexican family that was most likely headed by Leopoldo Carrillo, took precedence over the law, as children were socialized into non-Apache kinship structures.[115] Certainly the logic of seduction functioned in this case and in those of the other children who were not returned to their families. Saidya Hartman notes that seduction displaces and euphemizes violence.[116] Howard was seduced by the emotion of the situation. The desire of the leading families of Tucson who purchased Apache captives to retain their property (even if that property was integrated into the families) is grounded in emotive terms—what Hartman calls the bonds of affection[117]—rather than in the law, for it was illegal to buy Indian captives or own slaves in 1872. Affection and benevolence trumped the rights of the Apache families to their children and this "embarrassment," to quote Howard, ultimately protects the good name of a Mexican family, their special interests, and the fictive kin they acquired through the illegal purchase of a captive Apache child.

In his own defense, Carillo, who raised a captive girl, used the language of Christian benevolence, capitalism, and the law to further his claims to the family's *criada*, or servant: "I do not know that these captives are articles for sale; those that I know have been obtained from their captors by exchange, but not by actual bargain and sale; the citizens have obtained these captives from their captors more as an object of charity, and giv[ing] them a Christian education, but they are not treated as slaves."[118] Making the criadas into subjects of exchange rather than objects for sale shows, on the one hand, a kind of anxiety and uneasiness about the lawfulness of having captives in the home and, on the other, a desire to call them family to justify their captivity. Christian benevolence and the desire to save these children from their savagery, so to speak, separate their captivity from its economic aspects and obfuscates the illegality of keeping Apache children from the biological families who wanted them returned. Patriarchal power, Christian benevolence, and the family are conflated to show, as Carrillo stated, how "these captives are contented and do not desire to return to the Apaches; all I have seen will cry if told they are to be sent back; I know of ten cases in this town; many of them will deny that are Apaches."[119] While the voices of the captives are mediated by the desires of the patriarchal benevolent father (Carrillo), one wonders why the appeal made for keeping the captives is an affective rather than a juridical claim. Carrillo deploys affection in lieu of a legitimate juridical claim, the adoptive family's grounds for parental rights to the criadas. I further read the statement, "these captives are contented and do not desire to return to the Apaches" as an affective confusion of internalized racism and fear of separation from the new family on the part of the child captives, or rather Carrillo's projection of racism and affective confusion onto the brown Indian bodies of the captives. If the children had paid any attention to localized and extremely racist discourses about Apache savagery that circulated so blatantly among Tucsonense Mexicans or simply had been told that their Indian families did not care about them, it would be to their benefit, if they were to survive in the Tucson community, to claim they were not Apache

Indian and instead identify with their adoptive Mexican families. Thus the supposed contentment and the bonds of affection mobilized by racism and disidentification stand in for a juridical claim because it was illegal to possess child captives.

In her testimonio Alvina Rosenda Elías Contreras, a daughter of Jesus Elías, stated that many men brought home captives from the massacre but that they were later returned to the reservation.[120] For example, "Jimmie Lee brought back two which he gave to his sister, Mrs. R. G. Brady and she raised them. They were later married to Mexicans and the daughter of one of them is now a chambermaid at the Congress hotel. The captives who were not returned stayed of their own will and not because they were forced to."[121] Elías himself had a captive Apache boy in his possession at one point in time. That boy, named José Elías, "lived with [Elías] until he was 15, then he died of fever in the Santa Rita Mountains where he and father had gone for lumber."[122] So even though individuals like Elías and Lee actively agitated for the extermination of Apache adults, the taking of criadas into the family demonstrates how children were thought to be salvageable because their Indianness could be socialized away. They could nonetheless live normal Christian lives as Mexican subjects who were among the working poor, for example, chambermaids at places like the Congress Hotel in Tucson or bearing the name of the adoptive parent who had exterminated their kin.

Tucson attorney James E. McCaffery, acting on behalf of Gen. O. O. Howard,[123] went to visit Francisco Romero and Carrillo a year after the massacre. He wrote in a letter,

Each of these gentlemen had one of these captives in his family, and each of them said that the child was considered by him as his own flesh and blood, but that he would give it up if necessary and General Howard respected them and told me what he had before said to me in regard to not requiring the return of the captives who had parents and but said it would be necessary to have them all at Grant on the 21st of May to show the Apaches that they were dealing with them in good faith. On the 21st the captives mentioned to wit were taken to Camp Grant as the parties named understood, to be claimed by their parents if living.[124] At the conclusion of the talk with the Apaches, and when it had been ascertained that none of these children had parents living General Howard ordered all the children to be delivered to the Apaches . . . and the immediate execution of the order was only stayed because all the children struggled to get away from the Indians, and their screams were heart rending. On the next day General Howard decided that the children should remain at the Indian Agency at Camp Grant in Charge of the Agent until the matter could be referred to the President for his decision, and so the case rests at present. These people ask that you will do what you can to secure the return of these children, because they (the children) are now Christian, and it is an outrage upon Christianity and civilization to *force* them back into the savage heathenism of the Apaches, and because they have no natural guardians and they deserve to return to their adopted parents, where they were well cared for, and where General Howard knows they were being educated as Christians. We do not desire to take these children upon a writ of habeas corpus, as that would be claimed by General Howard to be an effort on our part to break up his negotiations with the Indians; we have confidence in the permanency of his peace with the Indians, but we will do nothing to disturb it.[125]

While the logic of General Howard's agent suggests that the state attempted to provide a kind of due process for these child captives to be returned to their families, the fact was that their families had been murdered, making it impossible to return the children to their biological parents. In other words, the logic of the Camp Grant massacre, facilitated by the state, was designed to displace children and civilize them because there was no alternative. It also suggests that placing children with families of their original cultural group was not enough. State intervention in American Indian family life was achieved by destroying it.

Having no Apache family base, the captives ultimately would not pass on cultural knowledge of the tribe to their own children. Instead, they were socialized as Mexican and often married Mexicans to ensure that civilized cultures would be propagated, the state and its actors thereby preventing such cultural traditions from being replicated. In this destruction of cultural reproduction, the fact that "all the children struggled to get away from the Indians, and their screams were heart rending" reminds the reader of the affective registers of family.[126] As the children were integrated into Mexican families and in a sense became their flesh and blood, they developed affective bonds to their new parents, actively severing their emotional ties to their Apache kinspeople. Finally, the social privilege of Mexicans who were permitted to keep the children communicates how, in the juridical arena, Mexicans wielded symbolic power equal to that of their Anglo counterparts. That they could keep these children via state intervention suggests that, unlike their Apache counterparts, they were citizen subjects in the eyes of the nation-state. The juridical aspects of these cases must be noted in that Aravaipa and Pinal families and their children were not recognized by the state as rights-bearing subjects. It was thereby virtually impossible to contest that the children were taken despite the federal ban of 1868 on Indian captive trading, and this, in turn, justified the emotive or affective registers as substitutes for state evidence and action.

THE DIMENSION OF SEXUAL VIOLENCE

While the child captives elicited a discourse of Christian benevolence, rescue, and salvation in the name of civilization, those killed in the massacre represented a politics of lack of use value. Because the victims at Camp Grant were almost exclusively women, we begin to understand the sexual and gendered dimensions of violence and exchange that had a specific regional grounding of discourses of indios bárbaros and class formation in the Arizona–Sonora borderlands. As the anthropologist Ana María Alonso reminds us, continuous conflicts between colonists and Apache Indians, which continued until 1886, overdetermined the structure of northern Mexican societies and forced the emergence of a distinct ethnic identity. Speaking of Chihuahua, Alonso argues that norteño Mexicanos invented a tradition of origins that affirmed their whiteness.[127] This norteño regional identity, much like that of Tucsonenses, created a social class of Mexicanos who not only identified with the privilege of whiteness, but also affirmed and reinforced their social class in opposition to indios bárbaros, concretely embodied in the Apache women who were attacked at Camp Grant.

Allowing barbarous, savage Apache women to reproduce and raise their children into adulthood was in and of itself a threat to territorial stability. It meant larger numbers of Apache who would need to sustain themselves. Instead, the sexual politics of preventing reproduction through death by massacre speak to the fact that the violence was not about exchange and renewal but about decimation and destruction, suggesting that Aravaipa Apache women did not have any social or economic value. The colonial logic of the attacking party and the killing of women and children at Camp Grant literally ended the possibility for future generations to exist in large numbers. A successful colonial project would entail the "defeat of the alien 'other' [Apache]—whose presence had in the past organized a morally binding framework of social relations and legitimized a 'warrior people paradigm' " within which Tucsonenses of Mexican descent saw themselves as Indian fighters.[128] This war for civilization created discourses in the period that claimed Apache women socialized their children to hate whites and Mexicans, only fueling the self-fashioning of Mexicans as warrior people and their further fashioning of the

Apache and Apache women in particular as a sign of barbarity.[129] The ability to reproduce is criminalized by the Tucson vigilantes acting to protect private citizens and private property. I use the treatise *Criminal Woman, the Prostitute, and the Normal Woman* (1893) by the Italian criminologists Cesare Lombroso and Gugllelmo Ferrero to suggest a broader, transnational set of ideas about barbarity from the 1870s and to demonstrate how marginal territories such as Arizona can or should be placed within transnational circuits of social scientific (pseudoscientific) knowledge. *Criminal Woman, the Prostitute, and the Normal Woman* was written at the time of U.S. military campaigns of Indian removal. Speaking about the character of criminal women, Lombroso and Ferrero wrote, "It is sad but true: among brutes, savages and primitive people, the female is more cruel than compassionate, although she is not as cruel as the male."[130] Given that the Apache were considered the ultimate savages, Lombroso's and Ferrero's logic forges the discursive link between criminality, cruelty, and reproduction, the argument ultimately used to rationalize the killing of Apache women at Camp Grant.

However, some of the defendants' court testimony tells another story of gender, one in which the rules of masculinity and femininity did not apply. As if anticipating the moral outrage over the killing of women and children, Joseph Felman in his court testimony recounts a different narrative: "In these attacks [one] can't distinguish the females from males; all look and dress alike."[131] In Felman's testimony there is an eerie kind of gender equality, in the sense that the raiders used the Apaches' androgynous dress as a means of making males and females equal in appearance and stature. Couching the argument in terms of sex and gender androgyny contests how the event and its impetus are remembered in official memory. It further makes forms of political killing an acceptable form of reprisal for economic losses ostensibly caused by indigenous populations in the nineteenth century. In addition, because the attack was an ambush, it alleviates the attackers of culpability from the gender code of morality that would spare women and children in the context of combat.

Still, the majority of the accounts produced by both Apaches and U.S. military officials have a clearly delineated set of gender and racial politics that stresses the centrality of reproduction and labor as threats to a stable nation-state. The citizens of Tucson painted the Apache women who labored at the army post harvesting hay in exchange for rations as overbearing and the Apache men as correspondingly lazy.[132] What most accounts fail to mention is that in the period before Apache women began harvesting hay, it was Mexicans who brought in the hay for payment by the U.S. government.[133] The labor of savage women had displaced Mexican labor and participation in capitalist exchange, most likely causing a great deal of resentment in the Mexicans who had held these hay contracts as Lombroso and Ferrero argued that the "savage woman is sometimes a warrior, and she often takes an indirect part in war, doing heavy agricultural work that would otherwise fall to men."[134] From a Western perspective, Apache women took on masculine labor roles by performing agricultural work at Camp Grant in order to provide their families with clothes and food. In this sense, the violence enacted upon them was reasserting the traditional Western and U.S. gender order. The historian Cornelius Smith, Oury's biographer, disavowed any inherent gender politics in the violence the raiders enacted: it didn't matter if the Apache who were killed were women and children, "they killed every Apache in sight, and these were squaws, children and a few old men. To the Papagos, it made no difference; an Apache was an Apache, male or female, small or large. To the Mexicans it made little or no difference either."[135] The discourse of savagery is turned to reflect Mexican and Papago cruelty from an Anglo-American perspective, making the alliances all the more necessary because they were believed to be part of the nature of these racialized groups despite the fact that Tucsonenses were doing everything they could to disassociate themselves from Indianness and its attendant savagery.

If discourses of savagery played a large role in the construction of the Apache women and children as having a propensity for criminality, so sexuality helps explain why some of the women were raped before being killed, a fact that is overlooked in most accounts of the Camp Grant massacre. Apache women transgressed a number of Western and U.S. ideals of what constituted womanhood at this historical moment. In this logic, their role as primary laborers emasculated Apache males and desexualized them even though within their own cultural context it was a normal distribution of labor.[136] In addition, Apache women often had control over raiding and socialized their male children to be warriors.[137]

These complex gender relations among the Apache suggest that rape was used as a weapon to sexually dominate and reinstate a Western gender and sexual order vis-à-vis Apache women during the massacre. The testimony of Conant B. Briesley was the only eyewitness account that acknowledges the sexual violence that occurred during the massacre:

Lieutenant Whitman then ordered me to go down to the Indian camp to render medical assistance and bring down any wounded I might find. I took twelve men (mounted) and a wagon and proceeded without delay to the scene of the murder. On my arrival I found that I should have but little use for wagon or medicine; the work had been too thoroughly done. The camp had been fired and the dead bodies of some twenty-one women and children were lying scattered over the ground; those who had been wounded in the first instance, had their brains beaten out with stones. Two of the best looking of the squaws were lying in such a position, and from the appearance of the genital organs and of their wounds, there can be no doubt that they were first ravished and then shot dead. Nearly all of the dead were mutilated. One infant of some ten months old was shot twice and one leg hacked nearly off.[138]

These scenes of excess are represented in medical or clinical language. While Briesley's testimony might seem sympathetic to the Apache who were killed in the massacre, the reality is that he was operating in the capacity of medical examiner and had little or no use for his healing expertise, for the bodies were beaten beyond recognition and repair. His testimony euphemistically refers to rape as ravishment. Perhaps the use of the word *rape* in an official report in 1871 was impolite, yet the official medical language of objectivity relies on the bodily evidence of mutilated sexual organs to give that euphemism some force in conveying the specific sexualized violence enacted against the women's bodies. While these images evoke injustice, Briesley was simply documenting his visual observations as part of his job as the post surgeon. He was trained to write official medical accounts in emotionless language.

When Whitman went down to the camp on the morning of May 1, it was "burning and the ground strewed with dead and mutilated women and children."[139] In his official court testimony in *United States v. Sidney R. De Long*, Whitman gave a more detailed description of what he encountered that May morning in 1871:

I should say that I saw about 30 or 40 dead bodies, nearly all women and children. . . . I saw the dead bodies of several women that I recognized. The dead bodies of the women were lying in different positions. Generally the bodies were found as they might have fallen when shot running. Some, I'll state positively two, were lying on their backs entirely naked and shot through the breast apparently with pistol balls. One body had three or four arrows sticking in it besides the probable death wound of musketry. I also noticed bodies of women, with the skull smashed. My judgement was that the women had been first wounded and subsequently killed. I judged that because in addition to the pistol shots or gun shot wounds their skulls had been broken. I saw the dead bodies of children—perhaps 6. They had died of gunshot wounds. I do not recollect where the gunshot wounds were. I recollect one child perhaps two years of age with the arm nearly cut off. . . . I had seen and examined battlefields before. The fight presented every appearance of a sudden attack, no attempt to escape and no resistance. I have no knowledge of the parties that did this killing.[140]

As a custodian of the Camp Grant Apache who was acting under the authority of the U.S. Army, Whitman could have been a sympathetic witness, but his testimony is given in an official reporting style. Whitman's detailed court testimony nevertheless demonstrates the excessiveness of the violence. The performative function of power is exaggerated to the point that tremendous labor was exerted in the killing of the women and children. As a profound message about an utter power imbalance, "bodies . . . were found as they might have fallen when shot running." Whitman's language contains and manages the excessiveness of the violence, and in some ways constrains its gendered implications.[141] While the testimony reveals that masculinity and femininity were enacted as social practice within this battle, it also shows that the boundaries between adversary and noncombatant were irrelevant. The strewn colonized indigenous bodies are represented as helpless and dependent. In addition, the descriptions seem to render the excessive violence as an insult to Aravaipa masculinity and femininity alike. Perhaps an attack on unprotected women and children while the men were away was designed to undermine the men's identity as defenders of their homes and families.

By enunciating metaphors of trauma and terror, Whitman's and Briesley's testimonies preclude any possibility of survival and recovery or any sense of restorative justice.[142] The government documents neither deny rape outright nor offer definitive, absolute confirmation of sexual violation. As Whitman says, "Some, I'll state positively two were lying on their backs entirely naked and shot through the breast apparently with pistol balls." While Whitman does not speculate on why or how the women's bodies were stripped naked, the logic of the event is that they were both raped and tortured, unspeakable violations the testimony neither denies nor confirms. The official government documents are confined to giving clinical meanings and representations, which somewhat predetermines the limits of what can be said about the Camp Grant massacre.

Within the truth regime of the late nineteenth-century court system in Arizona, Whitman's testimony fell on deaf ears. After all the statements were taken, the jury deliberated for only twenty-one minutes before declaring the defendants not guilty. The verdict was the product of a structure of denial and mediated truths and of a state that enacted its own forms of censorship about the severity of the violence that occurred at Camp Grant. The decision to not name sexual violence and state-sponsored physical violence for what they were rewards brutality and shows how the court case and the historical record directed national memory to forget the massacre. The symbolic meaning of the violence does not circulate in detailed form either, signifying that the incident is something most people want to forget as one of those unspeakable episodes in the history of both the U.S. and imagined Chicano nation.

Official BIA documents and Briesley's report are the only ones to detail what happened to bodies in the massacre. The ravished, bullet-riddled bodies of Apache women demonstrate how rape was used to differentiate the bodies of these racialized, sexualized women. The bodies of these women were used to confirm the domination of their attackers, who left the victims' genitals exposed and mutilated. Such acts of war, Scarry argues, mark "an early line of separation between civilization and its antithesis, [and] it is clear that both torture and war still belong together on the side of decivilization, since each requires human hurt in the analogical verifications of its fictions."[143] The beaten-in skulls of women and children, the raped bodies, and the exposed sexual organs prove that pain is an integral part of war's effectiveness. In order to demonstrate that their rules of civilization were the only ones that applied, the Anglos, Mexicans, and Papago not only killed the representatives of the people who threatened their ideas of civilization, but also resorted to acts of torture which announced their domination of the Aravaipa and Pinal Apache in the visual and political arenas. The episode marked yet another moment when indios bárbaros received what they supposedly deserved in the cycles of exchange and violence in the U.S.–Mexico borderlands. These mutilated bodies were on display and served as proof of the attackers' power to the men who returned to the camp after the massacre, demonstrating one way in which different versions of imperial rivalries unfolded throughout the Americas.[144]

The senseless mutilation of the infant who had "half its arm hacked off" and who was ultimately murdered demonstrates that the goal of the massacre was genocide. One of the witnesses in the trial admitted as much: "I had no love for the Apache Indians and would like to see them exterminated if we could not have peace without."[145] There is no need to kill an infant, for how can an infant possibly harm a nation? How can an infant who can't even feed itself be a threat to a community of individuals who have guns, stock, and real estate? This is the civilized ideological bent of genocide and warfare that is quite uncivil. A mutilated infant body is substantive proof of inhumane acts of power. Cutting off an infant's arm is a gruesome way of taking life from the body and destroying the individual's physical mobility in a social process of differentiation. The scholar of state-sponsored violence Leigh Payne argues that sadistic texts are rare because perpetrators seek to disguise their sadistic pleasure. She argues further that even when evidence of sadism exists, the perpetrators often fail to find an appropriate text to excuse their acts.[146] In the case of the Camp Grant massacre, what strategic value does the sadism inherent in hacking off a child's arm hold? How does one explain the unspoken delight of dismembering a child? As Payne suggests, texts that fail to disguise sadism do not make sense.[147] So instead of constructing a number of texts that contradict themselves or do not make sense, the testimonies during the trial and the military reports avoid naming the sadism by not speaking of what such killing must have evoked. Symbolically, the violent murder of these children communicates the desire to completely destroy the future of the Apache bands and leave the bodies as visual confirmation of the power of those who committed the massacre. At the same time, that the attackers could get away with doing so shows how such acts were normalized within the context of the violent economic and social exchange of the Apache removal wars of the late nineteenth century. In Oury's biography Smith implicates the Mexicans and Papagos in the worst of the killing: "There was no checking the Papagos now. They killed every Apache in sight. . . . To the Mexicans it made little or no difference either. Too long the Apaches had raided the little towns in Sonora, lifting Mexican scalps, and leaving whole families of dead Mexicans for the vultures to pull at. Side by side, the Papagos and Mexicans killed, hard-faced, vengeful, resolute."[148] In Smith's summation, the savagery of the moment, of the acts of killing, engulfed both the Mexican and Papago participants; perhaps he was appealing to scientific racist theories by implying that both groups had the same potential for savagery as the Apache they slaughtered. In any case, he totally absolved the Anglos of culpability and solidified the notion of their supposed civility.

One of the few Apache accounts of the massacre, recorded by an anthropologist of the Apache, Grenville Goodwin, does not discuss the sexual violence of the event either. Sherman Curley, a member of the Aravaipa band who was a young man at the time of the massacre, described the pandemonium that ensued as the the massacre occurred. The Aravaipa and Pinal Apache had been dancing the night before to celebrate the uniting of their peoples under the protective care of the Camp Grant army post:

> There was a big ridge above their camps, and one on the other side too. During the night, a big bunch of Mexicans and Papagos opened fire on

them while they were still dancing. They killed a lot of people this way. They all scattered. The scouts and soldiers down at Camp Grant didn't know what was going on. I ran into the arroyo. I had my bow and arrows, and I pointed at them as if I was going to shoot. This scared some of the Mexicans and Papagos back, who were after me. I ran on, trying to get away, but four of them followed me, but they did not kill me or hit me. . . . I ran to one side of the mt. top, and stayed there. Some others who had gotten away were on the top of this mt. also. . . . The next day one man went back to the place where we had been dancing. He found lots of bodies of dead Apaches there. Some of the women and girls who had long nice hair, they had cut a round place right out of the scalp, leaving the hair on, and taken it away with them. I don't know why they did this.[149]

Taking scalps signifies no desire for peace and negotiation; rather, it was a brutal means of punishing the Aravaipa Apache band. Similarly, with regard to Spanish tactics of warfare against the Apache in eighteenth-century Texas, Juliana Barr argues that "Apache women form the category of noncombatants [did not] merit exemption from harm and instead [were] viewed . . . as targets for enslavement. . . . Spanish officials ignored the fact that warriors would not allocate the male-defined tasks of warfare to women."[150] In nineteenth-century southern Arizona, however, the Mexican, Papago, and Anglo combatants did not see these Aravaipa Apache women as worthy of enslavement or captivity; rather, they were targets of extermination, proving their lack of social and economic value. In the mediated words of Chief Eskeminzin to Indian Commissioner Collier, "They think the people of Tucson and San Xavier [the Papagos] must have a thirst for blood. They seem to always be pursuing them. They think that as soon as the commissioner has gone, these people will return again and try to massacre them."[151] So while the logic of barbarity worked to justify the attack on the Aravaipa at Camp Grant, Chief Eskeminzin essentially calls the raiders savages, reappropriating the very discourse used to rationalize the slaughter of his people.

Curley's description of the scalped women is another marker of a particular form of gendered violence. His special attentiveness to the mutilation of "women and girls who had long nice hair" conveys Aravaipa cultural values about beauty and femininity.[152] To obliterate the gendered body of a noncombatant indigenous woman is to acknowledge the connections between "hair, spectacle and looking relations that are raced in their very nature."[153] Curley's focus on the women's hair demarcates a racialized spectacle of difference marked by scalping. The women were already dead, their bodies riddled with bullets, their skulls smashed. Why take scalps? And who took them? If the Papago warriors took the scalps, then the act was part of a larger symbolic economy of exchange value. As a means of showing respect for the dead, the Papago held a scalp purification ceremony whereby the scalp was to live with the warrior who took it.[154] But what if the Anglos and Mexicans were the scalpers? Taking scalps was not a part of their cultural practices, so if they did so the Mexican and Anglo participants were marking excessive violence as an indicator of an emerging disciplinary society that punished errant indigenous women's bodies, perhaps in a system in which the colonizer turns the tools of Apache warfare (for it was assumed that Apaches scalped all of their victims) against their originator.

The relationship between exchange, the body, and violence was exposed as a part of traditional Papago war practices. María Chona recalled another war song her father sang when he returned from making war against the Apache; it tells how and why men assigned a spiritual meaning to such gendered killings, especially in their purification ritual: "Alas! / Something I know? Clearly I know / I killed an Apache woman / She was crying and now light has come to me."[155] This ritual song has many possible interpretations, particularly as regards the relationship between gender and sexual violence. It represents an active deconstruction and reconstruction of the relationship between the Papago warrior and his victim, and a practice of spiritual reflection through the body of the dead Apache woman. Yet the death ultimately represents the highest expression of power. In her article "Not an Indian Tradition: The Sexual Colonization of Native Peoples," Andrea Smith argues that colonialism itself is structured by the logic of sexual violence. As the Papago, Mexicans, and Anglo-Americans were enlisted in a collective colonial project of massacre, they actively participated in the colonial structure that advocated sexual violence as part of its logic. At the same time, the Papago war song implies, if one identifies American Indians as an ethnic group, that intraethnic violence was a part of everyday life.

The majority of the historiography written about the massacre omits descriptions of the mutilated, raped bodies of women and children, which reinforces the idea not only that native peoples are a "present absence" in the U.S. colonial imagination, but also that U.S. colonial imaginaries are formed through acts of forgetting histories of racialized, sexualized violence.[156] Elliott Arnold's novel *The Camp Grant Massacre* (1976) is one of the few accounts to acknowledge the role of rape in the massacre and portray the sexual violence in detail. The novel describes what Lieutenant Whitman observed upon arriving at the scene, "He only saw women. Some of the women had been stripped.

Their legs were spread apart. Their thighs and bellies were mottled with sperm. Whitman could make out only a few of them. The clubs had made almost all of them anonymous."[157] To make a body anonymous by physically destroying its face, the feature that most distinguishes one person from another, is a way to minimize the implications of rape. Furthermore, the women's bodies are situated in a particular history of discipline achieved through colonization. That is, Indians are subjects to be disciplined, and destroying their sexual agency is the ultimate form of discipline. Still in *The Camp Grant Massacre*, Arnold denies that the Anglos and Mexicans could possibly have been among the rapists. Rather, Lieutenant Whitman suggests, "There must have been savages involved in this. They raped the women but they considered them unworthy to receive their sperm" because a number of the women's thighs and stomachs were streaked with blood and semen.[158] Elizabeth Grosz argues that "detachable, separable parts of the body—urine, feces, saliva, sperm, blood, vomit, hair, nails, skin—retain something of the cathexis and value of a body part even when they are separated from the body. There is still something of the subject bound up with them—which is why they are objects of disgust, loathing, and repulsion as well as envy and desire."[159] In the images of raped, semen-streaked women's bodies we see a direct imposition of one body on another. As Grosz states, sperm and blood are simultaneously objects of desire and disgust. Rape is an act of destruction against an object of both desire and disgust. The semen is public, visible confirmation of rape and further symbolizes the sexually charged nature of the killing of these Apache women: one cannot be imagined or carried out without the other. There are also nationalist implications for such a fictional representation: the idea of nation is fortified through eliminating threats to national security. In other words, the U.S. nation based on capitalist reproduction is consolidated through the scene of violence. Further, the fictional account renders extreme sexual violence, unspeakable in the realm of historical documentation, audible. It is the form of fiction that allows for violence to be expressed in a national imaginary that did not represent such images because they question the way nations consolidate themselves.

In some ways such manifestations of masculine aggression, argues Alicia Schmidt-Camacho, are a rational expression of contradictions of gendered and, I would add, racialized codes of governance.[160] In calling such violence rational, I do not mean in any way to condone the Camp Grant massacre. Rather, the event rationalized rape, physical dismemberment, and tortuous deaths as being necessary for personal security. Rape and physical violence inscribe social power upon bodies, which is reflected in how Arnold further imagines the scene: "Some of the more attractive Aravaipa women won a respite of a kind. The avengers worked unangrily. They were drugged with dedication. Age and sex and size meant nothing. Each enemy counted the same as every other enemy in the tabulation of the calendar sticks."[161]

Anglos and Mexicans are completely and problematically absolved of responsibility for the sexual violence both in Arnold's account and in the official accounts written by Anglo participants, which do not mention rape, marking a distinct line between Indian savagery and non-Indian civility. Schellie's *Vast Domain of Blood* tells a similar story: "A Papago threw himself upon an Apache girl, yet in her teens, and tore the clothing from her body and raped her. Another San Xavier man entered that wickiup then, and the first pinned the whimpering girl's arms to the ground while the second took her. And when they were finished they crushed her skull and slashed her breasts and fired bullets into her ravished body."[162] To displace the onus of sexual violence onto the Papago replicates a number of biologically based discourses of Indian savagery and further denies the processes of colonization in which, according to Smith, it was through "sexual violence and the imposition of European gender relationships on Native communities that Europeans were able to colonize Native peoples in the first place."[163] In other words, placing the responsibility for the sexual violence against Apache women exclusively on the Papago raiders is a colonizing trick that denies the effects of colonial systems of gender, power, and violence. Regardless of whether or not Mexicans and Anglos committed sexual violence during the massacre, participation in a colonial act of aggression effectively purchased Mexican inclusion in the capitalist class of citizens that believed eradication of the Apache threat would bolster their position economically and socially.

Yet the accounts contradict the displacement of culpability onto the Papago.[164] In 1871 it was illegal for Indians to possess firearms, and yet Schellie says, "Bodies were stripped. Bullets were fired into corpses, arrows shot into them. Nearly all the dead were mutilated."[165] Since the Papago were the ground troops committing the massacre, and they may have had guns, the fictional account raises the possibility that the Anglos and Mexicans who possessed firearms were also the ones who committed the rapes and shot the women. This account exemplifies what Scarry calls "the graphic image of the human body [which] substitutes for the object of belief that itself has no content and thus itself cannot be represented."[166] The images of raped, dead bodies secondarily violated by bullets in Schellie's fictional representation, which quite possibly came from the Mexican and Anglo participants in the raid, and by arrows, which must have come from the Papago (even though the historical accounts say they carried only war clubs), exemplify that this raid was not just about sexual violence but about torturing the dead, and by extension the surviving Apache who were later to be confronted with the violated bodies of their sisters, wives, mothers, and children.

Here, the Apache body becomes a text that is almost unspeakable but that haunts the history of this gruesome historical moment, which also contradicts the Anglo descriptions of the Papago and of themselves as civilized peoples. Papago oral histories of war support the finding that excessive physical force was used during the massacre, but they say nothing about sexual violence: "When our men go toward an Apache, they do not just walk. They leap. . . . You must take care of yourself until you have tamed that power or it will kill you. You could not stand against arrows with such power around you. You would be a sick man. You would fall. So they painted their faces black to show what had happened. They carried black paint for that in little deerskin bags. They stood away from the others, and other men who had killed came and joined them."[167] The Papago had a long-standing history of violent exchanges with the Apache, who had often raided San Xavier not just for horses, rations, and cattle, but for women as well, which explains why they had developed warfare rituals specific to the Apache. Not just the physical violence of the events, but spiritual dimensions of power as well, translated into the exchange of human bodies.

The construction of the San Xavier Papago as civilized in the national imaginary is an oppositional construct of a social history that is eerily silent about sexual or other types of violence in the Camp Grant massacre. In the textbook approved by the tribal government for use in O'odham schools, *Sharing the Desert*, there is little mention of the incident, and what mention there is is devoid of detail: "This group made a rapid march by night to Camp Grant. . . . In a surprise attack, the posse killed a large number of Apaches. The army commander at Camp Grant reported that the posse killed 21 women and children, but other reports indicate that as many as 125 people died in the raid. The victorious took nearly 30 Apache children to Mexico and sold them as slaves. Of those abducted and sold, only 6 children were eventually returned."[168] This tribally sanctioned history leaves out details of the violence, perhaps suggesting that it was culturally sanctioned as part of an exchange economy.[169] Perhaps the reporting of this history reflects how "Indian communities faced growing pressures that increasingly prompted violent decisions," including, at this historical moment, the normalization of violence as a social practice.[170]

Historically, there are a number of references to Apache women's sexual and gender identities. Accounts from the 1860s contradict the discourses of sexual lasciviousness, rape, and violence around the Camp Grant massacre. Capt. John C. Cremony, an army officer who worked among different Apache bands as part of the U.S. Boundary Commission during the 1860s, stated that "the award for female chastity is given to the Apaches. During a period of about two years, when hundreds of them were under our charge, and mingling freely with our troops, not a single case occurred, to the best of my knowledge, wherein an Apache woman surrendered her person to any man outside of her tribe."[171] Although feminist theorists would point out that a number of rapes and sexual encounters during military occupations likely went unreported because of the threat of further physical violence and power differentials, Cremony's tone suggests that chastity and womanly virtue guided the Apache women's behavior. This fact would make rape an especially powerful punishment. Oddly enough, Cremony's narrative of Apache female self-possession counters the standard narrative in which women are portrayed as victims of male oppression.[172] Somewhat in line with late nineteenth-century Western notions of Victorian womanhood, the interlocking frameworks of race, gender, and sexuality temporarily overturned discourses of the primitive in articulating Apache female subjectivities as being rooted in sexual agency. Cremony absolves the men of the U.S. Army, whether Anglo or Indian, of any thought of sexual violence against their captives, shutting down any possibility of questioning the complete male domination embodied in the colonial project of taming the Apache.

The press makes little mention of Apache women, focusing exclusively on masculine sexual politics: "Self preservation prompts us to slaughter him on sight."[173] Preserving one's economic welfare is a way of reinforcing one's masculinity and prowess. The death of one group of men and women at the hands of another literally halts the possibility of the former to reproduce and, in particular, to produce warriors. In addition, Apache masculinity was viewed as a threat to white womanhood: "He is supplied with a comely White matron to his slave and take a blooming damsel to his wife. . . . There is no happier lot than that of the nation's protégé, the pampered Apache in Arizona."[174] Destructive and threatening masculinities are projected onto Apache men, especially with regard to the capture of white women and sexual relations with them.

Apache, Papago, Mexican, and Anglo-American masculinities and femininities seem to have played a huge role in how the dynamics of violence played out at Camp Grant. Masculinity, argues R. W. Connell, is "at best, the formation . . . within the family . . . treated as a moment of reproduction of the gender order. At worst, an ahistorical masculine essence, as unchanging as crystal, is set up as a criterion against which social arrangements are judged and generally found wanting."[175] This binary notion of masculinity, while it deconstructs the static idea of what is masculine, nonetheless is a binary that allows for little discussion of racially bound questions of masculinity, sexuality, and gender within the complex social world surrounding the Camp Grant massacre. Sources from the 1870s do not discuss the complexity of Apache gender roles. Rather, Apache masculinity and femininity were imagined through ideas of savageness and a base desire to commit violence against others. Only much later, through Goodwin's work with the Western Apache in the 1930s, did people begin to understand how gender was pivotal to understanding why the Apache did what they did to sustain their social organization. Goodwin's field notes open a window onto social expectations about gender in Apache communities and how they changed because of U.S. imperialism.[176] His interviews also demonstrate that Apaches didn't construct their notion of masculinity in opposition only to that of Anglo men, but also to that of Mexicans and other indigenous groups on their own terms. Apache women mobilized warfare and raiding as cultural practices by praying for the safety of the warriors while they were away. If a man was not married, his mother and the sisters who still lived with him prayed for his safe return and success; a married man's wife and elder daughters performed this ritual.[177]

Apache masculinity was constructed around providing for the community through hunting and raiding. Similarly, Anglo-American and Tucson Mexican masculinities were defined by providing resources to their families and communities while exerting claims to citizenship; but they did so in formal economies. While the massacre indicates that there was some overlap in social practice around masculinity in southern Arizona in the 1870s—in defending their resources men were defending their heteronormative gender roles—the key difference lies in the desires of Anglos and Mexicans to continue amassing property, resources, dominance over trade routes, and social positioning. Even though dominant discourses of the Camp Grant massacre argue otherwise, warfare was not an illogical process for the Western Apache. It was a way to seek reparations for spiritual, emotional, and economic losses; namely, the loss of other Apache clan and family members. Almost all of the violent skirmishes that were reported to Goodwin in the 1930s were acts of retaliation, whether by an organized war party or in response to being shot at during a raid. This mirrors the response to the Camp Grant massacre, when men went on the warpath.

These narratives about the gendered, sexualized, and racialized politics of violence and the telling of history contain many lessons. As many scholars have noted, history is always already mediated by the desires of the tellers of the narratives. I have tracked the inconsistencies in the historical fragments that survive from the complicated narratives of the Camp Grant massacre. What is abundantly clear with regard to the Mexicans and Papago who participated in the massacre is that their citizenship was dependent upon the interplay between capitalism and race. Furthermore, Apache women's subjectivity is erased in the majority of these narrative fragments, reinforcing Usha Zacharias's argument that "women as citizen-subjects are often erased through two ancient tropes of feminine sexuality—only the husband and lover are acknowledged as nationally significant actors."[178] In the Camp Grant case, the women are represented as rape victims, torture victims, dead wives, and children. In some ways, Anglo and Mexican participation obliterates the indigenous subjectivities of both the Apache murder victims and the San Xavier and Pan Tak Papago who were the majority of the participants in the massacre, which absolves them of guilt.

The nameless Papago members of the raiding party—only fictitious first names appear in the court documents—stand as a testament that Indians occupied a tenuous position in the nation and in the Arizona Territory. Their participation in the massacre secured temporary citizenship for themselves and other populations, but not the right to long-term citizenship. The only Indians with any of the traditional identifiers of subjectivity in the documents are the chiefs. Chief Galerita, who led the Papago into battle, and Chief Eskeminzin, one of the leaders of the Apache band attacked at Camp Grant, are the two Indians who receive the most mention in the documents. By replicating the universal Anglocentric subject of history and feminism in which two Indian men represent the group,[179] the documents further problematize celebratory discourses of mestizaje in Chicano nationalism precisely because a clear distinction is drawn between the mestizos (Mexicans) in the raid and the Papago and Apache Indians.

Homi Bhabha argues that "the political unity of the nation consists in a continual displacement of its irredeemably plural modern space, bounded by different, even hostile nations, into a signifying space that is archaic and mythical, paradoxically representing the nation's modern territoriality, the patriotic, atavistic temporality of Traditionalism. Quite simply, the difference of space returns as the Sameness of time, turning Territory into Tradition, turning the people into one."[180] The Camp Grant massacre suggests a plurality of modern spaces: Arizona was a land of vast mineral and land resources for Anglo pioneers. Meanwhile, Mexicans were trying to retain what they had gained through Spanish colonization of the New World. Arizona was the homeland of the Apaches and Papago. The Camp Grant Indian massacre is the embodiment of a collision among hostile nations with divergent ideologies about order, civility, gender, and the value of life. In marginal territories such as Arizona, which had a distinct Spanish and Mexican history of failed campaigns to turn indios bárbaros into Mexicans, ambitions were quickly replaced motivations championed by acquisitive forces in the United States: capitalism fueled competition for control of territory.

In a presentation to the Arizona Pioneers Society in 1885, Oury quoted Elías as saying to him, "I have always been satisfied and have repeatedly told you that the Camp Grant Indians were the ones who were destroying us. . . . See your countrymen, they are the ones who have money to furnish the supplies necessary to make a formal and effective campaign against our implacable enemies. I know my countrymen will vouch that if arms and ammunition and provisions, however scant, are furnished them, they will be ready at the first call."[181] While Elías distinguishes Mexicans from Anglos in the territory, their site of agreement is concretized in the planned attack against the Camp Grant Apaches.

Government Indian policy was even more steeped in the interests of capitalism and imperialism after the Camp Grant massacre than at any time before it. The BIA *Report of the Commissioner of Indian Affairs* for 1872 expressed similar sentiments: "The freedom of expansion which is working these results is to us of incalculable value. To the Indians it is of incalculable cost. Every year's advance of our frontier takes in a territory as large as some of the kingdoms in Europe. We are richer by hundreds of millions; the Indian is poorer by a large part of the little he has. This growth is bringing imperial greatness to the nation; to the Indian it brings wretchedness, destruction and beggary."[182] For the Mexicans and Papago who participated in the Camp Grant massacre, such Indian policy offered a temporary reprieve from being swallowed up by the greed of U.S. expansionism. Once the Indian wars ended, however, Mexicans and Indians in Tucson were reduced to a disenfranchised social status that changed their relations with Anglos forever, especially after the arrival of the railroad.[183]

The sources do not reveal many firsthand stories of what Mexicans, Apaches, and Papago said about the Camp Grant massacre. Mostly their voices are filtered through the pens of Anglo narrators in the historical record. So where does this leave scholars methodologically? The reader is left teetering between the epistemic violence created by the sources, in which women, Mexicans, Apaches, and Papagos very seldom speak for themselves, and what can be gleaned without putting words in their mouths. The Camp Grant massacre shows how economic problems are often blamed upon racialized and sexualized peoples. Mexicans and Papagos purchased political and economic enfranchisement in the Arizona Territory, however temporary, through physical and sexualized violence against the Apache. They sought not only economic gain but racial differentiation from indios bárbaros; and, most important, all three groups, Anglos, Mexicans, and Papagos disciplined the savage Apache braves through the violation of the bodies of their women. Chicano nationalism cannot ignore this in its romanticized history of Mexican mestizo resistance to Anglos.

3 ✳ Spaces of Death

BORDER (ANTHROPOLOGICAL) SUBJECTS AND THE
PROBLEM OF RACIALIZED AND GENDERED VIOLENCE
IN JOVITA GONZÁLEZ'S ARCHIVE

> In the Borderlands
> You are the battleground
> Where enemies are kin to each other;
> You are at home, a stranger,
> The border disputes have been settled
> the volley of shots have shattered the truce
> you are wounded, lost in action
> dead, fighting back.
> "To live in the borderlands means you."
>
> GLORIA ANZALDÚA, *BORDERLANDS/LA FRONTERA*

Jovita González's body of work, loosely classified as anthropology, provides a textually based discussion of gendered and racialized violence, nation, and the body in the context of Texas. In 1930 González graduated with a master's degree in anthropology from the University of Texas, the first Mexican American woman to do so. She subsequently conducted fieldwork in the South Texas counties of Starr, Roma, and Zapata, producing one of the few scholarly archives about the U.S.–Mexican border by a Mexican woman in the early twentieth century.[1] She published only with the Texas Folklore Society, and, although she received a Rockefeller Foundation Fellowship, her work was not circulated to a mass audience.[2]

González's archive locates itself within the political and social geographies of the U.S.–Mexico border.[3] Her critical inquiry centers around space, which, as Doreen Massey describes it, "is a sphere of multiplicity, the product of social relations and if those relations are real material practices, and always ongoing, then space can never be closed, there will always be loose ends,

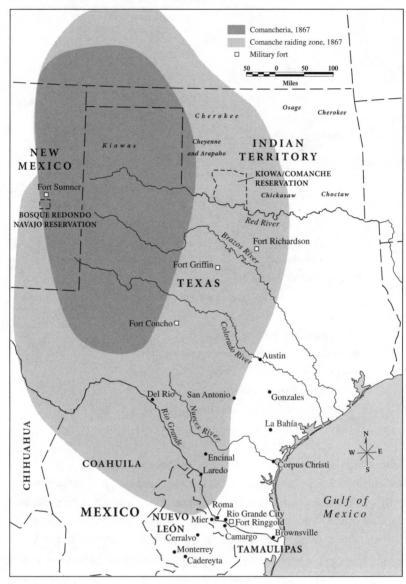

MAP 3 Map of Jovita González's Texas with details of the Comanchería

always relations with the beyond, always potential elements of chance."[4] How the U.S.–Mexico border influenced social relations is at the core of González's work on violence.

González was clearly invested in her anthropological subjects as people of the border whose lives were governed by violence. Her work represents the meeting of multiple ideological modes of thinking, as relevant to the political production of identities on what she calls the "Texas–Mexican frontier," that is, the "lower Rio Grande Valley [which] 'became a little independent republic.' "[5] González's representations of this contact zone, like the materials in her archive, are truly conflicted in the way they engage with communities in a territory where death defines life, a space that has changed political and national affiliations five times, all within less than one hundred years of her writing. On one hand, her texts attempt to correct the discursive and epistemic violence enacted in representations of "Texas-Mexicans" (the term she used in her thesis). Yet the texts enact their own form of epistemic and discursive violence through the stock caricatures, outright denials, racist portrayals, and erasures of African Americans and Texas Indians and through the generic portrayals of "Aztec" Indians that populate her observations.

Instead of arguing over whether González should be positioned as a Chicana/o studies foremother, a feminist visionary, or a racist elitist, I want to look at how the racism in González's texts provides an alternative narrative of the historical period in which she wrote, on the one hand, and how these racist musings complicate a feminist positioning of her work within Chicana/o studies, on the other. Chicano studies scholars often overlook this facet of her work for a very important reason: to acknowledge the racism in González's work would undo the claim that her feminist scholarship of border people was revolutionary or progressive. For at the core of the field of Chicano/a studies is a kernel of resistance to Anglo hegemony. González's amazing work on gender replicates a racism that is considered the exclusive property of an Anglo-American rhetoric of nation.

While feminist scholarship on González has noted her ability to embrace a progressive agenda about gender freedom and nascent Texas-Mexican questions of national liberation by documenting and celebrating communal traditions, one gap in this criticism is in the discussion of González's racism toward non-Texas-Mexicans and non-Anglos. Most recently, both María Cotera and Louis Mendoza have provided incisive readings of González's scholarly and fictional work in the novel *Caballero* (which she cowrote with Eve Raleigh) and of her anthropological work with the Texas Folklore Society. Mendoza and Cotera both firmly place González's work in a tradition of resistance.

Cotera's book *Native Speakers* contains two chapters on González. Cotera is invested in linking González to other early twentieth-century women of color, particularly anthropologist and folklorist intellectuals such as Ella Deloria and Nora Zeale Hurston as representatives of third world feminist discourse. Their work, in Cotera's view, is a useful platform for discussing the mechanisms of empire and colonialism as well as the anticolonial and antiracist political and cultural movements that emerged in the early twentieth century.[6] Through a productive model of comparative scholarship that avoids a colonizing gesture by settling on a discussion of confluences and convergences in Hurston's, González's, and Deloria's writing, Cotera argues that the methodology of the three writers reveals the emancipatory politics of their representational practices. In order to carry out this project, Cotera turns to U.S./third world feminist scholarship, to "illuminate their divergent approaches to unmasking the 'relations of rule' that have shaped both colonial and anticolonial discourses in the twentieth century."[7] What is interesting about Cotera's appeal to women of color feminist thought is that although it is clearly a break in identification with Chicana/o nationalist thought, the theoretical framework is nonetheless steeped in the rhetoric of resistance. Turning to the coalitional and foundational women of color feminist project represented notably by *This Bridge Called My Back*, Cotera suggests her method mines the particularities and differences across ideas of nation, race, and historical context without assimilating others' experiences to our own. The basis of the women of color feminist methodology that Cotera proposes is not a naturalized bond based on racial affinity, but a common context of struggle.[8]

By locating González's work within woman of color scholarship and deploying corresponding methodologies, Cotera accomplishes several things. First, and most persuasively, she argues that when scholars engage with cultural workers like González, we should deploy a different set of methodological concerns, for women like González and the scholarship they produced "have been disappeared from our national imaginary"—and, I would argue, have been disappeared at both the U.S. and Chicano levels—because they challenged disciplinary, aesthetic, and ideological norms.[9] Second, locating González's body of work within a woman of color feminist tradition erases the binaries that would suggest that race or gender would undermine conventional notions of resistance, providing a revolutionary optic to address the complexity of what Cotera calls border texts.[10] Third, Cotera reads González's texts (such as *Caballero* and *Dew on the Thorn*), as having theoretical affinities with a U.S.–third world feminist practice, and on that basis she argues that it has a much older genealogy than the cultural nationalist movements of the 1960s.

Mendoza, on the other hand, is invested in placing González's coauthored novel *Caballero* squarely within a Chicana/o literary tradition that was and continues to be invested in a history-writing project as practice. He traces this genealogy through a canon that includes Américo Paredes's *George Washington Gómez*, Antonio Villarreal's *Pocho*, and the Tejana poet Teresa Palomo Acosta's revisionist history of Chipita Rodríguez to refashion how the conversation on resistance takes shape in the field. *Caballero*'s most important contribution, Mendoza argues, is its critique of intracultural and intercultural gender and class relations. Building on this claim, Mendoza goes on to say that the resistive quality of the work derives from the imaginative representation of the time frame of 1848–50 in which *Caballero* alters our understanding of the history of the period and of Chicana/o literature through the form of the romance.[11] Mendoza convincingly shows how the novel stages social conflict between Mexicans as "preexisting hierarchies of privilege based on social status, gender, and race."[12] The romance form, characterized by the centrality of love plots between Texas-Mexican women and Anglo-American men and the role of matriarchs within the Texas-Mexican family, makes up the two formal representations that critique masculinity and femininity as operating social constraints. Ultimately, Mendoza argues, *Caballero* affords a mechanism for imagining the conditions and form of an emerging oppositional consciousness in the transitional period of the Mexican War. But interestingly, the term *oppositional consciousness* was coined by the Chicana feminist Chela Sandoval in her articulation of a U.S.–third world feminist agenda in the 1980s.

My digression into Cotera's and Mendoza's readings of González is not meant to undermine the efforts of Chicana/o feminist scholars active in literary recovery projects. But based on these two theoretical perspectives, I think a whole different set of questions present themselves: What does it mean to locate González's work within a late twentieth-century intellectual formation such as U.S.–third world feminism? What gets silenced, highlighted, and lost by applying a contemporary theory to a body of work that predated U.S.–third world feminism or Chicana/o resistance narratives by sixty years or more? What does locating the novel *Caballero* in the pantheon of Chicano/a literature do to valorize González's position as an intellectual? Moreover, how does this valorization, based on the claim of resistance, eclipse the question of racism in González's work? Why locate González's body of work as a precursor to or as part of an unbroken continuum of resistance that has been articulated through the channels of both Chicana/o nationalism and U.S.– third world feminism?

As my readings show, González's special brand of Texas-Mexican racism was no doubt a product of her historical moment and of the Texas-Mexican national imaginary that she reports on, interprets, and captures so effectively in her work. However, this is where my critique diverges from Cotera's and Mendoza's arguments. U.S.–third world feminism and the discourse of resistance in Chicano studies both imply a critique of racism. Not just Anglo and Mexican racism but racism among and between people of color, something González's work does not perform, no matter how progressive and solid her critique of gender inequality or of racist encounters between Anglos and Mexicans.

González's corpus is reflective of a border anthropology that produced an intensely intersubjective kind of knowledge derived from a diversity of voices, a feature characteristic of early twentieth-century anthropology as a field; it reflects and refracts a kind of racism that was class-based in nature but also inherent in the ethnographic practice of her time.[13] González establishes knowledge through multiple forms of representation: folk tales, ethnographic studies, the novel, and short stories. The cultural practices of the Texas– Mexico border are the all-encompassing concepts guiding González's work. My goal is to offer a different reading of her work, one that neither focuses exclusively on masculinist figures nor attempts to frame her work as a feminist discourse.[14] Her illuminating work on gender oppression as it relates to Texas-Mexican women and children stands in contrast to the overt racism revealed in generic representations of Aztec Indians as stand-ins for disappeared Indian groups of Texas (the Comanche, Kiowa, and Lipan Apache, in particular) and African Americans. Overall, the blanket discourse of resistance does not adequately apply to González's body of work. Her work might also be called imperialist nostalgia, nostalgia for a past when conquistadors of aristocratic means ruled the land, an attitude which sets up a desire to maintain a kind of racial and class structure that originated with early imperialist practices in New Spain.[15] At the same time, her reimagining of the Mexican nation in the United States (Texas) can symbolically be taken as an outright refusal to acknowledge the implication that Mexicans would have to assimilate to U.S. cultural norms following the annexation of Texas and the Treaty of Guadalupe Hidalgo. The racial and class structures González laments—in which generic Aztec Indians know their place to be one of inferiority and blacks exist outside of multiple national imaginaries, even though the nation, be it Mexican, U.S., or Tejano, was built on the backs of slaves—existed in the borderlands long before the area was annexed to the United States. The existence of this Texas-Mexican national imaginary disturbs the idea that U.S. colonization was complete. Imagining a Texas-Mexican nation within an American one signifies that multiple regional and national ideologies can coexist within one space.

The most contested categories of regional and national identity and nationalism in González's work are based in representations of speaking subjects who are actually or symbolically dead in the U.S., Mexican, and Texas-Mexican national imaginaries. Texas history is haunted by stories of physically and psychologically battered, dispossessed, and maligned figures. González's archive ultimately meditates upon the disciplining of renegade bodies as a social and spatial practice. In telling the stories of violated subjects in late nineteenth- and early twentieth-century Texas, González provides an alternative narrative to the traditional story of the clash between Anglo and Mexican men because she focuses on Texas-Mexican women and children who, according to the historian Elliott Young, like "African Americans and Indians . . . held little or no political or economic power on the border."[16]

In ethnography, much as in literary texts, "some data are chosen, others omitted."[17] González's omissions, substitutions, and unlikely shifts in storytelling are often Freudian slips that mask narratives of violence and subjection. In particular, the erasure of Indians and blacks as historical subjects in the making of South Texas complements references to the bodies of the socially dead, because both groups have the potential to disrupt the social order of Tejano hegemony. In contrast to the claims made by Cotera and Mendoza about the resistance politics and third world feminist politics of González's work that uphold a particular Chicana/o nationalist agenda, her stories of the spiritual other world, women possessed by evil spirits, Plains Indian creation myths, displaced African Americans, and errant Aztec Indians, González accomplishes, according to Sharon Holland, a "most revolutionary intervention into conversations at the margins of race, gender, and sexuality [which] is to let the dead—those already denied a sustainable subjectivity—speak from the place that is familiar to them."[18] Those who exist outside of a cultural system are as good as dead to those who do not recognize them as citizen subjects, and it is often through González's racist gaze that they are allowed to speak. Figures of the socially or physically dead represent a forgotten and unresolved past. Nonetheless, my focus on narratives about the socially dead, the abject, is a feminist critical move to complicate how we understand peoples governed by the very gendered, racialized practices in South Texas between 1870 and 1930. González's overarching argument against Yankee imperialism makes the stories of the dispossessed (noncitizens) more politically urgent because violence is at the core of their displacement, but this comes at the expense of racism enacted in representations (or the lack thereof) of blacks and indigenous peoples. At the same time, her selective forgetting of a historically and regionally accurate array of indigenous communities in Texas attempts to smooth over a very violent and problematic history that Chicana/o and Latina/o cultural studies, as a field, needs to address more effectively.

Short narratives such as González's master's thesis of 1930, *Dew on the Thorn*, and her personal papers reflect upon the impending threat of violence against women, children, and racialized others (not just Texas-Mexicans) who can't always speak for themselves. These narratives show that the border constitutes a terrain for a complex set of narratives about subject formation. This power of the border, the ways in which subjection is created because and in spite of the border, produces what Judith Butler calls subjection's "fundamental dependency on a discourse we never choose but that, paradoxically, initiates and sustains our agency."[19] González's identification of "border people" demonstrates a "power that at first appears as external, pressed upon the subject, pressing the subject into subordination, [and] assumes a psychic form that constitutes the subject's self identity."[20] Thus, González's narratives become disciplinary, especially for racialized and gendered subjects. Stories of madness and alienation are crucial to how we understand the policing of social deviants who were, not surprisingly, often women, Indians, and African Americans, by further removing them from the rights and benefits of citizenship and community.

Holland has shown that "our border is a constant space of death and terror [and] . . . discovering who resides in the nation's imaginary 'space of death' and why we strive to keep such subjects there" is of the utmost critical importance.[21] As space and violence aid in the construction of a specifically U.S.–Mexican border experience for people of color, Holland points to the ways in which those socially dead speaking subjects continue to remain at the margins of the society that defines their subjectivity. Texas-Mexican identity is oppositionally constructed at the expense of Indians and blacks in South Texas. González's stories show how the ruses of power make lower classes, racialized individuals, and gendered subjects more susceptible to intimate violence. Both the presence and absence of Indians and blacks in scenes of nation building—and their violent erasure from what could be called the Texas-Mexican national imaginary—compete with U.S. and Mexican visions of national history. These competing imaginaries are pivotal to understanding the violent interface of race and gender in the borderlands.

González maintains the racial hierarchy of dispersed peoples that origi-nated within the Spanish ideological framework of social and racial inequality whereby the *gente decente*, or *criollos*, were at the top of the racial and social hierarchy, mestizas/os were in the middle, and Indians (both Mexican and North American) and African Americans were at the bottom. Maintaining this hierarchy entails a difficult, anxiety-ridden process of cultural revision, espe-cially where African Americans and North American Indians are concerned. Such stories reveal how violence differentiates marked bodies in the social economy. González's novelistic text *Dew on the Thorn* includes a myth about a spurned, lovesick Indian maiden that explains how the Great Spirit of the Plains creates order in the natural world. In this narrative, the call of the turtle-dove to its mate is identified as the vanished or morphed body of the Indian maiden: "Yes, once the turtledove was an Indian maiden. She was in love with a shepherd lad, but he wandered away with his flock and soon found another love. The lovesick girl mourned and wept many moons for her faithless lover. The Great Spirit took pity on her and changed her into a turtledove.[22] And ever since then, when the dew is upon the earth or when the evening star makes her appearance in the twilight, the soft mournful cry of the dove is told."[23]

In this case, it takes the divine intervention of the Great Spirit to deliver the dishonored and abandoned indigenous woman from her pain and the bonds of proper femininity. But the elements that stand out most in a feminist reading of the narrative are the focus on the spurned Indian woman and her bodily and spiritual transformation. As a dove, she can escape the possibility of being rejected again and experiencing further violence and pain. Also central to the story, however, is the fact that within the context of the larger project of *Dew on the Thorn* the Indian maiden is rendered invisible and void of a gender identity through her transformation into a mourning dove. These doves, like the Indian maiden, "haunt the prairies" of Texas, a signal that Indian removal did not occur that long ago.[24]

González continues to wrestle with a Plains Indian story tradition, one that is presumably a hybrid of Comanche and Kiowa, but the Indians themselves are displaced by generic, universal Indians or generic Aztec Mexican Indians, even though the mythology is not. For example, the so-called Indian cook Ambrosio, who, according to Tío Patricio, "was in the kitchen sucking the raw marrow from a pile of fresh bones and singing his wild Indian songs," is a starkly racialized and demonized masculine contrast to Tío Patricio's poverty-stricken life as a Texas-Mexican shepherd. Patricio thinks, "Plague take the heathen Indian . . . why can't he take a nap like a well behaved Christian should?"[25] In both these references, the tribeless, untamably masculine Indian heathen is the ultimate marker of savage cultural practice, one that is not mythologized or celebrated in oral folk traditions. It is also a reference to a cannibalistic past not that far removed from present Indian behavior. Ambrosio's unintelligible, untranslatable "wild songs" become the justification for a normalized racial and gender hierarchy in the South Texas borderlands and for the fine racial and class distinctions between Texas-Mexicans and Indians. When things go wrong with the rain cycle, Ambrosio is blamed: "Just you wait, Don Francisco and that Indian cook of yours is to blame. A thousand devils take him where he belongs!"[26] In response to the curses of his Indian employee, the Haciendado's query is met with more racialized, cultural rage: "He's been singing his songs, songs of Satan they must be too. And when he sings it rains, a story this time it is sure to be. Oh, just look at him, he must be calling his heathen gods to help him."[27] The communal perception of Ambrosio is noteworthy for the tremendous amount of agency ascribed to his Indian voodoo, which supposedly had the potential to change weather cycles and cause storms, two critical phenomena in a rancho economy. Further, the cultural difference in religious beliefs is positioned as Satan's work, making the savage Indian masculinity, his songs, and his powers pathological. When Ambrosio is finally asked to speak for himself before his master, he replies, "Singing, master? I no sing. Ambrosio think. . . . That no singing master, Ambrosio think aloud. He think he is Aztec warrior. Spring come soon, cactus bloom, flowers will smell and Ambrosio think of his home in far Xochimilco. . . . Of Aztecs walking, walking many years. Looking for rich land, for lake, for eagle on cactus."[28]

But as Cotera points out, *Dew on the Thorn* takes place between 1904 and 1907, so one must ask what González is trying to represent through Ambrosio and his masculinized Aztec Indianness if he was in fact from Xochimilco, a suburb of Mexico City? The South Texas rancho at the beginning of the twentieth century was light years away from the historical moment of the sixteenth century, when the Aztecs ruled Xochimilco, Lake Texcoco, and Tenochtitlán (now Mexico City). In Ambrosio's appeal to a far-off homeland and an Indian empire of Mexica peoples that had not been in existence since the beginning of the Spanish colonial period some three hundred years earlier, we can see that González favors a Mexican national story and its nostalgia for the dead male Indian warriors of the past, rather than the living Indians of the early twentieth-century Texas-Mexican present. In the mid- to late nineteenth century Texas was the disputed homeland of the Comanche, Lipan Apache, Kickapoo, and Kiowa, but González offers up an Aztec instead.[29] Even though Texas Indians had relatively recently been relocated to Indian Territory, González's narrative completely writes them out of the mythological past of Texas. Instead of playing a part in the making of Texas history or its present, González's Indians are either generic, detribalized caricatures of a universal Indian savage or an Aztec, both of which are carefully differentiated from the Texas-Mexican people that populate her texts.

In sharp contrast with Tío Patricio's disdain for the heathen Indian Ambrosio, González turns to the harmless folk tradition of the Spirit of the Plains and the spurned Indian maiden to shift readers away from the bloody, socially complex world of the Texas borderlands, where Mexicans, Indians, and Anglos were battling over land and resources. Eliding the history of Comanche and Kiowa raids that dominated the history of Texas in the mid- to late nineteenth century, González makes generic Aztecs stand in for the Comanche, Kiowa, and Apache of Texas, who in 1867 were violently dispossessed of their traditional homelands and removed to reservations in Indian Territory and whose "wild and intractable" ways were, in fact, an enactment of social and territorial claims.[30] Describing the Indians on the rancho as detribalized Aztecs completely contradicts the earlier narrative of the spurned Indian maiden as a reference to Plains Indians that were removed from their territories, telling us the invisibilized twin history to the history of the imagined Texas-Mexican nation-state is dependent on the erasure of Plains Indians and the foregrounding not of the present but of a colonial Mexican Indian past.

The active historical erasure at work is quite salient given that as late as 1884 people in Texas were still filing reparation claims with the U.S. government for Comanche and Kiowa raids.[31] In 1885 the secretary of the interior stated that

a stronger more potent objection to concentration of [Indians] in the Indian Territory exists than any yet given, and that is the fierce and uncompromising opposition which this proposition meets in the almost unanimous sentiment of the white citizens of the four great states of Missouri, Kansas, Texas, and Arkansas, which surround this territory . . . and although representatives from other states of the union might believe that concentration of the savage Indian tribes of the country in the Indian Territory would be best for the Indians and greatly relieve the treasury . . . I would not advise such a step.[32]

National opposition to an Indian Territory and to savage North American Indians no doubt informs the shadowy presence of Plains groups in González's mythological works. Loss of land and power was a plausible threat if all the Indian warriors in the territory banded together to strike out against settlers in Texas, Kansas, Arkansas, and Missouri. The borderlands historian James Brooks notes that the "Rio Grande borderlands stand as one case of how successful capitalist expansion in the nineteenth century depended in some part on the creation . . . of a place and process organized around systematic thievery."[33] As late as the beginning of the twentieth century many distinct Indian nations, including the Kiowa, the Lipan Apache, and the Comanche, were still haunting the national consciousness with their raids into Texas; González's cultural substitution of the generic, universal Indian heathen or the Aztec for these Indians violently displaces the history of organized thievery Brooks discusses. And that history was not so far removed. On June 15, 1872, staking a claim to land and capital in Texas, Quahada and Coochchotellien Comanche raided government corrals in San Antonio, Texas, and stole livestock valued at $3,687. As late as January 1888 the state of Texas was reimbursed in the amount of $927,177.40 for "an estimate of appropriation for the payment of the amount found due . . . for expense of suppressing Indian hostilities" between 1866 and 1882.[34]

González's master's thesis constantly makes reference to raids by North American Indian on the border. For example, a fortress was constructed in 1851 to give protection from Comanche raids. At the time her thesis was filed the fort was still standing "in the main street of San Ignacio," Zapata County.[35] Her spatial memory is contradictory, as the metanarrative of the Spirit of the Plains actually refers to another narrative about displaced North American Indian tribes. Instead of focusing on the spatial claims of North American Indians in her thesis, she writes at length about Juan Cortina's resistance in South Texas, which was immortalized in corridos and in Chicano nationalist, androcentric narratives,[36] while completely ignoring the fact that in 1858 a group of Texans led by Cortina annihilated the state's last remaining encampment of Karankawa Indians, rendering the tribe essentially extinct.[37] By erasing the contradictory and violent relations between the Indian nations that inhabited Texas (Cortina's slaughter of the Karankawa) and uncritically putting Mexicans at the center of the historical narrative (Cortina's last stand in Brownsville), González denies the complex interplay of colonial and imperial structures in the social and cultural making of the Rio Grande Valley and elides the fact that Texas-Mexicans were often initiating the violence against indigenous peoples. González's Spirit of the Plains and representation of the generic Aztec Indian Ambrosio recall the spatial memory of the other inhabitants of the Texas-Mexican borderlands who were violently displaced but are historically represented as an absconded presence of the living dead who haunt Texas history.

Even if these tribes were not visible inhabitants of the Rio Grande landscape at the time González was writing, their stories and the memory of them were still present spatially (by her evoking of the Spirit of the Plains). As N. Scott Momaday writes, "Imagining is determined as well by racial and cultural experience. The Native American's attitudes towards his landscape have been formulated over a long period of time, a span that reaches back to the end of the ice age, the land, *this* land, is secure in his racial memory."[38] While some might read Momaday's assertion as essentialist, he is keenly aware that land or space—whether the fort erected in San Ignacio in 1851 to defend against the Comanche, the depredations of the Kiowa and Comanche in Texas from the 1860s to the 1880s, or the curious absence of living American Indian citizen subjects in González's narratives—forms the social basis for historical memory that is embodied in space.

Conflicts about what constitutes an Indian in González's South Texas are further complicated in *Dew on the Thorn* when the figure of the Indian becomes a Mexican one in her description of the project of making Mexican Indians into good Mexican boys (that is, citizen subjects). Education becomes a way of preventing the deterioration of Texas-Mexican cultural values.[39] As the students are educated about imperialism in world history through stories ranging from Greece to "the 'robbery of Texas by the insidious cupidity and avarice of the Colossus of the North,'" (that is, the United States as obnoxious overseer), it becomes obvious that the heart of this community is governed by Texas-Mexican cultural values.[40] The sense of place and spatial geographies is acute and sensitive:

> [The teacher] related to his boys the past greatness of the indigenous races; he told them of the city of the Aztecs, the heart Tenochtitlán, that had surprised the Spanish conquerors with its splendor and wealth. He told them of the valiant prince Cuauhtémoc who, when tortured by the Spaniards because he would not reveal the hiding place of Montezuma's treasure, had merely smiled and said, when his anointed feet were placed over the burning coals, "Verily this is no bed of roses." He unfolded the miracle of the dark Virgin of Tepeyac, the blessed mother, who as an Indian maid appeared to the Indian Juan Diego as proof of God's love for his Indian children. It was an Indian boy, Pípila, he said, who set fire to the strong Spanish fortress of Granaditas when the patriot Father Hidalgo was fighting for our own independence, it was Morelos. A man with Indian blood

who carried on when all hopes for freedom were lost. It was a pureblooded Indian, Benito Juarez, who struggled for our sovereignty when French aggression threatened Mexico and today, he ended, "it is a mestizo, Don Porfirio Díaz, who directs our destinies. So you see my boys, the heritage of the race of bronze, the race of strong heroic men. Viva la Raza de Bronce! Viva Mexico! Viva Don Porfirio Díaz."[41]

In stark contrast with the Indians removed from Texas, these Mexican Indians are not connected to Texas as a part of the United States. According to González, they had no land base or claim to the land in Texas. Instead, their claims to citizenship and history are located in the pantheon of Mexican history: Hidalgo, Morelos, Juárez, and Díaz. These indigenous Mexican peoples had little relationship to the national discourse around North American Indians in Texas. González's Indians are immigrant Mexican Indians (whose tribal affiliations are never mentioned) who were part of the debt-peonage system that Texas ranching economies relied upon in the late nineteenth century and the early twentieth. They had no political connection with Quanah Parker, the last chief of the Comanche, with the Great Spirit of the Plains, or with U.S. Indian removal policies. They believed in La Virgen de Guadalupe, Mexican independence, and the expulsion of the French from Mexico.

The stark contrast between Mexican Indians (González's *peones*) and savage North American Indians can be seen in three areas. First, Mexican Indians are educable and gendered: they attend school and learn about the participation of civilized Indians such as Mexico's first indigenous president, Benito Juárez, in the nation-building project of Mexico and Mexican masculinity. Second, Mexican Indian boys don't boast about scalping and raiding; they are the children of laborers who contribute to the local economy. Last, in the school for Mexican Indian children, they are educated in nation building which reinforces the idea that they are safe remnants of the past who do not threaten the present social order or class structure. Unlike the vanished Kiowa, Comanche, and Apache, these generic Mexican Indians, ostensibly the descendents of the extinct Aztecs, are a part of González's imagined Texas-Mexican nation, where they will be productive citizens and laborers.

González anticipates the early Chicano nationalism of the 1970s by presenting a vision similar to that of José Vasconcelos's notion of *la raza cósmica*, expounded when he was minister of education in Mexico in the 1920s. The passage quoted above locates the reader in the late nineteenth century and early twentieth, when Porfirio Díaz was dictator of Mexico (1880–1910), and praises a genealogy of full-blooded Indians and mestizos who were leaders in Mexico.[42] González recognizes the critical importance of Indians in Mexican history and how that history allows for the participation of Indian children in the educational system as part of the making of Texas-Mexican masculinity linked to the national imaginary. More problematic than the nascent nationalism that emerges in this passage as a gendered position of masculinized citizenship, however, is the lack of any criticism of the Porfiriato in the teacher's genealogy. Díaz was in fact a mestizo, but he was responsible for selling out Mexico's economic interests to U.S. capitalists and was also the driving force behind Mexico's attempt to exterminate the Yaqui Indian population in Sonora (see chapters 4, 5).

González portrays a narrative of Indian resistance as the story of the Mexican nation but does not acknowledge Mexican or Texas-Mexican racism against indigenous peoples. Still, the cost of nationalism is the glorification of some events and the erasure of others. *Dew on the Thorn* creates a national fantasy of sorts because she expends so much energy subverting Mexico's Indian heritage in her master's thesis and her other personal writings. In an unpublished essay entitled "Quienes somos," González takes great pains to locate the Texas-Mexican heritage in the conquest of New Spain. She writes, "Spain wished to colonize the land between the Rio Grande and the Nueces River. This land was infested with barbarous Indians, some of whom were cannibals. Even though many Spaniards lived in the New World, no one wished to come to the land of Texas, as it was called in those days. Spain was anxious to colonize this land, for fear that the French would acquire the land."[43] Even though *Dew on the Thorn* recognizes and even celebrates indigenous contributions to Mexican national history, the prehistory of Mexican Texas in "Quienes somos" identifies barbarous, cannibalistic Indians as the factor that deterred colonization of the territory between the Rio Grande and the Rio Nueces. González's essay notes Spain's competing interest in colonizing Texas. The aim in colonizing this land was not simply to Christianize barbarous Indians (most likely Caddo and Karankawa)[44] but also to prevent the French from expanding their territory beyond Louisiana. The contradictory messages in González's work suggest that indigenous peoples were not always celebrated but in fact were seen as detrimental to the development of New Spain and the later Mexican nation. The unpublished "Quienes somos" and the story about making Indians into good Mexican boys demonstrate that in the social and cultural imaginary of Mexican Texas and New Spain indigenous people have been excluded from equal participation as citizens. Instead, as either an obstacle to national development or at best as a citizen in the making, they have been imagined and treated as something other than Texas-Mexican or Mexican.

González's vision is in keeping with that of Vasconcelos, who argued for the whitening of the race. Vasconcelos advocated the breeding out of "negative" indigenous characteristics to form la raza cósmica.[45] The narratives in *Dew on the Thorn* similarly represent the social process of national consolidation of identities—making Indian and Mexican male children into good cultural citizens—and show that supposedly Indian stories and storytelling are integral to borderlands culture. Yet González's bold, if historical, representations of the racist attitudes toward Indians in Mexico and the United States certainly debunk the idea that Chicana/o resistance literature and politics must essentially recover or celebrate indigenous roots. Or, more precisely, González's immigrant Indians are constant reminders that Mexico's indigenous past is connected to the conquest of the Americas, that Indians are celebrated only as primitives of the past, not as its present.[46] They are identified first and foremost as Mexican Indians and secondarily as peones existing on the margins of rancho culture. They are living critiques of racialized gender (Indian masculinity) and labor inequities and also represent the vanished Texas Indians who were removed through the U.S. reservation policy. In claiming González as a feminist icon of Chicana/o nationalism, Chicana/o studies must claim this anti-indigenous vein in her scholarship as well.

In addition, African Americans make only sporadic appearances in González's work on the Rio Grande Valley, suggesting that they were not stakeholders in the power struggles over South Texas. When Texas was annexed in 1845 it was a slave state, and at the start of the Civil War as much as 30 percent of the Texas population was enslaved. In the 1850s Mexico offered safe haven to fugitive slaves who escaped across the border, and border towns like Laredo and Rio Grande City were originally settled by Afro-mestizos.[47] Yet González's rendering suggests African Americans or Afro-mestizos did not exist in Texas, or at least not in South Texas. African Americans and Afro-mestizos mark a different type of masculinized form of racism and a unique period of U.S. history that seems almost isolated in González's archive. One event that is mentioned is the race riot between Texas-Mexicans and African American soldiers stationed at Fort Ringgold in Rio Grande City in 1899. The conflict arose over a gambling hall dispute in which a police officer and a group of Mexicans hit an African American soldier over the head and shot another. But González elides these details in recounting the event in her M.A. thesis: "Immediately trouble arose between the colored troops and Mexicans, who resented their permanency in the town. Conditions grew tense, the Mexican population took the offensive and as a result the Negro troops raided the town."[48] That González reports the event in terms starkly different from those used in newspapers and other sources—for one thing the event was much more violent than she indicates—reflects the fact that she sees African Americans and Afro-mestizos as ancillary to Texas history; racism toward African Americans is an elided part of Texas-Mexican history.

The *Chicago Tribune* reported the townspeople's firing on the troops stationed at Fort Ringgold on November 22, 1899, as follows:

When at the close of the Spanish war the department sent two Negro regiments, the Twenty-fifth Infantry and the Ninth Cavalry to Garrison Texas posts, a general protest was raised. The Mexican population at once became hostile towards the Negroes. This tension between Negro soldiers and the Mexicans resulted in a fight between the Negro soldiers and the Police in Laredo some four weeks ago. . . . Of late some of the soldiers have written letters to friends here saying that their position at Ringgold was unbearable, that the people of the town were tormenting them, and had even fired shots from the town into the reservation. . . . On Monday night the men got possession of the rifles and ammunition and commenced a desultory firing. Instantly all lamps went out and the people began to barricade themselves in their own homes. The shots were directed principally at the saloons and gambling dens and these quarters were quickly deserted.[49]

Although African Americans and Afro-mestizos had served on the Mexican side during the U.S.–Mexico war and the Mexican government had invited them to settle in the northern frontiers in cities like Laredo and Rio Grande City during the period of the Mexican Republic in Texas, the Fort Ringgold riot demonstrates deep-seated racism that cut both ways. The incident showed a multidirectional racism of blacks toward Mexicans and of Mexicans toward blacks inhabiting Rio Grande City at the turn of the twentieth century. According to the version of the story in the *Tribune*, the hostility toward the African American soldiers at Fort Ringgold grew so extreme that Mexican townspeople in Rio Grande City attacked them. The soldiers at the fort convinced their commanding officers to allow them to use arms in retaliation, and they engaged in an armed conflict with the townspeople.

Other reports state that the black troops from the fort fired on defenseless women and children in the city, and they blame the Negro soldiers for instigating the riot. These narratives claim that the Negro soldiers were disgruntled over their gambling losses at a saloon and botched an attempted robbery to recoup their losses. Two of them were shot and one was murdered. The Mexican women who were supposedly cavorting with the African American soldiers, an original source of the tensions leading up to the riot, were said to be prostitutes who only went with black men.[50] Another version of the triggering of the riot is linked to Mexican American support of the Puerto Ricans and Cubans during the Spanish-American War. The company of Negro soldiers was sent to encircle the town, not to protect Mexican Americans but to police them and dampen their sympathetic identification with Spain against Yankee imperialism. These three competing versions of the Fort Ringgold riot show how racial incidents are narrated differently to obscure culpability. Some of the Tejano hostility toward African Americans surely is attributable to the soldiers' disciplining function along the border. After all, were the soldiers there to protect the Republic from Mexican and Mexican American sympathy with Puerto Ricans and Cubans fighting in the Spanish-American War against the United States or to protect the townspeople? Tejano hostility is understandable; some of their animosity toward the black soldiers entering their towns and socializing freely with Mexican American women was also attributable to the Tejano racism against blacks that was a legacy of the Spanish colonial caste system as it related to the intersection of race and masculinity. More interesting are the ways González glosses over the tendency toward racial conflict when blacks were stationed in predominantly Mexican communities in South Texas. This erasure not only minimizes the differences that played out in the Fort Ringgold riot, but also glosses over the fact that Mexicans distinguished between Afro-mestizos and Afro-Americans in the shared colonial history of the Texas borderlands, especially in border towns like Laredo and Rio Grande City, where 40 percent of the towns' founders claimed Afro-mestizo identities.

As the complicated history of race relations in Texas illustrates, African Americans were not considered full citizens of the U.S. nation-state or of the Texas-Mexican national imaginary González recorded. In *Dew on the Thorn*, the narrative of Pedro's journey to Sugarland, Texas, the modern-day home of the Domino Sugar Factory, recalls another type of exploited body in the history of the Americas, the descendants of slaves:

> There was something strange, he said, that he could not understand. Not all Americans were white. He had seen some as black as coal who had wool for hair and big, thick, purple lips. He had gone to one of their dances; but had not been able to stay long. They smelled like buzzards after they had been feasting on carcass and the odor was so strong he could not bear it.

No, he was not mistaken. He was sure they were Americans. Did they not speak English? He had not stayed long at Sugar Land. The dampness was making him have chills. So he had hired himself as a section hand. . . . he had been told that if he ate salt pork he would soon learn to speak English. Bah! What a lie! He had eaten it only days and had only learned to say "Yes."[51]

How was it possible that this other nonwhite racial group he encountered in Sugarland bewildered Pedro? Blacks were a longtime part of the Texas scene. According to Martha Menchaca, in Texas "most slave owners ignored the [emancipation] law, others found ways of complying without releasing their slaves."[52] New to Pedro, this type of American, a dark-skinned descendent of slaves, disrupts his construction of a brown–white racial binary based on region.[53] He also begins to understand that the white-skinned type is not the only kind of American. What follows is a stereotypical caricature of blacks that echoes the popular representations of African Americans through the cultural practices of minstrelsy and films like D. W. Griffith's *Birth of a Nation* (1915), the very images the director Oscar Micheaux tried to counter in his film *Within Our Gates* (1919).

The way Pedro describes African Americans establishes a great divide of racial difference. In some ways, his virulent deployment of scientific racism, comparing their body odor to the smell of a dead animal and describing their "thick, purple lips," expresses the overt racism toward blacks prevalent in U.S. society at the time.[54] The myth that blacks preyed on the dead established a symbolic association of meaning. Such an argument, Holland states, denies them a sustainable subjectivity: "Their presence in society is, like the subject of death, almost unspeakable, so black subjects share the space the dead inhabit."[55] While Pedro's representation does not reveal any feeling of racial or political solidarity between himself and other people of color, he does recognize that they share a lack of voice or presence. Blacks speak English and yet don't have the social capital that usually comes with linguistic proficiency. Pedro has internalized scientific racism and feels superior to blacks, yet he is still treated just as poorly as they are, being fed salt pork and bread. He is fooled into believing the food is good for him because it will help him learn English faster. This racial joke should create a moment of recognition for Pedro, an identification of the ways in which both Mexicans and blacks, if read through contemporary Chicano understandings of race, have been oppressed by the same colonial and capitalist systems. Instead, he distinguishes himself from the African Americans in Sugarland, believing he is somehow better than they are. Menchaca would argue that González's construction of black-ness does not "include Blacks as important historical actors." But in fact González does not deny "their presence in the history of Mexican Americans," as Menchaca suggests; rather, she caricatures them by deploying popular U.S. stereotypes that reinforce racism, thereby allowing Mexicans like Pedro to believe they are just a bit higher in the U.S. racial hierarchy.[56]

SOULLESS WOMEN: RACIALIZED, GENDERED,
AND SEXUALIZED VIOLENCE

González's archive contains several stories about physical violence being car-ried out against the bodies of Texas-Mexican women in the name of order and social norms, and she discusses the implications of their children witnessing such acts. Functioning outside of the spaces of normative community inter-actions and practices, such women are deemed soulless because they cannot participate equally as citizen subjects. Abjection takes on a spatial dimension in these stories, as the soulless are geographically, emotionally, and physically displaced through acts of denial and transgression. Julia Kristeva argues that abjection is "articulated by negation and its modalities, transgression, denial, and repudiation."[57] Drawing on psychoanalytic theory that begins with the law of the father, the secondary repression is the gap between the primary trauma and the secondary trauma, based in the sublimation of an original object.[58] Here, the primary oppression is that original object of rejection of González's soulless women: patriarchal power structures. The secondary ob-ject of repression is the "repelling, rejecting; repelling itself, rejecting itself. Ab-jecting of the gendered, racialized, sexualized self outside of the context of politics, for this process is the pathology of the politically powerless." Further, as Kristeva asserts, "the abject is that pseudo-object that is made up before but appears only within the gaps of secondary repression."[59] Abjection ultimately transforms the abject from subject to object position.

González seems most concerned with the effects of corporal punishment and abjection because they affect both the one who suffers this disciplinary action and those who witness it. Corporal punishment of women and chil-dren may normalize inequality, and yet the repetition of these narratives makes the violence highly visible and abnormal, reifying the abjection of the subject. In *Dew on the Thorn* physical and psychological violence are por-trayed as an acceptable remedy for Doña Rita's melancholic behavior. The disciplining of this deviant body is carried out while her child secretly wit-nesses the event. Doña Rita's corporal punishment instructs her body as to how it should function properly:

When Cristóbal was little, eight at the most, his mother took sick. It was a strange malady; she turned yellow and would neither sleep, talk, nor eat. She just laid in bed staring at the ceiling of the room. What she saw there, if anything, must have been terrible for occasionally she screamed out fearful words and shook her fists at the beams. Don Ramon, her husband, who knew a great deal about home-doctoring, thought at first it was her heart. He gave her a brew of *totonjil* and powdered deer blood for nine consecutive mornings, but that did not cure her malady. This he followed with a *cenizo* tea, which as you know, if left outdoors to be cooled by the night dew will cure any liver trouble. But that did not make her feel any better. The poor man, not knowing what else to do, came to me for advice. Full well did I know what ailed Doña Rita; she was bewitched; but those things are better left unsaid.[60]

The narrator implies that Doña Rita's malady is psychological (although perhaps in fact it was hepatitis or yellow fever),[61] a disease that generally cannot be detected on the body or via physical pain, except via hysterical symptom. Her only physical symptom is the yellowing of her skin. Using his knowledge of holistic herbal treatments, Don Ramon initially treats his wife for heart and liver dysfunction, maladies that can also cause a yellowing of the skin. When Doña Rita does not respond to these traditional treatments, a *curandero*, or indigenous, syncretic doctor of the spiritual, is called in to exorcise the malady from her body. The cultural silence around Doña Rita's condition relegates it to a private matter of shame and guilt. The narrator implies that the bewitched person is weak and susceptible to violence and evil behavior and thus her malady is embarrassing and unspeakable.

The cure comes in the form of a graphic ceremony that violates the sovereignty of the body in order to treat unidentifiable symptoms of illness and abnormality. Doña Rita's exorcism emphasizes the physical brutality that was carried out against the bodies of women but not against those of men. In none of these texts are exorcisms performed on men who cheat on their wives, who are silent, or who sexually abuse their female servants. As Doña Rita's story is told, the storyteller refers to the cultural silence overshadowing the condition of the bewitched, yet when the actual cure is administered Doña Rita's screams cannot be silenced and must be ignored: "He told Ramon to go to the creek and gather all the chili peppers he could find; he was to make a fire with them, close all the doors and windows, and place Doña Rita by the open fireplace. The suffocating vapors would either choke or drive the evil spirits away. This done he was to whip her with a rawhide rope folded three times, made from the hide of a black steer. . . . Tio Anselmo told Ramon not to mind Rita's screams at all. He would be merely chastising the evil spirit that possessed her."[62]

The screams break Doña Rita's inappropriate silence as the men try to nurture her back into reproductive labor by physically trying to erase her depression and ill health. Physical violence presents a way to understand depression, hepatitis, or yellow fever. Here, the confluence of medical treatment and torture, between the alleviation and the infliction of pain, is collapsed in the recommended cure. Religion does not justify the process, so the curandero provides a violent home remedy. The power dynamics in the beating and abuse of Doña Rita's body are so unequal that the voice of the tortured, afflicted subject is to be ignored during the beating and suffocation. Doña Rita neither consents nor speaks; she is simply subjected to the exorcism. This scene of subjection is a perfect example of what Richard Brodhead calls "disciplinary intimacy," wherein there is an extreme personalization of disciplinary authority.[63] The violence is doubled: Doña Rita suffers the physical effects of the beating and her child bears the psychological scars of witnessing the torture:

> In the mean time, unseen by anyone, Cristóbal had entered the room, hidden by darkness. His little pale face streaked with tears as he watched his mother writhe with agony under the cruel blows of his father. Her screams ceased; she fell in a merciful faint. For months she was more dead than alive. I think she would have died too, had it not been for young Cristóbal who, with the pale sorrowful face of the crucified, sat by her bedside day and night and looked with eyes that saw nothing. She recovered, but, and this is the thing that we dare not say, the grandmother finished in a confidential whisper, "it is thought that the evil spirit that left the mother took possession of the boy; for since then he goes about silent, looking at the world with the haunting eyes of the possessed. What is worse he shuns his father Don Ramon. Cristóbal hates his father."[64]

Doña Rita is beaten into unconsciousness. The reader does not witness each blow, but the child does. The violence of the moment causes a psychic break for Cristóbal in which he identifies not with the power of his father but with his mother. He is as terrified as if he had witnessed a death, an execution, or a slave beating in which the master wants his property, his wife, to behave in a certain way. Doña Rita should be happy, attentive, and talkative, not morose, silent, and despondent. "At the moment of trauma," argues the trauma scholar Judith Herman, "the victim is rendered helpless by overwhelming force. . . . When the force is that of other human beings, we speak of atrocities. Traumatic events overwhelm the ordinary systems of care that give people a sense of control, connection, and meaning."[65] The child witness takes on his mother's pain because he cannot escape the weight of the violence. The mother absorbs the physical pain that forces her to break her silence, and the child, concealed by darkness and undetected, witnesses the cruel blows dealt in the name of righting the social order of gender, of restoring the mother and wife to perform her domestic labor. Their trauma robs them both of speech. The mother has ceased to be a mother or to claim her right to her child, and the child in turn shuns his father as the family unit, the site of reproductive labor, disintegrates through violence. The child, through this violence, rejects the standard gendered order of patriarchy by identifying with his mother from this formative moment onward. This event alludes to a collective memory of violence and cultural misunderstanding in which women were beaten for not adhering to cultural norms and gender expectations. The patriarch's attempt to reestablish his own gendered sense of order in the family, to reestablish familiarity with his wife, turns against itself, in that power is always already about the father and not the mother. Furthermore, the child subject is obliterated. This new economy of violence operates in an older belief system that did not understand that maladies like depression, yellow fever, and hepatitis have psychological effects.

The possession or bewitchment and the communal silence about it are broken only by whispered gossip, bodily utterances, and González's actual recounting of the story as folklore, a form based on retelling.[66] While Cristóbal and Doña Rita remain silent, their silence registers a kind of protest that speaks volumes without actually naming intrafamilial violence. This silence undermines romantic representations of the Chicana/o family in the story of Doña Rita's illness, which is announced to the community as an object lesson of discipline. From the time he witnesses the violence at age eight until he is fourteen Cristóbal is governed by silence. Each encounter with his father or story about patriarchy and its effects on women demonstrates how a scene of violence, once witnessed, refuses to be buried. The only way Cristóbal partially heals his trauma in the narrative is through caring for his mother. The violation of mother and child rips the family apart, negating the possibility of "the family becom[ing] a locus of resistance, the building block for communities of people racially oppressed and otherwise."[67] Cristóbal formulates his own pattern of behavior against violent patriarchal regimes through his hatred of his father. The only power Cristóbal has in this system is to deny that his father exists and to mourn the losses of both his father and the caring and engaged mother he once had. His care for Doña Rita literally enacts what Butler calls the process of keeping "the dead object alive, but to keep the living object from 'death,' where death means the death of love, including the occasions of separation and loss."[68] This reading of melancholia follows a Freudian view: "In spite of his fourteen years there was something about Cristóbal that made him act and appear older. A certain sadness, a certain indescribable melancholy permeated a spirit which should have been young. His long, thin face, pale and sad, had the ascetic beauty of a medieval saint, and his black, haunting eyes had neither light or sparkle. He spoke in monosyllables, never laughed and his smile, when he smiled, was bitter. It was the smile of a soul that weeps."[69]

Cristóbal becomes the figure of the abject; he is a misunderstood, melancholy child that is perhaps queered.[70] If the mother's despondency is in fact a depression that denaturalizes her gendered position—makes her inattentive to her gendered duties (housekeeping, tending to the children, and having sex with her husband)—then the son's mimetic identification with her substantiates this denaturalization of gender roles and thus queers him. He refuses his rightful role identified with the masculine power of the patriarch (his father), opting instead for the queered or feminized role of caregiver. The melancholia of Doña Rita's children turns their gender identification against their sex. The women argue, " 'He is bewitched.' . . . 'And possessed by an evil spirit beside,' said another. 'They say he talks to the dead.' 'Yes, at night he and three devils play ball with the eyes of sleeping children who have been naughty during the day.' "[71] Cristóbal's condition might best be described as melancholia secondary to experiencing loss. According to Butler, loss is "the condition of uncompleted grief. The foreclosure of certain forms of love suggests the way that the melancholia that grounds the subject signals a complete and irresolvable grief. Unowned and incomplete, melancholia is the limit to the subject's sense of pouvoir, its sense of what it can accomplish and, in that sense, its power."[72] In a reaffirmation of the power system that caused the child's melancholy, one of the women suggests, "If I were his father I would whip the Devil out of him," returning us to the scene of torture and violence against his mother and, by extension, against Cristóbal.[73] By this time Cristóbal understands the inequality of gender relations and views male–female interactions as violent.

If one reads Doña Rita and Cristóbal as two more of González's gendered, racialized figures of the living dead in the Texas-Mexican national imaginary, subjects that occupy a space between life and death, then the story functions to reconstruct the life of a voiceless woman through her child's care giving. In this narrative González does more than fashion a folktale: she critiques the ruses of violent power that disfigure both the literal bodies of women and children and their formation as subjects within the structure of the family and the larger structure of the community. In response to Cristóbal's hatred of his father, Tío Patricio was "somewhat worried because he could not dislodge from the boy's mind, the unpleasant thoughts about his father."[74] What Tío Patricio did not understand was the insidious ways in which abuse formed Cristóbal's sense of self in relation to his father. He does not recognize trauma as a form of abuse. As Herman argues, "Child abuse takes place in a familial climate of pervasive terror, in which ordinary care taking relationships have been profoundly disrupted."[75] Tío Patricio does not take into account this rupture of familial roles in his attempt to regulate Cristóbal's beliefs. While in some contexts this might be a step toward recovery, González's narrative reveals that the silence surrounding Doña Rita's beating has infiltrated every aspect of family life. According to Tío Patricio's version of the story, Don Ramon's whole family was damaged by his act of extreme physical violence against his wife:

His two daughters are like mournful doves; they are always sad and the youngest child, my little mouse, has inherited his mother's illness. Doña Rita was once possessed of an evil spirit, but my master whipped it out of her. That was five years ago and Cristóbal saw it done. Since then he cannot stand to be near his father. . . . But he worships Doña Rita, and whenever she is not well, the child will sit by her bedside and never eat nor sleep. Don Ramon has brought the doctor to see him, but the child remained the same. The women at the ranch wag their tongues and say that the evil spirit that left Doña Rita possesses the child now. . . . Everyone . . . suffers from *susto* at one time or another. I understand why so many people die in town. People get a susto, explained the shepherd, when they have been terribly frightened, or when they have had a shock. At times when the shock is very great the spirit always leaves the body. I know that this is what troubles my Little Mouse. He has all the symptoms. He is pale, he does not talk much and at night has terrible dreams of spirits and ghosts. He lives in constant dread of being bewitched.[76]

Tío Patricio uses the language of medical diagnosis and bewitchment to explain this phenomenon. But the victim and the traumatized witnesses— Doña Rita and her children—remember the event in their bodies through their pained state of being: pallidness, an inability to speak, and the torment of bad dreams as queering effects that turn their gender against their sex. This is the second time her story is told. As storyteller, Tío Patricio is distanced from the event, which enables him to theorize about how negative energy can be transferred between people and how susto accounts for the family's melancholia.

The dead and specifically the living dead tell people things they do not know about themselves and their history. As marginal people, the living dead symbolically teach us about power inequities. Cristóbal, his sisters, and his mother all loom large in this Texas-Mexican community as people who are mournful, are living dead, and are contextualized by the presence of illness. Doña Rita's beating is not justified; rather, it is described as a reaction to her susto, which translates into "shock" in English. Susto is a culturally specific way of interpreting states like depression, shock, alienation, or fright. Tío Patricio describes the separation of body and spirit, a split subjectivity caused when "the spirit leaves the body" in an instance of susto.[77] This separation of the spirit, or the material essence of the soul, from the body that contains it accounts for the alienation and loss I discussed earlier—this is abjection. While beatings like the one Doña Rita suffered deny their victims a sustainable subjectivity, interpreting the "spiritual possession" as susto opens the door to a bit more sympathetic and less violent interpretation in the Texas-Mexican cultural framework. As Tío Patricio says, susto is common, normal, even though the beating and its effects suggest otherwise.

Doña Rita experiences such extreme physical and psychological violence as being based on issues of discipline and its relationship to intimacy. Doña Rita is disciplined for her failure to fulfill her gender responsibilities, and the beating takes place in the intimacy of the home and takes shape as a form of care: Don Ramón turns to the curandero presumably out of love for his wife. The most brutal forms of violence come at the hands of people who are known to the sufferer, which makes the trauma even more unbearable.

González's treatment of social mores in regard to education and women's roles as she observed them in her ethnographic work can serve to introduce my reading of the next story of the living dead. Michel Foucault argues it is no coincidence that in the Victorian period educational and other types of institutions, prisons, for example, became sites of punishment and discipline that were hidden from public view.[78] Educational institutions as disciplinary structures are no doubt what set the tone for another of González's stories about soulless woman.

In her master's thesis González traces the history of public and private education in Cameron, Starr, and Zapata counties, beginning with the Convent of the Incarnate Word, which opened a school for girls in 1853. St. Joseph's School for boys was opened in 1886. Both schools enrolled the daughters and sons of "conservative Texas-Mexicans of the border."[79] Public education was far more advanced in Cameron County than in Starr or Zapata counties because the capital of Cameron, Brownsville, was a commercial center. Up until roughly 1905, "the wealthy sent their children to the schools in Mexico, principally in Monterrey and Saltillo, those in moderate circumstances sent theirs to private Mexican schools in Texas. . . . This was a way for the border people to retain their racial characteristics and character intact, parents took the necessary steps to attain this end, and this was to give their children a Mexican education" in Texas.[80] In other words, it was expected that the elite would give their children a proper Mexican education, even if that meant sending them outside the geographical boundaries of the Texas-Mexican home community.

In *Dew on the Thorn*, Lucia chooses education over marriage, is administered a love potion, and goes mad as a result. This story represents a larger Texas-Mexican social commentary about the limited options for women outside of marriage and the disciplining they undergo for making such choices. According to the community, "it was thought best to forget" the incidents surrounding Lucia's madness. Her story is not a generic narrative that cuts across cultures; rather, it shows culturally specific Texas-Mexican problems that arise when patriarchy controls women's bodies and desires, political, educational, or otherwise. One of the vaqueros recounts that Lucia was joyful and curious, intelligent and proud, and the narrator describes her as being "full of devilment":

> She had spent most of her life in a convent school in town and when she returned to her father's ranch, she lacked no suitors. *But she did not want to marry. She wanted to go away to school, college I think they call it, and learn all that is found in books.* It would have pleased her mother if she had married Fernando, the master's nephew. But she paid him no mind; not that she was a flirt and liked to play with men's affections; she just did not love anyone. Neither did she pay attention to another suitor she had in town. He was a much older man, a widower, I believe, who had lots of money. Some say he made it smuggling, others said he was a gambler. Anyway he was a man that could not be trusted and Lucita hated him. Hearing that the girl was to go away he came to the ranch and asked for her hand officially. He was not discouraged at their refusal. It is said though, he swore he would have her some way or another. She laughed at this; but her mother was somewhat perturbed, fearing that he might use some dark means to win her.[81]

Lucia's refusal of her suitors and of a life that would reinforce familial relations of power through a marriage to the master's nephew devalues the upper-middle-class ideals of proper womanhood. Instead, she seeks liberation through education, which is the way not to become a better wife but to avoid becoming a wife altogether. Her experience in the convent school laid the foundation for the only alternative available to daughters during this time: the occupation of teacher. Yet the social economy only temporarily allows Lucia to believe she will avoid marriage and obtain her freedom through education. González's ethnographic work tells us that, even within convent schools, texts such as *Preceptos peculiares a las niñas* (1900) disciplined women even within the supposed space of freedom within the confines of school. Granted, this was religious education. For example, Lesson 4 states, "In all actions, one must manifest modesty. Don't cross your knees or sit by forcing your spine against the back of the chair; procure the descending nature of the dress so that it covers the leg and advert the eyes with obedience because it is a very ugly thing to look with barefaced effrontery, and that is the mark of a lost woman most certainly." Modesty, above all else, governs and disciplines the bodies of young educated girls, for there is nothing more perverse and immoral than a young woman looking directly into the eyes of a man. As this convent school lesson indicates, the body is a social text that renders gender as a spatial practice. There are even further problems for this disciplined body if the girl or woman does not follow a traditional heterosexual lifestyle.

Lucia is an allegory of discipline for wanting to be educated rather than to marry. González again presents a struggle in which men desire literally to own and control a body they cannot call their property. The spell cast on Lucia is symptomatic of how active bodies are made docile and inactive through domination. Her rejected suitor sends her a letter infected with a love potion. On her way to the train station en route to "some school where teachers are made," Lucia's father "had noticed how pale she turned, but she offered no explanation as to the contents [of the letter], neither did he inquire. A letter from some lovesick suitor, he thought, and let it go at that." Similarly, one might see Lucia's stunned silence as an attempt to avoid what Anzaldúa calls the repercussions of bad breeding: "Having a big mouth, questioning, carrying tales are all signs of being mal criada."[82] Silence becomes a function of both class and gender. The father does not question because it would be improper, and the woman does not reveal the threat her suitor poses for fear of being thought *mal criada*. The physical transformation of Lucia's countenance, her pale face, and her body language indicate that she is deeply disturbed. However, polite cultural practices of the upper classes lead the father to "let it go." The father drops her off at the convent, where she will live in the protective care of the nuns as she continues her education: "Sometime after midnight the whole convent was awakened by the girl's screams. The nuns found her screaming and beating her head against the walls of the room. A doctor was called, but there was nothing that he could do. No doubt the powders sent in the letter had already entered her brain. The doctor had to place her in a straitjacket and in that condition she was brought home to her mother."[83] The story can be read as one of revenge by a spurned lover, but also as one of a woman being punished for having ambitions beyond the rancho and marriage to a man she does not love.

Mirroring the embodiment of Anzaldúa's shadow-beast in her description of the Coatlicue state, Lucia's "spin into madness" can also be read as a formation of dissident subjectivity that is abnormal within this cultural framework. Her body literally bears what Anzaldúa calls "la seña, the mark of the beast."[84] In the words of the narrator, Lucita "became as wild as a beast, could not walk like a human being, but crouched on the floor and lapped her food the same as an animal. She jumped on all fours about the padded room and dashed her body against the walls. Her mother realized that some evil spell had been cast upon her and to make sure, placed a crucifix under her pillow and she who had been so religious screamed at the sight of it. The priest from town came to see her and when she saw him enter she flew at him scratching his face and spitting on him."[85]

On the surface, Lucia descends to uncivilized, unladylike behavior because of the spell. She is a shadow of her former self and of her image as a representation of virginal womanhood. Instead, she now embodies the spirit presence of violence. Alienation from her own body mirrors the description of fear Anzaldúa gives in her paragraph on the "no name woman" (see chapter 1).[86] After citing the fear of having no name and many names, Anzaldúa discusses the ways in which Lucia's body can betray the self. Her desire to be educated is betrayed by her body's succumbing to the spell. Her simultaneous embodiment of and alienation (abjection) from her body function is a way of contesting the spell. Lucia refuses to sink into a melancholic state like Doña Rita, producing the appearance of madness and the "change that had come upon her." If the spell had worked and she had accepted its terms—namely, falling in love with the rejected suitor—she would simply have left the convent for a melancholic marriage to the old man.

González posits madness as a viable, although physically brutal, subject position. While the narrator focuses on the physical brutality of Lucia's transformation, in a feminist reading of this story one needs to focus on the story's result. For the narrator, "the little hands I so loved to see, the little fingers once so pink and nimble were out of joint and hung yellow and limp like a calf's tail. . . . The shaven head, the black curls had been cut off because she pulled her hair out by the handful, the look of madness in her eyes, the face distorted and bereft of all beauty. She would not lay down even when death was upon her, she continued jumping and leaping like a frog. She died crouched on the floor like a sick lamb."[87] While the narrator is terrified by this bodily shift— from the ideal representation of womanhood to a woman who lacks beauty and dies alone and alienated from her community—what becomes most apparent in this story is that Lucia's suffering is caused entirely because she wanted an education instead of marriage to a vile old man.

In the aftermath of Lucia's death, her family discovers the truth about her madness: "After the funeral, the mother examined all the letters and she found the one she had received. It was from the rejected suitor and was covered with a yellowish powder. What can be done about such things? The scandal would have been too great. *It was thought best to forget.*"[88] The desire to forget the bodies of tortured, murdered, and maligned women, as Holland argues about Toni Morrison's *Beloved*, is "a cruel and self-centered process."[89] In Lucia's case, forgetting is another violent process wherein the memory of the dead is repeatedly violated in order to preserve a sense of normalcy. Family honor is more important than the injury that took Lucia's life. Well-being and social justice are sacrificed in the name of social graces. This process of "disremembering,"[90] this act of attempted erasure, links to a tradition in the regional and national imaginaries in which the subjugated bodies of women of color present object lessons that must be retold at the most inopportune moments to discipline other women, even when the majority of the community is making a concerted effort to forget them. At the conclusion of the narrative, the men say, "That's the queer thing about it, you fall in love with the person who owns [the spell] whether you want to or not."[91] But Lucia does not fall in love with the old man; instead, her madness, like Doña Rita's silence, represents her fight to preserve her desires and will as a political subject. The issue here is not that Lucia is silenced but that her voice is unintelligible; like Doña Rita's illness, Lucia's voice mirrors the self-inflicted and institutionalized torture that result from resisting power external to the body. Her refusal to marry renders her mad because her refusal of marriage is a form of social death. González's multiple representations of these injured racialized women trace a storytelling tradition of women who are physically persecuted, who become figures of abjection. While the stories of soulless women unseat the Chicana/o and Tejana/o familial romance of national consolidation through the bodies of women, González's retelling of these stories as cautionary folktales seems to participate in disciplining as well.

González's chapter "The Woman Who Lost Her Soul," raises fundamental questions about gender and subjectivities on the border: Who or what has made the protagonist of this story believe she has lost her soul? What gendered religious and cultural practices allow such communal alienation to happen?[92] I believe that this story is an allegory for the disenfranchised, fallen women of the border who live on the margins of Texas-Mexican rancho society: without a nation, without a home, without a family, in between cultural and actual citizenship in the United States and Mexico. "The languorous indolence pervading the atmosphere was that easygoing way peculiar to the Mexican temperament. This quietude and stillness was broken by a childish cry, 'La Desalmada, La Desalmada'—literally, the woman without a soul."[93] La Desalmada, whose actual name is Carmen, represents an inversion of the La Llorona story. The displaced woman does not cry out to punish people when she makes her apparition-like appearance in the community. Instead, the community cries out at the sight of her, and their fear continues to alienate the young girl as she enacts her own self-disciplining at every turn.

The community develops a fear of the abject when, at the sight of the Desalmada, "the girl on the porch, presumably frightened, dropped her guitar and crossed herself. The children in the schoolyard ceased their play; even the youths ran into the yard, roosters under arm. As the cry of alarm floated down the narrow street, the same demonstrations of fear were shown."[94] Life's daily rhythms and rituals stop, as if time stands still, with the appearance of La Desalmada. This story represents oppression in the spatialized community. Women and children view La Desalmada in violent terms as a dangerous threat to communal morality. In "The Powers of Horror: Approaching Abjection," Kristeva argues that "the abject simultaneously beseeches and pulverizes the subject, one can understand that it is experienced at the peak of its strength when that subject, weary of fruitless attempts to identify with something on the outside, finds the impossible within; when it finds that the impossible constitutes its very being, that it is none other than abject."[95] Building upon Kristeva's notion of the abject, I hold this to be the most extreme form of rejection, when the subject realizes that there is no one to identify with and that no one identifies with him or her. Suspended in time and place outside the living, the figure of the abject, the woman without a soul finds it impossible to identify herself as anything but a void and thus enacts her own kind of self-disciplining.

" 'Maldita, maldita,' she heard them yell, shaking their fists at a woman in black. The woman stopped as though in fear. She drew a black shawl over her face and in a moment disappeared into a dark alley."[96] This particular Texas-Mexican community's cohesiveness and identity as good, moral people have been formed through exclusion of La Desalmada. One can read the dispossessed woman without a soul as symptomatic of the twin projects of nation building and community building. Such projects, argue the editors of *Between Woman and Nation*, are "always predicated upon Woman as trope, displacing historical women" so that the formation of communities and nations is dependent upon ostracized, abject figures like La Desalmada.[97] She is not known as a woman with a name and with cultural citizenship; instead, she is defined by the fact that the community believes she doesn't have a soul. Here, nation and community are built in opposition to the symbolic figure of La Desalmada. Her anonymity is what allows La Desalmada to haunt the community; her name has been replaced with a description of her in which the "I" no longer exists. Her name invokes Anzaldúa's no-name woman, whom the Chicana feminist critic Norma Alarcón describes as a project to discover one's identity as generative in both positive and negative ways.[98] In an effort to redeem the girl and her unknown name, Don Francisco, who has no knowledge of La Desalmada's story, follows her home: "He ran after the woman determined to find out more about the strange incident he had just seen." The scene of abjection, the violent alienation of this girl from the community, instills in Don Francisco a curiosity, and he chases her, much as in the La Llorona story, in which men are intrigued and then the spirit turns on them: "Stumbling over the rocks and rugged cracks, he followed the fleeting black figure almost hidden by the darkness. . . . He followed fascinated by a morbid curiosity." Don Francisco's "morbid curiosity" becomes an adventure as he tracks her through deserted streets, wanting to know what the black figure truly is. Arriving at her hut, he asks to be let in. She replies, " 'But you cannot come near me, Señor. I am accursed. I am La Desalmada.' 'La Desalmada?' 'Yes[,] the woman without a soul.' 'That's why I must see you,' Francisco replied, humoring her, not having the least idea what she meant." Don Francisco does not understand the gender-specific meaning of being without a soul: that she is a fallen woman. Carmen recreates her rejection and becomes the site of self-discipline by trying to prevent any interaction with Don Francisco, and she effectively reproduces her own abjection: "But Francisco could see that the woman before him was beautiful, but beautiful in an unearthly way. Her face, pale as wax, reminded him of the face of an ivory medieval statue. Her eyes were black, fathomless pools, shimmering like black diamonds in the night."[99]

He is rendered speechless at her beauty, for she is not like anything in the world of the living. Erotic power is the only kind of social power she wields, again marking her as outside of Anglo and Texas-Mexican male circles of political power. In the style of a confession, La Desalmada offers to tell her story, but only so that "others may profit by my sinful actions. . . . But you must promise to tell it again and again."[100] This story can serve as a cautionary tale, so that others do not repeat her mistakes. However, there is an insistence, in this case, by González that speaking the story will counteract the narrative of silence. Each time La Desalmada insists on her story being told she effectively counteracts the power of the unspeakable, especially in the Chicano and Tejano national romance, as such a narrative would be an embarrassment to patriarchy and to the men and women who actively identify with and benefit from it. By repeating the story of her abjection, La Desalmada will become more real, perhaps regaining a semblance of her life prior to being disciplined. Candidly she admits, " 'Yes, Señor, I have no soul,' she said with the simplicity and conviction of a child."[101] But what does it mean to be soulless? Butler describes being without a soul in relation to disciplinary power in *The Psychic Life of Power*: "The transposition of the soul into an exterior and imprisoning frame for the body vacates the interiority of the body, leaving that interiority as a malleable surface for the unilateral effects of disciplinary power."[102] Recuperation of the soul can be achieved only by recognizing the discursive power that prevents the subject from comprehending how it is being formed by disciplinary power. Disciplinary power exerted by the community makes Carmen cease to be Carmen and to become La Desalmada, the figure of abjection. Only after Don Francisco hears the narrative and speaks to the priest is the girl's name revealed to be Carmen. The soul is supposed to be the essence of the human being, the ultimate reflection of interiority, the thing that ascends into heaven when the body is dead. In the Catholic context of this story, not having a soul means that one does not have the internal goodness to be saved by God. Her belief that she has no soul imprisons Carmen in a hell on earth.

La Desalmada has not always been without a soul; she had one before she was expelled from the community. As she tells Don Francisco,

Once I had a home and was happy, and because my parents had no other children, I was spoiled and selfish. Our friends considered me beautiful and were proud of me. . . . The praises of those who knew me turned my head and I became arrogant and haughty. My admirers were many. . . . Like all the girls of my class I lived a life of seclusion. But what does that matter when flashing dark eyes speak? I encouraged all, but I accepted no one. Why did I not marry? Because my perverse nature wanted the only thing I could not have. I loved the only man whose love was prohibited by all that was true. I loved Julio, the promised husband of Rosario, my best friend. My eyes told him what my lips could not utter. Every evening when all was quiet, he came to the raja of the window to talk to me. At this time something happened that made me more determined than ever to keep Julio for myself. . . . Why should she have everything while I had nothing?[103]

González chronicles the girl's fall from innocence when Julio returns her love. In naming her life choices as perverse, La Desalmada has internalized the community's view that a woman enacting her own desires is perverse and has bought into reproducing the oppression she experiences. La Desalmada cites her selfishness, her secluded life, and her love for Julio as her sins. The community sees her sin not as desiring Julio but as having everything and wanting more. The tale's object lesson comes from the community's insistence on policing her desires and directing them onto appropriate objects. Carmen/La Desalmada is a woman consumed with guilt because she acted upon her forbidden desires: she loved her best friend's beau. Such a distrust of desire and of the body leads to living in constant fear of sin and to being policed by a moral system that rejects female desire and the female body. Anzaldúa argues that "the Catholic and Protestant religions encourage fear and distrust of life and of the body; they encourage a split between the body and the spirit and totally ignore the soul; they encourage us to kill off parts of ourselves."[104] Anzaldúa articulates a split subjectivity that separates the rationality of the mind from the body, naturalizing the separation of body and spirit. To González, La Desalmada embodies this mistrust of the body and its desires. While the actual events of Carmen's dishonesty and the death of her best friend cause guilt, that guilt, with the help of the social and political imagination of Carmen's family and the community, transforms her into an oppressed and burdensome beast.

To adhere to the standards of female sexual desire Carmen tells Julio she can no longer see him: she must reject the very thing she desires so that Julio's and Rosario's marriage can take place. La Desalmada says,

I let him see the enormity of our sin and our wickedness and I urged him not to see me again. . . . But in spite of the heartache, I felt free and lighthearted because of my sacrifice. As Julio kissed my hand in a last farewell, Rosario came in. She did not say anything. . . . Early the next morning as I was watering the flowers in the patio, Rosario came in, pale as death. She gasped a few words and fell at my feet. She was dead. She held something white in her hand. It was a note to me. "You have tortured me on earth," it said, "my spirit will torture yours from Hell!"[105]

In a reversal of subject positions, Rosario speaks as the living dead through her note, avenging her betrayal. The image of the dead, virginal Rosario calls to mind a woman's vendetta against another woman, what Sonia Saldívar-Hull calls male-identified behavior.[106] This Texas-Mexican Catholic belief system places the blame on Carmen, the fallen woman who is not a citizen subject, instead of holding Julio equally accountable for his sexual desires.

"No sooner was Rosario dead than my soul began to be tormented. . . . Call it remorse, call it Hell or what you may, my soul was in agony," Carmen says.[107] Anthropologists, among them Akhil Gupta, have written of this transference of souls from one body to another: if "one dies unexpectedly the memory of the past is still alive" and attaches itself to another being or animal.[108] La Desalmada takes on the dead girl's pain out of guilt:

My parents, disgraced because of the shame that had befallen them because of my bad behavior, disowned me and I was shunned by our former friends as one unclean. My mother took to her bed and when she was buried a few days later, my father and I were the only ones who accompanied her to her resting place. My father left town but I could not. Something, some unknown force kept me close to the grave of my victim. Now I am as one unclean, a living corpse, for my soul is with my victim in hell. I cannot eat, I cannot sleep. I tramp the streets in hopes that the weariness of my body will make me forget.[109]

Speaking in terms of alienation and abjection, La Desalmada believes not only that she is responsible for Rosario's death, but also that through her transgressive behavior she has killed her mother and driven her father away. The story is in effect González's commentary on the ways in which religious and cultural beliefs punish women for their intimate relationships but not men. Julio does not suffer for promising his love to two women; instead, La Desalmada carries the burden of gender inequality in her abjection.

La Desalmada haunts the community as it tries to erase her presence, but Rosario comes to haunt her: "Then I see her as I saw her last. Her eyes pierce mine like a dagger and with a cry of anguish her voice rings out, 'My spirit suffers in hell because of you.' I wake up in despair—Oh! The agony, the suffering and the remorse of a lost soul!"[110] Haunting in this case blurs the boundaries between spiritual torture, mental anguish, and reconciliation to one's actions and their consequences. The effect, which might be called hallucinations or spiritual possession, leaves La Desalmada unable to distinguish who she is from what she has done. The past intrudes on the present every time Rosario's dead face appears to her. If one's soul and mental stability are dependent upon community acceptance, then social interaction participates in the obliteration of the subject, as it was known prior to the discovery of guilt. The space of community here is regulatory and policing. As Mary Pat Brady has argued, "The use of space to naturalize violent racial, gender, sexual and class ideologies" is nothing new.[111] Further, in *The Melancholy of Race*, Anne Cheng argues that "social relations live at the heart of psychical dynamics and . . . the complexity of those dynamics bespeaks a wide range of complicated, conflictual, interlocking emotions: desire and doubt, affirmation and rejection, projection and identification, management and dysfunction."[112] The binary relations Cheng identifies dramatize the psychic power of the social. The very notions of being human and of being a man or woman are formed through social relations. Hence, La Desalmada's struggle can be understood as a fight to reclaim her original subjectivity, which has been displaced by guilt and abjection, in the form of these paired terms.

Symbolically, Carmen is a sign of guilt and transgression, a woman who desired more than what she had. We may look at her as reflective of Judith Herman's notion of captivity, where surveillance enforces a structure of repetitive guilt, where the guilt keeps reproducing itself in an unending cycle. This process, according to Herman, "produces profound alterations in the victim's identity."[113] As the embodiment of abjection, Carmen completely fears the people of the community. She is outside of the domestic economy, being neither a nun nor a married woman. She has been displaced from all social and domestic intercourse, the two spaces in which women's participation matters most. Even after the priest absolves her of her sins, La Desalmada consults a witch doctor: " 'My soul,['] she said, [']was in the liver of a toad, and only through many incantations would it be restored to its proper place.' As she said the last words her eyes became distorted with fear. Like one in pain she shrieked, her trembling hand pointing to a dark corner of the room. 'It comes—it comes—for my soul!' A toad hopped into the middle of the room blinking its eye solemnly. . . . 'My soul is gone—my soul is lost.' "[114] Her fear of the toad signals another blurring of boundaries where spirits are transferred to nonhuman objects, where subjectivity is pathologized outside of the realm of the human or individual control.

Upon hearing La Desalmada's story, Don Francisco sees it as his social project as communal patriarch to redeem the abject, not by changing the gender and race system that causes her oppression and disenfranchisement, but by removing her from the oppressive context. Don Francisco speaks with the priest, who says he blames her parents more than her for the abjection she experiences. When Don Francisco and the priest come to restore her to the community of humans, Carmen is still in disbelief. The priest says, " 'I, Father Jose Maria, say this to you: your soul is safe. It is in God's keeping. You understand?' 'You mean I am free?' "[115] Once Carmen is taken out of her netherworld of the soulless, she joins a new community that accepts her as Carmen, not La Desalmada. She has an opportunity to recuperate the "I" that was lost through her abjection. In this new environment she does not direct her rage against herself or continue to control herself according to cultural norms. Through the intervention of Don Francisco and the priest (who embody the power of patriarchy) Carmen is rescued from wandering the streets and from her apparent madness but not from the oppressive gender system of power. Among González's stories of women who are tortured by their communities or by sexual violators, La Desalmada is the only one in which the woman is redeemed. The story is a critique of the cultural double standard of desire that erases Carmen's subjectivity, again suggesting that the soulless and socially dead are not political stakeholders in border life and that these socially dead subjects are more often than not women.

CONCLUSION

González argues that her generation of Texas-Mexicans "bring with them the broader view, a clearer understanding of the good and bad qualities of both races. They are the converging element of two antagonistic civilizations; they have the blood of one and have acquired the ideas of the other."[116] But she says little or nothing about Afro-mestizos, African Americans, or American Indians or about the specific place of women in this convergence. Instead, she focuses on the two competing nationalisms and dominant races, Anglo-Texans and Texas-Mexicans, and cultures of the United States and Mexico. While scholars can read her focus as an act of discursive violence for what it elides in terms of race and gender, we should remember that González was a product of her historical moment. Nevertheless, scholars must examine these other stories as the means by which socially dead subjects speak from a place of death, to show how Indians, both Plains tribes and the Aztecs of Mexico, and blacks, both mestizo and American, uncomfortably haunt the Texas-Mexican national imaginary. Much like Josefa/Juanita, they become subjects only when they are physically or metaphorically disciplined and wounded, and thus they occupy psychic space as the socially dead subjects of the actual space of South Texas.

Both the presence of these figures and their violent erasure in scenes of what could be called the Texas-Mexican national imaginary compete with U.S. and Mexican visions of national history. These competing imaginaries are pivotal to the underlying history of violence in the borderlands and to understanding this space of death. The silence in those narratives about the violent past warns us of the ever-present suffering and pain of living that is compounded by the contested existence of González's border people, especially border subjects who were outside the nexus of Anglo and Texas-Mexican male power regimes and thereby outside of González's Texas-Mexican national imaginary.

Here, social death, erasure, and actual physical death position racialized, sexualized, and gendered individuals to speak only from their relationship to violence. Some of the foundational myths González reiterates depend upon narratives of vanished cultures and disfigured bodies. In particular, these narratives erase North American Indian groups and marginalize African Americans to make their foundational fictions a seamless narrative of racial harmony that in reality was anything but.[117] The literal space of the border becomes the locus where González constructs a social history that begins with the arrival of the Spaniards and the colonization of the New World. Battered bodies nevertheless loom large in Texas history: the slave body and its descendants, the Afro-mestizo settlers of Laredo and Rio Grande City, the disappeared American Indian body, generic Aztec or Mexican Indian peones, and the bodies of displaced and battered Texas-Mexican women and their children. González's work situates her anthropological subjects within a nexus of complicated colonial regimes, one in which we move from simple hegemonic pictures of the folk to stories of the violated socially dead who, through the very presence of their gendered, racialized bodies, shift the discourses of citizenship and rights into discourses that defy the definite terms of Spanish and Anglo-American colonization. In this close examination of González's scholarly contributions I offer a critique of gender and the author's racist musings, in order to make evident how the discourse of resistance is insufficient. Chicana/o studies scholarship must develop new paradigms for its analysis of history and folklore, especially in the face of González's work. She replicates a hegemonic vision of Spanish caste and U.S.-based race relations in her rendering of the Texas-Mexican national imaginary, one that incisively critiques gender inequality but that colludes with rather than offering a critique of U.S. and Mexican racial ideologies.

PART TWO ✳

Like the silence surrounding Mexican and Indian forms of racialized violence in the Camp Grant massacre and Jovita González's erasure of non-Aztec Indians from the historical record, the actual social and discursive practices of the Mexican and U.S. governments vis-à-vis the Yaqui Indians in the Arizona–Sonora borderlands between 1876 and 1907 remain relatively unmarked in Chicana/o, Mexican, and U.S. national histories. This silence surrounding Porfirian-era genocidal projects obscures the role of institutional violence, torture, and sexual violation in a regionally specific history of removal that was officially declared by Porfirio Díaz on November 18, 1886, to be "equivalent . . . to initiating a war of extermination, because the Indian prefers death to exile, and faced with the prospect of being driven from his home, he will fight to the death."[1] The daily correspondence among consulates, state departments, and military officers demonstrates that this call for state-sanctioned violence, which triggered the Yaqui Indian wars, was the result of a wavering but nonetheless ever-present desire by Mexican (and by extension U.S.) venture capitalists and their government to make resistant bodies into what Foucault calls "docile bodies," a project that was never quite completed. The plethora of materials and correspondence in the archival record about governmental policies expresses the gravity of the political and economic situation forged by the Yaqui wars and other social crises (for example, the war with Guatemala in 1885, Apache raids into Sonora and Chihuahua, and the caste wars in Yucatán). The majority of the correspondence cited here follows a pattern of action on the part of the state and its actors, essentially asking for a response to Yaqui movements that caused social disorder. At the same time, this excessive surveillance demonstrated how space and bodies became increasingly measured and tracked as a part of the Porfiriato's charge toward modernity. To take full measure of this material and to painstakingly chart a single, well-chosen example and do a measure of justice to the history, I divide the last half of the book into two chapters.

In chapter 4 I examine government policy and military agency records from Díaz's regime and U.S. archives to show how hegemonic narratives of nation erase scenes of violence as points of origins and substitute genealogies to underwrite the unequal power relations within traditional hierarchies of families, labor, and nations based on a clear goal of achieving modernity.[2] By tracking deportations, confessions, and military maneuvers, I uncover how Mexican officials' enactment of state-sanctioned violence upon Yaqui subjects was and continues to be effectively hidden from public view as this history is shuttled to the side in favor of the history of the Mexican Revolution. The chapter shows the necessity of analyzing gendered and raced state violence; of challenging foundationalist conceptions of agency and resistance; of moving beyond the assumption that all talk about the border is necessarily trans-national; and of taking Latino studies in general and Chicano and border studies in particular into Mexico and into Mexican archives. Moving through these archives and episodes in the chapter, I examine the forging of railways in and between the United States and Mexico; the letters of Mexican military leaders as they prosecute their campaigns against the Yaqui; the specific case of the Yaqui leader Cajeme; the photos of lynchings of Yaqui; gun running and the regulation of U.S.–Mexico migration; Yaqui deportations to Yucatán; and, finally, the forced confessions and torture of Yaqui prisoners, all with the aim of presenting the nature of the state as multidirectional and the Yaqui insur-gency as a response to that omnipresent, colonially minded, modernizing Mexican state.

In chapter 5 I place these hidden records in dialogue with Montserrat Fontes's novel *Dreams of the Centaur* (1995) a literary text that is invested in exposing the large-scale, state-sanctioned violence and countering the eerie silence in U.S., Mexican, and Chicana/o histories of the late nineteenth cen-tury and the early twentieth, histories dominated by the Mexican Revolution and the containment of U.S. Indians on reservations. My readings of these collective texts reveal the long experience of violence that pervaded the lives of the Yaqui and others living in Sonora during the Porfiriato.

The Yaqui Indian wars, which are rarely acknowledged by the nation-states that enacted the violence, once again contradict the Chicanos-as-Indians par-adigm as the Yaqui Indian population was disciplined for the benefit of the Mexican mestizos on both sides of the border. The documents I examine can be viewed as a transnational narrative of violence. Through them I seek to address how racialized, gendered subjects emerging from the Yaqui Indian wars persist in narratives and histories of Mexican, U.S. and Chicano na-tionalism, whether they are acknowledged or not.[3] By tracing patterns of information, I attempt to explain why there was and continues to be historical amnesia and a persistent denial of the genocidal violence carried out against the Yaqui by Mexicans, other Yaquis, U.S. Mexicans, and Chicanos—all of whom are often ahistorically theorized as people of color. Much as in the Camp Grant Indian massacre discussed in chapter 2, the historical truth is that racial or national affiliation did not confer solidarity; rather, affiliations were driven by economic need.[4]

My readings of these texts center upon what might be called migrant subjects, or racialized, sexualized, gendered *subalternos*, in the late nineteenth century and early twentieth.[5] And while Yaqui individuals do not often emerge in the archives speaking for themselves—for their voices are often mediated by the masculinist discourses of the military, media, and diplomats—the traces that remain allow one to piece together a sketch of the politics of violence that shaped subjectivity during the Porfiriato. In official Mexican government documentation, subalterno emerges in the 1880s to describe Yaqui indigenous subordinates. While a discursive link can be made to theorization of subaltern identities in the contemporary period, the nuances are not the same.

My discussion is grounded in notions of transnational relations, conflicts, and identities forged in the U.S.–Mexico borderlands. I look at the extensive policing of the Yaqui peoples as an institutional practice of the Porfirian-era government. The paper trail, or literal body of evidence, shows a wavering consciousness and severe anxiety on the part of Americans, Sonoran Mexicans, and the central Mexican government about efforts to contain and exterminate the Yaqui because they posed a threat to a modern vision and enactment of Mexico.

In chapter 5 I also theorize the concept of stripping the body of flesh and memory, developing a theory of subjectivity based upon the extreme physical violence portrayed in *Dreams of the Centaur*. This theory accounts for place and memory in the flesh as modes of making genocide known within the context of the Mexican government's war of extermination against the Yaqui people. This theory accounts for unspoken practices in multiple national histories that strip the body of flesh and memory, whether by actively misrepresenting the histories of genocide and violence against indigenous bodies, by erasing them altogether, or by destroying the body with physical violence. Thus, trauma theory and Foucauldian notions of pain and imprisonment figure heavily in my analysis. I also consider how the concept of stripping the body of flesh and memory parallels the histories of ongoing indigenous wars against the Mexican and Spanish governments for more than 250 years and of Yaqui deportation to the henequen plantations of the Yucatán Peninsula.[6]

Dreams of the Centaur systematically names what is unspeakable in U.S., Mexican, and Chicano/a histories of the borderlands. Representations of excruciatingly painful violation of Yaqui bodies, I argue, demonstrate how women, men, and children became the instruments of their own oppression and the oppression of others because of the predicament of embodiment. This racialized subjectivity, tied to the brown Yaqui body, worked as an always available target of government surveillance and violence in both Sonora and Arizona. Fontes's work of cultural fiction reinterprets the bloody massacre of Mazacoba in 1900, revealing the ritualized violence enacted by Mexican troops as they ambushed and slaughtered Yaqui families in their sacred homeland; at the same time it offers a queered history of female masculinity that serves as an alternative to the exceedingly masculinist discourse of the archival documents.[7]

The ultimate goal of chapters 4 and 5 is to take the powerful moment of Indian history out of the distant past to demonstrate how Yaquis shaped modernity. These chapters write against epistemic violence that socially constructs the timeless, authentic Indians and the legacy of violence that often narrates them as victims of modernity. Indian wars in the U.S.–Mexico borderlands did not end in the nineteenth century. Rather, the Yaqui case study shows a three-century-long struggle for autonomy and nationhood as concrete enactments of subjectivity.

4 ✳ Transnational Histories of Violence during the Yaqui Indian Wars in the Arizona–Sonora Borderlands

THE HISTORIOGRAPHY

> The indigenous tribes are the eternal curse of the state of Sonora; they give us not a moment's rest.
>
> GEN. FRANCISCO P. TRONCOSO, *LAS GUERRAS CON LAS TRIBUS YAQUI Y MAYO*

> Torture, which contains specific acts of inflicting pain, is also itself a demonstration and magnification of the felt-experience of pain. In the very processes it uses to produce pain within the body of the prisoner, it bestows visibility on the structure and enormity of what is usually private and incommunicable, contained within the boundaries of the sufferer's body.
>
> ELAINE SCARRY, *THE BODY IN PAIN*

The interlaced history of three nations—the United States, the Yaqui (Yoeme), and Mexico—tells a story of power, for the power to narrate or to choose not to narrate is in itself an extreme act of control, a way to maintain a selective symbolic order. Keeping records of genocide locked away in archives, not accessible to the average citizen, is a national act of historical repression. That is, if information is sequestered, removed from national dialogues about citizenship, it can be ignored or forgotten. Aside from the works of Evelyn Hu-DeHart, Edward Spicer, Kenneth Burke, and Kirsten Erickson in English and recent publications in Spanish by Raquel Padilla Ramos and Javier Gámez Chávez, there has been sporadic dialogue at best and utter silence at worst about the Yaqui in U.S., Chicana/o, and Mexican historiography and cultural studies. Further, the materials from this period were produced in a highly masculinist discourse, dominated by the voices of men who were invested in reinforcing the relationship between gendered forms of power and nation-

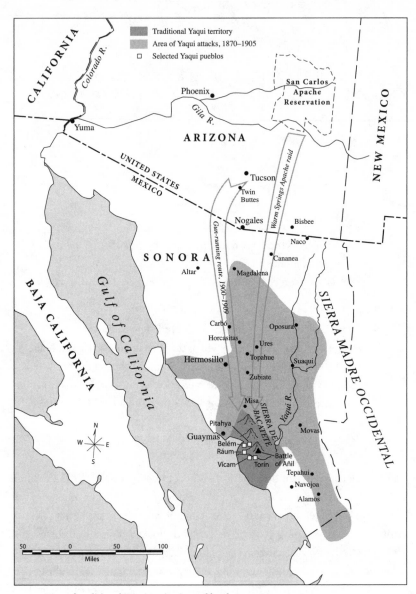

MAP 4 Map of traditional Yaqui territories and battles, ca. 1870–1905.

hood.[1] Given the masculinist nature of the records and my particular invest-ment in a gendered critique of this historiography, engagement with archival sources in Mexico and the United States is necessary to understanding all the factors that produced a hostile climate for the Yaqui at the turn of the twen-tieth century as well as how such history complicates a Chicano nationalist depiction of the past that unproblematically claims indigenous origins.

In this chapter, the reader is taken through a kind of thick description or thick depiction of the multisided, multidimensional quality of state violence against the Yaqui while highlighting their uncanny ability to consistently battle, baffle, and destabilize the Mexican nation-state by enacting their own vision of nation in the process. The chapter examines how and why state actors exhibited a high degree of fear of the Yaqui and more generally of their own failures and inabilities. The existence of such fear is notable because scholars very rarely think of the state as being fearful nor do we automatically assume indigenous peoples were actively shaping modernity. My interest in these moments has to do with recasting and analyzing the masculinity of state power and violence to demonstrate how the Yaqui skillfully undermined the national imagining of the Mexican state, poking holes in the top-down model of nation and empire that defined the Porfiriato.

In addition, the chapter maps what can be learned from Mexican archives, coupled with those in the United States, to provide different commentary on Chicana/o history and narratives of transnationalism. While the chapter vac-illates between making expansive theoretical claims and a sharply materialist set of connections between the archives and the histories they describe, I do so to show the micro- and macro-level implications of power at work and to establish a larger transnational model for history writing.

SÍNTOMAS DE ALZAMIENTO/SYMPTOMS OF REVOLT

Even though the Yaqui helped rid Mexico of the French in 1866[2] and were the major component of the labor force in the mines and haciendas of Sonora in the nineteenth century,[3] they continuously showed "síntomas de alzamiento" (symptoms of revolt), especially in the mid-1880s, 1899, and 1900–1908. The contradictory nature of Yaqui allegiance produced high anxiety for Mexicans and Americans invested in developing Sonora.[4] As a result of their perceived social deviance and "obligados a persistir en su estado de salvajismo" (per-sistent state of obligation to their savage ways), they became particular targets of state-sponsored violence during the Yaqui Indian wars.[5]

While I refer to this period as the Yaqui wars, the struggles were not always named as such in government documents. As the Native feminists Andrea

Smith and Luana Ross argue, genocide is not always named as such and has never been against the law in the United States or, I would argue, in Mexico.[6] These Yaqui, Sonoran state, and Mexican federal military campaigns were not always formal and often reflected conflicts between the desires of the state governments of Sonora, Sinaloa, and Chihuahua; the U.S. and Mexican federal governments; and Yaqui rebels. Moreover, government military action against the Yaqui was often retaliatory, a response to raids in the Guaymas Valley. Yaqui raids demonstrated a sustained Yaqui imagining of subjectivity and nation tied to self-determination and economic sustainability, even if at the cost of ranchers and miners in Sonora. The Yaqui valley is of historical importance to them because they see the land as sacred. As long as the Spanish, Mexicans, and eventually American venture capitalists stayed out of it, the Yaqui were willing to cooperate with the abovementioned imperialists. But the Mexican- and U.S.-backed encroachment in the Yaqui valley during the 1870s and 1880s was perceived as a declaration of war.

When U.S. investors, backed by Mexican government officials, began entering the Río Yaqui area and forming railroad and farming companies with venture capital, the nation headed by Porfirio Díaz deemed it necessary to eliminate any obstacles that would prevent such development in the state of Sonora.[7] Díaz was obsessed with making Mexico modern. On November 11, 1880, a formal agreement was reached on a plan to develop Mexican railroads without granting a monopoly to any party. At the negotiating table were, among others, Matías Romero, the Mexican ambassador to the United States; Ulysses S. Grant; Tomás Nickerson, a representative of the Compañía de Ferrocarriles Mexicanas; Samuel E. Huntington, the chairman of the Southern Pacific Railroad; and Edward D. Adams, a representative of the Compañía de Ferrocarriles de Sonora Central.[8] The agreement that was eventually reached allowed almost all U.S. railroad companies with southern routes to build rail lines as far as the border and then subsidize the construction of a corresponding Mexican line.

The desire to "construct and exploit" the land through the building of railroads was hindered by the Yaqui.[9] The Yaqui were said to be a "hazard to land travel" because they populated the routes and were often hostile.[10] If anything, Yaqui rebellions and raids, a direct result of the railroad construction in their homeland, contested and reinforced the idea that the Mexican and Yaqui nations were distinct and autonomous. Mexican Minister to the United States, Matias Romero, often wrote to President Díaz, making sure he was aware not only of all the press coverage of the Yaqui but also of the actions they were taking.[11] This extensive documentation by Mexican officials of

Yaqui rebellion contradicts Benedict Anderson's paradigm about the forging of the idea of nation outside of print culture. Yaqui and Apache uprisings were a direct enactment of an idea of subjectivity and nation in contradistinction to U.S. and Mexican nationalism, and announcing their rebellion in print threatened the territorial integrity of U.S. and Mexican nationalisms while galvanizing xenophobic patriotism. The Mexican government was never quite able to establish complete authority over the territory inhabited by the Yaqui. The Yaqui defined their nation not through print culture but rather on the basis of a national imaginary forged through armed struggle.

As Leigh A. Payne has shown, the implied but never stated criminality behind government and insurgent violence is part and parcel of the informal dirty wars of submission in the Americas, particularly in their documentation.[12] The idea of Yaqui criminality was in place by the early 1800s, when revolutionary leaders like Juan Banderas, a Yaqui chief executed in 1833 for trying to unite the Yaqui, Pima, and Opata tribes against the Mexican government, were labeled "individuals as criminal as their customs. They are more worthy of punishment and misery . . . their crimes cannot be left unpunished."[13] By contrast, Mexican state-generated violence was delicately lodged in the language of euphemism. Reflecting a somewhat fluctuating attitude about violence and the implied criminality of the state, officials were clear to place the onus for their own acts on the rebelling populations: the "need to delouse [the Yaqui River region] of the criminals that promote disorder requires other preventative measures" that justified a violent institutional response.[14] During this protracted series of wars, the generals mostly spoke of necessary combat against Yaqui *salvajes* (savages). Others downplayed the action by referring to the "history of the Yaqui revolution," speaking of war and nation but doing so euphemistically.[15] These euphemisms evade an outright discussion of these violent conflicts or war and locate the violence outside of war, which both destabilizes the idea of the Yaqui as a nation while at the same time marking the conflicts as being outside of national concern, that is, on the periphery of the Mexican nation. From euphemisms scholars see state violence as a diffuse or broad-based set of discourses and practices; not so much an oppression or subjection issuing from a singular source with one interest or goal in mind but as an incredible range of uneven, if powerful, tactics of violence that need to be concealed to present a veneer of democratic practice and benevolent nation. Further, domestic and international political realities require executives and national administrators to translate the mythological language of nation into a technocratic target language that absolves the nation of wrongdoing by creating a politically acceptable discourse.[16]

Strategic Yaqui attacks upon the Guaymas Valley and Mexican forces, including Federal Auxiliary forces, Sonora national guard troops, and National Army troops, both distinctly drew energy away from Mexico's desire to establish itself as an industrial, advanced nation, and on the opposite front, to protect Yaqui autonomy.[17] Yaqui revolution in essence was about sustaining autonomy and economic stability and enacting an imagined vision of nation that portrays themselves as full-fledged historical actors, which was incongruent with the desires of the Mexican nation-state. Subaltern action gets produced indirectly through state communiqués, showing that the state's desire to forget through processes of national rhetorics of state violence in practice had the opposite effect.[18] The desire to forget was part of state formations of modernity, and yet consistent Yaqui disruptions of modernity show that process as never quite complete.

At times Mexican military generals and even the secretary of foreign relations articulated differing Yaqui political subjectivities, ones outside the realm of criminality, either to manipulate the situation or to enact a campaign of total subordination. Secretary of Foreign Relations Pedro Hinojosa wrote the following to the military commander of the first zone in the north, Gen. José Carbó: "The Yaqui are already a civilized people [so one should not] treat them savagely, since they will become nomads and it will be necessary to wage a very difficult and costly war of extermination. Thus, they ought to turn away from their raids and sneaky thievery. They should not be provoked nor should war be waged on them by burning their homes and laying waste to their fields, since this will only frustrate them, so that they will not want to return to being in a country at peace."[19] Several conflicting visions of Yaqui subjectivity and their relationship to the nation are established in this passage. In the midst of the skirmishing and conflicts between the Mexican government and the Yaqui, Hinojosa articulates Yaqui identity as civilized, meaning settled as opposed to migratory, and he admits that militarization of their homelands had forced a nomadic lifestyle on a nonnomadic Indian population with a land base. He also underscores the ferocity of the Yaqui, suggesting that to provoke them will lead to a war to end all wars. Under the leader Cajeme, who, in 1876–87, led the Yaqui in an extended war against the Mexican state and those who sought to control and confiscate traditional Yaqui lands, Yaqui settled and developed farmlands, dug irrigation ditches, settled the eight pueblos, and developed a tax base. These were the factors Hinojosa cited as making the Yaqui civilized, for a tax system is the ultimate mark of a developed society. And while numerous scholars of Yaqui culture, including Erickson, assert that the "Yaqui are decisively a part of the modern world (their group identity arguably forged in the crucible of a modernizing nation-state), and that heightened awareness that identity's multi-faceted nature is a modern phenomenon," government policy suggested otherwise. Despite Hinojosa's clarity on the matter, many bureaucrats went against his argument about the Yaqui as civilized people in dealing with their sovereignty.[20] In arguing that the government should not treat the Yaqui as savages, Hinojosa makes the case that they should be treated better on the basis not of human rights considerations but of the cost of such a project. Apparently genocide was expensive, and in order to achieve peace the Mexican government would need to stop chopping down their fields and burning their homes. Herein lies the predicament: Yaqui were sometimes seen as productive members of society but could never be, in the eyes of the Díaz regime, individuated citizen subjects because they could not be socially controlled.

Hinojosa's musings stand at the ethical and economic crossroads of the Mexican government's multipronged efforts to make the nation-state modern: at this decisive moment physical coercion, military intervention, corporal punishment, and the imposition of a harsher penal system paved the way for what Díaz and his cronies believed would bring modernity to Mexico.[21] What the Porfiriato did not consider was how dissident Yaqui subjects helped shape that modernity.

An official military campaign was reopened against the Yaqui in the mid-1880s. On March 19, 1885, General José Carbó recommended to Díaz that they "definitively subjugate and pacify these Indians to the obedience of the government, organizing their villages in accordance with civilian law.[22] In order to achieve this without spilling blood, it is advisable to open the campaign with a sufficient number of troops to repeat to the degree that would make their importance known. In this way, it is almost certain that they would submit without a fight."[23] This document attempts to cloak state-sponsored violence in the technical language of military strategy, but it produces the opposite effect. Phases like "subjugate and pacify," "obedience to government," and "submit without a fight," patently communicate that physical force will be part of the campaign, undercutting any possibility of Yaqui surrender without a fight. National consolidation, at its core, required state-sponsored violence. Even though the text hints at violence as an implied part of military strategies of submission, it does so tentatively, as if trying to convey benevolence to yet another Indian group. How can one use a military surge of troops and not expect to spill blood? As the documents that follow indicate, such an outcome was and continues to be utterly impossible.

These veiled suggestions of criminality, violence, and nonviolence stage the fluctuating attitude of the Mexican military and government in relation to the Yaqui population. One of the most obvious and instrumental ways in which both the state of Sonora and the Mexican army and nation attempted to distance themselves from a potentially genocidal project was by transforming Yaqui activity from what they deemed criminal and unnecessary violence to making them into agents of the state. Transforming the revolutionary and autonomous mindset of the Yaqui could be achieved by putting them in the military and socializing them to be productive members of the nation-state (even though a great many of them were already working in the mining and agriculture industries). Such plans often backfired.

For example, Cajeme, at first venerated but then feared, became a military force in the Mexican army in the 1860s.[24] According to Ramon Corral's biography of Cajeme, at the age of fourteen, José accompanied his father and others from Sonora on the gold rush to Baja California norte in 1849. When he returned to Sonora about two years later he had learned English and had defended himself in armed conflict. He was enrolled in the first Colegio Sonora and subsequently learned to read and write Spanish. He began military service in 1857 at the age of eighteen with the battalion Fijo de San Blas, composed of Yaqui, Pima, and Opata. There had been few battalions like this one in Sonora, most likely because Banderas had tried to organize these Indian groups to rebel against the Mexican government in 1837. During the last years of his service, 1867–68, Cajeme was a captain in charge of one hundred men. Cajeme took part in one of the bloodiest Mexican military campaigns against his own Yaqui people from late 1867 through 1868. Without detailing the extreme violence or Cajeme's physical enactment of it on behalf of the Mexican nation-state, Gen. Francisco P. Troncoso wrote, "This fight in the Rio Yaqui, which saw many battles and the Indians were chased incessantly. The merits acquired by Cajeme, gave him official employment, and he was given command of a company formed with Indians."[25] Descriptions of the bloody violence are kept to a minimum and are euphemized, showing what Elaine Scarry argues about violence outside of an official war between nations: "What is first of all visible is the extremity with which or the extreme literalness with which the nation inscribes itself onto the body; or (to phrase it in a way that acknowledges the extraordinary fact of the consent of the participating populations in conventional war) the literalness with which the human body opened itself and allows 'the nation' to be registered there in the wound."[26] While this government report does not describe the wounds suffered by Yaqui in the attacks, they are registered by the nation on Cajeme's body as he carried out genocidal violence against his own people. He became an agent of the Mexican nation, and the psychological wound that such violent activity created no doubt influenced his later turn to violent defense of Yaqui autonomy against the Mexican nation. Perhaps this was Cajeme's way of enacting a galvanizing drive or dealing with loss, which David Eng and David Kazanjian have argued represents the hopeful and hopeless aspects of history.[27] The turn away from institutionalized war in service of the Mexican nation toward guerrilla warfare to achieve Yaqui autonomy was no doubt a way of remembering and mourning what remained, which was a fragmented, dispersed, displaced group of indigenous people.

In 1874 Cajeme became *alcalde mayor* (local territorial governor) of the Río Yaqui territory.[28] The government put him in this position thinking he would, after his military service, pacify his people. He did create a tax system for the pueblos, a commercial market with outside traders, and a system of organized village governments. But he also waged war when these institutions were threatened. The Mexican government and U.S.-based investors did not count on Cajeme rekindling a long history of maintaining Yaqui independence. Cajeme's turn to defending Yaqui autonomy was an enactment of grave losses, and both the absence and implied representations of extreme physical violence provide us with a new site for theorizing subjectivity in this nineteenth-century borderlands context. The unspeakable quality of violence registered in Cajeme's and other Yaquis' experiences in the Mexican army is regularly implied through official government orders stating "la necesidad de pacificarlos" and "será necesaria la efusión de sangre" (the necessity of pacifying them; it will be necessary to spill blood).[29] The necessity to pacify the Yaqui and the knowledge of future bloodshed initiated a state-sanctioned, painful process of violation of Yaqui soldiers and the Yaqui population in general. The scenes of subjugation in the historical documents are only alluded to and only become concrete through photography and occasional extended descriptions.[30] Details of the violence against the Yaqui can be found in the correspondence leading up to Cajeme's capture and public execution. Gen. Ángel Martínez wrote the following to Díaz: "Certainly, I have not wanted to use any rigorous measure against Cajeme, because I am thinking of taking him to the Río Yaqui and there, presenting him before the indigenous masses so that they will be convinced that their chief is in our hands, and after that I will subject him to the punishment that he deserves."[31] And on April 21, 1887, the Mexican military did exactly that; they took him by ship to the Yaqui River and marched him through all the pueblos, arriving at Cócorit on the twenty-fifth, where he was publicly executed by a firing squad.[32] For the state, Cajeme's public death march was meant to punish the Yaqui people as a collective by making an example of him and proving he really was dead so that people couldn't use rumors of his survival to incite further rebellion. Public death by execution, however, may have served the Yaqui people as another concrete opportunity to use this moment of loss to mourn, remember, and imagine a future free of executions and constant battle with the Mexican military. The Mexican government thought the execution of Cajeme would bring a final peace to the Rio Yaqui, that there would be no more *cabecillos* leading the fight against the nation: "You want the capture of Cajeme to be definitive, so that you can win in the Yaqui and Mayo Rivers."[33] Instead of being a triumph in the Yaqui and Mayo rivers, the death of Cajeme provoked an "adamant refusal of closure," for within a few months Yaqui rebels were actively raiding and skirmishing with the Mexican military.[34] Even if Cajeme's body "was exhibited in all of the pueblos comprising the Río Yaqui" with the intention of discouraging rebellion, stripped of his agency, this action had the opposite effect.[35] The execution precipitated "mourning without end, [for] melancholia results from the inability to resolve the grief and ambivalence precipitated by the loss of the loved object, place, or ideal"; the acts of war by the Yaqui following Cajeme's death are the manic expression of such melancholia.[36]

One can read Cajeme's life story in multiple registers: as emblematic of a Yaqui refusal to be silenced and a never-ending process of mourning enacted through warfare; as a feeble attempt of the Mexican government to exhibit state power by displaying the dead body of a leader who was both beloved and sometimes hated; as an expression of sovereign collective and individual indigenous subjectivity most visible in death; as a raced subject that is considered unequal and inferior; or as one of the quotidian displays of violence as everyday practice. However, what the display of Cajeme's dead body most emphatically communicated was the fear he evoked in life and how that fear was temporarily quelled in his death. Cajeme's dead body symbolized the triumph of modernity over barbarian forces, the overlaying of the Mexican nation-state onto the Yaqui nation, rendering it dead like their leader. Instead of a lament, the displaying of the body of Cajeme was a punishment and a warning to Yaqui Indians to abandon their misplaced alliances, a reminder of how nation-state formation was and continues to be predicated upon violence against indigenous bodies.

In July 1885 General Carbó reported that "the state of poverty and misery of the rebels had taken away their spirit, and . . . Cajeme is actively preparing for war because he feared that with the arrival of two battalions of federal troops, it would be expedient to open campaign."[37] The Mexican national project to pacify the Yaqui backfired several times over, and Cajeme's switching of allegiance was and continues to be the ultimate symbolic embodiment of such failure.[38] The Yaqui were made to undergo specific, diffuse, and directed forms of violence because the nation-state, both the United States and Mexico prescribed particular gender roles and race and class statuses that they did not adhere to in their everyday cultural and social practices. The violence against them was very much a process of using deportation and wars designed to restrict their autonomy and mobility.

Commenting on Gen. José Otero's letter dated March 5, 1885, Díaz parenthetically notes, "The origin of the Yaqui rebellion was the provocation of the Prefect of Guaymas, who protects some rebellious Indians corrupted by their leader. We are feeling the aftermath now: one of that gang of Yaqui ransacked and destroyed his hacienda, called La Noria. He believes that the Federal Government ought to seriously focus its attention and free Sonora of those Indians."[39] Díaz seems tired of the pleas and requests for help in subduing Cajeme and his rebellious Indians. Blaming the inconsistent policy on the prefect of the First Military Zone—who one minute protected the Yaqui by valuing their labor in the copper and silver mines and haciendas, and the next admonished them for attacking and looting the hacienda that employed them—Díaz harshly states that in some ways Sonora and its hacendados got what they deserved. He describes the conflict not as a war but as an Indian uprising, an isolated incident located outside the realm of national concern or national priority.

Díaz's frustration was a direct reflection of his reluctance to recognize the Yaqui nation as such. Doing so would acknowledge that the Yaqui, as a separate nation, had a history of autonomy through treaties with Spain that preexisted Mexican national formations.[40] Díaz declared in 1872, "Let the Yaqui nation die in a war, but if they recognize their mistakes, let us pardon them through a surrender that ensures forever the tranquility of the State, and that they remain capable of making amends for the damages that they have caused the Towns of the West. This recommended altruistic action cannot be hidden from the eyes of the government of the State."[41] In this passage Díaz simultaneously affirms *and* denies the Yaqui nation, which must be vanquished, at one moment, and then pardoned and forced to make amends to the Mexican nation at another. Referencing Joseph Roach's arguments about the unspoken, in which the unspeakable is not rendered inexpressible but is forgotten in a deferral of memory, each denial of Yaqui autonomy provokes an acknowledgment of it.[42]

In fact, as late as 1885 Governor Luis Torres of Sonora wrote to General Carbó, several times restating the pleas he had already made to President Díaz:

"I have written to the president, bringing him up to date about these events and talking to him in terms of the need to undertake a formal campaign until we achieve complete submission of the Mayo and Yaqui tribes to the commands of the government."[43] Torres's complaints were based on his desire for federal intervention and a formal campaign. That is, the state of Sonora was not capable of mediating or controlling the retaliatory violence generated by Yaqui enactments of sovereignty and subjectivity. Rather, the nation, Mexico, needed to be called in to quash physical enactments of Yaqui autonomy.

Writing to General Carbó on June 24, 1884, José Montesinos, a former alcalde of a municipality in Sonora, explained that "the president told me that given the circumstances that the nation was facing, without resources and at election time, he believes that it is an unjustified adventure to wage war against the Yaqui, who never bother anyone, and the campaign would demand a greater number of troops than he currently has under his command, [this is] something that he is unable to facilitate at the present time."[44] As demonstrated by Montesinos, Mexican opinions on the Yaqui conflict were diverse and actually fluctuated, depending upon the economic and political state of the nation as a whole (for example, elections, border wars with Guatemala, U.S. Apache raids into Mexico, and so forth), reinforcing Sonora's historically marginalized position as a border state. Interestingly, Montesinos states that the Yaqui "never bother anyone," completely contradicting the discourses about their savagery originating from Sonoran locals, the military jefes, and even some members of the central government. Carbó's skirmishes with the Yaqui are labeled "su campaña," or his campaign, by Montesinos, making them personalized and thus separate from national concern. This was Carbó's personal vendetta, not necessarily reflecting or in consonance with the desires of Sonorans who lived where the war was being conducted. Sending troops to aid Carbó would not serve the nation or local residents well at this moment, according to Montesinos. The Yaqui problem, it seems, was a conditional one, sometimes becoming a national issue, at other times being eclipsed by issues more important to the nation.

The Porfiriato and its military were also frightened by Apache threats to the nation-state. A problem dating back to Mexico's infancy as a nation, the Apache raids peaked public interest between 1883 and 1885 because they interfered with the campaigns against the Yaqui and commerce networks in the north. On March 18, 1883, Díaz's secretary general wrote to General Carbó, mentioning the hostile tribes of the Río Yaqui and the Apache issue.[45] During 1883, when Chato's band of Warm Springs Apache fled the San Carlos Apache Reservation in Arizona (the same place the Camp Grant Apaches were relocated to) into Mexico, plundering along the way, the Foreign Relations Secretariat and the governors of Sonora and Chihuahua were worried about individual property loss but feared a unified Indian rebellion even more.[46] They believed these renegade Apache could help the Yaqui overthrow unstable state governments along the U.S.–Mexico border, and consequently in 1883 federal troops staged a massive attack against the Yaqui in the Sierra Madre of Sonora. Government officials were fearful that the Apaches were moving from Chihuahua into Sonora to aid the Yaqui in their fight against the Mexican government, which is probably why the Mexican federal offensives increased.[47] Clipping files amassed in Mexico's Ministry of Foreign Relations reflect the Mexican national leaders' heightened anxiety about an indigenous rebellion, which would have negative implications for U.S. and British businesses located in Sonora. The unsolved Indian problem on the U.S.–Mexico border created an unstable climate for foreign investors.

In April of that year the Mexican army made several forays into the Sierra Madre, including one in which eight hundred men pursued Cajeme's men, who numbered more than three thousand.[48] In May 1885 the army continued "violently the preparations to open the campaign," amassing fourteen hundred federal soldiers and eight hundred soldiers from the state of Sonora. The troops were sent into the Yaqui pueblos of Misa, Pochote, Mapole, La Pitahaya, and Potam in the midst of the Indian dissidents, where, on May 15, they attempted to round up the families of the three thousand warriors.[49] By 5:00 p.m. they returned with seventy-seven Yaqui in total: eighteen men, twenty-five women, and thirty-four children, a small number considering the large number of warriors targeted. No mention is made of where the prisoners were taken.[50]

The rounding up of Yaqui families then turned ugly, as the Indians quickly reacted to the military action. The Yaqui were familiar with the terrain and possessed a degree and variety of arms that the soldiers were unprepared for. In June 1885 the column of soldiers

met with the greatest number of rebellious Indians, calculating their number at between 4,000 and 5,000 men who are defending the land, armed with around 12,000 rifles of various calibers and systems, as well as a regular number of pistols, and the rest of them armed with arrows—In my opinion, this is an ignorant and timid enemy. In order to dislodge the enemy from its advantageous position, it would be enough to have the valiant and selfless soldiers that were under my command, if not the force that I have had the great honor of leading. It is my belief that the expedition of this column has made patent to the enemy that despite the high number of insurgents, the Supreme [Federal] Government, with its loyal servants, knows how to make itself felt against those who destabilize order and the public peace.[51]

The report, written by Col. Lorenzo García, contradicts Ambassador Romero's claim that there was no fighting in Sonora.[52] García says the enemy is ignorant and timid after he catalogues the Yaquis' stock of rifles, pistols, and arrows, which seems like military posturing. If the Yaqui were as ignorant and timid as García claims, they would have avoided combat and fought only with arrows, being unable to procure firearms. Rhetorically, García attempts to privilege the prestige and intelligence of his men, even if they don't always follow his orders, to minimize the Yaquis' skill and expertise in warfare. Such a rhetorical strategy taps the Mexican discourse of *indigenismo* with its always already submissive Indians.[53] García stresses the capacity of the supreme government and its loyal servants to quell a rebellion of subalternos, even though in the battle the Yaqui suffered only nine deaths out of four or five thousand troops. García states that the army has the situation under control, which it clearly did not, given both the very low Yaqui death toll and the fact that armed Yaqui efforts for self-determination continued well beyond the beginning of the Mexican Revolution (1910). But the larger question is whether it is permissible for military commanders to admit to weakness and fear in official documents, especially if the rebellion they are fighting is clandestine. What would it mean for García to admit defeat and concede that the Yaqui were, in fact, intelligent, rational, thinking subjects with a different vision of nation and autonomy? To admit such fear would disturb the foundational discourses of Mexican independence: mestizaje and indigenismo and the hierarchy of the dominant, politically and economically astute mestizo elite above the subordinate, politically and economically dormant Indian.

Still, in 1885, a year of sustained conflict and violence, General Carbó did admit to Díaz that he had concerns about Yaqui military strength. In an official report Carbó states, "I have told the Secretary of War about a skirmish that was verified yesterday around dawn between the federal forces and a group of five hundred Yaqui, at a point in the Valley of Guaymas . . . the Indians were on their way to attack the Jaimea hacienda, and eighty men went after them. . . . These events will give you an idea of the true character of rebellion among these tribes, and the need to asphyxiate it by means of force."[54] Arguing for the use of extreme force in the campaign, Carbó reveals that even federal forces, the most elite fighters, can't match up with five hundred Yaqui warriors. Enacting their own vision of citizenship, the Yaqui may have felt that the real character of their uprising was an exercise of rights by means of warfare. In some ways, we might be able to consider these small defeats suffered by the Mexican army as a disruption of normalizing ideas about citizenship and masculinity tied to Mexican mestizo identity. The battles no doubt created a sense of fear that the Yaqui campaign was a never-ending struggle, but they also contested what constituted a masculine citizen subject at the moment, as the Mexican government viewed Yaquis as a subordinate ethnic group, not as tribal or national citizens equal to mestizo citizens.

Carbó admitted to being afraid during the Yaqui campaign when he wrote to Díaz, "I have already begun to send forces against the Yaqui, and I have established a camp in the Los Pilares Sierra, which is one of the Indians' strongholds. I must undertake this campaign with great precaution, because the enemy is much greater in number than the force that I have available, and under no circumstances, do I want to expose myself to a calamity."[55] Lizbeth Haas has argued that in the colonization of California during the Spanish period, the Spaniards governed by imposing fear, religious practices, and a set of suffocating punishments and restrictions.[56] If one reads Mexico's handling of its Indian populations as practical residues of the Spanish Empire, then Carbó's words of caution in the Yaqui campaign ultimately signal fear embodied in the potential for loss. In this case, mourning represents an active loss of power, resources, military bodies, and, most important, of the sense of a strong Mexican nation. But in a way Carbó's account of such a loss of power can be thought of as a kind of narrative of mourning, in the sense that moments of national foundation represent lost coherence and purity; they often have a paradoxical quality of mourning their loss before it has even been constituted. Carbó's summation reveals a fear of another kind: Yaquis were interrupting a particular vision of national development, on the one hand, and, on the other, that Yaquis were using this moment to assert their alternate vision of their own nation was very important. Every time the Mexican military lost a battle with the Yaqui in Sonora there was a depletion of resources and an active weakening of the ideal of the Mexican nation. After forty years of battle those Mexican losses had to have elicited shame, fear, and anxiety that the nation could not contain dissident indigenous subjects, who in every violent skirmish were not only fighting a battle over land and culture, but also asserting a political vision about citizenship.

Governor Torres tells a different story about the Yaqui rebellions and the Mexican nation in his correspondence with President Díaz and General Carbó. Torres was in constant contact with Carbó and offered information about the battle General BonifacioTopete had with Cajeme's forces at El Añil, lamenting a prior defeat in his campaign against the Yaqui and commenting that this victory by under-general Topete was well done.[57] Thus the documents constantly shift between anxiety over battle losses and assertions of Mexican governmental and military superiority. Even though Torres assures Carbó that the loss is unimportant, an earlier letter dated February 26, 1885, suggests the opposite. Complaining that the Yaqui had again attacked the principal haciendas in the Guaymas Valley (the same haciendas they worked at in times of peace), Torres appeals to Díaz for help, claiming that quelling the raiding was beyond state military capacity. Torres wrote about "the Yaqui and Mayo Indian uprising and the extremely violent situation that it has justifiably created in the state. . . . I am in charge of it, Mister President, and I hope that you will do me the favor of having confidence in this plan."[58] This unsettling narrative that wavers between state dominance and indigenous dominance shows that the military was unable to regulate, track, and monitor guerrilla warfare. What was far worse was that it was Indians, subalternos, who frustrated military officials while creating a public climate of fear and loss in Sonora.

In whom did Yaqui attacks cause fear and why? Gen. Walter S. Logan, a New York City lawyer sued for embezzlement in 1907 for his involvement in the Yaqui Land Company, an irrigation enterprise, that capitalized $1.5 million in profits, delivered a speech at a banquet in honor of Mexican Minister to the U.S. Matias Romero.[59] In it he articulates why Yaqui attacks caused fear and loss for Mexicans but were symbols of the past for Americans: "No one who reads the story of these [Yaqui] Indians, who sees their fierce, indomitable love of freedom, who follows their heroic struggle for independence, and notes the sublime courage with which they welcomed death upon the battlefield rather than submission to the Spanish monarchy or the Republic of Mexico, cannot help but drop a tear over their fate. . . . The march of progress is powerful and relentless."[60] Since the Yaqui wars did not cease until the Mexican Revolution, Logan's desire to mourn an object, for political purposes, that is actually not dead or lost, seems ironic to the reader. The psychoanalytic critic Anne Cheng has argued that "mourning implies the second killing off of the lost object. The denigration and murder of the lost object fortifies the ego. Not only do we note that 'health' means re-killing an object already lost, but we have to ask how different is this in aim from the melancholic who hangs onto the lost object as part of the ego in order to live."[61] Strangely enough, the gesture to "drop a tear" for the lost Yaqui nation and their "fierce, indominable love of freedom" requires the incessant killing and rekilling of the Yaqui in symbolic terms. In order for companies like Logan's Yaqui Land Company (the corporation functioning like a person in this instance) and the U.S. and Mexican nations to continue living through capitalist development, they have to kill and rekill the lost object (the Yaquis and the Yaqui nation). In this instance, mourning and loss are necessary components of losing the object, killing it, and stabilizing the nation. Yet the continuance of Yaqui attacks until the 1910s shows that these mobilizations were expressions of Yaqui autonomy and of their questioning of Mexican and U.S. national mourning of an object that was subject to hatred and thus needed to be killed so that it could be mourned.

Within a context of disrupting the desired hegemonic national mourning of a not-so-lost lost object, we can turn to accounts of Yaqui attacks, which often had two purposes. First, they were often launched to secure provisions like clothing and food because the settlement of Mexicans and Americans along the Río Yaqui had displaced the Yaqui from their homes. Second, attacks were often retaliatory reminders to the Mexican, American, and Sonorense governments and their citizens that Yaquis would not tolerate the capitalist expansion of irrigation, mining, and land speculation corporations on their sacred lands. On September 30, 1901, a telegram was sent to the prefect of Guaymas reporting an assault: "The president of the ranch advised last night by telephone that yesterday at 7:30 pm Yaquis rebeldes assaulted two washerwomen who were about to go to the *arroyo hediondo* that is very close to the villa where there were taking dirty clothing to be washed. The Yaquis stole all of the dirty clothes. Later, the municipal president ordered that 10 men go out to pursue the assailants to see if they could catch them, teach them a lesson, recover what they robbed and protect the other laundresses that are here at this port."[62] The stealing of clothing without injuring the laundresses signals a few important things about Yaqui attacks. First, theft of dirty clothes can be read as quotidian acts of survival. Stealing was an alternative to trade at an economic moment when it was dangerous for Yaquis to seek provisions through traditional trade. This attack was carried out for purposes of subsistence, not to physically harm anyone. Scholars can also read it as an enactment of politics in support of a larger rebellion against the Mexican state. As the historian of U.S.–Mexico Indian wars Brian Delay has argued, historians need to think about politics "as a process, one of establishing and pursuing public goals . . . Despite their differences, the Americans, Mexicans and independent Indians . . . were all engaged in political endeavors."[63] While the state saw stealing clothes and assaulting the laundresses as a barbaric attack of *indios rebeldes*, an act of incivility, an act that they could never "teach them a lesson about," the theft was very calculated. The politics of rebellion required planning, preparation, and execution, exposing warriors to potential capture. The clothes could have been used by Yaquis to pass as Mexican when crossing the border or to trade for ammunition or simply to cover their war-ravaged bodies. The theft shows the vulnerability of Mexicans to Yaqui raids at a local level, while at the same time signaling that not all Yaqui raids were meant to inflict physical violence or to carry out a political vendetta.

There is something quite poetic about stealing dirty clothes. In an ironic twist, virtue is rewarded and the vice of the state is temporarily punished as the Yaqui thieves aren't captured. Yet there are many other accounts of Yaqui violence taken to extremes in their attacks in Sonora, showing a politics of vengeance and retribution at work. During the 1880s under Cajeme's leadership these acts of violence were directed at the colonizing presence in the Río Yaqui. In an article entitled "Cajeme Asserting His Jurisdiction," the *Washington Post* reports that the Yaqui chief "burned a number of boats seized from the white settlers along the Yaqui River on the 14th instant [of February 1885]. It is reported that a number of ranches have been burned between the settlements and that part of the river over which Cajeme claims jurisdiction by bands belonging to his tribe."[64] Three days later it was reported that the Tamiopila and La Misa ranches near Guaymas were burned to the ground, which precipitated an attack by federal troops on the Yaquis in that area and resulted in "the Indians [being] routed."[65] Burning these ranches and boats to the ground serves as a direct critique of colonialism and capitalism. While power and control are rendered ineffective through the destruction of property, the representational strategy positions the hacienda owners in a victimized position. The article firmly represents the failure of empire through an extreme display of Yaqui subjectivity: what better way to disrupt Mexican and U.S. imperialisms than by destroying the economic systems in Sonora's haciendas? The effort to eradicate the site of private property, even though Yaquis were often laborers on Sonorense haciendas, marks what the historian Ranajit Guha has called the alarm and interventions phases.[66] Within a state of alarm and intervention regarding Yaqui destruction of haciendas in the sequence of events, fear and shock spur state action. Further, the communal and national outrage provokes not sympathy for the Yaqui insurgents defending their land but increased desires for security and large-scale war.

But even more important to the project of this book are the ways in which the press tries to attribute the insurgency to an individual, Cajeme, shifting us away from a vision of collective political subjectivity. Under Cajeme the Yaqui had an organized military with cavalry, infantry, and artillery forces that controlled the river, so why turn to burning haciendas to the ground? The article relies on the rhetoric of savagism and lower intelligence to suggest that Cajeme single-handedly masterminded the burning of the haciendas. It says nothing of the collective of individuals who aided in the burnings, who planned the secret, undetected guerrilla attack. Furthermore, the haciendas were not ransacked before they were burned, suggesting that these acts were about a collective of peoples literally destroying institutions both to send a political message and to make political gains in order to maintain their autonomy. Violence directed at institutions that were imagined by Yaquis to be the base of the economy, symbolic of the state and national governments but also private capital, shows how they imagined their insurgency campaign against empire and the state. Yaqui insurgency-based violence and the immediate Mexican counterinsurgency attack suggest that the respective strategies in using violence were different in scope but not in scale. Both used mass mobilizations of formal military structures; however, "Cajeme's assertion of his jurisdiction" used clandestine tactics directed at institutions like haciendas and military and at private property to hurt hated enemies.[67] Instead of massacring entire groups of random people to actively disrupt Mexico's national narrative of mestizaje by eliminating the very institutionalized manifestations of state and capitalism embodied in the haciendas, the Yaquis sought to destroy the very institutions that sought to destroy them.

In a plan to counteract the hostile, violent climate engulfing Sonora, Carbó made one of his many pleas to Díaz. Unofficially, however, Díaz's marginal notes give a different view of General Carbó's work in the First Military Zone: "Reduce the troops because I cannot offer more because the truth is no single step will follow."[68] Díaz's government was financially strapped in 1885 because of a border war in the south between Guatemala and Chiapas, a national war that took precedence over localized Indian wars on the fringes of empire. It didn't matter how much fear and violence ruled the social and economic climate in Sonora, the northern frontier was a lower priority than the southern because the Yaqui wars were presumably contained within the Mexican nation-state.

But more than Yaqui Indian wars was happening in the state of Sonora in the 1880s. The generals on the battlefront in Sonora often argued that the atmosphere of violence was propagated not just by the Yaqui but by local political jefes as well. Often generals and political bosses in Sonora conflated political infighting among the elite ruling classes with the Indian question, using their military power to mitigate local factions of power. These tensions between actual Indian violence, on the one hand, and abuses of power, on the other, are best articulated by Carlos Ortiz, a former Sonoran political boss himself, who wrote to President Díaz appealing to the nation to protect his interests. Blaming the Sonoran government, Ortiz argues that

> for more than two years, not only members of my family but also some of my political and personal friends have been the victims of an unjustified persecution on the part of the government of Sonora. These acts put me in the position of entreating you most earnestly to be kind enough to give me some letters of recommendation to Generals Topete and Lorenzo García, federal chiefs in Sonora, on behalf of those of my friends who, at the same time, are the most persecuted, . . . some violent or unlawful act, above all today with such serious difficulties having originated with the Yaqui and Mayo tribes. . . . Now, I take the liberty of addressing you in writing about that request. . . . I clearly see that taking advantage of the opportunity of the recent and unfathomable rebellion of the Yaqui and Mayo Indians has begun to unfold the new and the most terrible persecutions against my friends, being much to be feared that for this purpose, they count on the help of federal troops.[69]

According to Ortiz, half the time it was difficult to tell whether the violence originated with the Yaqui and Mayo or with the corrupt state government. He essentially accuses Generals Topete and García of abandoning people like his family and friends, leaving them defenseless against Indian raids, but also against attacks from other infiltrators.[70] Ortiz calls on a sense of Mexican nationalism and national belonging to cement personal and communal material security as one means to persuade Díaz to use his power to protect his interests against other elites trying to take advantage of the situation.

Exercising his power with the president as a former Sonoran political boss, Ortiz uses his family and political network to lobby for national intervention. They are battling not only the Yaqui but corrupt political bosses in the state as well.[71] In a complicated exposition, Ortiz tries not to blame the federal government for his and his friends' economic problems and inability to do business because of both the rebellious Yaqui and Mayo and other "persecutions." Ortiz essentially says the Sonoran government is incapable of handling the situation. Calling upon Díaz to send memos to the commander of the First Military Zone and Sonoran military forces, Ortiz implies that presidential power is the only way to force these disparate military forces to put their own political gains in abeyance so that they can quell Yaqui resistance. Ortiz also refers to his own tenure as former prefect of Alamos, at a time when the Yaqui were presumably more manageable, again implying that the current state government and military are completely incapable of solving the Indian problem in Sonora.

Ortiz further complains that General Carbó and Governor Torres left Alamos and its residents virtually defenseless on April 20 and 21, 1885, by removing federal and auxiliary forces.[72] Citing Carbó's incompetence, Ortiz pleads with Díaz:

No person who knows that place, however ignorant he or she might be, could conceive that, in a plan for a campaign against the Yaqui and the Mayo, it would be possible to adopt a measure that leaves the most important district in the state so badly exposed to their ferocity, without any element of defense. To the contrary, everyone knows that from the most remote places in which there has been an Indian rebellion, and when it is a matter of launching any kind of military operation against them, the first decision adopted has been that of waging war with the competent forces of the town of Navojoa, because it is considered a strategic point of great importance and key to the district of Alamos.[73]

Ortiz privileges the district of Alamos as the site of commerce and development and the home of loyal citizens of Mexico because of its rich mineral deposits, fertile farmland, and large Yaqui population to labor in these industries. Ortiz gives a secondary, underlying current of critiques of Carbó's ineptness as a military strategist, showing a bifurcated vision of what was important to different communities during the Yaqui Indian wars. Ortiz believed it was the responsibility of the federal and auxiliary troops to protect the seat of the district and its businesses from Yaqui pillaging.[74] On the other hand, Carbó's use of Navojoa, an outpost thirty-one miles from Alamos, as a base of operations for tracking the Yaqui into the Sierra Madre demonstrates that the military priority was to wipe out the Yaqui. But since Carbó failed, the attacks did not stop.

Ortiz insults Carbó's masculinity by questioning his military decisions:

For two-and-a-half years, while that State has been sleeping, he has continually kept a garrison of federal troops in Navojoa, and it has been sufficient to put the Indians back in line. If he has now changed his mind, whatever may be the pretext he invokes, I can assure you, Mr. President, that the true motive behind his determination is none other than the passion for revenge; since [he acts] spitefully against those wretched inhabitants because they have no love for him, there is friendliness toward the Governor who leads the State for some years now. I have been threatening to take a similar determination, with the objective of doing them the greatest harm possible.[75]

Ortiz further accuses Carbó of "political persecutions" and self-generated pretexts for vengeance, remarking on his personal political ambitions in the state of Sonora, something a federal general should not have.[76] Carbó's dishonorable enactment of policy, argues Ortiz, suggests that the generals were more consumed by their own masculine culture of aggression, power, and passion for revenge than by the welfare of Sonora's citizens. Carbó's decisions as a military strategist are reduced to excessively egocentric, uncontrollable emotions.[77]

Most important about Ortiz's critique of Carbó is that it shows a schism between elites over ideas of nation. To Ortiz it is more important to protect the citizens than to eliminate the Yaqui, whereas to General Carbó the nation must rid itself of racial and cultural difference. Ortiz's letter to President Díaz illustrates how the vision of capital-holding elites was less abstract than those of military elites. Ortiz wants security and prosperity for his people, which does not require the annihilation of indigenous difference. But because General Carbó sees Yaqui attacks and sovereignty as an affront to geographical and national integrity, the military is carrying out a masculinist national agenda hinged on race, not on the citizenship claims of elite mestizos. Ortiz's dissent shows an interesting contrast between the elite mestizo classes of northern Mexico that actually work against each other.

Ortiz argues that "the Supreme [Federal] Government entrusted him to establish in Sonora the most abnormal system of terror that could possibly be imagined, in order to suppress manifestations of the public spirit, either by true law or tyranny, and even in order to take vengeance on the unfortunate inhabitants because they do not applaud the incalculable abuses that have continued to be committed for more than three years, even before he was given the most remote pretext for these measures involving terror."[78] The concrete relationship between state-sanctioned violence and the larger Mexican project of modernity often negatively affected even people like Ortiz, who were recognized as citizens. A military and political tyranny of its own affected not only the lives of supposed legitimate Mexican citizens like Ortiz, his family, and his cronies, but Yaqui and Mayo lives as well. Terror and fear inhibited not only capitalism and free enterprise but also basic everyday life.

Even upper-class, landowning Mexicans in Sonora were trapped by the rhetoric and domination of coloniality propagated by a corrupt (according to Ortiz) military presence.

Criticism of political abuses in the form of excessive violence came from both the U.S. and Mexican press, which questioned the tactics of state-sponsored violence. Mexican consulates in the United States and the secretary of foreign relations were preoccupied with these reports, for bad publicity about Mexican barbarity no doubt hindered capitalist investment and the nation's march toward modernity. The San Francisco consulate believed that these articles "in general, in a tone less hostile to our government would limit these supposed announcements of depredations; and focus on the peace settlement without doubts about the pacification of the Yaqui."[79] Consular officials were constantly trying to make it seem these violent encounters, whether fictitious or not, were minor concerns. Gravely concerned with stories appearing in the United States, the Mexican consulate in San Francisco reported that U.S. perceptions represented the Mexican government as

having undertaken various wars of *extermination in which women and children have been included in the general butchery [la carnicería]*. This policy has done nothing more than to intensify the Yaquis' hatred towards the Mexicans, a hatred that those who have survived these successive wars have transmitted to their progeny. It is very clear that the Yaqui are today as far from being on the decrease as ever, and the problem of subjugating them, and of developing resources in the territory that they occupy, seems no closer to a solution today than it was when the Republic declared its rights and sovereignty.[80]

The evoking of butchery of bodies, a fierce metaphor for violated dead bodies of Yaqui women and children, simultaneously accomplishes two things. First, such violent practices reveal that Victorian presuppositions of the sanctity of women and children held no sway in this war, and, in fact, the prevention of reproduction was targeted as a mechanism of genocide.[81] This strategy created in the Yaqui even greater hatred of the Mexican government. Yaqui women, it was assumed, would teach their children, with the death of a family member or assassination attempt that they survived, to hate the Mexican government. Government practice embodied in the *carnicería* of bloodshed is what taught Yaqui children to hate Mexicans, not just the social conditioning from their mothers. The delicate balance between wanting the Yaqui to stop hating Mexicans and stopping the war is circumvented, in this passage, by the assertion that the Yaqui were no more subjugated in 1906 than they had been in the past, a constant reminder that Sonoran natural resources could not be developed as desired. Even though the American newspaper report names the carnicería of violence and hatred, this is the very thing the Mexican government tried to cover up. Yaqui desires for sovereignty and rights, often enacted in raids on haciendas for supplies, constantly triggered Mexican military counterattacks, creating a perpetual cycle of warfare that took a toll on Yaqui and Mexican alike.

An article of April 27, 1902, in the *Arizona Daily Star* about the deportations of Yaquis to Yucatán criticized the Mexican government's inhumane and misguided emulation of U.S. policy toward Geronimo's Apache. The piece was quickly condemned for being full of lies by the director of the Mexican consulate in Tucson, Arturo Elías. The article was a public relations fiasco waiting to happen because it argued that

> the government of Mexico, it seems, sends into the same exile the Yaquis, the good, the bad, and the independent, the industrious, the organized, those who obey the law, without there being any reasons taken into account for their good or bad conduct. This causes general displeasure among the good and industrious Yaquis, many of whom have risen up in order to protest against such unjust practices by the government. In recent weeks, the government has issued some extremely strong warnings. The Yaquis are taken prisoner wherever they may be and put on a ship in Guaymas headed for Yucatán, and they say, moreover, according to rumors, that once they are on board ship, they never again set foot on land unless it be the ocean floor. If this is true, the Mexican government's policy and manner of working for its cruelty, its barbarity, and its injustice has no sanction anywhere in the civilized world. The Yaqui Indians are the most industrious, the most responsible, honorable, and virtuous of the working class in Sonora. They should not be pulled from their homes. The state's mining industry, in which so much American capital has been invested, must not be deprived of such an industrious class of people.[82]

In his rebuttal, Consulate Arturo Elías adamantly refuted rumors of genocide but did not respond to the accusation that all Yaquis, good and bad, are targeted indiscriminately: "The government provides them with land and with tools to till it, and only in extreme cases, when they refuse to adapt to a peaceful, honest occupation, they are drafted into military service. There is no basis for believing the rumor that some of these Indians, put on ship in Guaymas, never reach their destination because they are thrown into the ocean to perish. Let me make a suggestion, Mister Editor, and that is that you

FIGURE 2 "The Scourge of the Yaquis." *Harper's Weekly Magazine*, May 2, 1908.

demand that your informant reveal the source from which he got this piece of news, which unjustifiably slanders the [Mexican] Republic that I have the honor of representing."[83] Mexican government officials went to great lengths to dispute the slightest accusation of barbarity. In effect, such discourses create a discontinuity of history between violence as a cultural practice and how Mexico wanted to be seen by its northern neighbor.

Historical denials of state-sanctioned violence, such as Elías's portrayal of a democratic policy toward the Yaqui, is undone by photographic archives that picture the lynching of Yaquis. Set in the context of yellow journalism, "la prensa alarmista," and sensationalism in the United States and Mexico in the early twentieth century, the photographs of Yaqui lynchings and executions come not from Mexican sources, but from U.S. newspaper clippings in Mexican archives (the Secretaría de Relaciones Exteriores). In fact, the Mexican press strongly criticized U.S. journalism, especially as it pertained to representations of Mexico.[84] As exhibited in full-page articles in the *Los Angeles Times*

(May 13, 1906), the *San Francisco Sunday Call*, *Harper's Weekly* (1908), and the Sunday *New York Herald* (January 31, 1909), torture and its public documentation in photography were essentially used to ascribe a premodern barbarity to Mexico and its twentieth-century Indian policy; extremely violent U.S. Indian policies of only a few decades earlier were overlooked in the process.

Manufacturing an image of a "barbarous Mexico," to borrow the title of Kenneth Turner's exposé of Yaqui enslavement and exploitation at the hands of the Mexican government and transnational capital industries in Sonora (funded by U.S. dollars), also justified intervention by the United States in Sonora through capital improvements. The perception of U.S. civilization in the United States hinged upon an image of Mexican barbarity, most graphically conveyed in photographs of executions and lynchings of Yaquis. Those images facilitated the denial of the lynching of African Americans as a simultaneous cultural practice in the United States.[85] With all of these various political and psychic displacements at play (U.S. exceptionalism that denies its lynching of African Americans, Mexican barbarism in its Indian policy, Mexican modernity versus Mexican premodernity) and given the intertwined transnational histories of racial violence and modernity embodied in execution, lynching, and deportation, the actual content of these photographs requires careful consideration. My reading is situated between a critique of the lack of transparency embodied in photography and the documentary nature of these photos. Critical discussions of war and punishment are useful here to illuminate the ways in which the Yaqui endured torture and bodily violence and in which these tortured bodies remain outside of official national histories of Mexico and the United States.

Most interesting about these photographs is the lack of an explanation of their content. The articles accompanying them say nothing about why or how the lynchings and executions occurred. Instead, they focus on talk of Americans who have been robbed and Mexicans' retaliatory attacks on Yaqui insurgents in Minas Prietas and to the east of the Sonora Railway line, explaining the rebellion and its origins. The reader is asked to make the cause and effect connection between the "Stupid [Mexican] Soldiery" and the executed bodies of the "Red Raiders of Sonora." Making light of why Yaqui raids happen, the writer, Allen Kelly, again brings up American exceptionalism but this time related to its handling of the Apache conflicts. He wrote, "To compare the wretched Mexican convict-soldier with the American trooper is absurd."[86] Kelly ignores that Geronimo, Victorio, and any number of Apache leaders eluded U.S. authorities for long periods. He also selectively forgets and romanticizes the U.S. cavalry's role in Apache subjugation in his haste to chastise

FIGURE 3 "The Scourge of the Yaquis." *Harper's Weekly Magazine*, May 2, 1908.

the premodern, criminal, recalcitrant Mexican fighting forces charged with keeping Sonora safe for capitalism.

Within this context of the discourses of a barbarous Mexico and an exceptional United States, I want to shift my focus to discuss what the photographs signify in the larger Mexican and American nationalist projects of forgetting violence. The United States chastises Mexico even as African Americans were still being lynched in the country in record numbers. Meanwhile, Mexico declared Sonora free of Yaqui insurgents and safe for capitalism while Yaquis were automatically lynched or deported. The photos represent how flesh is mutilated or betrayed by forces outside of the body and in a public context, making pain legible while avoiding a description of the social structures that ultimately created these dead bodies. The processes of torture, the physical destruction of the body by an outside force, also acted to break down the mind of the tortured as well as those of the people who witnessed and sensationalized the violated body. These photos emerged in certain U.S. media markets as exposés or perhaps in sympathy with the Magonista movement preceding the Mexican Revolution.[87] Yet images of the Yaqui body in pain at the hands of the Mexican government serve to displace attention from the brutality of the United States in its Apache campaigns. The photos of dead Yaquis erroneously obviate contemporary race problems in the United States; furthermore, the photos decontextualize how executions and lynching happen, suggesting they are not random but associated with a larger structural process of differentiation.

Pockets of the Mexican media were, however, critical of public executions and lynchings as a method to break down the willful rebellion of Yaqui subjects. On May 3, 1906, the newspaper *La Bandera Sonorense* in Urés, Sonora, called the violence embodied in these photos "a work of extermination, cruel, systematic, that no longer seeks to finally and totally pacify and to put down but to exterminate the Yaqui pueblo." *La Bandera* recognized that public displays of military and government power to destroy the bodies of Yaquis with impunity show a larger systematic desire not just to pacify this disgruntled indigenous group but to finally wipe them out. In publicly inflicting pain, the torturer (as a stand-in for the state) gains ethnic, gender, religious, or national superiority over the tortured and gains visible power. Through public displays of power, the reading audience learns that the individual body is destroyed by state power. Michel Foucault's *Discipline and Punish* cites the mid-eighteenth century as the period when public execution decreased as a form of capital punishment.[88] Foucault argues that more hidden forms of discipline and violence take precedence over public punishment, but he does not say that the hidden forms completely supplant the public ones; rather, they continue to exist alongside each other, but in a different relation to one another. Between emergent surveillance and discipline, on the one hand, and persistent corporal, public punishment, on the other represents a mode by which states ensured their reproduction in the Americas at this point in time. What is most striking about the opinion expressed in *La Bandera* is that they are in accord with "final and total pacification" of the Yaquis but not extermination. While the power mechanizations I discuss here are absented from the photos as if they were self-explanatory and transparent in their meaning, they still provide evidence of the disjunctures on the Yaqui question. The photos, in a quite detailed and unavoidable fashion, demonstrate that the state was invested in a project of annihilation of indigenous people as the means of making the state modern. The lynching photos directly challenge nationalist visions of Mexico in relation to indigenous peoples: extermination of the Indian in mestizo Mexico would allow for modernity to be achieved. For the people of Sonora, there is a concrete business interest and desire of Foucauldian modernity—one in which medieval forms of control have been added to the rationalized means of so-called pacification. The real problem comes in the idea that government troops betray the Mexican nation's message of modernity in practice through their colonial displays of state power. The difference between extermination and total pacification should be seen as oppositional practice in the larger scheme of empire, especially when we are reading lynching photographs.

Such photographs as evidence are rare. More common within the archive are discursive tracts denying state-sanctioned violence and torture of the Yaqui. In both a dispatch to General Torres, the military commander of the First Zone, and a newspaper article published in Arizona, Consul Louis Hostettler argues the exact opposite of what the photos suggest: "Having felt an interest in the condition of the Yaqui Indians, that were returned from the United States, I am pleased to report that they are well treated and seem to be perfectly content with their treatment, I find they are at the jail in Magdalena, and all of them are in the best of health."[89] Hostettler went to see the prisoners because "there was a rumor circulated on the street here that these Indians had been tortured and shot by the Mexican officials, but the report shows that rumor false."[90] Hostettler attempts to settle the record on torture by denying its existence. But instead, his assertion (as a stand-alone document that was also reprinted in the newspaper article) unsettles the account of violence, making the line between accountability, public knowledge, and the state even more tenuous.[91] The attempt to make the violence unspeakable or invisible in official U.S. and Mexican national discourses ultimately names the thing that is denied, so that the absence of torture is felt but not formally acknowledged.

Sometimes the Mexican government perceived the U.S. press as writing with "both malice and tenacity that have been exploiting public opinion in the country, striving to impress the alleged impotence of the general and local government to pacify, subdue or exterminate the Yaqui."[92] Already somewhat fearful of impending economic losses, American investors in Sonora wanted nothing less than to hear they were part of a government plan to exterminate, pacify, or subject the Yaqui because they had already done so with their "own" Indians and were now suddenly above such actions. However, this did not stop U.S. journalists from taking an interest in the Yaqui situation. *Collier's Weekly* for March 11, 1905, featured an article entitle "The Last of the Yaqui," which touts itself as an "anthropological excursion" through the Sierra Madre on which a reporter was allowed to accompany Mexican military officials as they brought Yaqui prisoners to the Río Yaqui:

> At the little deserted town of Bacum the cavalcade halted only long enough to execute ten Yaqui men and boys by hanging them to trees, without a hearing or explanation. It was sufficient to be adjudged guilty of being a live Yaqui to have the death penalty inflicted in the most revolting form and in the quickest time. These men and boys were brought out with their arms closely pinioned and a rope around their necks, the end of which was thrown over a convenient limb of a nearby tree, tied to the pommel of a soldier's saddle, and the horse, spurred into a run, immediately jerked the poor victim into eternity.

The article goes on to detail the institutionalized process of lynching. It glibly demonstrates Mexican military irrationality and a propensity for violence, as anyone gendered male could be lynched "without hearing or explanation." Further, it illustrates that the conflict was a competition between notions of masculinity and nation that played themselves out on Yaqui bodies hung from trees.

But fear of losing U.S. capital investments did not stop the Mexican government's all-out war on the Yaqui. In an article from an unidentified U.S. newspaper, translated and stored in the general archive of the state of Sonora in *Reclamaciones de extranjeros* (Foreign reports), this information leaked out of Sonora in 1906, tracking the gruesome details of the Yaqui campaign:

> Strange fruit is seen on many of the trees in Sonora's beautiful and fertile fields, strange and horrible like the "acorns" in the reign of Louis XI in France. A single branch often holds two or three dead Yaqui Indians, rocking in the wind, with their heads fallen to one side and their beards on their chests, and always revolving around the tree and its horrible fruit is a buzzard, and sometimes a dozen of them. The dead Yaquis rocking in the breeze are warnings from the Mexican government for the rebellious natives in Sonora, who, nevertheless, forcefully and resolutely increase their desire for independence, month after month, while their reputed chief, John Dwyer, the American mining expert, waits, trusting in the political event that will follow the death of elderly President Díaz. The dead Yaquis suspended from the branches in Sonora are not the only admonition to the rebels. Each month, half a dozen of the tribe's brave warriors are marched by a military escort from the prison in Hermosillo to a field beyond the city, and there, as publicly as possible, they are militarily executed.[93]

Several aspects of this article about the lynching of disobedient Yaqui and their rebellion against the Mexican nation are noteworthy, the first being the conspiracy theory that an American miner, John Dwyer, was their political jefe and that he wanted to use the Yaqui to annex Sonora and create a sovereign nation for the Yaqui. Several reports from the Secretaría de Relaciones Exteriores articulate anxiety about Dwyer because somehow the presence of American funds, support, and leadership made Yaqui rebellion doubly dangerous.[94] Mexico had already experienced two fiascos in which it had ceded territory: the Mexican War of 1846–48 and the Treaty of La Mesilla. Suggestions that Dwyer was using the Yaqui to annex Sonora no doubt reminded the Mexican government of its failed colonization policies that caused the loss of more than half of its territory to the colonial power to the north. Opening a wound of historical trauma by means of such a suggestion only reminded the Mexican government that it had not only been unable to stop U.S. colonial powers, but also was incapable of asserting its own colonial designs in its own territory because of Yaqui resistance. Further, suggesting that the military leader of the Yaqui was a gringo is another effacement of Yaqui subjectivity, a denial of their ability to rationally carry out warfare against a sovereign nation like Mexico. The Mexican frustration and anxiety over its failure to carry out its colonial projects within its borders was taken out upon the bodies of Yaqui insurgents through torture and lynching. The references in this article to the strange fruit of the trees bearing hanged Yaqui bodies are among the few descriptions in print of the Yaqui body in pain. Some argue that the text draws on African metaphors about strange fruit hanging in the trees in Abel Meeropol's poem "Strange Fruit" of 1930 and in Billie Holiday's recording of the song version on Columbia Records in 1939, but this news clipping about Yaqui lynching, published in 1906, predates both of these texts by twenty-five years.

The haunting nature of the strange fruit metaphor reinforces why it was necessary for the government to constantly preach that the Yaqui wars were over, precisely because they were not over. At a dinner held in Washington, D.C., on December 12, 1891, in honor of Matías Romero, the retiring Mexican Minister to the United States, who served as a diplomat sporadically from 1860 until 1898, the keynote speech, entitled "The King of Yaqui Country," seems to regard the Yaqui and their wars as a thing of the past. The king of Yaqui country was not Cajeme or any other Yaqui for that matter. He was Don Carlos Conant, a wealthy venture capitalist who was the son of a New Hampshire–born man and a Sonorense woman. Conant quickly tired of the class struggles and political wars engulfing Sonora in the 1880s because he was on the wrong side of the battle; he fled to Chihuahua, only to return at the request of Díaz. With much drama and flair, Walter S. Logan proclaimed to the American audience, "We come again to 1886. The Yaqui have been conquered and scattered. The country which they have claimed and defended for untold centuries is now for the first time open to settlement by civilized man. But what is to be done with it? . . . To reclaim these required the construction of vast irrigating works, the expenditure of a large amount of capital and the work of a great organizer,"[95] and that person was none other than Conant, Díaz's former soldier and general manager of the Sonora and Sinaloa Irrigation Company, the first company to bring private capital into the Río Yaqui for agricultural development. In his revisionist history designed to persuade American venture capitalists that Sonora was a safe investment, Logan stretches the truth. In 1886 and 1887, as numerous letters between Díaz and Generals Carbó, Topete, and García attest, the Yaqui may have been scattered, but they were not conquered. On January 22, 1887, when more than one thousand Indians surrendered, Gen. Pedro Galván wrote to Díaz declaring the Yaqui campaign over.[96] Yet the peace was formally broken in 1899 with a declaration of war by the leader Tetaibate, suggesting that eruptions of Yaqui insurgency continued through the Mexican Revolution.[97] But this continued rebellion on the ground did not stop the grand, optimistic narrative of a Sonora open for North American investors.

Supposedly Conant told Díaz he would spearhead colonization efforts:

"on one condition—that every surviving Yaqui shall be guaranteed his freedom, and that I may select some favored spot on these lands you give me, and invite their original possessors back to enjoy some portion of the country which has so long been theirs." The president himself desired this consummation quite as much as Don Carlos; and so as a result of the great grant or concession of 1890 to Don Carlos Conant of the lands and the river rights of the Yaqui, Mayo, and Fuerte Valleys of Sonora and Sinaloa, that the Yaqui and Mayo Indians, then driven from their homes in exile, scattered over the face of the country, eking out a precarious existence where they can and starving where they must, are to be invited back to the homes of their ancestors, their ancient occupation of tilling the soil.[98]

Narratives of imperial benevolence like this one create a story about great Mexican male industrial capitalist saviors who gave the poor displaced Yaqui people their land back and says nothing of the economic causes behind the wars that displaced them in the first place. The supposed "Empire of Don Carlos" signals the second coming of colonialism in Sonora, but this time funded by Yankee dollars and constructed by Yankee architects and captains of industry. The explicit purpose of the dinner was to praise Romero and get Yankee dollars flowing into Mexico. Discursively, the visions of Mexican and U.S. development of northern Mexico are aligned doubly through the bodies of the Yaqui: first, through their removal via genocide and deportation and, second, through the returned and redeemed. Rebellious bodies are removed; grateful, industrious ones are returned.

Somewhat in line with this "exceptional" benevolence, after the battle of Añil in 1886, which the Mexican army believed would squelch the Yaqui resistance, the troops occupied the Río Yaqui, eventually offering land to the surviving families.[99] But this generosity did not last for long. General Martínez wrote to Díaz,

I do not put great importance on these [battles], and if I feel that the Yaqui, not knowing their own interests, have rejected the generous protection that the Superior [Federal] Government has offered them, but moreover, I am glad, to a certain point, because they themselves have indicated the conduct that I ought to observe in the event, a thing that I could not do when I saw them accept the act of submission, influenced without doubt by the presence of our troops, since the conviction in which they have contracted these Indians which have resulted in their work, but still we have to punish their insolence and pacify with the Mayos to secure the peace in this river valley, Mr. President, to give a good lesson to these ingrates, a lesson that they will not forget in many years.[100]

In threatening the Yaqui with punishment for their insolence and rejection of the terms of military occupation, General Martínez shows how thin such a promise of protection was. Although the Río Yaqui was declared Conant's concession and the theater of his work (the Empire of Don Carlos), the fact remained that this empire was always at risk of falling to the supposedly conquered Indians. Mexican and U.S. imperialisms mobilized the language of benevolence or reconquest or both, but in financial terms and with a kind of ambivalence and fear, with the Yaqui always lurking in the background as a potential threat to empire's stability.

The ambassador's dinner, "A Mexican Night" was designed to abscond the fact that the Yaqui were still waging war in Sonora in December 1890. Essentially writing them out of Sonora's history except as the recipients of Anglo and Mexican benevolence, "A Mexican Night," the dinner honoring Romero, was an institutional erasure of multiple Yaqui attempts to publicly enact subjectivity through warfare. "A Mexican Night" recast the Yaqui struggle as an ancient battle, one having little or no effect on Sonora's political, economic, and social climate in the industrial reconquest of the 1890s. It is an attempt to write Yaqui agency out of the historical narratives of Mexican and U.S. venture capitalism as they were intimately intertwined.

Even if Conant were the capitalist savior of Sonora, and Mexican and U.S. officials had declared Yaqui rebellion finished, it is clear that the Yaqui struggle was highly visible to both U.S. and Mexican officials, even though both state departments tried to contain press articles about the wars and violence. After the major battles of 1885 and 1890 and the massacre in Mazacoba in 1900, the deportations began and thus the discourses along the U.S.–Mexico border shifted to the question of immigration and surveillance. Vice Consul Máximo Gavito wrote to the governor of Sonora,

> There has not been any immigration of Yaqui through the consular district under my charge. The Yaqui that are in the railroads in Bisbee and the woodcutting camps have been well known in those parts for more than 10 years, and they have not moved from these places. But in the event that it comes to be observed that they enter these camps both as miners as well as railroad workers, I will have the pleasure of communicating that, and moreover, of monitoring them in case they might wish to penetrate Mexico once again. For another thing, I will report to the federal and civil authorities along the Mexican border, so that they may be on alert, and in the case that the Indians are armed, that the officials may apprehend and confiscate their weapons and war ammunition. I will also notify businesses generally in the consular district that is under my charge, so that they may advise me immediately in case some Yaqui buy arms, with the objective of impeding them from entering Mexico with those weapons.[101]

This shift from military actions to immigration control and wholesale vigilance marked a moment of increasing technologies of counterinsurgency. Federal and civil forces as well as private industries and municipal governments could and did use the telephone and other new technologies that enabled monitoring of populations to track the movement of Yaqui employed in local industry, especially if they might be running guns between the United States and Mexico to fuel their armed struggle.[102] But even if people weren't running guns, "indios Yaqui sospechos[os]" without passports were often apprehended by local governments as part of state and national efforts to curtail the untraceable armed Yaqui struggle.[103]

After the incident at Mazacoba the Ministry of Foreign Relations was trying to do damage control relating to Yaqui attacks with the U.S. government and the Mexican president. Mexican consulates in the United States were a part of the surveillance apparatus. After deportations began, the director of the consulate in Phoenix sent the following letter to the Secretaría de Relaciones Exteriores:

> Having recently received reports about the presence of more unknown Yaqui Indians in *rancherías* [small settlements] in the southern part of my consular jurisdiction, whose movements seem to be suspicious enough; in fulfilling my duties, I believed that it was certainly wise to carry out a rigorous investigation, with all the prudence and reserve that the case requires, in order to make certain said reports, to put me immediately in route from Sonora, to the person in charge of monitoring that part of the border through which it is likely that those Indians might return, as is supposed, in order to procure their apprehension and their delivery to the respective authorities.[104]

Private enterprises, such as U.S.-owned and Mexican-based mining companies like Treadwell and the Cananea Consolidated Copper Company, would send telegrams to the Sonoran state and Mexican federal governments regarding any sightings of potentially threatening Yaquis, sometimes demanding that troops be sent to protect mining interests and other times simply warning the government of a potential insurgent attack.[105] Private security forces were created to protect haciendas from raids, with the express intent of policing the workers as well as those Yaqui circulating in the immediate area. For example, in June 1904 police at the Hacienda La Galera reported to the municipal president that "some old, peaceful Indian servants had been absent from that Sheriff's office during the days of the rebellion, and as soon as the rebellious Indians withdrew, there returned to the aforementioned hacienda all of the servants who had been hiding, perhaps with the objective of avoiding all communication with the insurgent Yaqui that were hostile to the government, but if this authority judged it appropriate to order the apprehension of the referred-to servants, it would do it in a public way, putting them at my disposition."[106] The disappearance and reappearance of older, "peaceful" Yaqui servants at this hacienda nevertheless raises suspicion, precisely because their absence coincided with a time of revolt. Age did not excuse people from being suspected as rebels; in fact, circumstantial evidence collected by public and private policing contributed to a climate for desired control. On June 21 of the same month, Florencio Robles and six national guardsmen under his command were not able to capture any of the elderly Yaqui at the Hacienda La Galera, because the levels of surveillance did not always function correctly. Yaqui guerrilla strategies often trumped these technologies and the military was outsmarted several times over.[107] This discreet shift in how surveillance took place was marked by the emergence of new institutions in both the United States and Mexico at the beginning of the twentieth century: police forces, *rurales*, Arizona Rangers, the Border Patrol, and consulates all practiced new technologies of surveillance, the mechanisms of modernity that eventually quelled the Yaqui rebellion.[108]

One of the foremost preoccupations of both the Arizona-based Mexican consuls and the Seretaría de Relaciones Exteriores was the fact that Yaqui were passing for Mexican mestizos and purchasing guns, cartridges, and supplies in Arizona to smuggle into Sonora. The year 1905 was filled with conflicting information about Yaqui violence against Americans colonizing Sonora, Mexicans in Sonora and Arizona, and general assaults against the Mexican nation. At the same time, Yaqui racial passing also turned into a debate about immigration and deportation.[109] A letter of January 5, 1905, from the consul at Yuma, Arizona, to Foreign Relations Secretary Ignacio Mariscal reveals that gun-running by Yaquis posing as Mexicans was a serious problem. "The authorities here told me . . . that a law prohibiting the sale of arms and ammunition to the Indians, existing as it does in the Arizona Territory, they would try to demand its fulfillment by the town's business owners. However, these officials encountered a serious hindrance in satisfying my wishes, because it is not so easy for them to recognize the Yaquis, since each time that they come around here, they come dressed like the Mexican workers walking around these places are accustomed to dressing, and so it is not easy to tell them apart."[110] There is a troubling racial, ethnic, or national slippage between being Mexican and being Yaqui for both Mexican and U.S. authorities precisely because the Yaqui were effectively performing Mexicanness to get across the border, buy arms, and return to Mexico. The resemblance between Mexican worker and Yaqui insurgent demonstrates the inability to physically track, confirm, and discern racial and cultural characteristics as well as the tenuousness of the all-important ways in which the Yaqui stealthily participated in the cross-border labor market by performing Mexicanness, which in turn fortified their armed struggle.

Even though Arizonans could be fined or imprisoned or both for selling arms to any Indian, this did not prove a hindrance to the Yaqui. Further, the Arizona consulate's attempt at racial profiling is quite ironic in its description:

Undoubtedly, a lot of weapons and a lot of cartridges have been brought into Mexico in the past for that purpose, both by the Yaqui as well as by their sympathizers, but this has never happened openly, nor has it been permitted by any official, so that the authorities in Arizona are justifiably anxious that nobody helps out the rest of the Yaqui. . . . Although, as is probable, the Yaqui do not know that this law will apply to them with equal force and even more, because this is a reason for believing that the sale of these arms and bullets is against a friendly government. The Arizonans who sell firearms have got to take care to examine each one of their customers [to see] if they are tall, with black hair, and brown skin, since many of the Yaqui are mistaken for Mexicans.[111]

The profile of a tall, dark-haired, brown-skinned person fits a broad range of people along the U.S.–Mexico border but still assumes a few things. Dark skin, dark hair, and tall height were supposedly not traits of Sonorans or Mexicans, who were supposedly light-skinned and short and had light eyes. The presupposition of the description is that in Sonora no Mexicans, only the Yaqui, are tall and have dark skin and dark eyes. The passage demonstrates the plasticity of supposedly stable, fixed categories like race, class, and nation. In census counts from 1906 Pimas and Opatas were described as "laborers in the farms, ranches and orchards . . . and live with their families and are confused with the families of the white race," thus classifying them as mestizo Indians. By contrast, this description labels Yaqui nonwhite, non-Mexican, and therefore noncitizens.[112] The Yaquis should be clearly identifiable to authorities because, whereas the Pimas and Opatas residing in the same district of Urés as peones "are intimately mixed with the whites and it is almost impossible to racially distinguish them," the Yaqui were presumed to be racially unmixed.[113] To suggest that Pimas and Opatas were mixed with and indistinguishable from whites also commented on their civility and assimilation. Pimas and Opatas had a long history of helping the Spanish, Mexicans, and even Americans fight against the Apache, Seri, and Yaqui in Sonora, which in some ways facilitated this reporting of them as white. Admitting slippage in the Yaqui case—that Mexicans were Indians and Indians were Mexicans—would ideologically undermine the very goal sought in conducting war against the Yaqui Indians. Subduing Indians because they were not considered mestizos or Mexicans with citizenship rights was the way to continue the distinction between Yaqui as Indians and Mexicans as mestizos.[114] As the consul complains, "We cannot wait for the success or failure of their offerings because when any Yaqui goes to Yuma, they need to be completely stopped but they are often invisible to police agents, and when I have seen them in the streets myself, I have not had the occasion to know them either."[115] If neither Mexican consular officials nor police officials at the border were able to identify these insurgents, how could a government quash their armed resistance?

There was also fear that Yaqui were mixing among Arizona Indian tribes and reservations as well. American officials could not tell if they were Yaqui rebels or not or if they were American Indians, Mexican Indians, or Mexicans. Slippage between identity categories and phenotype could not be overcome, even within the established U.S. reservation system or institutional policing at the border. While Mexican and American officials tried to police the bodies of Yaqui crossing the border, the fact that they were blending in with U.S.-based Indian populations in Arizona and Mexican populations on both sides reveals that such systems were never totalizing and always porous.

Passing was not just a social problem but a political problem because the sense of an unbounded, untraceable enemy disrupted state-formation. If the U.S. and Mexican officials could not tell the difference between a Yaqui and a Mexican, how could they stop the arms trade or, more important, how could they carry out an effective project of genocide if they were killing the wrong people? Passing became such a problem that the Tucson consulate hired a private detective, paid with Mexican government funds, to investigate the sale of arms and track suspicious Yaqui-"Mexicans." Not surprisingly, the private detective was a Mexican American, Oscar Carrillo, who had a reputation of "persona activa y de Buenos antecedentes," perhaps a precursor of the modern-day Border Patrol.[116] The turn to a private investigator demonstrates the Mexican nation's inability to police its border and the Arizona Territory's inability to enforce its laws about the sale of arms and weapons to Indians. What does it mean, then, for Mexican consular officials to admit that "the Yuma Police Department has offered me help, to finally defeat the arms trade, it is possible, but these authorities do not know our Yaquis, and I don't believe that there is anyone here who knows them like we do and don't you think the success that they may obtain is doubtful if not impossible?"[117] The consular official, C. Fernández Pasalagua, expresses concern that he could not depend upon U.S. law enforcement officials to tell the difference between a Mexican and a Yaqui, but then again neither could the Mexican officials at times.

In his submissions to the consulate in Tucson, Detective Carrillo detailed his surveillance based on general observations about Indian insurgents and Tucson merchants.[118] He had nothing to report: "I kept vigilance from the 16th to the 20th in a store that sells the apparatuses of arms and weapons in Twin Buttes, that is about 30 miles from Tucson, where they did not register one sale, even though there are 16 Yaquis working in the town."[119] Pima County authorities took the charge to stop gun-running seriously as well. District Attorney Dick stated to the *Tucson Citizen*, "Information has reached me to the effect that the Yaquis or their agents are procuring arms and ammunition from local merchants, which enables them to carry on their cruel warfare in Sonora, torturing and slaying Mexicans and Americans alike and doing great injury to mining properties in which American capital is heavily invested. I am to loathe to believe that any of the Tucson merchants have willfully and knowingly supplied arms and ammunition to the warring Indians."[120] As in the wartime economy that supported the carrying out of the Camp Grant massacre, Tucson merchants benefited from the Yaqui arms trade in southern Arizona at the turn of the twentieth century, regardless of the fact that it was illegal to sell arms to any Indian. District Attorney Dick refers to the good citizens of Tucson as being deceived into selling arms to Indians, thereby publicly denying that economic need might trump obedience to the racist law. Further, he accuses the Yaqui of torturing their victims, Mexican and American alike, to reinforce the dire need to control the arms trade and Yaqui bodies on a larger scale.[121] That Yaqui were being sold guns and ammunition suggests that capitalist interests displaced the patriotic practices of citizens. Merchants of Tucson were selling arms to Indians, and the famous Ronstadt family was unabashed in their interest in doing so. José Ronstadt, while in the custody of the Tucson consulate office, explained that "it seemed to him an injustice that they would be prohibited from selling arms and ammunition to the Papago Indians, given that they were not at war with the Yaqui. He talked in general, without distinction to race, and moreover, that there existed the certainty that the Papago had been serving as agents to the Yaquis by providing them with weapons."[122] Indian conspiracy did not concern the Ronstadt family of merchants; they, like "business owners in Cananea, Sonora, Mexico, were empowered to sell a certain quantity of weapons and ammunition each month, which, without ongoing monitoring of the market and with the sellers taking advantage of the license, it was impossible to ensure each time that they were not surpassing the limit and selling more weapons than the determined amount."[123] The market, not border or Indian policy, drove the desires of the merchants, who surely benefited from the Yaqui struggle.[124] Nor did racism toward Indians affect whether or not someone sold arms to the Yaqui. Ronstadt's testimony indicated that arms were not being sold to Yaqui just on the U.S. side of the border, but also in Cananea, Sonora, disrupting any idea about uniformly hostile Sonorense sentiments toward the Yaqui and their war. We can conclude that these ambivalent attitudes toward trade and commerce with Indians and Mexicans were the very things that made Yaqui rebellion possible for such a long time. The U.S. reservation system, the extensive social and economic networks of the Yaqui, the Yaquis' ability to pass as Mexican, and the easy availability of arms on the border facilitated Yaquis' participation in transnational circuits of power. Their movements couldn't be marked and contained until they were deported. This wasn't the only genocidal plan in the works.

Some might call the Yaqui deportation scheme a conspiracy to eliminate the Yaqui rebellion, while others would call it state-sponsored genocide. The earliest evidence about the project of Yaqui deportation was from 1886. The brainchild of Gen. Angel Martínez, deportation was seen as a way to "to break with their traditional habits and customs, which still have some points of similarity with savagery. To carry out my proposals, it perhaps might be good to confine to various parts of the Republic all those Indians that are notoriously marked as being incorrigible . . . we need to make it impossible for them to return to these rivers where their residences are, a motive for agitation and uprising and whose bad consequences would be squelched when the Yaqui arrive in Yucatán."[125] Although this project did not materialize until 1901, when rebels began being deported out of Sonora, and was not implemented on a mass scale until 1902, several things in Martínez's treatise on deportation are notable. Echoing the ideology behind American Indian industrial schools and the reservation system itself, Martínez advocates for a logic of spatial control. Removing the Yaqui from their land base and making them work on farms in Colima or Yucatán that belonged to Martínez's friends solved three distinct problems.[126] First, Yaqui ties to land they regarded as sacred, communal, and defensible would be destroyed; second, the labor shortage in Colima would be alleviated; and third, Martínez's friends could reap tremendous profits with free Yaqui labor to further develop an underpopulated, underworked farmland. So while the project of deportation was seen as a national solution to a national problem, at the personal and local levels it was a way of reinforcing the *patronato* (or legal entitlements through the patriarchy embodied in government).

At the very least, deportation was a cultural genocide in the sense that it segregated members of the same cultural group with the stated intention of destroying collective memory and community imaginings of an autonomous Yaqui nation. By some estimates, including those of the historian Evelyn Hu-deHart, roughly 2,000 Yaqui were deported by 1907, but an official number was never recorded.[127] A sample of deportation documents from 1902–9 suggests the number may be much higher. In a report from 1885 the entire Yaqui population was estimated at 20,000.[128] The land survey of 1900 conducted by La Comisión Geográfica Exploradora and led by Col. Ángel García Peña counted 7,606 Indians in the Yaqui River valley.[129] Seven years later the first census of the Porfiriato, on June 21, 1907, tallied 2,723 Yaqui in the state of Sonora. A 17,000-person drop in population over a twenty-two-year period represents an 86 percent decline. Furthermore, Yaqui land rights had been significantly diminished. In a statistical notice of 1906 for the Guaymas district, of the 3,546 (a sign that figures fluctuate from year to year based on deportation, migration, and resettlement) Yaqui counted in the census, 1,680 farmed or occupied 37,000 square meters of land in Cócorit, Torin, Potam, Cumuripa, and Bacum, suggesting that more than half of the district's Indians were urban.[130] The creation of an urban Yaqui population was a survival strategy that signaled a dwindling connection to a Yaqui rural space of autonomy. Urban Indians in the United States, for example, lack the legal protections available to federally recognized tribal groups with a land base and thus develop their own means of self-advocacy.[131] There have never been Indian reservations in Mexico, but the Yaqui are the only tribe to be recognized by the government as having a land base. In the colonial Mexican centers of power, indigenous elites had a stake in power and policy, but this was not true for Yaqui in Sonoran urban centers like Hermosillo or Guaymas.[132] A move out of the Río Yaqui or one of the eight pueblos into an urban center was not a demonstration of civic participation as an indigenous person. Rather, it was propelled by economic security and perhaps a cultural and social disassociation with Yaqui rebels. At the same time, the centralized nature of cities surely made surveillance of Yaqui populations there much easier. Municipal police, a limited geographical area to patrol, and an influx of state and federal troops made it possible to monitor the Yaqui population in a way that simply could not be duplicated in the eight pueblos or the sierra.

One can surmise that the threat of deportation indeed created the phenomenon of Yaqui urban migration. The process of deportation was initiated in 1902 after the battle of Mazacoba. In a letter to Díaz, the newest commander of the First Military Zone, General Martínez, "reports that the situation of the Yaqui is desperate and they are perpetually hiding in the Río Yaqui. In my opinion the solution to put an end to these rebels will be to embark them to a distant place; but as this turns out to be expensive, we will ask the Sonora headquarters to cover the expenses for the shipment and maintenance of the

TABLE 1 Place of imprisonment of Yaquis by age and gender, 1902–1905

Place of imprisonment	Age in years	Male	Female	Total
Penitentiary of Hermosillo	0–5	46	40	86
	6–11	20	28	48
	11–15	12	4	16
	41–80	0	3	3
	Subtotal	78	75	153
Public jail of Hermosillo	0–5	1	2	3
	6–11	0	3	3
	Subtotal	1	5	6
Total		79	80	159

Source: Data are a composite for the years 1902–1905, from the FMGR at the AGN.

exiles."[133] Yaqui living conditions were terrible and enabled the government to frame the discussion of deportation as a response to a desperate social need, another message of benevolence. As a military officer, Martínez was well aware that the cause of the Yaqui wars was that the Yaqui refused to leave their land, and thus relocating them far away would be a devastating cultural and political blow. Even if it would cost the state of Sonora a huge amount of money to move and maintain them, it certainly would require fewer military personnel and less vigilance, making the state safe for capitalism.

Several lists of deportees by classification show the blanket effects and cultural decimation intended by the process of removal. My statistics are based on a sample of roughly sixteen hundred cases. They show particular patterns of number, gender, and age distributions of the deportees that help expose population and cultural impacts. December 1902 marked the earliest push for deportation.[134]

Some of the earliest deportation lists were organized by sex and show a preponderance of adult male deportees. On December 31, 1902, 207 men were scheduled to be deported along with 79 women and 51 children.[135] Some deportation lists contain only names, while others give ages, locations of birth, and other personal information are given. Details are scarce on the list for December 31, 1902. Shortly following the deportation of December 31 was a group of Yaqui children who had been distributed ("niños Yaqui que se han repartido"). These children, much like those who were seized in the Camp Grant massacre, were given to prominent Sonoran families to raise by order of the secretary of state.[136] The same people who were able to demand state

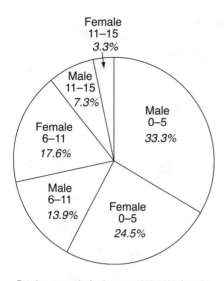

Female
11–15
3.3%

Male
11–15
7.3%

Female
6–11
17.6%

Male
0–5
33.3%

Male
6–11
13.9%

Female
0–5
24.5%

Data is a composite for the years 1902–1905, from the FMGR at the AGN. Total sample size is 273 youths.

FIGURE 4 Yaqui prisoners and deportees by age and gender.

troops from the governor of Sonora at a moment's notice to protect their investments (such as the Luken family) were given permission to raise Yaqui children as wards of the state.[137] It is not surprising that civilian individuals wielded the power to control military troops and absorb child captives into their labor force or family. Simply put, deportation practices are a perfect example of the individual rights embodied in capitalist citizenship advocated by the Díaz regime for white Mexicans. The individuals investing in development and their corporations were granted every courtesy by the Mexican government and military, including access to children who could be absorbed into proper families as objects of filial affection and servants.

In the data sample, there are multiple cases of children being imprisoned with their mothers, with their entire families, or with other child captives in Hermosillo (see table 1, p. 218). Officially called prisoners of war, child prisoners or deportees emerged early in the process of dislocation, in 1902 to be exact. By the time child prisoners had been kept in the Hermosillo jail for two years, their social position raised other social and ethical dilemmas. The Sonorense government asked for a doctor's report from the General Municipal Hospital regarding Yaqui child prisoners. A paraphrase of the report of Agustín A. Roa reads as follows: "I went to the Headquarters of the detachment of the 200 Battalion in this port, and the referred-to doctor having done the respective inspection, he believes: that the causes of the deaths of the Yaqui children

TABLE 2 Site of Yaqui capture and seizure, by age and gender, 1902–1905

Place of capture	Age in years	Male	Female	Total
Hermosillo	0–5	75	56	131
	6–11	28	42	70
	11–15	18	8	26
	41–80	0	3	3
	Subtotal	121	109	230
Rayon	0–5	3	2	5
	6–11	3	1	4
	11–15	2	0	2
	16–21	1	1	2
	22–30	2	2	4
	41–80	2	2	4
	Subtotal	13	8	21
Total		134	117	251

Source: Data are a composite for the years 1902–1905, from the FMGR at the AGN.

are diarrheas resulting from their detention and by infectious intestinal fevers; the overcrowding in which these families are found, along with the lack of medical attention, has had a strong effect on the development of these diseases."[138] The illnesses experienced by imprisoned Yaqui children were the result of many factors. The average per-prisoner allowance for care was $0.75 Mexican pesos. Even in 1904 this was not enough to provide children with a healthy diet. Micronutrient deficiency is thought to be one of the main causes of diarrheal diseases and over time can also affect cognitive development.[139] Further, prolonged exposure to viruses contained in feces and contaminated water and with limited areas in which to circulate most likely further impaired the health of the children. The benign neglect was brought to the attention of Governor Rafael Izabál, but he did not change the policies much.

While the circumstances are not identical, the high child mortality rates in U.S. Indian boarding schools show a similar trajectory of illness and death. Children at the San Carlos Day School who had tuberculosis were, according to the historian David DeJong, rarely given medical examinations, and if they were, the exams were superficial and provided a diagnosis but no treatment. Tubercular children were kept at the school until the last stages of the disease and then were sent home to die.[140] The BIA documents DeJong analyzes evoke the word *murder* uncomfortably, but nonetheless "subjecting them to such tearful mortality is little less" than murder.[141] While sick Yaqui children could not be sent home because their homes had been destroyed by warfare, keeping them in unclean, cramped, unventilated prison conditions only contributed to the spread of disease and death. On April 25, 1904, 26 children, along with 34 men and 27 women (87 total), were brought to the jail in Hermosillo. On April 30, 1906, just five days later, 54 Yaqui children between the ages of one and thirteen arrived at the jail. The jail was designed to hold 300 people, and those 54 children were accompanied by 39 women and 34 men, totaling 127 prisoners.[142] The constant influx of Yaqui prisoners unquestionably led to overcrowding, another factor undermining the health of children and adults alike. The future of Yaqui children was seen as unimportant, for the Mexican government's policy made sure they had no future. Instead the hidden institutional status of imprisoned Yaqui children allowed for lack of regulation or reform. The mortality of imprisoned Yaqui children did not amount to a social cause requiring change. Ultimately, decreased Yaqui populations and fewer children being born to Yaqui families meant fewer people to rebel against the Mexican government.

As the plan for Yaqui removal continued, a prison in Hermosillo was constructed specifically for holding the Yaqui ("La prisión de Hermosillo fue construida por prisioneros Yaqui y establecida para ellos").[143] But the main problem that emerges, in my analysis, is not its actual structure, overcrowding, or daily workings, but the social problems and the fact that families were separated and disrupted: "Men and women are separated from each other and the same with the children, leaving them in prison, even when their parents have been deported."[144] As the Mexican government tried to resolve its Indian problem through deportation, it created another huge social problem—it orphaned countless Yaqui children: "What ought to be done with these children is one of the most serious facets of the problems that the Mexicans are trying to solve. For now, they say that there are close to 300 of them in Hermosillo, and most are too young to look after themselves, and they are absolutely without assistance, except what the government can give them. They cannot be sent to Yucatán, where the natural conditions are bad, nor can they be returned to the Yaqui region, because no one was left there who can look after them."[145] Shifting from Indian rebellion to a social problem of displaced children, the article openly admits that the living conditions on the henequen plantations are intolerable, which proves that deportation to this locale was intentionally genocidal in nature. These uncared-for children are living illustrations of the government's desire to break up Yaqui institutions, including their local governments in the eight pueblos, their kinship networks, and their ceremonial cycles. Leaving small children stranded without any caregivers demonstrates how one political problem (stopping Indian rebellion) created a whole host of other social problems for the state. On the basis of the traffic in Yaqui children as prisoners and their role in the civilizing and modernizing of Sonora, one can say that the deportation system was a more measured and processual means of destroying the family to preserve capital-based institutions that did not include preservation of the Yaqui family.

Destruction of the Yaqui family was a primary goal of deportation. Deportation lists were at times quite sophisticated, in that they tracked not only gender and age, but also where the prisoners were taken from.[146] Additional censuses of passive Yaqui workers were constantly taken to track the exact number and location of Yaqui bodies in the state of Sonora. The patterns of these prisoner listings tell us about the accumulated practices of the state and open a window on to the government's desires and the effects of deportation and imprisonment on Yaqui populations at large. One list from 1902 records eleven prisoners taken from Valle Carrero and seven from Tecoripa.[147] Young boys, or *muchachos*, had their own category as well, perhaps signaling the precarious nature of their relationship to the state. One of the "Listas de muchachos que se van a deportar" showed that eighteen boys between the ages of seven and fourteen were to be sent to Yucatán, because it was thought that by the age of eight Yaqui were capable of carrying out war against the Mexican government. Of those eighteen boys, six had the family name Yoqui-hui, presumably brothers and cousins being taken from their families and forced into labor outside of Sonora.[148] The Mexican government expressed its eagerness to have the young boys be managed because they teetered on the edge between childhood and manhood and thus between being a warrior against the state or an instrument of the state. In the same group forty-two women were slated for deportation, and nine had the family name Yoquihui, probably the boys' mothers, sisters, aunts, and cousins.[149] In the cumulative data set the surname Yoquihui had one of the highest frequency occurrences of all.

Mexican officials also used the category "Yaqui rebeldes que se van a deportar" (Yaqui rebels that will be deported). What were the criteria for distinguishing between a Yaqui who was a *rebelde* (rebel) and one who was a *pasivo* (passive)? And how is the rebel different from the regular deportee? From the confusion about racial passing to the elderly Yaqui workers who disappeared from the haciendas that employed them and then reappeared after periods of intensive warfare there seems to be little logic or identifiable characteristics of difference between a rebelde and a pasivo if you were a male

TABLE 3 Most common Yaqui surnames of deportees and
captives by gender, 1902–1905

Male surnames	Frequency	Percent	Female surnames	Frequency	Percent
Buitimea	87	7.3	Yoquihui	189	27.8
Álvarez	72	6.1	Valenzuela	46	6.8
Valencia	69	5.8	Álvarez	39	5.7
Buitemea	67	5.6	Buitimea	29	4.3
Molina	62	5.2	Molina	26	3.8
Valenzuela	61	5.1	Seamo	25	3.7
Matus	57	4.8	Flores	19	2.8
Bacasegua	28	2.4	Sehua	11	1.6
García	26	2.2	Buitemea	10	1.5
Flores	23	1.9	García	10	1.5
López	18	1.5	Matus	10	1.5

Source: Data are a composite for the years 1902–1905, from the FMGR at the AGN. Total sample size is 1,187 males and 680 females.

over the age of ten. Unless one was caught in possession of a gun, running guns, actively doing battle and being taken prisoner, these were the obvious markers of rebellion. However, men and man-children were rounded up from haciendas on the basis of suspicion and confessions solicited under duress and fear, suggesting that one could be considered simultaneously pasivo and potentially rebelde. Categorization was fluid and based on the potential for insurgent activity against the state. Some prisoners, such as José María López, taken from the penitentiary, were labeled as being loco, which implies that the state may have had its eye not just on insurgents, but on other social outcasts such as the insane.[150] Yet even that is debatable because the connection between madness and the civilizing impulse, especially as it relates to indigenous populations, has its own narrative of discursive and physical violence.

That incarcerated Yaqui were deported to Yucatán indicates that Sonora did not want to be responsible for any Yaqui, whether criminal, bronco (wild rebel), loco, pasivo, female, or otherwise. But this measuring of Yaqui dispositions raises another question: how did the state know who was crazy, who was rebelde, and who was pasivo? The lists of "Yaqui rebeldes que se van a deportar," from 1902, give no explanation as to how or why the government determined they were rebels. The lists simply give the names of 227 men, most of whom have at least one relative on the list with them.[151] Perhaps these deportation rolls are a governmental enactment of the unspeakable; that is, they reference the rebel Yaqui and assign them a subjectivity by naming them as dissident subjects, but the reader is not privy to the rationale or bureaucracy that discerned a rebel threat to the state. The accounting system required that they be named, and this state act of ascribing a discernible identity to Yaqui deportees is a simultaneous act of stripping individuality, as all rebels were lumped together. In sum, they were treated as rejected wards of the state, to be shipped off to a different kind of penal system, one that required harsh manual labor.

In some cases, however, the record tracks Yaqui confessions, reminding one of another ritual of violence that was a precursor to deportation, for the form of confession has its own special logic of terror. The form and meaning of these confession transcripts are worth analyzing because they reveal the power of state technologies of violence cloaked in softened official rhetoric. In December 1902 several "Declaraciones de los Yaqui complicados en el Distrito de Magdalena y del Altar" were compiled, in which one informant's confession produced a domino effect of arrests. Yaqui Javier Rivera confessed that he was traveling without a passport and had no employer:

He confessed that he was at the house with intent to go north and that some had given him provisions and said that the party that we were following came from the house of Juan de Loreto who lives close to him and that he only came to his house. That Loreto had a 50 caliber Remington. That in Las Caporales there are two women whose husbands are not there. That in La Galera de León Serna there are two relatives that protect the armed insurgents, one whom they call El Poblano, and another named Eulogio. That in San Lorenzo there are four Yaquis that work with Manuel González and he had seen them come to their houses. That in El Alamo close to Las Pedradas, there are various Yaqui that receive campesino sympathizers and that go out with them. That La Barajita is where the Yaqui broncos go down to return to those with whom they work in El Ranchito de León Serna, that between them is Miguel Mariscal, one of the worst of all of them. That in Las Pedradas there are two bad ones, one named Pedro and the other he doesn't remember the name, but that he has seen viewed that shipment. That in Las Planchas de Plata there are two relatives working that go out and that almost all are bad and go to buy arms.[152]

The confession has several purposes. The power dynamics and effectiveness of the confession rely upon the victim's desire to survive. Judith Butler has argued that this desire " 'to be,' is a pervasively exploitable desire" in which the subject creates his or her own logic as follows: " 'I would rather exist in subordination than not exist' . . . where the risk of 'death' is also possible."[153] Butler's view of subjection and subordination reveals several things about the function of Yaqui confessions, the first being that the confession is a direct result of the desire to be, the desire to live. Giving information was a desperate attempt to circumvent the all-too-real possibility of death. If the confession did prolong life, it was a prolongation funneled into a different system of exchange, that of controlled labor on the henequen plantations of Yucatán. After making such confessions Yaqui were rarely returned to Sonora and set free to return to their lives. Instead, the confession delayed death and recast their role in the larger Mexican nation and labor market by dislocating them from their land and placing them in a contained space to which they had no emotional or cultural connection. The only connection to be made would be that of laborer, a choice between life and death; the confession determined which mode of existence would stand.

Similarly, a confession document from 1906 is actually labeled "Denuncios de Yaqui rebeldes," marking how the process of confession involved the denouncing of others in the hopes of saving oneself:

Already at the last minute to remit the indigenous Yaqui Juan José Bacase-hua, Jesús Amarillas, Juan Valenzuela, and Nicolás Buitimea that refers to my note of this day, underwent further questioning because of Bacase-hua's confession, who through the interpreter Teofilo Romero, was in charge of the vigilance for those of the tribe in this mine. He said the following: that Miguel Buitimea (who is also known by the name of José María Jiménez), suggested that if he should need supplies all the time, he should always go to [Buitimea] with the Yaqui, replying to Bacasehua you do not need anything.[154]

First confessions were mediated through an interpreter, obscuring their meaning and potentially criminalizing prisoners. Second, some of the Yaqui had an alias to protect their identities in the struggle against the government, although many indigenous people had names in their own language and Spanish names when they were among Mexicans. While Buitimea denies further involvement with Yaqui insurgents, he states that Bacasehua has continued his insurgent activity. The formalistic aspects of the confession mark a process in which the "visible is the extremity with which or the extreme literalness with which the nation inscribes itself onto the body; or (to phrase it in a way that acknowledges the extraordinary fact of the consent of the participating populations in conventional war) the literalness with which the human body opened itself and allows 'the nation' to be registered there in the wound."[155] Without revealing if in fact a physical wound or wounds were inflicted to gain this confession, the document shows how the formalistic practice of the confession is a way of inscribing the state on the body, its own kind of psychic wound. Buitimea's denial of participation deflects attention away from his own body and onto the body of Bacasehua. Additionally, the confession informs the state, as Foucault would argue, because a confession results from believing that one is guilty. As Bacasehua's body is labeled a rebel body through his confession, Buitimea is temporarily spared physical violation through betrayal of another Yaqui body. The physical reality of the prisoners' bodies is ever-present in the way that they are constantly referenced by name. In contrast, the body of the guard or military officer, perhaps the torturer, is absent from this document except in the actual recording of the prisoner's words, marking an extreme differential in power. While Buitimea's and Bacasehua's subjectivities become visible through the confession, the subjectivity of the recorder of the confession is made secondary. This gap in power between the two reflects how the prisoner, even if temporarily liberating himself from torture, has no voice except within the confines of the confessional form. Silence, in this case, is objectified and becomes the grounds for punishment; the prisoner is forced into betrayal of self and others. Furthermore, the space communicated through the confession presents contested ideas of masculinity: the absented, invisible yet present, hegemonic mestizo Mexican masculinity presides over that of the Yaqui, setting up a hierarchy of racialized gender stratification among men.

In a social movement based on ideas of self-determination and bodily preservation, confessions like this one had not just localized effects for the prisoners but also a ripple effect on the entire group of Yaqui insurgents. This betrayal of self and others in the struggle is what led to deportation and execution, reducing numbers and the population as a whole. Yet the confession continues:

> The same Bacasehua, I declare Basilo Buitimea was invited to go to the Sierra, telling their agreement to two or three others, but that they should go with him, and that he did not know if they would go. What else is mentioned here, they knew the teacher Ignacio Mátus (who was hung by Mexican forces), was an accomplice of the Yaqui and where the said Mátus went, was the house of Marcos . . . whose last name was ignored, in the Realito and another of the same name Marcos that lives in the same Realito, are the accomplices, just like Francisco Álvarez, who also was brought in from the same Realito. Consequently the vehement suspicion of com-

plicity of all the Indians mentioned, with the exception of the two named Marcos, who did not go on the walking trip of the group of Indians denounced by Bacasehua even though he was saying that they were all a part of it in the interrogation. This same Juan José Bacasehua along with another Indian named José, who is the servant of Fernando Flores of El Realito, also has a woman and daughter, is neither to be found in the appointed place and that another Indian by the name of Antonio Valenzuela, neighbor of Suaqui a well-liked young man who only has one daughter, went to Cacimiento most certainly, where the interrogated lived, to ask for supplies which he never gave because he is very poor and cannot even maintain his daughters, this individual came to his house, without arms, and after the said Valenzuela came to the mill at Suaqui she supposedly came to buy bread and was known by some of the *peones* of Candido who were also servants and he saw them come two times for the *pascolas* [Easter ceremonies]; they actually never came, but he saw them in the same evening.[156]

The structure of the confession creates a web of social relations, implicating not just the four men who have been brought in for questioning, but men like the supposed cabecillos, or leaders, Mátus and Marcos and the conspirators Valenzuela, Flores, Álvarez, and Bacasehua, who supposedly have been running insurgency operations out of their bosses' ranchos in El Realito. In addition, Butimea makes sure to mention that Valenzuela and Flores both have daughters at their places of employment and that Flores has a wife. While the confession seems to be situated in a masculine discourse of war and exchange, the gendered aspects of the rebellion are demarcated: women and daughters are evoked as a means of power brokering. That is, Butimea situates the daughters and wives of Flores and Valenzuela within the chain of rebellion and conspiracy, marking them as rebel bodies because of their patriarchal and spousal family ties. The confession also had the potential to open the women's bodies to sexual violation. The confession, according to the scholar of the Argentine dirty wars Frank Graziano, is a performative discourse, as the form solicited and "reaffirmed the veracity of the repressors' ideology."[157] Thus the confession is really not about guilt but about the reproduction of the state, a kind of loop that ensures its own existence, justifying the violence against the individuals, silencing what they had to say.[158]

When a bit of the narrator's or inquisitor's voice is finally heard, it is only to summarize Butimea's statements about himself: "At the same time, it should be noted that the same Basilio Butimea, which is not the referred to, is married to the daughter of the named teacher/ringleader Ignacio Mátus, who as it is said, was executed. All of which is for me to put them in the realm of your knowledge."[159] This is not Butimea's final piece of confession but rather a summary of the interrogation that implicates his family ties as the backbone of the insurgency. By revealing that he is married to the daughter of the "maestro" Mátus, Butimea exposes his family to potential state-targeted violence (deportation, execution, rape, starvation) while affirming a commitment to the movement. These confession documents are rare and set the stage for the pro forma mass deportations that occurred frequently between 1902 and 1909. At that point the state relied on confessions not only to determine guilt or innocence but to justify nationalized violence, rape, torture, and deportation as necessary evils to make the nation-state safe for capitalism. Confessions, ideologically, reinforced state action as a rationale for counterinsurgency tactics of the most extreme kind against the Yaqui. Even though entire Yaqui families were being shipped to Yucatán, whether or not they were confessed rebels, the confessions served as a justification for the practice of deportation in the national and international media.[160]

What is left out of this document is the process by which the confession was solicited. In a report labeled "Reclamaciones extranjeros," the process of soliciting the confession is detailed and labeled as torture.[161] Presumed to be a translation of an American newspaper article or investigation, it states, "Some of the most depraved warriors are obliged to go before a line of a group of perhaps 100 prisoners and they tell them to confess that they killed the man whose mutilated body was found by the soldiers. All of them deny having done this. Then one is chosen, directly accused by the soldiers, and they will pardon him if he confesses and points out his accomplices. . . . All of the soldiers try to force a confession out of him. He is tied to the pillar [or post] his fingers toward the back, twisting the arms, or he is tortured in some other manner until he finally gives in and confesses his guilt. Generally, he is willing to point out those who are guilty, choosing, certainly, the same Indians that the soldiers have designated."[162]

The ritualized nature of the lynchings and violence was steeped in codes of masculinity and femininity. After a Yaqui had been shot by a firing squad,

> they throw a rope over the arm of a tree, an end of this is hung around the neck and the other end is tied to the saddle of a Mexican soldier. When the soldier walks, the Indian is raised off the floor and stays hung, rocking the body. Then the rope is tied to the tree, leaving the body hanging until the rays of sunlight kill it, or until the love of a woman makes it lively enough

to take it down and give it a proper burial. Many of the hanged bodies as an example to other Yaquis, are treated this way. One woman, after the game that has caught her husband, and saying goodbye until he is executed and the soldiers withdrew, then came from a hidden place; and cautiously takes the body, opening a grave with her bare hands if necessary, which is much better than leaving it for the birds.[163]

Torture is overwhelmingly present to the individual experiencing it, more emphatically than in any other human experience. Quite poetically, executed Yaquis are saved only by the light of dawn, a woman's love, or Christlike redemption. Shifting into the realm of the romantic or the elegy of mourning and loss, the language appeals to tropes of heteronormativity, religion, faith, family, and rebirth. The language simultaneously downplays and mourns the violence as part of a larger trope of Christlike allegory. The moral codes of loss and state-sanctioned violence are doubly conveyed through the message that execution is wrong, but only through the poetic language of the dawn's light, Christlike redemption, and a woman's love. The three things that reveal the excessively punished body to the world mediate the scene of violence through love, Christian symbolism, and care of family. Yaqui women hide and witness the execution of their loved ones, then attempt to recover the body. They take the body from the tree, enacting a particular ritual of mourning and loss that is completed with a proper burial, a grave dug with her own hands. Saving the body from becoming carrion is a means of remembering the human value of the victim, who was already dead but hung as a warning to others, while avowing the dehumanizing nature of these kinds of deaths. Such a "return" to the value of the family to avoid nihilism, argues Sandra Soto, is "a familiar construction of the always already existing, functional, intact, and peaceful family coming undone by prolonged exposure to . . . external dysfunction."[164] While Soto argues that the discursive return to the family in another context is the result of the social construction of family outside of capitalism, she convincingly demonstrates how capitalism *is* absolutely dependent upon the reproductive labor of the family, especially in the production of sexism and heteropatriarchy.

In this description of Yaqui women's labor to preserve memory and humanity by rescuing the body of a family member, the author ascribes the traits of civility, religion, and spirituality to Yaqui women. Heteronormative women's labor is reified as a deliverance to civility. In the moment of loss, such care for the dead body is an inscription of civility and institutionalization of the practice of caring for the dead to the figure of woman, who was deemed the ultimate savage by the Mexican state. Civility, rationality, and compassion are ascribed to Yaqui women because of the universal institution of family. Further, the appeal to the family brings the Yaqui into capitalism, providing what Soto calls the destruction of the classic pastoral family.[165] In this temporary reprieve from a discourse of Yaqui savagery, Yaqui lynchings and executions represent state savagery that leaves the dead body as evidence of radical subjectivity for the mourning Yaqui woman who retrieves the body that is its result.

The U.S. press had different views of Yaqui deportation and torture, vacillating between a critique of the Mexican government's unnecessary brutality toward them and expressions of a desire to keep Yaqui in Sonora because they were the best workers in American mines. The Arizona-based newspaper *The Oasis* had this to say: "The hostilities 6 years ago imply that he did not think possible for them to recover their former possessions and even suggesting that they might agree to settle in any other state outside of Sonora."[166] That other state to settle in (Yucatán) was not a choice but cloaked language for describing deportation. The *Arizona Daily Star* reported on April 27, 1904, "There has been some very harsh measures enforced by the government during the past few weeks. Yaqui are being taken wherever found, and sent to Guaymas and shipped off, 'tis said to Yucatan but rumor has it that they are not supposed to ever touch land after boarding the vessel unless it may be at the bottom of the sea. If this be true the policy and action of the Mexican government will not receive the sanction of civilization, because of its cruelty, injustice and barbarity."

Yaqui were accused of retaliatory violence in reaction to the Mexican government's widespread deportation practices. Two brothers, Ramón and José Contreras, were presumed to be assassinated by "los bárbaros Yaqui," and a detachment of Nacionales were sent to look for their murderers. At 4:30 p.m. on the afternoon the detachment was sent out, the cadavers of the Contrerases were found, "in complete state of decomposition, the scene advertised that they were cruelly killed, martyred and punctured with sticks; that in order to carry their remains was necessary accordingly to cremate them."[167] A day later, the owner of Tienda de Boston, proprietor of Fleischer y Smith in Sonora, wrote to the Sonoran governor with a similar complaint: "The Yaqui are robbing and killing many, I want to say to Governor Izabál personally, we have several Yaqui here, who say they are pacified [*manzos*], but they are but the evilest of all, but there are few in this region who are not, I can assure you.... At the same time, tell the governor that in case he sends the soldiers, order the Captain to stop at my house."[168] Many Sonorense had access to state power and therefore could ask the state for protection from raiding Yaquis while at the same time employing their kinsmen. In order to continue their armed struggle against the Mexican government, the Yaqui needed supplies. Raids against haciendas were a regular part of retaliatory violence. At the end of 1904 the Hacienda el Pópilo was attacked for a second time by ten well-armed Indians. They robbed the Tienda de Rayo, taking with them four firearms (two carbines, one Mauser pistol, and a Remington used by the Mexican infantry) and ammunition that was supposed to be used for defending against the Indians. Later that same day the municipal president received further notice of Yaqui activity: at Rancho el Cato they robbed the house of Manuel Amado, "also leading his horse to be saddled and re-shoed; and was also raided and robbed by the workers of Don Manuel F. Cubillas when in transit to la Mina Sultana at Carbó."[169] One might consider Yaqui attacks in the context of deportation as part of a cycle of violence connected to borderlands exchanges, what the historian James Brooks has called a systematic redistribution of wealth and power across indigenous and European communities.[170] Clearly, Mexican authorities wanted to prevent transfers of capital and goods to the Yaqui because they did not benefit institutional-level American and Mexican capital exchanges. However, Yaqui violence systematically redistributed resources to them while generating a wartime economy for Mexico. So even though there was a loss of lives on all three sides (Mexican, American, and Yaqui), violence was its own economic factor, one that produced subsistence for some and growth for others. The Yaqui did not collude in long-range profit maximization strategies in the capitalist development of Sonora. Rather, the cost of revolution and the potential loss of life were far more valuable than collusion with the state.[171] The violence brought with it grave economic costs and benefits in terms of human capital.

Yet literate, property-owning citizens of some wealth living in Sonora and Chihuahua complained to the federal government about the excessive and unnecessary nature of state-sponsored violence. Highly critical of the state government, they had no qualms about taking their complaints to the highest level. José Montesinos wrote to Porfirio Díaz, calling the events in Sonora "an unjustified adventure to wage war against the Yaqui, who never bother anyone, and that campaign would give a greater number of troops than he currently has under his command, a thing that cannot now be facilitated."[172] Critiquing official national policy generated from the geographically distant capital, Montesinos is in the minority. He states the Yaqui were harmless, most likely implying their high value in the Sonoran ranching and mining economy, where their labor was indispensable and unequaled. When Montesinos calls the conflict a war, he locates the problem in the *transnational* realm between nations and identifies the violent conflict as spurred by U.S. capital interests in Mexican Sonora. Acting within a localized personal, social, and economic context, Montesinos testifies on behalf of the Yaqui, proving that there was not a complete disconnect between the Yaqui and the ways in which residents of Sonora imagined themselves: both were citizens of a Mexico whose central government was run by Díaz from Mexico City.

In a telegram to Governor Izabál, a group of thirty-six Sonorans lodged a similar protest, this time questioning the imprisonment and deportation of women, elders, and children as part of the government's strategy of Yaqui containment:

> Our Respected Sir: Before you, with due respect, we, the undersigned, explain that a hundred and some Yaqui are being sent to that capital, forty men and an equal number of women, some elderly and others pregnant, as well as sixty boys and girls between the ages of fifteen years and thirty days in great danger of perishing on the deportation road, along with sick children and pregnant women. We have founded reasons for believing that none of these Indians is guilty, and this belief drives us to entreat you to be kind enough to allow them to remain here under conditions that you believe appropriate for the greatest security in the intelligence we have received, we would happily put all the means at our disposal, according to the instructions that you would kindly communicate to the Prefect. We can assure you that we enjoy all the desired security and guaranteed rights so that we are pleased to extend our gratitude to you, since one or another isolated case that I regret occur in that other way anywhere in the civilized world. "Insecurity" only exists in the imagination of historic Mexicans and perverse foreigners. Your bidding and conditions will be highly appreciated by your fellow citizens, who offer you their loyalty and respect.[173]

In a highly sophisticated critique of insecurity, these Sonorans evoke the paranoid nation of the past and the wealthy neighbor to the north that provoked such paranoia. Paranoia, they argue, is not the stuff of modernity or civilization. Recent Yaqui violence is viewed as non-systematic, and they argue that there is no need to deport women, children, and elders. In essence, Montesino's letter and the telegram from the group of thirty-six Sonorans who wrote to Governor Izabál in 1906 asking for the release of Yaqui prisoners shows a completely different side of Mexican beliefs about the Yaqui conflict. Montesinos and the Sonorenses remind the government of the moral implications of deportation: the lives of elders, pregnant women, and sick children would be lost to the community who depended on their labor. But even more than a capitalist justification, this appeal to morality shows an ethic of care about Yaqui humanity and the right to live. Naming pregnant women and sick children shows a desire on the part of the Sonorenses for the Yaqui to have a future as a people within the confines of the Mexican nation-state as a national moral imperative argued from a localized, Sonora-based standpoint.

Much like Montserrat Fontes's novel *Dreams of the Centaur*, Ortiz's letter demonstrates the other Sonora, the one not governed by capitalist greed but by an interconnected sense of localized citizenship, regional identity, and subjectivity. Governmental sweeps of Yaqui workers employed in the hacienda system throughout Sonora and in the copper mines decimated the primary source of labor and destroyed Yaqui rights to self-determination.[174] Through mass deportations to the henequen plantations of the Yucatán Peninsula between 1905 and 1911 and the forced peonage and enslavement of the Yaqui,[175] the government sought to destroy the spirit of the Yaqui and their connection to their land and their bodies by making them isolated vessels of intensive manual labor.[176] The Yaqui were brought in to replace a shrinking Mayan labor force, who were, in essence, reduced to slavery in the henequen plantations after their last revolt.[177] Engaged in an increasingly profitable export industry, henequen hacendados demanded more bodies and cheaper forms of labor, and the industrious but rebellious Yaqui of the north were the perfect solution.

5 ✳ Stripping the Body of Flesh and Memory

TOWARD A THEORY OF YAQUI SUBJECTIVITY

I was more than naked, I was stripped of flesh and memory.

MONTSERRAT FONTES, *DREAMS OF THE CENTAUR*

In the previous chapter I detailed official state records and discourses from the United States and Mexico as a means of tracking silences, slippages, and denials that index the unspeakability of state-sanctioned violence against the Yaqui at the level of the national imaginary. Each of these forms of writing offers truths about the Yaqui and how their war for autonomy collectively shaped the modernizing discourses of vying nationalisms, past and present (Mexican, U.S., Chicano). But sometimes it is the unsettled quality of history, the unspeakable thing, taken up in other forms that can shine light upon what has been silenced. I want to turn to the novelistic form, for it can represent what the national imaginary has rendered unspeakable. This chapter is different from the others in the sense that the book as a whole is about the failure to archive a subaltern version of history, but here I focus on speech as an alternative to silence and the unspeakable that lies beyond public understanding for a reason. Mestizaje is recentered in this chapter as part of political interests, but not as a national fantasy of racial harmony. Instead I show the utter failure of mestizaje as a device of nation building because Mexican, American, and Yaqui violence demonstrates how racial categories of separation were maintained as difference. I speak against both the way the Yaqui genocide has been silenced and the impossibility of strategic and yet romantic evocation of mestizaje as nation (Chicano, Mexican, or U.S.).

State-sanctioned violence and torture of Yaqui insurgents are most eloquently represented in Montserrat Fontes's transnationally minded novel *Dreams of the Centaur*, which discursively and cognitively maps at great length the unspeakable scenes of torture and violence that are alluded to in the archives but not fully articulated in the historical record. It is one of the few

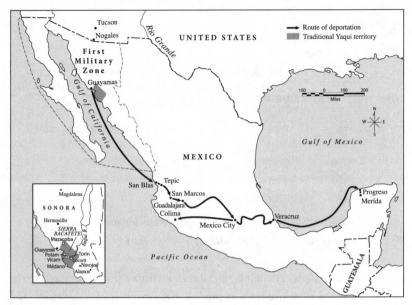

MAP 5 Map of Yaqui deportation routes and battles, ca. 1902–9.

literary projects that takes responsibility for Mexican and Mexican American violence against indigenous people without romanticizing either the past or mestizaje. It makes a concerted effort to critically think through the relationship between representation and torture. Such a literary intervention seems plausible only in the late twentieth century (1995), more than one hundred years after the Yaqui Indian wars, because at that historical moment there was no sense of national political urgency to make the violence stop. Had it not been for the Mexican Revolution, who knows how long the armed struggles of the Yaqui peoples would have continued? Violence and genocide, as national agendas, were operating as cultural practices with no bounds because they were what fortified the project of modernity in the U.S.–Mexico borderlands. Throughout the chapter, I juxtapose *Dreams of the Centaur* and historical documents to demonstrate the different kinds of ideological work these texts do in the cause of nationalism, on the one hand, and of the project of revisionist historiography, on the other.

It seems apropos that genocide as a social and political process in *Dreams of the Centaur* is represented as a means of communicating the pain, suffering, agony, and loss that sometimes escape words altogether. In the case of *Dreams of the Centaur*, formal literary devices (realist representation, stream-of-consciousness narration, and time–space ruptures through narrative prose) articulate that which has been rendered unspeakable in U.S., Mexican, and

Chicano national histories; they bring to light the nature of state-sanctioned violence in practice, implicate all actors in the production of unequal power relations, and to some degree even make readers question their own culpability as well. I use this literary text as evidence alongside military communiqués about Yaqui deportation and torture to show that traditional empirical evidence is sometimes not enough. When read alongside theories of trauma and pain, the violence of Yaqui displacement and genocide provides an alternative national imaginary from which to theorize loss and Yaqui subjectivity.

Dreams of the Centaur chronicles a history of the Yaqui struggle in the state of Sonora between 1885 and 1905 through the prism of quotidian violence. The novel imagines these struggles for survival extending over a three-thousand-mile radius that goes as far north as Tucson and as far south as the henequen plantations located in Yucatán. Two of the main characters, Alejo, a mestizo Mexican, and Charco, a Yaqui, are imprisoned, and in prison they discover they are half brothers. Both men are tortured, but Charco is explicitly targeted because he is half Yaqui and was picked up with a group of insurgents. In exchange for their release from the *bartolina* (a particularly inhumane prison built as either a cave in a mountainside or a hole in the ground with a metal grate over it), they become a part of the Díaz government's prisoner regiments that were used to round up the Yaqui for deportation to the henequen plantations. When they desert the army, they are imprisoned along with large numbers of deported Yaquis. Escaping again, they go to the Sierra Bacatete, a sacred and inaccessible Yaqui stronghold in the northern Sierra mountains of Sonora, and, in trying to warn the Yaqui leaders of the fate that awaits them as slaves in Yucatán should they not negotiate peace with the Mexican government, become involved in the bloody battle of Mazacoba (January 18, 1900). Through Charco's and Alejo's multiple forced migrations and the people they encounter along the way, the reader is confronted with several scenes of subjection in which racialized, gendered, and sexualized violence is articulated as part of the project of modernity and the imposition of the Mexican nation and U.S. venture capitalism upon the bodies of Yaqui subjects.

TOWARD A THEORY OF YAQUI SUBJECTIVITY

As I noted in chapter 4, there are few archival records in which the Yaquis speak for themselves, and even when they do their voices are always filtered through the colonial gaze of Mexican or American government officials or newspaper writers. As Gayatri Spivak, Louis Althusser, and others have shown, "The constitution and 'interpellation' of the subject not only as individual but as 'individualist' is not a transparent process, one where we can see the un-mediated voices of the subaltern."[1] As much gets displaced onto the Yaqui in public records, they become less important in their own right than as the sign of some other desires. In examining how *Dreams of the Centaur* proposes a way of thinking about Yaqui subjectivities I do not want to fall into what Spivak calls the "mesmerizing focus of the 'subject constitution' of the female individ-ualist" or subaltern subjects.[2] Rather, I want to look at all of the novel's discursive and representational practices that portray actions and communi-cate events differently from a project to recuperate subaltern voices but as a counterhistory. In other words, my reading of Yaqui subjectivities in Fontes's novel is less about finding celebratory examples of resistant indigenous men and women than about tracing the systematic structures embodied in military violence, torture, sexual violence, deportation, social pathologies of illness, and queered gendered performance that provide a different point of view, a way of reading the unspeakable register in another form, one in which the discursive fills the unspeakable gap in nationalist historiography, a kind of dialectical chronology that shapes the contours of memory.

The title of the chapter, "Stripping the Body of Flesh and Memory," comes directly from Fontes's novel. As a base line for theorizing violence and sub-jectivity, I want to suggest that "stripping the body of flesh and memory" marks the violent process and the physical site where subjectivity and an unaccounted-for historical consciousness are produced. Thinking in this way produces a corrective of sorts to the elision of violent histories from Mexican, U.S., and Chicano national imaginaries. The flesh-and-blood experiences of torture, of deportation, and of sexual violence represent the site of memory in a particular historical instance of war and violence. The novel articulates in great detail the information that official histories and records omit but that Yaqui oral histories tell, for much of Fontes's novel is based on her own research in the Yaqui archives.[3] State-wide punitive activities of nineteenth-century Sonora and how individuals who fought against the current of Mexi-can modernity experienced its savage wrath cloaked in the mantle of progress are at the core of the novel.[4] Imagining the Yaqui body in pain tests the limits of modernity's message by marking the lack of state-related freedom of Yaqui individuals. These scenes of subjection, to use the evocative words of the literary critic Saidya Hartman, represent how fine the line was between insur-gence and complicity for Yaquis at this moment in history. The way that pain is represented in the novel poses a series of questions about violence and subjectivity: what happens when one cannot shield one's body from its naked-ness? What does it mean to have nothing left but the flesh on one's bones, after being whipped within inches of death? When the body is ravaged by illness or hunger and the only thing left is bodily memory itself, how does one survive? As the previous chapter illustrated, these questions of interiority, survival, and punishment aren't necessarily the central concerns of the authors of government documents about the Yaqui Indian wars. Theorizing the relationship between the body and violence and among flesh, memory, and loss is my attempt to emulate the feminist critic Norma Alarcón, who in "Tradutora, Traditora: A Paradigmatic Figure of Chicana Feminism" speaks to the forgotten nature of La Malinche as a flesh-and-blood person.[5] Her reading of La Malinche moves scholars away from the male-centered nationalist image of La Malinche as an icon of the betrayal of the Mexican people; it does so by revealing how the body and thus the actual subject (La Malinche as a person) can be forgotten through nationalistic, male-centered discourse. Critics like Alarcón forge a connection between flesh and memory and put flesh back on the object, to force us to recognize that subjects such as La Malinche were historical actors rather than transparent, albeit potent, symbols of failed nationalisms. Instead of reifying discourses that violate while completely disregarding the actual subjectivity that is formed through the literal flesh-and-blood experience, critics need to look for the cognitive connections between mind and body, between flesh and memory and the traces of these subjects in all forms of evidence. Literary representations, like Fontes's, and those rare historical records of torture and of violations of the body demonstrate that quotidian physical violence produces psychological feelings of disembodiment. Those acts of "reading" torture and making such histories accessible through the juxtaposing of the historical and the literary can help the reader to understand the private and incommunicable parts of why nations—the United States, Mexico, and the imagined Chicano nation—selectively forget the roles they have played in intracultural, intranational, and transnational violence and genocide.

To take seriously the theoretical imperative of "stripping the body of flesh and memory," we may first recognize how difficult it was to be a completely self-possessed Yaqui individual in a moment when everything that Yaqui personhood stood for was at odds with Mexican ideas of modernity. The desire for self-possession was twofold. As the state attempted to impose its markers of modernity (containment, docility, and so forth) on the bodies of Yaquis in the late nineteenth century and early twentieth it attempted to strip the body of flesh and memory. Stripping the body of flesh and memory is a multidirectional metaphor for the state-sponsored violence that produced Yaqui subjectivity. Much like Josefa/Juanita (see chapter 1), the Yaqui insurgents are inaugurated as subjects in the historical record when they inflict violence against the nation-state and when the nation-state documents the violence it inflicted upon them. Stripping the body of flesh and memory marks the literal destruction of Yaqui bodies through death, deportation, imprisonment, torture, and lynching. The act of torture was literally a form of stripping the body, and its intended effort was to break the body of its sovereign will. The phrase also evokes the removal of bodies from a homeland where cultural memory is tied to land base. To literally remove Yaqui bodies is an active, state-sanctioned process that attempted to strip Yaquis of their cultural memory. The metaphor evokes the struggle to maintain bodily integrity as a subject in light of the violence experienced by this community of tribal peoples. Also breaking up families, stripping flesh from flesh was an imposition of cultural loss. Preventing people from working; deporting them into forced, uncompensated manual labor; and dislocating them from their land base are all acts that deprived them of self-possession and personhood, all forms of a mandatory forgetting of sorts.

Pain, memory, and loss are linked because they essentially work together to produce what the scholar of torture Elaine Scarry has called radical subjectivity. Erosion of the boundary between mind and body forges a sense of self created by physical and psychic violence. It moves the conversation away from a universal or humanistic subject and toward a highly specific subject formed through a particular set of multiple violent national conflicts, in this case, the Yaqui Indian wars and the pain they produced. Scarry argues that

> the radical subjectivity of pain acknowledges the simple and absolute incompatibility of pain and the world. The survival of each depends upon its separation from the other. To bring them together, to bring pain into the world by objectifying it in language . . . the pain is objectified, articulated, brought into the world in such a way that the pain itself is diminished and destroyed; or alternatively, as in torture and parallel forms of sadism, the pain is at once objectified and falsified, articulated but made to refer to something else in the process, the world or some dramatized surrogate of the world is destroyed.[6]

Here, radical subjectivity is the individual's experience of pain and its incompatibility with living. Scarry's analysis of the relationship between world making and the destruction or creation of pain leads to the notion that a radical self-awareness is produced through having pain inflicted upon the body from an outside source. But this radical subjectivity can be lost or denied when it becomes objectified, when we see pain as being separate from the body, as not forming part of the individual. To minimize or objectify the pain to the extent that it seems unreal or unbelievable, then is to run the risk of dramatizing the existing subject and the world it inhabits to the point of devaluing the claims about pain and subjectivity. Any attempt to represent pain necessarily objectifies it, and yet without writing about it we cannot gain access to histories of violence. In some ways, novelistic writing participates in the objectification of pain. At the same time, Fontes's socially conscious novel attempts to represent the Yaqui body in pain by presenting the emotive register of the individual who experiences such violence. There is not a one-to-one correspondence between literary representation and actual historical documentation. Rather, this draws attention to how the imaginative representation of fiction allows for subjectification or the psychoanalytic "I," the opposite of objectification (even though that is clearly the reason for violence, to make individuals into objects) to emerge as the one who experiences that pain and is constituted through that pain. That subject formation of the "I," which becomes a communal "We," speaks in the wake of national silence about the Yaqui genocide.

VIOLENT FOUNDATIONS

To open the novel, Fontes provides several framing devices: the definition of *centaur* from the *Larousse Encyclopedia of Mythology*; the lyrics to "El Corrido de los Durcal"; a map of the Yaqui deportation route from Guaymas, Sonora, to San Blas, Nayarit, then to Tepic, Guadalajara, Mexico City, Veracruz, and finally to Mérida, Yucatán; and the vision of a dead young husband chasing a Yaqui servant girl. By framing the text of *Dreams of the Centaur* with a mythology of "primitive populations of cowmen . . . their behavior was rude and barbarous, gross creatures, cruel and given to lechery and drunkenness," Fontes suggests that in this novel life in a frontier zone is constrained by an andocentric world of grotesque violence. Further, the corridor recalls a borderlands oral tradition, locating the narrative in a lexicon that John H. McDowell has called a mestizo cultural form associated with the rise of Mexican national consciousness, especially in relation to conflicts and violence between the United States and Mexico in the early twentieth century.[7] McDowell's definition of the corrido sets up an expectation of violence against Mexicans in the United States that unfortunately occludes mestizo violence against indigenous Mexicans. Yet, as McDowell asserts, the corrido form is characterized by a formalistic saturation with violence and an oral performative quality that provide a clue to how Fontes wants the novel to be read.

Further, the maps of the forced migration route of the Yaqui and the detailed image of Yaqui homelands points toward space and setting as active forces that foment events, action, and even subjectivity. Calling readers' attention to the physical manifestation of space, Fontes's map of migration and diaspora sets the tone for a history and literature that will track social activities, material things, phenomena, and processes that take on spatial forms. The map will not have meaning or significance unless one reads it and gives it meaning. Fontes's novel offers such a reading about the meaning people give to these places, how they understand their identities in relation to these places, and how subjectivity is ultimately connected to the physical manifestation of space.

The novel's last narrative frame reopens the question of violence, but from the perspective of individualized characters in the novel. Felipa, one of the protagonists and Alejo's mother, sees the face of her dead husband, José, "one afternoon when she saw Rosario, a Yaqui Indian girl—no more than fifteen—running through a row of orange trees. The laughing Rosario ran. . . . From where she stood Felipa could see the girl more clearly than who was chasing her. The girl and her pursuer zigzagged through the trees towards the back of the house. Soon the pair were out of Felipa's sight."[8] This scene creates a narrative gap and tension for some sixty pages, until the reader discovers that Rosario's sexual encounter and/or rape resulted in the conception of Charco, Alejo's half brother. Seeking to understand the relationship between histories of violence and literary production, I interviewed Fontes about her reasons for opening the novel with what could be interpreted as a rape. When I asked her about this scene she replied, "Many people talk to me about the 'rape scene.' Is it? Or is it a master playing, simply fulfilling his role, and taking what is his? In rancho economies in nineteenth-century Sonora, many of the servant girls had their first child by the master of the house. Is José and Rosario's encounter any different?"[9] While some might be disturbed that Fontes does not interpret the scene as depicting a rape, she points us to the embedded power dynamics of the historical period. The language, power structures, and society of the time do not afford Rosario, an indigenous servant girl, speech or voice to name her violation as rape. The power dynamics between the *patrón* and the workers are hierarchical, and sexual violation is permissible. Racial difference also plays a role in economies of power, representing the intricacies of a system in which Yaqui female bodies are not protected or respected in the same way that the bodies of married Mexican women are. In the larger context of the Yaqui Indian wars and Yaqui removal and deportation, Indian bodies are marked, available to members of the dominant culture because of the spoken and unspoken privileges Indians are denied, and they are hypervisible because those with power projected their sexual, capitalist, and other desires upon the bodies of Indians, especially Indian women. As I have shown in chapter 4, the intensification of guerrilla warfare and the lack of employment in the Yaqui Valley forced Yaqui laborers to become migratory and thereby brought women like Rosario into contact with *hacendados* like José. Social structures were reordered as Yaquis were forced out of their fairly insular pueblos and into slave labor, mining, and hacienda labor, where they were not always able to control their social and public interactions. One can read the scene between Rosario and José as an example of what Mary Pat Brady calls the ways in which poor, young women of color are disciplined for "being excessively mobile."[10] Brady goes on to argue that young, poor, working-class women of color, as visible figures in the market, cannot be raped, precisely because their bodies were coded as always already open. Rape cannot be used to describe Rosario's experience within the narrative because the young woman's body is considered a commodity, silenced by the powers that negotiate her ability to speak of a sexual encounter. This is not to say that the subaltern Rosario cannot speak, but that she is given discursive space only to laugh, not to exhibit any other feelings about the sexual encounter.

Regardless of whether Rosario may have accepted the situation as normative or viewed it as a violation, her pregnancy is entirely blamed upon the supposed availability of her indigenous, nonmestiza body. We never hear about the encounter from Rosario's perspective, nor do we know if the violation happened more than once. The silence and mystery written into the text in regard to this foundational moment show the reader the oppressive ways in which others control Rosario's reproduction, and violence is masked as being natural. The fact that Rosario is laughing as her pursuer chases her makes her seem complicit in her own violation, or perhaps that it is pleasurable. If we read this opening scene as a foundational moment that defines the gender and sexual hierarchies of power in *Dream of the Centaur*, then in this nineteenth-century world violence is normalized social practice. Like a manifestation of the repressed trauma of Rosario's rape, Charco's presence constantly reminds the reader of the opening scene of sexual encounter, even if the representation of the act of sex is banished from the text. Through the character Charco, José Durcal's illegitimate son who becomes the living evidence of power violations that silence Rosario, one has to acknowledge that something happened in the first place. In other words, sexual, physical, and psychological violence are subverted recursive signifiers but that constantly return when least expected, the defining tenet for the entire novel that follows. All of these framing

devices—the definition of *centaur*, the map, the corrido, and the chase scene—
locate the narrative genesis, and thus local and national histories, in an archeology of violence. I turn to the Chicana feminist scholar Emma Pérez's[11] use
of the term *archeology* (Pérez in turn draws from Foucault) as a way to signal a
discursive methodology of investigation that interrogates how multiple power
sources and nation-states use their power in a multidirectional, panoptic
manner.[12] The discursive strategies in *Dreams of the Centaur* offer an archeology of language in which Porfirio Díaz, the Mexican nation-space itself, U.S.
venture capitalists, and complicit Mexicans and Mexican Americans are the
invisible characters in the text that account for systems of violence past.

NATIONAL IMPOSITION OF POWER ON GENDERED, SEXUALIZED BODIES

In the spirit of examining social processes as they are played out in language
and literary representations and how Fontes's textual clues set up those processes, I turn first to an example of how radical subjectivities are produced
through violence, of how the nation inscribes its power upon the bodies of
dissident subjects in *Dreams of the Centaur*. In these scenes of subjection, the
power dynamics between Yaqui women prisoners and the guards who are
charged with watching them as they await deportation demonstrate how
gender and race are used as factors to limit bodily and social freedoms.[13] The
unequal power relations naturalize the force of the male gaze through surveillance and thereby place women in an especially vulnerable position. It
was not uncommon for undisciplined state auxiliary forces that lacked officer training to transport Yaqui female prisoners without supervision, which
opened the women to sexual violence. The soldiers were mostly criminals and
believed to be the vilest reflection of Mexican society.[14] A number of government records report that at the beginning of the mass deportations and
rounding up of Yaquis from haciendas, the women prisoners were separated
from male prisoners, suggesting that women and girls became potential targets of sexual violence based on their isolation and assumed gender subordination and inferiority.

Fontes's novel imagines how public surveillance became an occasion for a
contest of will as the Yaqui women tried to avoid further sexual exploitation.
In the novel, the *bartolina* soldiers come to mock the women as they are being
rounded up for deportation to Yucatán.[15] A sexualized contest between a
bartolina soldier and Luz María, a Yaqui girl, shows bodies colliding in destructive contests over nation:

A balding bartolina soldier is determined to have one of the Yaqui women. He tosses a lasso at his selection, a pretty girl—maybe fifteen years old. She grabs the rope around her ankles, yanks it out of the soldier's hands, then chases after him. Before he can out distance her, she loops the lasso under his feet, pulls, and brings him face-down into the dirt. . . . But the Yaqui girl stays mad. Before the soldier gets up, she's on top of him, keeps him down by driving both knees into his chest. She pummels his bearded face with her fists until two soldiers pull her off.[16]

In this confrontation, much like Josefa/Juanita's confrontation with Cannon before his death, it is the man who openly challenges the young girl to resist his desire for her. Because he is a soldier of the Mexican government, he feels a sense of entitlement to the bodies of indigenous female prisoners as he tries to take possession of government property, essentially political prisoners. Reversing the stereotypical narratives that represent indigenous women as passive subjects or as whores, Luz María is a warrior defending her gender, her race, and her nation, showing her deftness and skill by employing her only weapons: her brains and her body.[17] In articulating rage as a legitimate response to genocide and to the potential for rape, Luz María is defending much more than her body: "The women are counting on her and the bartolina soldiers are betting on him."[18] Symbolizing the warring Yaqui and Mexican nations in their struggle to control land and autonomy, Fontes inverts the gendered hierarchy of nation here by representing the Yaqui nation as enraged, feminine, and fierce while the Mexican nation is gendered as masculine, lascivious, and impotent.

Furthering the point of the novel's assertions, official Mexican government documents label Yaqui women's rage as socially conditioned and pathological. In his communiqués during the wars, General Troncoso wrote the following of Yaqui women: "With the Yori [the white] . . . the woman continues with threats . . . and when the child arrives to the age of eight or ten years, she says it to him and repeats it incessantly that Yori has killed the father, the grandfathers, the relatives, and they have eaten too its brothers; impressing this idea upon them and that the Yori must be killed."[19] General Troncoso, in official dispatches to the secretary of the army and navy, pathologizes Yaqui women's hatred of white men (Mexicans). Notice Troncoso's absolute distinction between Yaqui ethnicity as Indian and Mexican ethnicity as white, undermining the nationalist paradigm that Mexicans are mestizos. The term *Yori* renders Mexicans as unambiguously white. Fontes's representation of the fifteen-year-old Luz María fighting to preserve her bodily integrity reveals part of a historical trajectory of racialized and sexualized violence carried out by Yori men, and such a narrative offers a literary foil to General Troncoso's official historical attempt to pathologize Yaqui women for their rage.

The reader is taken step by step through this battle scene of nation against nation, or of woman against man, one that does not culminate in rape. Luz María refuses to become an object and maintains autonomy over her body no matter what it costs her. If other soldiers had not intervened, Luz María would have continued to unleash the collective rage she has harbored. Only with intervention does "the soldier stagger to his feet and strike her across the face."[20] The rare spectacle of a man and woman fighting in a highly contested public space underscores a sensationalizing desire to witness violence in a context that does not inflict pain on the spectator's body. The action recommences when "someone yells, 'Let her fight!' The soldiers let the woman go and she lunges at the soldier."[21] In this simultaneously erotic and violent scene the sexualized nature of the female body is temporarily displaced by violent acts of self-defense: "They bite fingers, scratch faces, kick and swing full force. Somehow the girl manages to stick her middle and index fingers inside his mouth and grabs hold of his cheek. He howls in pain as she spins him around, forces him to the ground and gouges at his eyes. Their clothes are nearly ripped off. Blood from her nose and lips colors her breasts. His eyes are swollen nearly shut. Bloody scratches X his chest."[22] The pretext of Mexican governmental order is shattered in this passage as the young Yaqui woman uses the few weapons she has—her fingers and her teeth—to defend herself. In images evoking dismemberment and disembodiment, fingers and teeth are isolated from the rest of the body and become weapons. Pain is registered in the soldier's uncontrollable howling, publicly undermining his masculinity. The scratches and blood also mark the body's pain. In singling out Luz María, the soldier signified his desire to use her body to affirm his sexual dominance but utterly fails to do so. In official government policy and statements, generals such as José Carbó, chief of the First Military Zone, claimed to "organize their pueblos without the result of spilling of blood, [by] agreeing to open the [deportation] campaign."[23] So while in theory Carbó argues for a civilized interaction with the Yaqui, Fontes's depiction of Luz María's battle represents implementation of policy as an entirely different matter, namely, as an extension of war and the sexual violence endemic to war.

The spectacle created by the fight demonstrates the importance of the act of witnessing violence committed against other humans. Here, race, sexuality, and gender collide as the pleasure experienced by the Mexican soldiers watching the fight is contrasted with Luz Maria's fight to avoid rape and maintain bodily sovereignty within the context of a larger Yaqui struggle to survive genocide: "The girl and the soldier crash again and roll on the ground. Every time the soldier pins her down, up she snaps and down he goes. He may be stronger, but he can't hold her long enough to end the fight. . . . The girl wins. She bests her opponent with a pair of short punches to his eyes. The soldier hold up his hands to signal enough."[24]

There are several noteworthy aspects of this passage. First, the representation echoes American press reports about the ineptness of Díaz's military regime. An article in *Harper's Weekly* from 1908 describes the regulars (like Luz María's opponent) as "a promiscuous soldiery: most of them serve in the army as a penalty for some offence committed against the laws of the republic and are sentenced to serve for such a length of time as their crime warrants. . . . It is easy to understand that such soldiers as these are not trained, have no patriotism and will not fight except for self-preservation. The soldiers are not drilled at rifle practice and they know practically nothing about the use of their firearms, except what they have learned in desultory shooting."[25] Steeped in the idea of Mexican barbarity, buffoonery, and premodernity, the symbolic defeat of the phallus embodied in the image of the soldier whom Luz María fights is no surprise; it is in keeping with the scathing account and assault on Mexican military masculinity expounded in *Harper's Weekly*, an attitude based in U.S. moral codes and an imperialistic gaze. The soldiers have no loyalty to their country and no ability to aim their weapons, and furthermore they are undisciplined and criminal, driven by sexual desires. They were "individuos que han prestado servicio de guardia custodiano los yaquis aprehendidos / individuals lent out or borrowed in service as custodial guardians for apprehended Yaquis."[26] Fontes uses U.S. imperial discourse both to critique Mexican military ineptness and to highlight Yaqui attempts at circumventing Mexican military power.

In this same scene, the reader encounters what Hartman calls "the constraints of the captive body."[27] A captive body is limited in its potential for agency; a captive body must find alternative ways to defend itself or face total domination. Although Hartman's analysis discusses the limitations of the slave body, the racialized body of a political prisoner like Luz María is in a similar position. Through her actions, she has a marked subjectivity as a political dissident because she resists the sexual force of the government embodied in the soldier's advances. Luz María is forced to perform her Yaqui ethnicity and culture as a brutal and bloody warrior, but only within the confines of the rules that govern her captive body. Interpreting this scene, in Hartman's words, as an effort to "alleviate the pained state of the captive body," is one option, but this interpretation may be too celebratory because, although Luz María has avoided rape, she has actually opened her body up to more violence.

Once Luz María is declared the winner of the fight, the Mexican government intercedes and corrects the absence of order to restore masculine dominance. The men cannot allow the Yaqui girl to claim victory over the Mexican soldier; it is unnatural in this world: "A *rural* steps forward and strikes the back of her head with a rifle butt. Everyone is silent as she drops to her knees. A second blow breaks her front teeth. He drags her back to the circle. Two other rurales clap chains on the weary soldier's wrists and ankles and haul him away. The girl is howling angrily. Her yell fills the air that moments before held cries cheering her to victory or defeat."[28] Prior to this moment Luz María has not registered her pain verbally; only through the blood on her chest does her suffering register. She, like many other tortured Yaquis, chooses to maintain silence as an act of refusing state power. In an attempt to make pain visible, the novel displays Luz María's head being bashed with a rifle butt. The blow forces her to her knees in submission, as her legs cannot support her against it. She is forced to kneel before her oppressor. In corporal punishment, "populations whose bodies are used in the conformation process [of conventional war] can not have exercised any consent over this use of their bodies."[29] The power to survive and defend oneself is easily policed by two blows of a rifle butt. Unable to articulate her pain in Yaqui, Spanish, or English, Luz María's howl is the opposite of a silenced Mexican national history in which Yaqui women do no more than respond to violence with violent acts of their own: fight to the death to avoid rape. Nonetheless, self-defense initiates the betrayal of one's own body because the defense of Yaqui sexuality is a denial of the state vision of savageness that evokes violence and brutality. Bestial defeminization is rearticulated once she is beaten by the gender and national order that requires submissive femininity.[30] Luz María's moment of triumphant self-defense is superseded by the public display of her beating. In this scene of subjection, Fontes invokes the distinct Yaqui history of subjugation and the radical subjectivity produced through violent confrontations with sexualized patriarchy. It is the preexisting subject position that suggests violence is not what inaugurates Luz Maria as a subject. Rather, it is her fighting that suggests that the "I" subject formation exists prior to the violence and is only radically reinforced by defending oneself from violence.

This scene mirrors something recorded in the historical archive in a letter of 1885 to Díaz: "In all Districts of the State are being carried out the most scandalous attacks and disgraceful campaign against the Yaquis, who throughout Sonora are justified in their actions, but they are capable of performing even more infamous atrocities."[31] This is one of the few testimonies that allude to the "scandalous" violence employed to subvert the Yaqui, but, more important, this scandalous violence is still unspeakable, as the attacks are offered to the reader devoid of any detail. Unnamed violence briefly mentioned in the historical testimony and evoked in the scene between Luz María and the soldier represents an absent presence, one that is remedied by fictionalizing it (as speech) in an imagined fight scene that reinforces the idea that Yaqui subjectivity was enacted through self-defense and attempts to maintain bodily sovereignty.

Fontes's representation of Luz Maria's struggle to defend her bodily sovereignty ventures into the realm of the unspeakable, turning it into something spoken, unmasking historical denials of sexualized, racialized violence. Sexual violence and torture tactics were not always approved by agents of the federal government but nonetheless were used. Scholars argue that these tactics came into play because the majority of the Mexican soldiers were prisoners of the Mexican government. For example, in 1904, fifty-three government prisoners from states like Puebla, Guerrero, Guanajuato, Campeche, Zacatecas, and Veracruz, among others, were brought to Sonora for sentencing and then enrollment in the Mexican army in Sonora, most likely with the express purpose of taking part in the Yaqui campaign.[32] The anthropologist Ana María Alonso describes how, during Díaz's regime, the state had to recreate itself on the northern frontier by creating new types of institutions. The rurales, one of the military elements used to contain the Yaqui, were individuals of working-class origins who were correspondingly used as instruments of the state.[33] They did not hold land or political power in Sonora and therefore had little or nothing to lose by serving the government. Military service was the only way they could access state power. Making Mexico a "safe" place for capitalism meant wiping out all traces of nationalist movements that threatened to disrupt the modernization of the Mexican nation-state. As the number of rurales in Sonora increased, Díaz manufactured an image of this roving police force that proclaimed their "*machista* ruthlessness and invincibility, [which] made them hated and feared by subaltern groups and classes throughout Mexico."[34] Called "cutthroat soldiers" by the American press, a group of these soldiers who were on skirmishing duty in January 1900 attacked the house of one Nacho González, who allegedly had supplied the Yaqui with information.[35] Because they were unable to find and arrest him, "the soldiers tortured his wife and grown-up daughter and afterward ravished and killed them and set fire to the house."[36] In this economy of retaliatory violence, masculinity as sexual excess embodied in rape and torture seemed to be a significant way for individuals who had little to no authority as ground soldiers of the government to establish their power. Performances of masculine excess may have reflected these personal power imbalances. Nevertheless, these soldiers also performed such acts in the name of the state, for they were actors in army uniforms.

In another context, the feminist scholar Jasbir Puar has theorized the "unwitting collusions of nationalist sentiment and sexual torture" embodied in discourses of U.S. exceptionalism and the Abu Ghraib torture photos leaked to the U.S. press in February 2004. She argues that "sexual humiliation and ritual torture of Iraqi prisoners enabled the Bush administration to forge a crucial distinction between the supposed depravity of Abu Ghraib and the 'freedom' being built in Iraq." Puar goes on to argue that a fine line was constructed between depravity and freedom for the Iraqis and the U.S. soldiers who administered the torture and took pictures of the sexual humiliation, but that the discourse "attempts to paint the United States as victim," an America in danger of losing its moral authority.[37] Puar focuses on the sexual humiliation of Muslim men in Abu Ghraib as a direct affront to their religious practices based in Orientalist ideologies. Further, the sexual violence was part of foreign and military policy that emerged as an unsophisticated rendering of Arab and Islamic cultural difference. The sexualized violence enacted upon the other by military agencies, be they American in the twenty-first century or Mexican in the nineteenth, put the nation-state in peril precisely because, as Puar argues, symbolic representations of sexual violence or actual violence motivated by sexual desire in a wartime situation all take away the ability to ground power in moral authority.

Taking this lack of moral authority into account, Fontes's passage involving Luz María portrays not only a failure of wartime hypermasculinity but also a direct critique of the image of the rurales that Díaz tried to manufacture during his regime. The fight scene between the rural and Luz María also signals the failure of this state vision of a nation based in morality. It is the entrance of sexual violence on behalf of the nation as the disciplining agent of the amoral Yaqui subject that allows for the freedom of some (those who economically benefited from Yaqui removal) and the unfreedom and depravation of others, the sexualized Yaqui prisoners. But this scene also reminds the reader of the small ways in which the Yaqui remained self-possessed individuals in the wake of violence against their person.

TORTUROUS NATION, TORTUROUS MASCULINITY

But the scenes where power circuits are temporarily cut or impaired by the depiction of an amoral, feeble, lascivious Mexican nation are coupled with depictions of a demasculinized and tortured Yaqui nation (embodied in the figure of the bronco or warrior), complicating visions of race, nation, and social hierarchies in the context of the Yaqui Indian wars. Fontes does not merely invert the colonial paradigm in celebration of the Yaqui. For example, Charco, who is half Yaqui and half Yori, is held in the inhumane bartolina prisons, where the government authorities constantly torture him to elicit information on the whereabouts of the leaders of the Yaqui rebellion. When asked how long he has been there, he replies, "I can't tell. Carrasco kept me tied to a post—day and night, . . . Ombliguito persuaded Carrasco to untie the reins they had around my neck. That's how I got here."[38] The punishment of his body erased linear time. Time and space are obliterated through torture as Charco is punished for his silence about the Yaqui insurgents: the horse's reins reduce him to the status of an animal. The "obsessive, self conscious display of agency" on the part of his torturer shows the absolute power of the guards over the prisoners as the physical punishment they inflict supposedly corresponds to the gravity of the prisoner's offense against the state.[39] These conscious displays of violence reinforce a language of supremacy. Small gestures that the average person takes for granted as intrinsic personal freedoms become the determining factor in whether the young prisoners will be allowed to feel like humans with agency. Still, Charco's torture continues, and the narrator states the obvious: "No one deserved to be tied to a post."[40]

Fontes's novel uses fictive representation to make visible the hidden history of torture in the everyday practice of the state under Díaz and of the Mexican military. A report by the U.S. consulate in Nogales confirms the practice of tying prisoners to posts as well as other forms of torture. After a Yaqui raid against Americans traveling through Sonora in which two men, Garret and Martin, were killed, several Yaquis were brought in for questioning by order of Governor Izabál, known for his Yaqui Indian fighting while he was the state governor.[41] The Indians were tortured one by one, according to the consulate report, with the intention of exacting a confession of complicity in the

FIGURE 5 Man awaiting punishment in a henequen hacienda drying yard, Yucatán, Mexico, ca. 1902–9. Reproduced with the authorization of the Mexican Instituto Nacional de Antropología e Historia.

murders of Garret and Martin. To the consulate, one punishment was especially worthy of commentary:

> Finally, I learned that he had reached the turn of Luis Pérez in the torture, whose hands were tied to a post, and that he had been kept face-down in the hot rays of the sun; they had tied a rope around his feet, whose ends were tied twice to the post, and soldiers, by order of the governor, secured the cord at the ends, leaving Pérez secured in this way, in horrible agony, and I observed the thermometer marking over 100 degrees. For over two hours one could hear his cries of pain around the city of San Marical because the torture took place at the center of town. . . . they informed me that Pérez had lost his reason, as a result of their actions, and that torture had ended. . . . One by one the assembled peons, I know, suffered the same torture, which lasted until they were placed in a position to say anything you would like them to. . . . The governor ordered them to be shot, to complete their suffering, and they even begged the soldiers to kill them immediately, asking them to take pity on them and spare them that suffering.[42]

Foucault calls torture like this an "instrumental coding of the body," and this was a twofold process in Pérez's torture. First, the body parts were individually objectified, tortured independently. Second, the injured body parts were manipulated in the process of isolating them, and, according to Foucault, they are thus "correlated together according to a number of simple gestures."[43] The total effects of torture suggest that the body is literally imposed upon by the power system of objects outside of the body itself, marking it as acceptable and legible for the state (that is, as docile). Luis Pérez's hands and feet were essentially hogtied, and he was standing up, hunched over but face down so that he could not see what happened behind him. Here, the body does its own work against itself because slight movements cause discomfort. Seemingly natural elements—the position of the body, the hot Sonoran desert sun, the central plaza of San Marical—are really not natural at all. These spatially determined elements all create the spectacle of torture. The spatial confinement served to torture Pérez, as his world was shrunken down into the tiny space around the post. At the same time, spectators no doubt observed this self-conscious display of state agency, as the privacy of one's body became a public spectacle. Because the torture took place in the center of the city, we are once again shown that setting and space are crucial to emphasizing Pérez's lack of power. The confinement wreaked havoc on Pérez's sanity, as his "yells were heard all throughout the town." But one could also argue that the extreme physical violence he experienced produced a sense of radical subjectivity, a hyperawareness of the body's limits as a living organism, and a stripping of masculinity. The hyperawareness shows how race and a lack of citizenship were inscribed onto the body performatively through the enactment of physical violence in a public space. Further, the public disciplining of the Yaqui body serves as a reminder not just to Pérez, who was tortured, but also to all other Yaquis, reminding them they could suffer a similar fate. In life and death, both Pérez's and Charco's being tied to posts expresses the extreme suffering and loss experienced by Yaqui political prisoners in a war of decimation.[44]

The Mexican army's practices were aimed at destroying Yaqui humanity through enactments of debasement. The torture was not uniform among the prisoners; it was specific to one's rank in the resistance movement, if this could be proven. On June 26, 1886, Mexican forces captured the cabecillo Bacilio Tableño, and after he was questioned about the resistance, which he denied any knowledge of, he finally confessed that more than six hundred armed Indians were located along different parts of the river. Instead of securing the end of his torment, "the prisoner was granted his liberty with a shot, because of his resistance."[45] Just like Luis Pérez and Bacilio Tableño, Charco is punished for his affiliations with the Yaqui; however, Charco is kept alive because of his phenotype. Because "Charco has blue eyes. . . . Carrasco won't shoot him or send him to the Yucatán."[46] The *federales* in the novel kill the disposable Yaqui prisoners who refuse to give the government information, but Charco is spared because his blue eyes signify his whiteness, his Mexican-ness. Although his blue eyes save him, his fierce loyalty to the Yoeme drives the continuous cycle of his torture. Given what this book has shown about marking Yaqui Indians as nonmestizo, the fact that Charco is kept alive because he is mestizo and yet tortured because he is Yaqui says something important about the logic of Mexican national projects. A mestizo individual allied with the Yaqui could perhaps serve as a way into the insurgency movement because he is read as mestizo symbolically and phenotypically signals that he is not a full-blooded Indian. Allegorically, he represents the future of the Mexican nation, but only if he can be turned away from the Yaqui insurgency movement and converted into an agent of the state.

The novel's narrator tells the reader how "the guards pull[ed] a bundle wrapped in a crude blanket off of the wagon. They held the ends and swinging, heaved the bundle into the cell. A guard reached in and jerked the blanket out before replacing the grill. . . . Bloody welts dotted the boy's back, legs and buttocks."[47] As the crude protection is ripped from Charco's mutilated body, the authoritarian power of the torturers is exposed in physical declarations of power mapped upon the flesh. According to Elaine Scarry, what is "remembered in the body is well remembered," meaning that the repetition of disciplinary practices carries not only a physical but also a psychological burden or loss.[48] Charco's reaction to the torture is to remain silent, and consequently he absorbs the steady infliction of further bodily punishment. It is as if his body, when being violently abused, communicates to his brain and mouth that he must remain silent at all costs—even at the cost of his bodily sovereignty. This is a different kind of silence from what I have described thus far in the book. Rather than an official silence imposed in government records to forget atrocity, Charco's silence is a metonymic Yaqui silence. That is, his silence is substituted for information about the insurgency against the Mexican military. At the same time, we can think of his silence as part of a larger, more general Yaqui silence allegorically in history because of a lack of trust in the Mexican nation. Yaqui silence was and perhaps continues to be a survival mechanism.

Within the time frame of Yaqui struggles for autonomy, Charco's torture is the direct result of the Yaquis' breaking of the Ortiz Peace Treaty. Tetabiate, the Yaqui leader of the Sierra Bacatete faction, signed this treaty on May 15, 1897. In a so-called act of submission, Tetabiate and his four hundred men agreed to recognize the sovereignty of Mexico's government, and, in turn, the government guaranteed the Yaqui would not be harassed for their past rebellion.

They offered the natives of the Yaqui River land in the Yaqui Valley that was far from the *ejidos*.[49] As Yori settlers increasingly encroached on the Yaquis' territory, and the Mexican troops were not withdrawn as promised in the treaty, regiments of warriors broke the peace in 1899.[50] One of the few documents I came across that was written by Yaqui peoples related to the broken trust of the Ortiz peace accord. Dated August 21, 1899, it reads, "Tell us now: what we want is that the whites and the troops leave our land. If they leave willingly, then there is peace; but if they don't, then we declare the war. Because the peace that was signed in Ortiz was with the condition that the troops and whites leave, and that they do not comply to it, to the contrary, instead of complying they want to remove our weapons. It is your luck now that you and all of the negotiators will be to blame for all the misfortune that has set on Sonora. Los ocho pueblos del Yaqui"[51] This is one of the few documents I found written in both Yaqui and Spanish that tried to compromise with the Mexican government. As we can see from the history and the representation of that history within Fontes's novel, Yaquis were forced to adopt insurgent tactics because no compromise could be reached. White Mexicans would not stay off their land and did not respect their autonomy. National policy and military operations reinforced the acceptable nature of such behavior.

In *Dreams of the Centaur* extracting evidence of the plans of the insurgent movement from Charco proves futile. Charco's knowledge of the whereabouts of the rebels opens up the complex web of relations that allow the torturers to temporarily disable his body in the service of extracting important information from him. Torture that pushed the individual to the brink of death was ideal, as the body could heal and recover, and the victim retained his usefulness as a potential informant. The bodies of the tortured are played off against each other to increase the power of the terrorist regime. Interpreting Charco's ethnic identity as solely or primarily Mexican on the basis of his blue eyes is a mistake. Just like those of the Yaquis who passed as Mexicans in order to purchase arms in Arizona (see chapter 4), Charco's loyalties are with the Yaqui, even when his body is read as Mexican and white. Yet the torture inflicted upon Charco's body concretely and politically links him to the Yaqui, which suggests his torture is not about his position as an informant, but about something else. The *guardia* seems to be trying to torture the allegiance to his Indian side out of him, literally torture him to the point that he gives up his Indian identity. His problem, as a mestizo, is that he fails to properly subordinate his racialized Indianness to his whiteness.

Another reference to the torture of Yaqui prisoners can be found in a special feature article in the *Los Angeles Times* entitled "Red Raiders of Sonora Hills: Guerrilla Operations of Bronco Yaquis in the Mining Districts." Published on May 14, 1906, the article appeared after Yaqui attacks were carried out against American miners and Mexican landowners in Sonora. Writing of the killing of a miner, the article reports that

> about a week after the killing of Williams, a roundup of Yaquis working in the vicinity of Carbo was made, and thirty Indians were arrested and taken to the penitentiary at Hermosillo, where a number of Indian men, women and children are held awaiting deportation to Yucatan. The Sonoran authorities said they believed they had caught some of the bad Yaquis in the band of thirty and it was intimated that the "third degree" would be worked on a few of them to persuade them to confess. If the "third degree" is what it is said to be, it is sure to produce any confession desired by those who work it. It is fully as effective as the "water cure" in the Philippines, a few years ago. The policy of rounding up "tame" Yaqui laborers employed near the scene of an outrage has been adopted because it is believed that the Indians take turns in going on the war path, and that a Yaqui may be tame one day and bronco the next, according to opportunity. . . . Yaqui servants who have been trusted for years by their employers, have been caught going out at night to join bronco bands and take part in murderous adventures.[52]

Once again we are presented with the singular importance of extracting a confession of information. The confession signals the real nature of betrayal: the body betrays itself by speaking and the sovereign Yaqui community by implicating them. But the way the confession is solicited here has special resonance because again the writer does not describe the actual methods of torture. Instead, the writer evades discussion of the methods of torturing the Yaqui by recalling another anti-imperial struggle involving the United States—the war in the Philippines. The three-second water cure, perfected in what at the time was the U.S. colony of the Philippines, was transferred from empire to empire.[53]

What is striking is that the effectiveness of a U.S.-invented torture tactic, developed in the Philippines to quell native resistance to U.S. imperialism, is compared to the effectiveness of tortures used in Mexico by the Mexican military to quell Yaqui Indian resistance. Tracing this comparison, we can see that the *Los Angeles Times* writer naturalizes and almost celebrates a late nineteenth- and early twentieth-century circuit of imperialism in which technologies of war and torture are traveling in service of quelling third world dissonance. This logic serves to mark Mexico's project of Yaqui extermination as not simply one of decimation but also one of empire and territorial expansion. The Mexican three-second trick, cousin to the Filipino water trick, was designed to unmask the disguised Yaqui "broncos," to prevent further "outrages," and to protect American miners. Also implied in the article are excessive brown, animalistic masculinities that the imperial forces could not contain. Bronco is the name commonly used for Yaqui insurgents. In this context in particular, *bronco* signifies excess, of gendered, racialized disorder that caused the Mexican military and Porfiriato much grief because it disrupted dominant conceptions of hegemonic masculinity and power. Although one might think such articles in the U.S. and Mexican press could have provoked social outrage, there was little reaction, and I suggest this is because the Yaqui nation was in the interstitial space within two nations. Sonora is nearly equidistant from the centers of U.S. and Mexican power (roughly 1,846 miles from Mexico City and 1,860 miles from Washington, D.C.), and this spatial separation was necessary in order for imperialism to unfold without question of ethics and morality. It is the distance from the center of power to the colony that allows for the three-second trick or the water cure to be ignored or go unquestioned.

In *Dreams of the Centaur* the three-second trick makes an appearance as well: "It's scientific. The man's mind tortures him while he waits for the next lash. Sometimes they faint. The mind does it. I tell you, if you wait six seconds, you'll never have to give more than fifteen lashes," the implication being that the prisoner will thereby be able to work the next day.[54] Further, referring to torture as a trick evokes child's play or a game, making torture seem like a simple, transparent situation with a clear winner and a clear loser. Fontes's use of this term lulls the reader into forgetting, underscoring both the scientific precision of torture and the rhetorical obfuscation of war. That people died from these imperial tricks, this chain of imperialism, a fact uncovered in American documentary journalism, demonstrates that Fontes's fictional accounts of deportation, torture, and violence are not far from the truth of what was going on in multiple sites of imperial domination against third world peoples around the globe.

Recounting another scene of Charco's torture, the narrator, Alejo, speaks from a place of empathy and caring but also from a politically critical standpoint that questions the destructive capacity of torture, a view completely absent from the newspaper accounts about Mexican imperial tricks: "Several nights ago, soldiers had again come for Charco. Though he was gone only a few hours, the boy had barely spoken since his return . . . And though Alejo had not seen Charco, the guard's consoling phrases told him the boy was seriously hurt. Alejo admitted he was relieved that it was Charco and not him Carrasco had sent for. Filled with remorse, Alejo vowed he would not leave the bartolinas without Charco."[55]

Charco's injured body is protected by cover of night, and his failure to speak communicates the fact that his bodily abilities to move and talk have been impaired. The signs of torture are cast as signs of absence or lack. Alejo's presence of mind, body, speech, and self-mastery contrasts greatly with Charco's lifeless body and seems to allow mourning of the loss. Someone else has essentially mastered his body. Marking the great difference between the half brothers, it is the Indian-identified Charco who loses self-possession through his torture, while his mestizo Mexican brother Alejo, a criminal convicted of murder, is saved by his Mexican skin. In torture, as much as in resistance, "repetition is an outcome, a consequence, or an accumulation of practice, and it also structures practice."[56] Here, the torturer's repeated acts of bodily mutilation (this is the second time Charo is beaten within inches of his life) become the everyday practices handed down by the repressive state apparatus. Nationalist cultural practice is structured in terms of violence against bodies in the novel, and racialization as indigenous seems to be the marker of difference. Charco's refusal to speak—his ability to remain silent, even under the severest physical pain—shows how he too is engaging in an accumulated practice of refusal. While Alejo, the witness, realizes that dissent equals increased torture, it is Charco's body upon which the power dynamics between Mexico and Yaqui are violently mapped out.

Yet sometimes criminality and its punishments were doled out equally to the two brothers. Alejo recalls a night when "he and Charco were bound, gagged, blindfolded and tossed into the pits."[57] When the sympathetic prison guard lets both boys out of their cells, Alejo is shocked to find Charco inert and lifeless, again marking the racial privilege and difference between them. As Alejo climbs into the pit he finds "the gruel the soldiers had poured down lay baked over [Charco's] head. He also understood why Charco had not spoken. The sides of his mouth were slit open."[58] Slitting the sides of the mouth would make it difficult for the victim to create air pressure in the cheeks to produce words and sounds. Such mutilation therefore makes every utterance excruciatingly painful and difficult. The silence, disfigurement, or dysfunction of Charco's mouth recalls what the Yaqui critic Delberto Dario Ruiz argues about "the realities of a cut tongue, [which] are especially disturbing." His phrase, "Teki Lenguas del Yollotzin" (cut tongues from the heart), describes the immense psychic pain of physically and metaphorically being stripped of speech.[59] For Ruiz, the process of being stripped of one's native tongue or the act of speech altogether is central to orienting and manipulating social interaction and, I would add, conceptions of subjectivity.[60]

Building on the physical violence against the social processes of being stripped of language that Ruiz describes, I read Charco's torture as an instance of his body being literally cut from language and cut by language, because the soldiers take away his ability to form speech altogether as racialized forms of punishment for his not telling them what they want to know about the Yaqui rebels. The lifeless body is an example of "discipline produc[ing] subjected and practiced bodies, docile bodies."[61] Charco's body is made into an object of docility because, in addition to the slits at the sides of his mouth, "welts covered the boy's legs, back and shoulders."[62] He has been beaten into submission and, even if he were conscious, he would be unable to communicate verbally without pain. Here, attempts at agency become painful for the docile body. These types of acts of torture that prohibit the body from maintaining itself as an active, autonomous entity were used in combination to break Yaqui dissidents.

The psychological terror of imprisonment under such harsh conditions makes a person feel completely alienated from his or her body; the aforementioned case of Luis Perez being tied to a post is a perfect example of this. Charco, as a political prisoner, receives the most brutal discipline and punishment. But despite the numerous times Charco is tortured throughout the narrative, his survival is indicative of something transcendent. "Alejo watched Charco walking with Ombligo at his side. How did Charquito do it? He recalled what Tacho said about horses and Yaquis getting their strength from the land. *Even in the pits, Charco's on Yaqui soil.*"[63] Charco's connection to Yaqui soil and his memory of place are far stronger than any beating or bodily destruction the guardia could inflict upon him. Such indigenous familial, communal, and spiritual land ties, as N. Scott Momaday says in *The Man Made of Words*, are characteristic of how "sacred ground is in some way earned. It is consecrated, made holy with offerings—song and ceremony, joy and sorrow, the dedication of the mind and heart, offerings of life and death. The words 'sacred' and 'sacrifice' are related."[64] Charco draws upon the sacred space of his ancestral homeland to survive his imprisonment. Through hundreds of years of conflict with Spanish missionaries and the Mexican government, the Yaqui have known where their land is and have carried it with them internally, even if Yoris occupy that physical space. By making the connection between sacred lands and suffering, Fontes acknowledges the fact that, for the most part, the state of Sonora has been founded through Yaqui labor, displacement, loss, and suffering. While the fight for Yaqui autonomy and land rages in the background, Charco's bodily memory reminds us of the importance of protecting sacred lands, nations, and the people who defend them.

When Charco and Alejo finally escape the bartolinas by enlisting in the Mexican army, the physical and psychological transition is marked by a spatial break that shows a narrative advance in time. They are put through one final Foucauldian ritual of bodily violation before they make the transformation from prisoners to soldiers. Alejo's younger brother Hector "witnessed Alejo and another young man joined to a chain gang of twenty naked men whose arms were strapped to wooden mesquite stakes. The procession stayed clear of Yaqui forests, making it impossible for any Yaqui insurgents to interfere with the government's work. . . . The men [went] on foot. Those too weak to walk were shot. Twelve survived the seven-day journey."[65] Naked and unable to shield their bodies from the harsh sun, infection, and abuse, the men are forced to march for their lives and prove they deserve to live. Those who cannot handle the journey are killed without remorse. In archival records the process of moving Yaquis was described as "individuals who drive the Yaquis" like cattle being herded.[66] Further, it becomes clear that the demasculinization and humiliation of subaltern and peasant classes was a necessary part of carrying the transformation from state offender to state actor. The ways in which such offenders were disciplined precisely functioned to reinforce the severity and brutality of the Yaqui insurgents and criminals by disciplining them with even harsher punishments than they inflicted upon their victims. This life-or-death march determines whether or not these men are worthy of being made into soldiers. According to Foucault, "The soldier has become something that can be made; out of a formless clay, an inapt body, the machine required can be constructed; posture gradually corrected; a calculated constraint runs slowly throughout each part of the body mastering it, making it pliable, ready at all times, turning silently into automatism of habit; in short, one has got rid of 'the peasant' and given him 'the air of the soldier.' "[67] Foucault believes that soldiers are made, that is, transformed, through discipline and automatism, which enables them to leave the past behind. Through this process of conversion the individual can be created anew as a subject.

But what happens when the transformation from citizen to soldier or prisoner to soldier is met with resistance? According to the scholar of trauma studies Laura S. Brown, the scenes of torture and state-sponsored violence qualify as "event[s] outside the range of [normal] human experience . . . the range of what is normal and usual in the lives of men of the dominant class; white, young, able-bodied, educated, middle class, Christian men. Trauma is thus that which disrupts these particular human lives, but no other. War and genocide, which are the work of men and male dominated culture, are agreed-upon traumas; so are natural disasters," but not when related to people of color, queer people, or women.[68] Brown's analysis of the relationships among race, class, and trauma illuminates an array of forces that contribute to the destructive power of events that occur abnormally. Oppressive forces caused by racial traumas or traumas related to gender, racial, or sexual orientations are considered disruptive traumas. She writes, "Feminist analysis also is to understand how the constant presence and threat of trauma in the lives of girls and women of all colors, men of color, in the United States, lesbian and gay people . . . have [sic] shaped our society, a continuing background noise rather than an unusual event."[69]

While *Dreams of the Centaur* extends itself to transnational traumas, to indigenous genocides that are unacknowledged yet perpetrated by first world powers, Brown's feminist ideas about trauma resonate in the scenes in which women are abused and in which Alejo and Charco are forced to make the transition from being traumatized to becoming enforcers of trauma. This transformation allows those earlier traumatic events to be remembered from a new subject position as soldier. Alejo says, "All I had to do to become a soldier was take a few paces. But while I was walking from one group to another, dizziness came over me. I staggered and fell. I was more than naked, *I was stripped of flesh and memory."*[70] In the moment of conversion from politi-cal prisoner to soldier, trauma is not a repression but the return of a "tem-poral delay that carries the individual beyond the shock of the first mo-ment."[71] The narrative structure of this scene enacts a temporal delay by displaying the residual effects of Alejo's accumulated psychological trauma. Alejo's stumbling in the scene of conversion is also marked by a curt narrative style. As the textual form mimics this new shock, the idea that Charco and Alejo "carry an impossible history with them, or they themselves become the symptom of a history that they cannot entirely possess," has the implication of being skinned alive.[72] The violent past comes to bear on the present, causing Alejo to lose control over his body and memory. To be stripped of flesh and memory is the recognition that the idea of becoming a soldier after soldiers have violently tortured the body is a psychic weight that is almost too much for Alejo to bear. Torture is destructive of the mind, and this destruction manifests itself in the body. It is a violent process of stripping maligned bodies of the blood memory and racial memory.[73]

Alejo describes how one person's dominance becomes another person's subjection or, more concretely, how "no dream is fulfilled without hostages, without victims, without blood," which Fontes says is the premise of the novel.[74] The Porfirian-era dream of mastery over the Yaqui requires one to actively forget one's own political convictions to become part of the national fighting machine. It requires active forgetting, something Alejo and Charco cannot do for their own political reasons. The gap between forgetting and remembering, between being a politically ethical subject with a moral consciousness and a state instrument devoid of critical faculty, is the enactment of painful forces on the body. Remembering has the potential to disassemble the national memory of complete domination. Memory is kept alive because it is carried as scars on the flesh; they are scars of memory that carry the loss as a part of subject formation, reminding us of the severely politically compromising positions people were put in during the Porfiriato and the suffocating nature of the responsibility that memory brings with it.

Fontes's curt narrative style marks this uneasy and traumatic transformation of character as never being quite complete, neither a total form of complacency nor outright resistance. The transition from abused docile prisoner body to docile citizen-soldier, with a spatial break at the beginning of part 2, shows the psychic effects of the violence not only for the Yaqui but also for Mexicans involved on both sides of the struggle. In fact, the Mexican army had trouble preventing soldiers from deserting during these wars because they were so long and often, in trying to defeat a dispersed Yaqui guerrilla force, abstract.[75] As the narrative tracks the psychic processes of Charco's and Alejo's transformation from prisoners to soldiers, the spatial/textual break indicates a shift in time and a shift in consciousness. Consciously marking a literal shift in identity, Fontes shows that the only way to escape the bartolinas is to inhabit the name, the "newly" reconstructed body, and the identity of another. "The change from criminal to soldier went smoothly for everyone, except for me," remarks Alejo.[76] In his new identity, Alejo says, "Color gives me no pleasure. In an airless hole below [the boat deck], Yaqui families and other prisoners are packed tighter than I was in the bartolinas. A sodden stench invades the air, flows through me, and unrolls itself across the deck. I shut my eyes and still see the faces of those we shoved into the lower decks. Shame clings to my palms."[77] Precisely because it is narrated from a privileged mestizo perspective the image of a Yaqui middle passage, where bodies are inhumanely packed into the hull of a ship so tightly that the air smells of rotten human flesh, marks a parallel history of slavery in the Americas that carries into the late nineteenth century and early twentieth, when empire, race, and genocide benefited those identified through their whiteness.

Disease and the smell of death preoccupy Alejo as a newly made Mexican soldier; even when he tries to escape this image, he cannot. As soldiers, Alejo and Charco are immediately asked to prove their loyalty to the nation by actively engaging in the torture of others, as if disease and starvation were not enough. Here, the former recipients of torture, Alejo and Charco, become the instruments who enact torture on behalf of the nation. Again, the dialectic between flesh and memory poses the tension that expresses the pain of re-membering. The pain of memory is carried in the flesh; forgetting would provide complete disengagement with the pain. The material presence of shame, manifested in the flesh of the palms, demonstrates the weight of guilt and how even if we want to escape them, certain memories are inescapable, and what is rendered or remaindered is a haunting sense of loss. Shame travels with Alejo as he recognizes his complicity in the government plan to extermi-nate the Yaqui people. His shame does not allow him to forget the innocent faces of the nameless Yaqui families who suffer below the ship's deck, even when he actively tries to forget. Instead of presenting a "wall of silent com-plicity" to military superiors and the Yaqui prisoners, Alejo and Charco con-stantly struggle with their proximity to violent death, precisely because it reminds them of their own past and the potential to be close to their own deaths again.[78]

Standing apart ideologically, but physically and socially placed alongside the other soldiers, Alejo and Charco are not men united in service to their country. Rather, they are men who escaped life imprisonment through mili-tary service. The other soldiers have been conditioned to be men who exploit those whom they perceive to be weaker. Indeed, they understand their mili-tary service as power to exploit: "They were no longer men. They raced rats, but to make sure they controlled them, they cut the tendons. When they spoke of women, they talked of parts. Nipples. Breasts. Crotches. Thighs. Buttocks. To them, women were for chewing, riding, piercing, swallowing, wearing. The men's night noises told me something had cut loose their souls. And though my eyes never absorbed their faces, their laughs told me these men belonged to no one."[79] These prisoner-soldiers are desperate men focused on destroying things outside of their existence in order to gain power. While they disable rat bodies or reduce women's bodies to parts, the novel shows the ways in which systematic apparatuses of discipline in late nineteenth-century Mexico did not actually rehabilitate supposed and actual criminals or allow them to regain a sense of humanity and a political consciousness. Rather, the men are a part of a technology of destruction. The reference to cannibalism—the desire to consume not just any flesh, but the flesh of women—also reinforces the notion that women's bodies are to be owned, consumed, and violated. The threat of rape and violation looms, as the criminal element has not been transformed into a fighting machine of brotherhood; or perhaps the fighting machine of brotherhood is predicated on the rape of and sexual violence against Yaqui women. It is the pain of others imagined and real that brings them pleasure, a mechanism to displace and disconnect their own bodies and psyches from their entrapment and pain. What unifies all of these destructive images is the fact that the soldiers are using physically destructive behavior to rework their memories in a way that is manageable even at the cost of the suffering of others.

The military, as an organization, was and is designed to discipline individuals, although in this particular context that motive failed both the soldier and the military prisoner. Foucault cites "the distribution of bodies, the spatial arrangement of production machinery and the different forms of activity in the distribution of 'posts' [that] had to be linked together" in order to continue disciplinary action.[80] The military posts or units are designed to have the soldiers police each other. But in Fontes's representation, they are too busy seeking pleasure through dismembering rats or imagining the sexual exploitation of Yaqui women's body parts to monitor one another. Surveillance works in groups because the disciplinary unit, in the constant knowledge that an officer is supervising all of the units, is responsible for every member. This system of discipline breaks down when soldiers are forced to act independently of the apparatuses of production. Here, the bodies of others are offered up as sites to gain knowledge of one's newfound power. Their own ugly bodily "hunger" allowed them "to feed on the bodies of unprotected women."[81] In effect, these men use the power of their bodies, the power invested in their guns and military uniforms, to dismember the bodies of rats and of Yaqui women, one and the same, in the name of both sexual pleasure and total physical domination. The idea that the posts work to police soldiers completely breaks down at this moment, when private sexual desires to rape and ravage overtake the public state's desires to detain the Yaqui women as a moral project of maintaining order in Sonora.

Juxtaposed with the image of the potentially abusive, newly made soldiers is the image of a group of Yaqui prisoners who aren't criminals but are treated as such because they are Yaqui. The Mexican government had set out to destroy Yaqui culture by eliminating the one cultural structure that was and is portable, the family. Especially after the battle of Mazacoba, orphans under the age of ten, according to numerous historical documents, began turning up alone in Sonoran municipalities, reflecting a genocidal project that took children from the parents and families that transmitted Yaqui culture and made them wards of the state. In a telegram to the secretary of state dated October 16, 1901, Municipal President R. F. Nieto of Hermosillo sent this message: "There are two little Indian boys, one of three months and the other of four years, and two little Indian girls of three years."[82] Nothing is mentioned of these children, their parents, or how they became prisoners, implying that they were viewed as bureaucratic casualties of the war and an opportunity for the state to intervene in the family.

Even when attempts were made to keep families together government control involved gendering. Fontes's novel grapples with this fact: "Yaqui women walking with their bodies straight, their belongings balanced in bundles on top of their heads. Their children walk alongside them. Herded separately in the back, hands bound, Yaqui males. Some no older than twelve."[83] Disassembling familial and communal units throughout the deportation process enabled the government to cut off what had sustained the culture and concept of the Yaqui nation from the years following the conquest into the twentieth century. In particular, Yaqui mothers were blamed for perpetuating the rebellion, for they inculcated in their children from birth an indelible hatred of all Yoris, educating and encouraging them to sustain the resistance.[84] In order to justify the brutality against Yaqui women and children, the Mexican government blamed the mothers for breeding and grooming the next generation to hate Yoris. On the same subject, the historian Evelyn Hu-DeHart further argues, "When the massive deportation took place, perhaps the single most important factor that weakened the Yaqui spirit was the wanton breakup of their family units."[85] By forcing male children to adopt the role of soldiers, they were disciplined "to establish presences and absences, to know where and how to locate individuals, to set up useful communications, to interrupt others, to be able at each moment to supervise the conduct of each individual, to assess it, to judge it, to calculate its qualities or merits."[86] The rupture of the family unit and the making of boys into soldiers forced male children to obey so that their mothers may live. Disobedience and obedience alike turn love into social death.

These scenes of state-sponsored violence against the Yaqui in *Dreams of the Centaur* can best be located in the series of fundamental questions they raise in both the novel and the larger context of this transnational history of violence. Alejo, the narrator asks, "Have you ever seen starvation? People's skin turns gray. Their eyes sink into their head. Their skin opens. Liquids come out of every hole that God gave us. And through all this, the Yaquis are silent."[87] When Alejo asks his family these questions, they are posed to the reader as well. In fact, in Yucatán and other ports of arrival, the local population often attributed the high rates of Yaqui illness to social pathology. While there is a short reflection on illness in *Dreams of the Centaur*, starvation and suffering on the deportation ships from Guaymas to Nayarit created huge social pathology in the receiving communities in the Yucatán Peninsula.

Another unexpected consequence of the deportation projects is that the removal of Yaquis from their traditional living conditions into cramped jail cells, train cars, ship holds, and dormitories, along with the diet of soggy, uncooked corn dough, gruel, and stale beans and tortillas they were forced to endure created high rates of illness among the deportees while they were en route to their destinations. I want to rebuke the "theories of Indians' inherent racial susceptibility, virgin soil, and degree of Indian blood," as the historian Christian W. McMillen does when he looks at the health crisis among American Indians and their high rates of tuberculosis around the beginning of the twentieth century. When scholars examine more closely the social pathology constructed around Yaqui illness in Yucatán, it mirrors McMillen's findings: "Explanations that argued that Indians possessed a uniquely high risk of infection not necessarily associated with poverty or behavior, but a risk embedded in their bodies, were common and compelling. They were also convenient: they meshed well with ideas concerning 'primitive' peoples' inability to remain in step with modernity and provided easy and plausible-sounding answers as to why Indians were so prone to the disease."[88] Setting aside racist musings, McMillen documented that abject poverty and changes in food, housing, and sanitation caused the high rates of tuberculosis among American Indians.

Describing the same period with a more focused data set, David DeJong examines mortality and illness in Indian boarding schools between 1878 and 1918 and explains why more and more Indian communities believed there was a strong correlation between the death of Indian children and Indian boarding schools. According to DeJong, "Children had to be kept healthy and alive if they were to have the chance to succeed in their planned American experience."[89] But there was also a contradictory logic operating. Because of the massive death toll in Indian boarding schools, life and the American experience were secondary to the death that such schools created en masse. The core issue of health in boarding schools was overlooked as strict codes of military discipline, inadequate diets, regimentation, routinization, and overcrowding were dismissed as possible reasons for high illness and high mortality rates.[90] The spatial containment in boarding schools is similar to that which Yaqui deportees experienced. Both groups were confined to measured, controlled spaces. The Yaqui deportation is made more complicated, however, because they essentially had much less control over their bodies as prisoners of war in comparison to the child wards in the state-sponsored racial uplift and assimilation projects of American Indian boarding schools. The Mexican government essentially created the conditions for numerous kinds of minor epidemics within deported Yaqui populations, and there was no sense of urgency about their illness precisely because these pathologies created a powerful rationale for keeping them in squalid conditions.[91] Containing Yaqui illness and making the population healthy would have meant recognizing the inhumane conditions of deportation and government policy.

Raquel Padilla Ramos, a historian of Yaqui insurgency movements, pays close attention to the race and class dimensions implicit in how disease and social pathology interfered with the perfect socioeconomic plan of deportation. The majority of the Yaquis were shipped by boat or train or traveled on foot to their destinations in Yucatán, and there was tremendous anxiety among the citizens of Yucatán about the desirability of receiving such a labor force and being exposed to the illnesses they brought with them. Yucateco newspapers consistently reported the arrival of new workers to the port of Progreso.[92] Even though Yucatecos had experience with deportation—that of the Maya Indians during the caste wars of the 1840s and 1850s—the Yaqui situation proved to be more complicated because of illness. Padilla Ramos tracks the role of illness but does not touch on the social pathology created by the Yucatán deportations. Yet the social pathology of illness shows how difference was crucial in perpetuating the pathology.

When *La Revista de Yucatán* reported on March 24, 1908, that "some of the Indians arrived in very bad states of health, of the degree that there were some who could hardly walk," the disease is traced back not to the Río Yaqui but to the port of Veracruz via the Mexican railroad station.[93] Notably, the transporters of these Yaquis had abandoned a cadaver at the Comisaría of the Colonia of Santa María de la Ribera and the Hospital Juárez under military authority.[94] Why would a local newspaper go to such great lengths to detail the illness and death of Indian slave laborers? It seems that the illnesses quickly became an epidemic of virus and yellow fever, and perhaps the corpse left in Santa María de la Ribera and the sick bodies that continued on to the henequen haciendas in Yucatán became scapegoats for other fears of the Yucateco populations.

Racial difference is perhaps one of the ways in which the Yaqui social pathology of disease emerged. But the deportation project was also pitched as the lesser of two evils: "It is required to do it this way because it is not achievable to suppress the rebels and keep them quiet, the peaceful population is suffering murders, robberies, and harassment of all classes. It is hard but necessary what is done with the Yaquis, ousting them from their territory and confining them where they cannot do wrong, before executing them en masse."[95] This was a twofold mission: saving Sonora from the Yaquis and killing Yaquis one way or another because it would be the easiest solution for the government. But if they were dying or getting ill on the way to Yucatán, what kind of message did that send the rest of the world about Mexico's so-called morality of modernity, especially if that modern mission of capital growth necessitated keeping the Yaqui alive and in good enough health to work? The conundrum of social pathology, epidemics, and labor shows various conflicting desires about what the deported Yaquis meant and what they were supposed to do and be.

On April 22, 1908, the supreme health committee sent Francisco Colomé to report on the Yaquis deported to Progreso and Mérida. He reported, "The department where they were sick of smallpox will be disinfected with vapors of sulfur, burning forty grams per cubic meter, and after having taken the necessary precautions so that the result here is complete. . . . Eleven were sick with a virus, with one death. . . . Besides the ten cases of smallpox that were cured there were a large number of patients with common illnesses who also were discharged, and many patients with smallpox and the virus."[96] The various diseases Colomé mentions—pneumonia, dysentery, intestinal infections, common colds, tuberculosis, anemia, congenital birth defects, and ulcerative colitis—attack the system in different ways. Some diseases were respiratory; others had to do with diet and the digestive system, with the weakening of the immune system, or with environmental exposure and transmission through close contact. Most interesting about these diagnoses and the decontamination of the barracks where the sick were kept is that both actions occurred via state intervention into localized Yaqui labor markets. Had the Yucateco government not sent someone to investigate, the diseases may well have gone undiagnosed and continued to spread.

While the government acted to quarantine the sick, Fontes's fictional account suggests that even the quarantining of sick Yaquis was exploitative. As Charco and Alejo are led around the Hacienda de San Jacinto de Yucatán they see the following: "Weak, lifeless men and boys move slowly through the rows, turning henequen fibers into the sun. 'What's the matter with them?' asks Charco. 'They look bad.' 'They say they are sick,' says Pacal, displeased. 'This is where the sick work. They get half pay.' "[97] In the brutal grind of the henequen plantations even the sick remain on the job, working at half pay. Everyone sleeps in the same dormitory, with no regulation of hammocks, no guarantee there were enough for everyone; there was no disinfection of cups, utensils,

FIGURE 6 Henequen plantation jail, Yucatán, Mexico, ca. 1902–9. Ethel Duffy Turner Collection. Reproduced with the authorization of the Instituto Nacional de Antropología e Historia.

eating and drinking instruments, work tools, or clothing. At the same time, the Yucateco state sanitation inspection puts the Indian body under further scrutiny, but only for temporary relief from disease. Labor practices in the henequen industry were unregulated, and it seems that Yaqui illnesses became news only when leaked to the local press. Not until their illnesses reached epidemic levels and became a threat to non-Indian communities was anything done at a policy level to counteract them. Harsh manual labor in hot, humid conditions, which the Yaqui were not accustomed to, coupled with poor nutrition and the circulation of the sick among the healthy caused the myriad illnesses. As Alejo says, "I'm thinking that Yucatán doesn't feel like Mexico," especially for indigenous and Mexican *norteños*.[98] The result was a henequen plantation that bred illness as a self-contained economic and epidemic unit.

The hacendados' desire for Yaqui labor kept sick and healthy Yaquis alike flowing into Yucatán, but did the Yucateco population in general want the Yaquis there? The newspaper reports on Yaqui illness lead me to believe there was not uniform acceptance of Yaqui labor; in addition, there may have been circulating discourses of biological inferiority because the Yaqui were neither native to Yucatán nor Mexicans, for pathology draws on social fear as its own form of evidence. Perhaps a kind of Yucateco nativism circulated in this period, in which scientific racism was emerging in U.S. and European eugenics movements. Evidence of biological race degeneration was mobilized to return sick Yaquis to Sonora at a later time.[99] Placing the pathology of disease on the Yaqui body is an active forgetting that, for example, there was a yellow fever epidemic in Mexico at the time, and many people were dying. The Yucateco papers target the racialized Yaqui body as the carrier of diseases without advancing a structural critique of the conditions that created the diseases in the first place.

HENEQUEN PAIN

Dreams of the Centaur also delineates the fate that awaited deportees in Yucatán from a different angle, showing the consequences of human suffering. The novel exhibits the culture of rumor, fear, and conspiracy that developed not just among the Mexican citizens of Sonora but among the Yaqui as well. Rumor in the novel conveys larger historical truths: "They're sending all prisoners—not just Yaquis—to work in the Yucatán or the Valle Nacional in Oaxaca" (Fontes 173) in the sugar cane fields, whereas the majority were sent to Mexico City to be sold to labor contractors to work in Tabasco or Yucatán state. As rumor turns into truth in the novel, corporal punishment looms large over Yaqui lives as they move from one penal system in Sonora to another in the Yucatán. Scenes from the henequen plantations make visible the pain that is often conspicuously absent in certain historical texts about the Yaqui.

Whereas Kenneth Burke's journalistic exposé *Barbarous Mexico* details the barbarity of the physical and psychological treatment of the Yaquis en route to Yucatán, such discussions are conspicuously absent from major historical works on Yaqui history by Hu-DeHart, Spicer, and Padilla Ramos. Perhaps wanting to avoid the yellow journalism or sensationalism that Burke is often accused of, Hu-DeHart and Padilla Ramos choose not to detail torture or psychological debasement as part of their narrative histories of Yaqui rebellion and survival. In *Dreams of the Centaur*, Fontes seems to strike a balance between the two. She delves into the penal culture of Yucatán, illuminating the psychological aspects of deportation, torture, and the putative culture of violence linked to labor without sensationalizing them and making them markers of subjectivity in moments of extreme duress.

Charco, Alejo, and their sergeant, Gustavo, decide to desert the Mexican army in Yucatán. They meet a Mayan coyote of sorts, Anginas, whom they depend on to get them papers to make the passage back north. Anginas reminds them that in Yucatán one kind of Indian suffering replaces another, earlier one. Anginas was a member of the Mayan resistance during the caste wars (1847–1910), and his outspokenness as the "talking cross" earned him an ugly fate: " 'The henequen kings took me prisoner. They let me live, but they put burning coals down my throat. As a lesson to the rebels I was dragged from village to village wearing a sign that said 'talking cross.' . . . 'Others had their hands cut off. I was fortunate. I learned to speak again.' "[100] The apparition in 1850 of the "Talking Cross cult" inspired the Maya of the southeast to continue the struggle against Yucateco criollos. This apparition, believed to be a way in which God communicated with the Maya, dictated that the caste wars continue. The cross appeared to the rebels beside an uninhabited cenote at the famous separatist capital of Chan Santa Cruz. The cross began to speak in Maya, announcing God's love for the Maya and promising them success. The cult became an inspiration that rallied lagging rebel forces in a war that lasted nearly a century. Anginas's appearance in the novel occurs in 1899, about two years before the rebel cause lost its political independence in Yucatán.[101] Anginas becomes the vehicle that informs Alejo, Charco, and Gustavo of a parallel history of indigenous revolt against mestizo Mexicans, but in the south, not in Sonora. A repentant talking cross, Anginas was tortured by means of coals thrust into his throat to take away his speech, the site of his agency within the insurgency movement. Charco is the only one who seems to understand immediately that the political struggle that decimated Mayan populations in the south explained why Yaquis were being imported: they were meant to compensate for the shortage of Mayan laborers.[102] Fontes nonetheless makes the reader do a little mental work to connect the Indian struggles against a hegemonic Porfirian Mexico in both the north and the south.

Anginas promises to smuggle the travelers out of Yucatán, but since Alejo, Charco, and Gustavo are norteños, taller than the Mayans and the majority of Yaquis on the henequen plantation, lighter skinned, and speak with a northern accent, he turns them over to the *majacol* (whipper) Martino, who takes them prisoner alongside the Yaquis who have been brought to Yucatán as slave labor.

At daybreak on their first day of imprisonment they are shown the contained expansiveness of the hacienda before they are brought to witness the punishment of four Yaqui men who were caught trying to escape the hacienda.[103] In a ritualized scene of violence every worker and prisoner is led to the plaza of the hacienda, where the foreman reads the following: "Running away is forbidden. Failure to meet your daily quota of 2000 leaves is forbidden. Abuse of a henequen plant is forbidden" but abuse of the Yaqui body was absolutely permitted.[104] In this economy of crime and punishment, every aspect of life was defined in terms of measurement, prohibition, and production. What is forbidden defines life, and the life of a plant that yielded one cent in gold per leaf was worth more than the lives of the Yaqui, Mayo, Coreano, Chino, or Mayan that picked it. Henequen production and profits skyrocketed around the beginning of the twentieth century. In 1877–78 a total of 10,471,318 kilos of henequen were exported. Twenty years later, at the beginning of Yaqui deportation to the henequen plantations in 1898–99, the output and exports had multiplied sevenfold to 75,183,816.[105] Profits increased correspondingly: in 1887–88 henequen export profits were reported at $31,978,090 pesos; in 1897–98 they tripled to $90,462,977 pesos.[106] These exports mostly went to Europe according to Francisco Bulues, solidifying Mexican trade relations internationally and illustrating that "Mexico has made progress and great progress."[107] But the *Revista de Mérida* reported in 1921 that the majority of henequen was being exported to the United States.[108] Nonetheless, henequen kings like Bulues argued for Mexican progress not solely on the basis of industrialization, but also from a commitment to agriculture, trying to secure their place in the future of the nation on the backs of Yaqui labor.[109] While they were enacting these desires through national discourse, agitating for free trade agreements with Britain and the United States, their on-the-ground employees were enforcing their agriculture-based vision of modernity in an exceedingly violent manner.[110] One could argue that in the context of the desire for increased productivity, output, and profits, Yaqui deserters in Fontes's novel are not just political prisoners doing forced labor; their attempts to escape threatened the profits and international economic prominence of Yucateco businessmen. Further, Yaqui deserters contradicted the visual demonstrations of control over the plantation system.

In the novel, public beatings serve to resignify criollo dominance, reinstating the institutional order. The majocol Martino "reached into the barrel, takes out several thick meter long ropes, and tosses them on the ground. He prods them with the tip of his shoe before choosing one, swinging it over his head until it whistles. When he's ready, he signals the guards to remove the first man's shirt, then give his back to Martino. I close my eyes and count the blows. Fifteen. Martino takes his time, making his movements large and visible to everyone, eventually all four prisoners lie before him."[111] In ceremonial fashion, the torturer's weapon, a simple rope made of henequen, the very product of Yaqui labor, ultimately becomes an extension of his body. The public torture becomes a pedagogical moment for the other Yaqui workers. They are not to abuse the henequen plant, run away, or fight. Otherwise, the beatings to near death will continue; the threat of death is used to increase the productivity of the worker and erase the possibility of revolt and disobedience. The foreman must perform his power with a weapon to make his power believable, prolonging the tension of the impending beatings by testing the strength and sound of the ropes; the psychological aspect of torture is designed to break down the mind, instilling uncontrollable anticipatory fear while simultaneously using the rope as a coarse and rudimentary instrument of torture.

No speech is involved in this performance of power. He "signals," and the guards respond by removing the men's shirts, the one barrier that lies between the skin and the lash. The tortured men "give their backs," allowing the overseer to take ownership of their bodies because the alternative is to be killed. The prisoners are objectified, removing the possibility of agency and denying subjectivity as racism's assumption of a transparent, static Yaqui subject takes hold in the forms of punishment. This convincing spectacle of power takes precedence over the pain the bodies experience as they receive fifteen blows from the lash. Ironically, the instrument of their torture is the finished product of the workers' production in the henequen fields showing that modernity and capitalism were not restricted to the northern border and U.S.-generated capital investments but were a countrywide project of development that depended on export capitalism to Europe and the United States. Capitalism and modernity are embossed, as it were, on the Indians' bodies, as one cannot escape his or her own body or the products of the body's labor.

To the witness of the torture, the pain is unintelligible; Alejo is able to describe only the beatings, nothing more. The reader is left with the sign that "all four prisoners' bodies lie before the" overseer, suggesting neither identification nor disidentification with the majocol or the Yaqui prisoners, a speechless rendering that what is left cannot be articulated.[112]

The signs of near death demarcate the fragility of the body as it is beaten into submission, an act which at the same time displays the pedagogical force of terror.[113] However, when Charco, Alejo, and Gustavo are once again asked to prove their allegiance to the henequen hacendados by branding Yaquis with a branding iron (a marker of ownership if they run away), the scene of refusal starts an all-out war between the representatives of the ruling class who run the plantation and the Yaquis and other workers who make the plantation run. Martino unties Charco and points to the Yaqui closest to them:

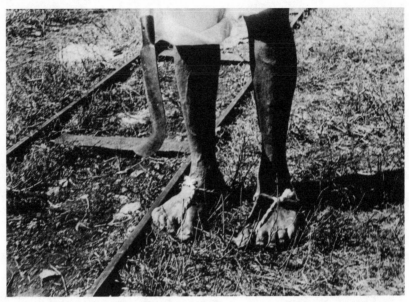

FIGURE 7 Feet of a Yaqui, unknown henequen plantation, Yucatán, Mexico, ca. 1902–9. Ethel Duffy Turner Collection, Reproduced with the authorization of the Instituto Nacional de Antropología e Historia.

"Brand him," he says.

Charco nods several times before voicing, "No."

"Here, in the hip," says Martino, slapping his own hip.

"Never," says Charco. . . . The first lash catches Charco by the ankles and brings him down. He quickly turns onto his stomach and buries his head in his arms. In silence, my brother takes six blows before his body becomes soft, inert. With his foot, Martino cautiously turns Charco over. . . . Martino looks at me. I steel myself; shake my head, "never." He unties me and I lie flat on the ground before him. The first lash catches me unprepared. I hear myself gasp. I bite my lip and prepare for the second blow. Pain echoes, moving in waves from the outside flesh to the body's center. The next blow yanks the pain back to the top. I lose the first wave somewhere inside me. My mind scrambles, crazily trying to keep track of each burning wave of hurt. And then another lick comes, and another, and I'm spinning in a swirl of singeing pain. I lift my head and my eyes lock with the Yaqui closest to me. I hang on, reaching to hide inside him, seeking to enter him through his eyes. I try to gather the surges that course through my body by driving my groin into the earth.[114]

As Alejo and Charco face the lash themselves rather than brand the Yaqui workers, the scene enacts what the cultural critic Judith Butler calls "one's own subordination . . . thus required to persist as oneself."[115] But the behavior of the two men shifts from Butler's logic where embracing the very form of power's "regulation, prohibition, suppression—that threatens one with dissolution in an effort to precisely, to persist in one's own existence."[116] Charco and Alejo "agree. Death first. Death, the cleanest, simplest measure" when forced to choose their own lives over those of the Yaqui being punished with the branding iron.[117] Here the "I" emerges not as a form of dependence upon abjection as a means of living; rather, the "I," or collective "We," is fashioned by a conscious decision to die rather than brand other humans like cattle. The refusal, through accepting their own death as the result of preserving Yaqui lives, shows that the branding ceremony is not an event without structural purpose. This is a vital part of the novel's refusal to make Yaqui peoples into objects.

Even after Charco's and Alejo's public beatings, the disagreement about the injustice of branding Yaquis is not resolved. In what follows, their absorption of pain as performance turns the power of the branding rod and its wielder on itself. They do not show the typical willingness to obey in performing acts contrary to their social and moral convictions.[118] Alejo says,

> I hear myself. "A la chingada!" I dive for the iron, grab it, and still on my knees, drive it into Martino's lower back, and hold. He stands paralyzed and yells "Pepe." Machete in hand, Pepe comes at us; Gustavo trips him, grabs the machete, and ends Pepe. Martino, legs rigid, stumbles forward. He drops the whip. Turning, he reaches for me. Charco lunges and hugs Martino's ankles, bringing him down. Again the iron. I bring it full force down on his head. Martino is silent. A bloody stain swells around his head. . . . I empty the bucket, fill it with straw from the stable, and toss coals over it. I tell the men, "Move. Burn the drying yard." In seconds the men pull on their pants and shirts. They take the coals and grab the whip and machete.[119]

The race riot of sorts that follows is the violent expression of the repressed anger, rage, and frustration over enslavement, where those who have been abused for months stage violence and anguish over power differentials by burning the henequen drying yard. Their mutiny is less sophisticated than Babo's in *Benito Cereno*, but nonetheless they take their master down with them. As the photos and government documents suggest, some weren't lucky enough to escape. Yet the novel's dependence upon violence as the thing that represents Yaqui subjectivities suggests the generative nature of these scenes in that they reveal when traditional gendered, racialized, and institutional power structures fall apart.

SPACES OF WARFARE ARE NOT JUST FOR MEN: REINTERPRETING
THE BATTLE OF MAZACOBA

The battle of Mazacoba occurred on January 18, 1900. It was for all intents and purposes a massacre, one intended to stop the small bands of Yaquis who moved between upper Sonora and the Sierra Bacatete, their traditional stronghold. There may have been another reason for the battle of Mazacoba, however. In an article called "Yaqui War Conspiracy" that reflects on the implications of the battle, the press reminds the reader that captive priests and Josephine nuns who were with the Yaqui on Mazacoba were later charged with conspiracy for not "disclosing secrets to which they had honorably bound by the Yaquis."[120] Being the proprietor of an immense ranch in the sierra, which was at that moment in possession of the Yaquis, the commanding general, Luis Torres (the future governor of Sonora), had a particular interest in punishing the clergy and the Yaquis at Bacatete.[121] His brother, Gen. Lorenzo Torres, owned a strip of land near Turbin; so did Ramón Corral, the Mexican secretary of state and future vice president.[122] Luis Torres wanted Yaquis off his land so he could freely develop it. With the resources of the Mexican government and more than four thousand soldiers—vastly outnumbering the Yaqui warriors and the more than one thousand Yaqui men, women, and children who were injured or killed in the massacre—the soldiers scaled the cliffs of the natural fortress in the sierra and dislodged the rebels, often through hand-to-hand combat. Some of the Yaqui preferred to throw themselves off the precipice into the deep canyon below rather than fall into the hands of their hated adversaries.[123] Relying on Yaqui oral histories and documents and on the basis of her research in Yaqui communities, Fontes's novel attempts to revise the standard historical narrative of the battle of Mazacoba.[124]

Gen. Lorenzo Torres's official report to the secretary of navy and war contrasts greatly with Fontes's interpretation of the event. Assisted by twenty-three Indians who guided the three columns of soldiers into the Bacatete, Torres exults, "the assault was conducted with perfect success, throwing the Indians from the positions they held and defended with tenacity, and in the center of the general fortification were many stone walls as forts, it was necessary to evict the enemy, little by little, until they turned in all its parts by the force of our troops, and sought out their exit in the fight."[125] Torres focuses on military precision and the procedural aspects of the battle, which he says were perfect. To call a military battle perfectly executed is to imply that the enemy casualties and prisoners taken constitute domination and loss simultaneously. After counting about four hundred dead Yaquis, the soldiers searched among the cadavers of the enemy, identifying the ringleader, Pablo Ruiz (Opodepe), whom, according to Torres, "the rebel Indians recognized as their supreme leader and who was without doubt the soul of the rebellion. In addition, some one thousand prisoners were taken, women and children for the most part, some of whom died en route from Mazacoba to Tetacombiate."[126] Viewing women and children as appendages or byproducts of the massacre, Torres focuses his attention on the dead leader Pablo Ruiz, suggesting there would be no further Yaqui rebellion because he was dead. He, like his predecessors, was obviously wrong.

The *Saint Louis Globe Democrat* newspaper reported retrospectively as follows:

It counts of a plan projected for surprise of some of the secrets of the Yaqui Indians, consisting this in the apprehension of a priest of surname Beltran and of four Josefina nuns that were residing with the Yaquis, being a follower of them. Upon being examined, they declared that they knew about a reunion that the Yaquis had intended to carry out a diabolical plan of attack against Potam, Torin, Medano and Cocorit with a thousand men for each population. . . . This news has caused a great sensation among the Mexican troops and everything possible is being done to destroy this project. . . . It is said that many soldiers are getting rich by this war and that a lot of the army national volunteers have asked that it change or end. The government gave 22,400 Mexican soldiers who left with a course for the [Sierra] Bacatete and they expect to have a formal battle with the Indians. There is great excitement in Mexico and above all in Sonora, with the recent treaty between Mexico and the Chinese; this treaty is completely unfavorable for the United States, due to the fact that the Chinese have obtained documents of Mexican citizenship with impunity and can be admitted to the United States. The Generals Luis and Lorenzo Torres have ordered to the troops to complete construction of barracks and dikes in the vicinity of Potam and Torrin, and there is the intention to establish there the general headquarters. The general, one Luis Torres, possesses a girdle of land near Potam, and the General Lorenzo Torres possesses land near Torrin as does the temporary Governor Izabál; before beginning the war against the Yaquis they found it difficult to utilize these lands due to the lack of water for its irrigation, therefore between its lands and the place where is found the necessary water for its irrigation is the land belonging to the Yaqui Indians, not having been able to obtain Indian permission to provide water to those lands through legal agreement. It was believed that an individual called Nacho González, who lived on the ranch of José Dracamonte, was submitting reports with respect to the position of the national forces, and soldiers were sent to apprehend him; they instead assaulted his wife and daughter and afterwards burned their shack. All the men of Torin, Potam, Cocorit, and Medano are obliged to carry weapons, and expect an attack by the Yaquis at any moment. Broderick continues to be elusive but still provides the rebels with arms.[127]

Set within the larger international context of Mexico's treaty with China, which naturalized Chinese citizens as Mexican in a moment when the United States policed Chinese immigration, the article discusses all the possible acts of treason that occurred in the battle of Mazacoba: Josephine nuns refused to give up Yaqui secrets, individuals like Nacho González were accused of sending word to Yaqui forces about the position of federal troops, and another American instigator, Broderick, is accused of providing them with arms. In addition to the main point of these transnational exchanges of information and bodies, one thing to take away from this passage is that the *Saint Louis Democrat* argues that several people in Sonora were getting rich from this war, including the state governor, Rafael Izabál, the Generals Torres and Secretary of State Corral. This is another clear example where war was the basis of borderlands economies: the battle of Mazacoba, while staged as an act to pacify Yaqui rebellion, was really about securing the wealth of a few political jefes with an act of genocide.

Fontes's revision of the battle of Mazacoba completely disrupts the standard Mexican historiography of warfare, especially the Indian wars as narrated by the so-called Great Generals like Lorenzo Torres, Ignacio Izabál, Jose Carbó, Angel Martínez, and Bernardo Reyes; or even by Corral in his biography of Cajeme. All of these narratives focus on men and masculinity as the proper historical subject. Fontes's reinterpretation of the bloody massacre of Mazacoba focuses on a Yaqui woman warrior, Pilar, who defied Western gendered notions of what it means to be a soldier.[128] The representation of a masculinized Yaqui woman warrior embodied in the character Pilar turns gender and power hierarchies on their heads, contradicting official historical narratives that are dominated by male figures. The presence of masculinized women in a space where Western culture does not imagine them to assert power, the battlefield, underscores how Fontes imagines that gender was queered (nonnormative) and nontraditional in these violent transnational conflicts, because avoiding genocide required this. Judith Halberstam, who coined the term *female masculinity*, has shown how masculinity and maleness are difficult to separate in the way they produce power, legitimacy, and privilege.[129] There was a clear political need for Pilar's female masculinity. Rather than a direct embodiment of the privileged, Anglo masculinity Halberstam critiques or an expression of a different kind of queer sexuality, Pilar's gender performance is more like an alternative masculinity, one that confuses Mexican military hierarchies, opens up spaces for temporary social justice, and "exposes the working of a dominant, heterosexual masculinity," which, I would add, is rooted in a particular vision of whiteness in written history.[130]

While genocidal war and female masculinity may seem an unlikely pairing, I would like to argue the opposite. When foreign investors, colonizers, and federal troops occupied the Yaqui homeland, the Yaqui wars were clearly about sustaining sovereignty and preventing genocide. The Mexican government was literally trying to replace their bodies in Sonora with the bodies of masculine workers and developers to make way for capitalism. Pilar's alternative masculinity defends against a hegemonic mestizo masculinity based in the intentional Mexican military destruction of Yaqui families. Her family is not a means of maintaining heteronormativity but rather serves as the basis of kinship networks and indigenous identities.

In Fontes's historical revision, Pilar leads Yaqui forces. She is the older sister of Juan, a Yaqui man pulled from the pile of dead bodies after the riot in the henequen plantation drying yard. Pilar "was a renowned warrior who had escaped from jail twice, once from a fort outside of Hermosillo and another time from Guaymas. She had fought hand-to-hand and disarmed her jailers, killing four. Then, dressed as a soldier, she had returned at night, causing chaos by freeing all the prisoners."[131] In this armed struggle for survival Pilar of necessity assumes a position of power, and the reader witnesses the deconstruction of the battlefield as a site of male meaning queered through gender-destabilizing behaviors. Her performance of masculinity, as a means of tweaking gender, exemplifies how female masculinity is a specific gender with its own cultural history rather than a derivative of male masculinity. Dislodging the privilege of masculinity from the male body and doing so within a Yaqui context, provides an alternative register of history that challenges the idea of an essential male masculinity that is formed by rejected scraps of dominant masculinity.[132] Because she's "been with the mountain bands [of Yaquis] most of her life[,] Yoris will pay five thousand pesos for her head."[133] These mountain bands of Yaquis are normally associated with excessive masculinity and warfare. Yet Pilar "wears a long faded calico skirt, a man's shirt—crossed cartridge belts around the chest—and hat with two hawk feathers in it."[134] She is not only physically strong, smart, and knowledgeable of the Mexican army's weaknesses, but also a pivotal leader in the guerrilla war because of her defeminized (or masculinized) body. She literally inhabits militarized "Mexican men's" spaces, performing masculinity by cross-dressing to evade capture. Her stocky silhouette, strong arms, and the fact that she is a woman throw traditional visions of militarized subjects into crisis. Her long skirt, faded from wear, contrasts greatly with her "man's shirt" and the ammunition belt strung around her body, obscuring the idea that Yaqui Indian men are inherently extremely violent with a propensity for war and thus inhabiting that stereotype but in men's and women's clothing simultaneously. She's not a romanticized Adelita of Mexican revolutionary lore; she stands alone as her own reference point and as a self-constructed figure in Yaqui nationalism. This is not woman's body co-opted in the rhetoric of a Western nation-state. Here, an indigenous woman's generative leadership constructs self and Yaqui nationhood through action, not symbolism. Rearranging both the image of the hyperviolent Yaqui Indian man and the Yori-hating Yaqui Indian woman, stereotypes that were thoroughly entrenched in Mexican and American media of the time, Pilar dons the physical vestments of femininity and masculinity at the same time, outwardly projecting a truly nonnormative enactment of subjectivity.

The most important feature of Pilar's dress is the hat with the hawk feathers in it. In symbolic terms, this signifier most strongly communicates her status as a respected warrior and her gender queerness: "Only defenders of the Yaqui territory may wear hawk feathers. The thick braids that trail down her back represent the power and wisdom of the woman who controlled the destinies of the tribe. Pilar is barefoot."[135] Marked with the sacred feathers that identify her as a leader, she leads her nation into battle with her body marked by braids, bare feet, a skirt, rifle cartridges, and a man's hat, signals of masculinity and femininity that in total equate to symbols of power and ambiguity. Pilar's female masculinity locates the warrior in a space where spiritual commitments to religion, community, and culture take precedence over individual needs. The life of the Yaqui warrior is a life resigned to death, long before that death happens in the service of protecting the nation. To be a warrior in some ways means a distancing from the general body of the community or tribal band, something not imagined as a woman's role.

Making the reading of gender ambiguous, Pilar "stands straight, heedless of the soldiers on the opposite mesa firing in her direction."[136] Facing the enemy changes her subject position; women do not merely care for children or give birth to nations. Pilar's gender-queering performance affects a rupture of "imperialism and the culture associated with it [that] affirm[s] both the primacy of geography and an ideology about control of territory."[137] Effectively placed on the contested ground of Mazacoba, Pilar's female masculinity challenges the imperial structure that relegates Native women to the role of tortured informant or breeder of children, useless to the imperial forces of production except for their reproductive labor.

Located within the space of the battlefield, however, Pilar is not exempt from being treated as a gender curiosity or oddity to the male gaze:

> Transfixed, Alejo watched her coil the rope as she strides to the very edge of the peak. She lays down the rope and takes up an old Winchester with a tubular magazine beneath the barrel. Standing erect, face calm, she grips the rough rim of the mountain with her toes as she fires fifteen rounds at the soldiers across from her. Finished, she spits. With an open hand, she presses the hat down on her head, Turning, she catches Alejo's eyes upon her. Embarrassed, Alejo wants to say something—anything—to her. Here, in the midst of the tumult, beneath a blanket of smoke, heat and the endless thunder of rifle fire, he wants to praise her. He opens his mouth, but words are useless before Pilar's stony expression.[138]

The battle of Mazacoba represented through a queered female body engaged in hand-to-hand combat with Mexican troops dismantles images of a totalizing, Pofirian-era military power that completely controlled the bodies of its citizenry in the name of development. Alejo cannot comprehend that as an indigenous woman, Pilar, puts her body in the line of fire. She simultaneously debunks the image of the heroic, male Indian warrior-savage (the Iztaccihuatl and Popocatepetl mythology in both Mexican and Chicano national iconographies, in which the Aztec warrior mourns over his dead Aztec princess after returning from battle) and instead shows a well-trained, masculinized female body that threatens the imperialist patriarchy.[139] Alejo's admiring yet stunned attitude was caused by his own beliefs in normative gender ideologies about war. In affirming his position as male agent, he originally believes his speech—that is, his affirmation of Pilar's strength and heroics— will somehow make them more real, more believable. The criollo dominance and privilege of speech, that is, as an entitled commentator whose words would authorize the reality of the situation are short-circuited by the simple display of agency, power, and control. In this moment, her "stony expression" silences the legitimating discourses of Yori male privilege and replaces them with the image of a gender-bending subject.

Pilar's gestures silence Alejo; his shock and awe cannot be registered in words. For this reason, amidst the battle in which hundreds of innocent people were slaughtered he wants to make himself visible to her: "He wants to see her, to prove himself to her. Why did she leave him here? He knows the answer, he's a Yori."[140] In stark contrast with the official military report by Troncoso cited earlier, Mazacoba in Fontes's novel is constructed as a space where Yoris have no place and where traditional gender conceptions do not apply. The desire to be seen, acknowledged, and accepted by the other only emphasizes the white male need for recognition. By ignoring Alejo, Pilar affirms that Mazacoba is her space, her people's space, and a place where Western gender and race hierarchies do not govern quotidian life or the battle itself. At the same time, Alejo is forced to abandon his somewhat naïve and benevolent fantasy of being a savior or peace broker for the Yaqui: he mumbles "Pendejo [idiot]! . . . Since they left for Bacatete, he has always seen himself on top of the mountain talking to the Yaqui chiefs Opodope and Tetabiate. He saw himself describing the voyage to Yucatán and detailing the treatment of the Yaquis. The chiefs would listen intently, and devise a plan to keep their people here in their homeland. Never had he envisioned himself climbing a mountain with heavy equipment choking him."[141] Here the narrative fantasy of the Yori who saves the Yaqui from impending doom is stopped short by the narrator's own critical reflection; Alejo calls himself a idiot for thinking that it would be easy to get to Bacatete, that he would sit with the chiefs and be the authentic reporter in the discussion of what really happens to Yaqui deportees in Yucatán. Alejo's critical self-reflexivity is an outright refusal to reproduce contemporary fantasies of mestizaje by positing a discourse of personal, and by symbolic extension, national responsibility for the Bacatete massacre.

Confronted with his whiteness as a sign of untrustworthiness, Alejo is forced into subordination by Pilar, out of respect and the sheer necessity of survival in the embattled war zone of Bacatete. Further, Alejo's masculinity is called into question as Pilar continues to emit a kind of masculinized power and mastery he simply cannot emulate: "He fumbles with his backpack, but he can't untie the leather straps around his chest. Pilar moves toward him. Out of nowhere she produces a knife and with a single thrust cuts through the straps. She hands him his backpack, wraps a hand around his neck, and leads him like a child to a narrow opening between the rocks."[142] Alejo is like a sullen child whose fantasy of accessing the power of Yaqui leaders is completely thwarted because he realizes he has no meaning as an actor within this context. Even though Alejo becomes marginal in this scene of battle, he still has the power to continue as the novel's narrator, which says something about his privilege but also signals that this is not just a Yaqui story but a Mexican story as well.

As the battle takes place, "bone fragments spray the air. A woman loses the top of her head, yet she turns and reaches her hand out to a child just beyond her. Another woman is shot through the neck. Her head drops, but her arms remain around a half dozen children."[143] Curt, blunt narrative style mimics the action as severed bodies try to protect the lives of children. Most people are not aware that many families caught up in this battle had sought refuge in the sierra to avoid deportation to Yucatán only to find themselves trapped on a precipice and awaiting death. Neither sparing readers the macabre images nor sensationalizing the violence, the narrative description straddles a fine line between representing state-sponsored punishment and loss. And yet when the narrator describes more of the Bacatete massacre as a scene of violence and death, it represents the experience of "a torn, hungry, thirsty pueblo."[144] Pilar appears not as a resigned member of the pueblo and instead "shoves the dead woman aside and leads the children away from the fort. . . . Gone is the solemnity of the moments before. The Yoris are on Mazacoba. People push, shove each other out of the way and over dead bodies. *A world is ending.* Alejo sees Pilar's eyes on him. He will not disappoint her . . . he gestures, *Can I go to you?* She shakes her head. With her rifle, she vehemently points him to the most extreme part of the mesa. It's an order."[145]

Amidst the madness and confusion Pilar emerges from the smoke to help children escape from the Yoris who invade Mazacoba. While Pilar sees Alejo as a potential ally, he can see her only as someone to impress. From his outsider position as a non-Yaqui, all he can think about is how he would like to be accepted by the ultimate other, a gender-bending indigenous subject. As Mazacoba shifts out of the hands of the Yaqui and into the hands of the Mexican government, Pilar is forced to take extreme measures to save children who cannot defend themselves; this moment of political solidarity is overshadowed by Alejo's desire to perform acceptably and to save the children. Alejo obeys Pilar's orders and shifts his culturally mediated thoughts about power relations, authority, and gender in Yaqui culture: "Anguished, Alejo watches her take her place among the warriors in front of the fort. Body low to the ground, she places one leg in front of the other. She's ready. Except that her hat with the feathers is gone. No, the person next to her wears the hat. Charco. Though filled with jealousy, Alejo sends an impulse of love to his brother, then follows Pilar's order."[146] In a rare moment when the narrator admits his jealousy and immaturity, he is able to transcend it. But why be jealous of people who have been consistently hunted by the government and are facing extinction? This is an interesting critique of Chicano and Mexican nationalism. The fetishization of both the revolutionary and the indigenous at this moment in Fontes's novel marks an inability to recuperate the indigenous as the mestizo Mexican or Chicano self. Alejo desperately wants to transform himself into a guerrilla subject, but history, Pilar, and Charco will not allow him to do this in a space that has historically been Yaqui. Their silent rejection reminds Alejo of "the ideal subject after a transcendental choice has been made and the revolutionary has left behind a pre-Revolutionary order of consciousness."[147] So Alejo's desire to leave behind his prerevolutionary consciousness and transcendentally choose an identity of revolution, a choice afforded to those with full self-possession, is completely short-circuited by his Yaqui comrades. This is not an essentialist argument here (that only Yaquis can be revolutionaries), but rather suggests that solidarity is based on the fact that Alejo is denied the right to become what the critic María Josefina Saldaña-Portillo calls "the authorized subject of insurrection."[148] In other words, Alejo may be able to narrate what is happening, but the Yaqui characters quite deftly and consistently deny him access to that authorizing power of appropriating the Yaqui struggle as his own. These narrative denials constantly remind Alejo of his history as the Mexican son of a rancher who employed Yaquis, the half brother of a Yaqui insurgent born of a rape that is neither confirmed nor denied, and a former criminal imprisoned alongside Yaquis in both Sonora and Yucatán. The political and social connections are present, but the differences also need to be respected. In Alejo's constant desire to be a part of the Yaqui insurgency, Fontes keeps him at arm's length to show us that solidarity is not a given; it is earned through an astute respect for and recognition of difference in the particular histories that all of us carry.

The world made of Yaqui resistance comes to an end at this moment of carnage and loss. The enormous loss is most deeply registered in how Pilar dies a warrior's death: "Everyone is staring at the empty space where the boy and girl jumped, and suddenly Pilar runs full speed at the soldiers and she grabs three around the neck and takes them down with her."[149] While for some this might signal the romantic vision of the defiant Indian resisting hegemony or seeking a power that extends beyond life and into death, I think Pilar is a representation of female masculinity that defies normative visions of combat and national identity.

Fontes also writes the Mazacoba massacre from a Mexican woman's perspective. A transition marked only by a spatial gap and curt phrases formalistically mirrors the battle's carnage: "The first body . . . is a woman, lying face down, arms outstretched. Felipa asks why she only anticipated finding males when at the day's end she saw every kind of human form fall from the peak. Maybe because these acts belong to men."[150] Felipa's belief system about masculinity and war do not allow her to anticipate what she sees. She believed that such violence against humanity was an act carried out exclusively by men against men, but the wounded prove otherwise, transforming the political stakes of the battle of Mazacoba from a contest over masculinity to one based on an ethnic community's genocide: "As she climbs the mountains this is what she sees. The bodies are in heaps, draped randomly, one on top of each other in such numbers that the soldiers are loading them onto two wheeled-carts they have hand-pulled through the thick ravines. She moves closer, lowers down the lantern over several individuals. Her pulse quickens. Her legs tremble. These aren't soldiers. She sees old people. Infants. Children. Entire families. Other than death, they share something else: they have been shot several times in the back."[151]

With a critical eye, Felipa finally understands that innocent people have been massacred and executed. Her identification with the dead babies, elderly people, and families who have been shot demonstrates her awareness of the outright genocidal violence committed at Mazacoba by the Mexican troops. "First light shows Felipa the battle's tally. Walking towards her must be a thousand people. In torn bloody rags, faces sooty, burned lips blistered, cut, they move slow in heavy silence."[152] In an act that counters her previous resentment toward the Yaquis, Felipa looks beyond her own experience, including a lifelong hatred of the Yaqui because they killed her mother and Rosario had a liaison with her husband, to see the need for political solidarity, as the Yaquis are being senselessly killed. Seeing the pained, violated bodies of others makes the violence real to her, generating a political consciousness and structural critique of the facility with which the state dictated life and death for indigenous subjects who disobeyed the state.

CONCLUSION

As late as 1928–29, some twenty-five years after the massacre at Mazacoba and the deportations to the henequen plantations of Yucatán, Yaquis continued to raid railroad cars, burn trestles, and pull up rails to impede the conversion of their sacred lands into public sites of capital production. These acts were meant to counter silence and combat the history of decimation of a people who left their mark by contesting the nation (the United States and Mexico in their joint capitalist ventures).

As chapters 4 and 5 demonstrate, the Yaqui had a protracted struggle with the Mexican government from the 1870s to 1910 that waned and intensified depending upon larger national conflicts and budgetary constraints. For my purposes, specific epochs and dates of battle show the height of institutionalized, discursive, and genocidal violence. In particular, 1880–86, 1899, 1901, and 1905 stand out as years during which Yaqui dismay with Mexican and Anglo intervention on their lands weakened local military forces and created incessant calls for federal intervention. At the same time, some of the letters written to the central government suggest that Yaquis were not a problem for Sonorenses, but a part of the quotidian operations of ranching and mining industries. Reading the archives of the Porfiriato and the United States and *Dreams of the Centaur* side by side makes the state-sponsored violence against the Yaqui people both visible and invisible in two distinct but interconnected national histories that conveniently forget such atrocities.

The Yaqui Indian wars of the late nineteenth century enacted state policies of violent, politically charged punishment that oftentimes stripped the Yaqui of certain bodily freedoms, in particular through forced deportation to the Yucatán Peninsula or, in more extreme cases, through lynching and execution. The Yaqui tried to maintain an autonomous Indian nation within the borders of the newly modernizing Mexican nation-state that was highly dependent upon U.S. capitalist development. The torture and public disciplining of the Yaqui offer evidence of how the nation asserted its identity.[153]

These transnational interests were complex because the mission of national consolidation and Yaqui removal during the Porfiriato reveal that the nation at that moment was unwilling to tolerate an autonomous Indian nation within the Mexican nation. By examining the different kinds of sources (government communiqués, letters, newspaper articles, photos, and fictional accounts), scholars see that the relationships between people are founded upon violence, providing some visibility to a little-known part of history in which Mexicans allied themselves with the Mexican and U.S. governments against the Yaqui, out of both necessity and development-related interests. These disparate texts do not excuse the acts of gendered, racialized, and sexualized violence. Rather, forced migration and self-imposed exile represent the choice between life and death and an interlocking history. The nineteenth-century Mexican borderlands of the Sonoran Desert and the Yaqui insurgents, who fought tooth and nail to protect their tradition, land, autonomy, and culture, form a complex portrait of the meaning of nation.

Judging by these documents, there was a distinct will to impose a state vision of reality. Witnessing, engaging with, representing, or imparting an understanding of the cognitive impact of pain inflicted through torture, sexual violation, or emotionally oppressive situations have to come from outside the state mechanisms of representation in order to force individuals to question traditional national narratives about Mexican, Chicano, and U.S. nationalisms. In particular, *Dreams of the Centaur* captures the limits and interests of a single nation or individual by teasing out the complicated nature of Yaqui–Mexican relations in the late nineteenth century with realist representation. By disputing regulatory definitions of racial and ethnic formations, Fontes shows that the policy of mestizaje was not what is now celebrated as the future of racial and cultural hybridity. Rather, mestizaje as a cultural and social outcome had a severe and violent cost. It becomes very clear that Yaqui Indians were not imagined either as Mexicans or as citizens of Mexico.

To return to the title of this chapter, to "strip the body of flesh and memory" describes the means by which violence not only aims to destroy the presence and vitality of the physical body, but also serves as a way to destroy the mind and its ability to recall a time that precedes the destruction of the individual mind and collective memory of a people and is a symbolic enactment of historical forgetting. But *Dreams of the Centaur*'s speech acts counter the unspeakable and show how stripping the body of flesh and memory was never completely realized in U.S. or Mexican national projects. The emotional trauma of such events and the physical violence of the events represented here force the reader to reckon with different levels and types of pain. These last two chapters grapple with the relationship between human bodies under conditions produced by nations that attempt to strip them of life and memory, not only literally but also figuratively. That is, the active forgetting of massacres and genocide was and is an active stripping of the Yaqui body of subjectivity, flesh, and memory, and when celebratory mestizaje is the focal point this project is effectively reinforced by U.S., Chicana/o, and Mexican national historical silences. The novel's allusions to violence and scenes of torture create a cognitive map from the bodily experience, making visible the oppressive regimes and forces that tried to erase people as subjects. I have tried to account for the oppressive world of the tortured body as part of the historical amnesia surrounding the Yaqui Indian wars. War was a measured way of containing dissident subjects. Even though the totality of losses in general and at Mazacoba in particular were intended to destroy the Yaqui as a people, the military record shows that they were not contained and stresses the measured, dehumanizing mechanisms of war.

Alongside the discussions of torture the novel represents Yaqui subject formation as both preexisting and resulting from violence. The communiqués, newspaper articles, and fictional accounts all suggest that Yaqui peoples saw themselves as sovereign agents of their own nation space from the beginning of these wars in the 1870s. Further, while Yaquis did not write the majority of these texts, we can glimpse what it meant to feel like and to be a racialized human subject of one's own making in the face of extreme state-sanctioned violence against an entire indigenous population. Herein lies the value of proposing that the evidence creates a constellation of Yaqui experiences, both collective and individual, that elucidate how subjectivity was not just the confirmation of self-making but also the way the state tried to unmake Yaqui selves through its political authority and violence.

The way in which national histories elide the Yaqui essentially *strip the body of flesh and memory* by not representing the Yaqui body in pain or the details of war. Coupling *Dreams of the Centaur*, military communiqués, and newspaper articles with a push back against Chicano nationalisms that imagine a distant Aztec Indian instead of a historical subject with geographical proximity to Aztlán does little to accurately represent Yaqui subjectivities in their historical context. These case studies, when juxtaposed, break the silence by showing that modernity and its social projects were not an Enlightenment discourse of autonomy and individual citizenship and rights; rather, Yaqui claims to self-determination were seen as undemocratic and contrary to the vision of the Mexican nation, for they lived outside of government obedience. The Porfirian-era project, which many Americans and Mexican Americans in Arizona were involved in, was not just a project of modernity, development, and active genocide, but a social project of intentional forgetting that transcended borders, cultures, and economic divides. There is much to be mourned in this history, and the process of reconciliation begins with acknowledging national and individual participation in the forgetting and establishing an active, honest, and open engagement with history.

✳ On Impunidad

NATIONAL RENEWALS OF VIOLENCE IN

GREATER MEXICO AND THE AMERICAS

Although the topic that concerns me most broadly is that of violence as both social practice and historical silence, I have kept my analysis focused on the late nineteenth century and early twentieth in the belief that a well-chosen set of empirical moments of violence in Chicana/o, U.S. and Mexican national imaginaries can reveal more about the unspeakable, historical change, and continuity over time and space than a wide-ranging atemporal survey. My secondary aim has been to model a kind of criticism that is self-reflexive and uses the tools of feminism and transnational studies to elucidate why certain events are silenced in the historical record and the processes by which they became unspeakable in the first place. These stories of the past influence the present critical conjuncture. I argue that scholars must change the ways we do our work but, in addition, I detail precisely how and why we need to change the kinds of questions we are asking about violence, gender, sexuality, race, and citizenship in the U.S.–Mexico borderlands from 1851 to 1910. Paradigms of mestizaje, resistance versus assimilation, and victimization have been exceedingly useful in the creation of an anticolonial discourse that comes out of ethnic studies intellectual work; without them, I might have nothing to talk about. But their institutionalization in Chicana/o, Latina/o, and borderlands studies has taken another turn; the romance of embedded multiple nationalisms has a seductive quality that directs scholarly literacy in a certain way and prevents us from seeing other things in engaging the archive of the past. So even when these attempts at mourning and reconciliation of the record and accounting for tremendous losses at the personal, communal, and psychic levels become locked into nationalism's seductive remedies, there are so many things we miss if we keep asking the same questions.

These are my broad preoccupations. I have plotted them through Josefa/Juanita's lynching in 1851, the Camp Grant Indian Massacre of 1871, the discursive violence and racism in Jovita González's oeuvre in contrast with her feminist gender critique, and the Yaqui Indian wars of 1880–1910. Fittingly, the manuscript begins and ends with discussions of lynching and public displays of violence as a way of breaking down the seductive romance of nationalisms and mestizaje and favoring the complexities and contradictions of each event in the multiple registers of their specific historical context. While the systematic and geographical contexts of Josefa/Juanita's lynching and Yaqui lynchings (in the context of larger deportation projects) are completely different, they nevertheless speak to a fifty-five-year period that had some continuity; public destruction of brown bodies was part of the repressive state apparatus in the greater Mexican–U.S. borderlands. As I often say to my students, state-sanctioned violence is always present; it is the technologies of violence that are always changing. Josefa/Juanita's lynching was about consolidating the idea of California as Anglo and part of the United States through public enactment of violence against a Mexican woman's racialized, sexualized body. To substantiate a similar claim about how the Mexican nation attempted to consolidate itself through the public lynching and torture of Yaqui bodies and to do justice to this history, I had to go to the political centers of Mexican life and politics to get this information.

Given the time I spent in Mexico City doing research and my social location as a Latina feminist based in Tucson, Arizona, while this book was being written, it would be disingenuous to act as if my thoughts have been engrossed only in racialized, sexualized, gendered violence in the late nineteenth century and early twentieth. Engaged readers will, without doubt, understand my irritation with new technologies of violence that are normalized to the point that perpetrators go virtually unpunished in the late twentieth century and early twenty-first. The contemporary practice of *impunidad*, is just as influenced by the past as it is by the present. My colleague and the chair of gender studies at the Universidad Nacional Autónoma de México, Marisa Belausteguigoitia, said it best, commenting on the number of decapitations happening in Mexico at large under the rubric of narcotrafficking and the militarization of the state: "The head of the nation is being decapitated" she calmly stated, with an incisive analysis that parallels the mission of this book. To say that the nation is disembodied through the literal violence of individuals being decapitated at multiple levels of society—whether they be the head of the state police being beheaded and displayed in front of the police station in the upper-class neighborhood of Polanco in Mexico City or violent images of individuals being dismembered, as in the *feminicidios* (the murders of women, or "femicides") in Ciudad Juárez—shows how Mexico publicly imagines itself in and through the media. As part of a larger public discourse of everyday life, much of this violence has to do with an ever-present U.S. demand for drugs, cheap labor, and deregulated commerce in a moment of intensive regulation and militarization of the U.S.–Mexico border. These interlocking relations have led me to believe that violence is a part of national imaginaries in the contemporary period in both Mexico and the Unites States. The recent panic over the North American Free Trade Agreement and how it directly facilitated the 2009 epidemic of swine flu geographically situates the violence in a backward, primitive, somewhat inferior Mexico. In actuality it was NAFTA that facilitated the relocation of a swine-processing plant owned by Smithfield Farms, a U.S.-based corporation, to Veracruz. Because there are no regulations governing the disposal of industrial waste in Veracruz the company can dump raw sewage into rivers and local water supplies. The resonance and echoes mark a chilling reality: our silence implicates each and every one of us when we fail to provide a structural analysis of the gendered, racialized, and sexualized politics of how these kinds of situations come into being and how they are articulated or not in public discourse.

It is this early twenty-first-century capitalist moment that links transnationalized monetary flows and violence between the United States and Mexico through economic practices like narcotrafficking, and feminicidio that bring us back to the individual body in pain and how that body is or is not linked to the larger national body. The national body (both Mexico and the United States) is dismembered; there is a fractured sense of the nation, and the fractured bodies of people put on display for public consumption communicate a kind of normalized regularity in the images. This is what I believe Belausteguigoitia was talking about; the juxtaposition of nation and violence, or rather the codification of violence as normalized state practices on the literal bodies of individuals. I argue that this is no accident and is in fact quite intentional, ushering in a new era of how multiple publics and national imaginaries are formed by violence, especially in this post-NAFTA moment. There is a double move here: violence against marginal individuals not recognized as citizens by nation-states does the work of national consolidation, and at the same time these broken brown bodies signal the fracturing of the nation in the contemporary period, when the rhetoric of global citizenship presupposes a universal citizen subject that is simply not reflected in the violence meted out against people. I suggest that the function of death and violence in the current Mexican, U.S., Chicana/o national consciousnesses is ever-present in this moment of a new kind of imperialism that the technologies that NAFTA ushered in, but something has changed. I would argue that what has occurred is a rhetorical, visual, and discursive shift in Mexican, Chicana/o, and U.S. media in particular, cementing a particular kind of multinational consciousness in which state violence is unabashedly operative, especially in the case of mass assassinations and impunidad, an "epidemic" of crime that goes back to the early 1990s and is centered in a locus of NAFTA, along the U.S.–Mexico border. The term *epidemic* is not meant to culturally pathologize how these deaths are examined, but rather to point to the mass quantity of murders and to their gendered, classed, sexualized, racialized nuances. Further, it is also important to point out that there is nothing sexy about this violence, but the formalistic structures of its reporting are quite seductive, potentially emptying the subjects and their contexts of meaning and making the risqué and the taboo "sexy" and interesting and potentially devoid of critical analysis. It may be helpful to end my reflections on violence in this historical continuum, those of the book dating from 1851 to 1910 within the operative context of impunity, the unabashed state use of violence, and the politics of NAFTA in the late twentieth century. I want to situate the story that I tell next as part of the intellectual problems of doing transnational feminist scholarship, demonstrating how ideas of race, gender, sexuality, and violence are incongruent in multiple national imaginaries (Mexican, Chicana/o, and U.S.) and need to be noted as such. This is a transnational story that has much to say about the convergence of politics and violence, both discursive and real, at this historical moment.

NOVEMBER 4, 2008

CNN was the last network to call Pennsylvania for Barack Obama at 7:39 p.m. The crowd in the Black Horse Tavern, an ex-pat hangout in Mexico City, erupted in screams of triumph. My colleagues and I had been following this election more closely than any other in our lives, and Obama's win made us feel more connected to our country than ever before. Cutting between the scenes of the Obama victory was Mexican media coverage of the crash in Mexico City of a plane belonging to the Secretaría de Gobernación. The accident occurred in broad daylight in one of the sprawling capital's most affluent sectors, Las Lomas, near the Paseo de la Reforma. The crash shut down the periférico, a major artery, and completely halted business. Thirteen people were killed, including the young politician Juan Camilo Mouriño, the secretary of Hacienda. Mouriño had been in charge of security during the government's violent battle with Mexico's powerful drug cartels, a battle waged ever since Felipe Calderón became president in the highly disputed election of 2006. About 10,475 people were killed in drug-related violence from December 2006 to March 2009, and kidnapping rates in Mexico are among the highest in the world.[1] The news reports began to speculate: was the plane crash an accident? or was it a form of the newly coined *narcoterrorism*, an incident of which had shocked bystanders at a Mexican Independence Day celebration in Morelia, Michoacan, in September?

The term *narcoterrorism* dates back to the 1980s and was first used to describe the situation in Peru; its use in Mexico dates to the start of President Calderón's war on drugs, in which the military has engaged in large-scale warfare with drug cartels. It seems that Mexico's northern neighbor influences the use of this term, in a Mexican context. The U.S. State Department has an extensive website detailing the governmental position on narcoterrorism, arguing that there are numerous examples of the "connection between drugs and terrorism."[2] In 2003 a Library of Congress Federal Research report arrived at the following findings:

> Mexico's drug trafficking and alien smuggling networks have expanded their criminal activities aimed at the United States by capitalizing on the explosive growth of transborder commerce under NAFTA and the attendant growth in human and merchandise traffic between Mexico and the United States. The growth in trans-border commerce, as manifested in soaring levels of overland passenger and commercial vehicle traffic, has provided an ever-expanding "haystack" in which the "needles" of illicit narcotics and illegal aliens can be more easily concealed.[3]

While the document argues that a concrete set of qualifiers exist to determine what constitutes narcoterrorism, it makes a connection between both the fear and the commerce generated by NAFTA. While terror is not evoked directly, the perpetrators who have committed crimes like smuggling drugs and immigrants are one and the same. Thus the report's finding conjures up images of violence, an unsecure border, murder, and bribed public officials. The fear of such crime and violence spilling over into the United States from Mexico is not unidirectional from north to south, for if there were no U.S.-based demand for drugs or immigrant labor, the fear and subsequent border policing of bodies and commodities would be a moot point.

As these two moments, Obama's victory and the death of the secretary in the plane crash, coalesced, another series of events happened in the Black Horse Tavern. Within earshot of a television crew, two men dressed in what is considered traditional Saudi men's dress began to sing and dance to the following chorus: "Los terroristas amaban a Obama! O-sam-a!" When my friends and I confronted the men about their mocking of Obama's victory and their intentional linking of his blackness to Muslim terrorists, the men claimed it was a joke that we supposed Americans (granted, the majority of us were U.S. minorities) could not understand. They told us that their behavior was not racist and that they were making a joke we simply failed to understand.

A few minutes later the disc jockey had a Memín Pinguín doll, complete with huge red lips, dark skin, and wide-open, oversized white eyes, perched at the corner of the booth. With each cheer from the crowd as Obama was declared the victor in state after state, he made the doll do a kind of minstrel ode to Obama, his idol. When my friend seized the doll, the DJ quipped that this was merely a joke in good fun and that, as Americans, we had failed to understand. To my colleagues and me, this was no doubt a strangely postmodern, nationalist yet transnational moment in which ideas about race, discursive violence, gender, sexuality, and nation collided in a quickly unfolding set of events triggered by the presumed narcoterrorist plane crash and the historic election of the first African American president of the United States.

It is no accident that Pinguín was censored in Mexico, as the Cuban-Mexican character's name was said to be a reference to the word *pinga*, or penis. Nor is it an accident that our interpretation of these events, which linked Obama to Arab terrorists and to a Sambo doll with its long, sordid, racist history of slavery and minstrelsy, through a North American lens was met by the disclaimer that racism does not exist in Mexico. As I continued to discuss the event with other people, some responded with fervor that Memín Pinguín is loved by Mexicans and that somehow the equation of Obama with what we read as a Sambo doll was not racist. If there is one thing that this book on violence has shown, it is that Mexicans, Mexican Americans, Anglos, and indigenous peoples are all implicated in hierarchical systems in which racism, gender, and sexual oppression are differentiating mechanisms that often create their own kinds of violence, be they physical, psychic, or discursive, often operating as acknowledged or unacknowledged institutionalized racism. Having racism literally written out of a Mexican national narrative was something my friends and I were not willing to tolerate at that moment when our transnationalized sense of historic consciousness collided with the "jokes we failed to understand."

The literal *choque*, or clash, of these moments of incredible national significance to both the Mexican and U.S. nations shows how discontinuities in analysis illustrate why we tragically fail to learn from each other. I am haunted by several things from my time in Mexico City: Belausteguigoitia's statement about the head of the nation being decapitated, the ways in which violence and racism against indigenous and African peoples are elided in national narratives; U.S. criticisms of Mexican racism at the beginning of the twentieth century toward its indigenous inhabitants, as if the United States had not brutally attempted to exterminate its own Indian populations only twenty years earlier; and news coverage of the plane crash on election night at the bar. The Mexican feminist scholarly discourse on violence and impunity vis-à-vis the Juárez feminicidos or the brutal and deadly assault on Ernestina Ascención, a seventy-three-year-old indigenous woman who was violently murdered and sexually assualted in Veracruz by the Mexican military, has much to teach Chicanas like me about an internationalist, antiracist politics that is different from identity politics.[4] These scholars have provided a tremendous body of knowledge that provides us a means for characterizing the failure of multiple nations in relationship to their most marginalized populations. At the same time, the jokes my friends and I "failed" to comprehend shut down the possibility of political critique because a joke is easily dismissed, is not intended to do harm. But when we take jokes seriously, as Freud argues we should because they are half-truths, there is a sense of injury posited through them. We see how Mexican public sentiment sometimes fails to take race and racism seriously in a "mestizo" nation. By taking a joke about race seriously we potentially have much to offer Mexican and U.S. analyses of the collapse of a legitimate state, where the possibility for civil rights and redemption is closed down through the mishandling of much larger institutional issues like the Juárez feminicidios or the aftermath of Hurricane Katrina. When Kanye West said that, in light of the structural violence of Katrina, George W. Bush doesn't care about black people, his words echo a parallel sentiment of what gets silenced or lost in the Memín Pinguín joke when directed at U.S. minorities in a Mexican context. Both West's statement and the Pinguín joke articulate a critique that the state and its majoritarian subjects do not want to hear: marginalized people of color have been literally silenced through their deaths and mistreatment, which represent utter acts of state failure. For example, the state failed the families of the murdered women in Juárez, who instead of going through the Mexican legal system, had to go to the Inter American Court of Human Rights in Santiago de Chile to be taken seriously because the Mexican and U.S. nations refused to recognize them.[5] In other words, these are the structural conditions of late capitalism that necessitate violence, both state and individuated, to maintain a kind of racialized differentiation.

What can one take away from a nuanced analysis of violence at the discursive, physical, psychic, and epistemic levels? Because violence orders how we analyze racial, sexual, gender, and class inequalities, it renders visible the unspeakable and demands more openness in a way that nationalisms, mestizaje, and resistance-assimilation do not. This is the reason my study turns to both transnationalism and feminism as a means of unmasking why certain histories remain unspeakable. To disavow racism in a symbolic act of minstrelsy or to disavow U.S. intervention in the everyday facets of border capitalism is to foreclose the possibility of mourning, of taking seriously the losses experienced at the hands of violence. The inability to reckon with our intimately intertwined national histories forecloses the possibility of reconciliation because individuals and nations on one side of the equation are not willing to take responsibility for the violence. If someone took responsibility for violence it would allow survivors of violence and their kin to mourn and move forward with a mindfulness about history. Instead, many of us run around making heroes and heroines of people who have literally survived violence and trauma. Mourning the losses, both national and individual, could perhaps provide the structural and institutional examination of violence as both a category of analysis and an intensive declaration of difference. I hope this book will open up a seriously sustained dialogue about violence, citizenship, mourning, and loss within Chicana/o, Latina/o, American, and borderlands studies so that we don't repeat the same stories and questions in the same way, creating an awareness while questioning, with care and reverence, all that has come before.

✳ Notes

INTRODUCTION

1. Hall, "Downieville: A Former Mining Town in the Sierra Revels in Its Golden Years," 27.
2. Ibid.
3. For an excellent treatment of the politics of race, class, gender, and economic outcomes in the central California gold diggings, see Johnson, *Roaring Camp*.
4. Hall, "Downieville," 27–28.
5. Parker, *Performativity and Performance*, 7.
6. I use *U.S. Mexicana* here to indicate that Josefa/Juanita was a Mexican in the United States in the period immediately following the annexation of California. She could have been a migrant from Sonora who came to work in the gold mines, or she could have been a native Californiana. *U.S. Mexicana* signals a nineteenth-century positionality for historical accuracy. To call her Chicana, Mexican American, or Mexican would be anachronistic and would fail to take into account the geopolitical complexity of her identity in the 1850s.
7. For an excellent study that debunks the idea that lynching was a means of carrying out justice in lieu of an institutionalized justice system, see Gonzales-Day, *Lynching in the West*, esp. 33–45.
8. I know of only three cases where women were lynched: Josefa's lynching in 1851, the lynching in 1881 of Cattle Kate during the Johnson County Wars in Wyoming, and the lynching of Laura Nelson in Okwmah, Oklahoma, in 1911. Gonzalez-Day also argues that of the lynchings he surveyed in California history from 1850 to 1935, people of color were statistically more likely to be lynched (26).
9. Guha, "The Prose of Counter-Insurgency," 339.
10. Ibid., 341.
11. Ibid., 345.
12. Coronil and Skurski, "Dismembering and Remembering the Nation," 84.
13. Roach, *Cites of the Dead*, 3; and Taylor, *The Archive and the Repertoire*, xvi.
14. Roach, *Cites of the Dead*, 4.
15. See Diana Taylor on the Milgram test in torture, in which people are shown to obey even if doing so requires them to go against their moral convictions ("Double Bind," 720).
16. Ibid., 715.
17. Scarry, *The Body in Pain*, 29.

18. See Foucault, *Discipline and Punish*, 197.

19. There are several excellent studies of the manifestation of trauma in survivors of violence. See Aldama, *Violence and the Body;* Blackhawk, *Violence over the Land;* Jacobs, *Victimized Daughters;* Hartman, *Scenes of Subjection;* Goldsby, *A Spectacular Secret,* especially the introduction; A. Smith, *Conquest;* and Herman, *Trauma and Recovery.* In particular, Berger and Berger, *Second Generation Voices,* discusses the ways in which a parent's Holocaust experiences sediment themselves in their relationships with their children and thus affect their capacity for intimacy. Even though the children did not experience the trauma firsthand, that trauma exists within families and leaves traces or social residue.

20. Herman, *Trauma and Recovery,* 33.

21. Glenn, *Unequal Freedom,* 2002, 2–4.

22. Gupta, "Song of the Nonaligned World," 71.

23. Brady, *Extinct Lands, Temporal Geographies,* 8.

24. Blackhawk, *Violence over the Land,* 8.

25. See De Vries and Weber, introduction, *Violence, Identity and Self Determination,* 2.

26. Kristeva, "The Powers of Horror: Approaching Abjection," 232.

27. Eng and Kazanjian, *Loss: The Politics of Mourning,* 4.

28. Coronil and Skurski, "Dismembering and Remembering the Nation," 84.

29. This masculinist discourse represents a trove of writing on Anglo-Mexican male relations, including Montejano, *Anglos and Mexicans in the Making of Texas;* De Leon, *They Called Them Greasers;* and Acuña, *Occupied America,* which have defined the contours of the field and become the canon for discussions about race, nation, and identity in Chicano studies. Rather than focusing on the development of this dominant strand in Chicano studies, I point to these texts as a way of shifting the discussion to other ways that Chicana/o studies have been practiced in the last forty years, in particular, a nod toward the transnational.

30. Hernández, "El México perdido," 130.

31. Del Castillo, preface to *Between Borders,* iii.

32. This book was part of a series called La Mujer Latina.

33. Ibid., iii and vii.

34. Ibid., xii.

35. Ibid., xiv.

36. Ibid., 13.

37. Coyolxchaulqui is the female Meso-American deity who was dismembered by her brother for plotting against her mother Coatlicue. La Malinche or Doña Marina was the Indigenous translator and eventual lover of Hernán Cortés who is blamed for the Spanish conquest of Mexico and the mother of mestizaje. Both figures are central to Chicana feminist theorizings of subjectivity.

38. *Between Borders,* 85.

39. Ibid., 87.

40. Ibid., 92.

41. Ibid., 105.

42. Chabram-Dernersesian, "Chicana! Rican? No, 'Chicana, Riqueña!,'" 267.

43. Ibid.

44. Ibid., 268.

45. Ibid., 269.

46. Saldaña-Portillo, *Revolutionary Imagination in the Age of Development*, 4.

47. Ibid., 5.

48. Ibid., 6.

49. Ibid., 8–9.

50. Ibid., 9.

51. Ibid.,141.

52. Ibid., 198.

53. Ibid.

54. Briggs, McCormick, and Way, "Transnationalism: A Category of Analysis," 633.

55. See Saldívar-Hull, *Feminism on the Border*, Alarcón "Chicana Feminisms: In the Tracks of the Native Woman"; and Chabram-Dernersesian "Chicana! Rican? No, 'Chicana, Riqueña!' " for academic models illustrating this call in Chicana feminist scholarship.

56. Pérez-Torres, "Miscegenation Now!" 371–73, 377.

57. Y. Padilla, "Indian Mexico," 22.

58. Pérez-Torres, *Mestizaje: Critical Uses of Race in Chicano Culture*, xv.

59. See Rodriguez, *Brown Gumshoes*; Aranda, *When We Arrive*; Kaup, *Rewriting North American Borders in Chicano and Chicana Narrative*.

60. Gaspar de Alba, "Book Review of *Brown Gumshoes*," 145.

61. A perfect example is a recent advertisement for a CD on the NACCS Southern California listserv:

> In Lak Ech, is a collective of Xicana artists, who would like to introduce you to our group and poetry and song CD, "Mujeres Con Palabra." As a group, we are seven Xicana Indigena urban women from the greater Los Angeles area that carry our cultura, community, and children close to heart, not to mention our degrees, danza trajes, and deep love and dedication to empowering Raza Womyn. Our work honors the rich artistic heritage of our predecessors and also brings the energy and flavor of today. We encourage you to incorporate the new generation of Chicana poetry and art in your class lectures, presentations, and assigned reading/listening. Our CD has been used in various college courses and can easily be incorporated into any Chican@, Women's, or Ethnic Studies class, not to mention History, Literature and Creative Writing Courses. We often say it's "a Chicana Studies Course in a CD." Professors have successfully incorporated the CD into curriculum and syllabi and we encourage you to do the same. The CD includes the best of this generation's Los Angeles Xicana flor y canto, with original poems from six women, and indigenous pow-wow style songs. The CD is a beautiful full-color 14 page codex with poetry and original artwork, all on recycled paper! Noted Chicana feminist authors Ana Castillo and Cherríe Moraga have both written noteworthy reviews of In Lak Ech's debut CD, "Mujeres con Palabra."
>
> "In Lak Ech will blow you away. In the tradition of Sweet Honey in the Rock, they are fierce warrior women who, like our ancestors, do battle with poetry and song, and thrown in the mix, some humor that also keeps us strong. !Adelante, Xicanas!"—Ana Castillo

"I am impressed at a heart level with the work of In Lak Ech because it responds to a Xicana-Indígenismo thirty-five years in the making. Blending Northern Native musical influences with Southern Indígena filosofía, the CD celebrates the myriad spiritual and political roads Xicanas have walked to acquire a living uncompromised identity and cultural practice in the United States."—Cherríe Moraga (Retrieved from naccs-scal@lists.naccsonline.org, June 14, 2008.)

62. Kaup, *Rewriting North American Borders*, 201.

63. Scott, *Conscripts of Modernity*, provides a provocative reading of C. R. L. James's *Black Jacobins* and the romance of revolution, most notably detailed in the representation of Toussaint L'Ouverture. In developing the concept of black vindicationism and redemption, Scott accounts for what gets missed and celebrated in accounts that romance the history of revolutions (see 83).

64. Laplantine and Nouss, *Mestizajes: De Arcimbolod a Zombi*. This book is actually a dictionary of mestizaje that explains why each object or phenomenon qualifies as mestizo or hybrid.

65. CPD, Legajo 11, 0026932, March 11, 1886.

66. CPD, Legajo 11, 0026933, March 11, 1886.

67. Bass, "Counterinsurgency and Torture," 233.

68. Hu-DeHart, *Yaqui Resistance and Survival*, 149.

69. "Es la raza azteca esa raza, y se la ve asentarse en el Anahuac, sobre un balle cubierto de lagos y arboleadas; see la ve combatiendo con los vecinos y organizado un ejército asombroso: pero hombres extraordinarios, y cubiertos de hierro, invulnerables a las armas de los aborigines, y que disponen del fuego del rayo (el arcabuz y el cannon), aparecen por el Oriente, aliados con sus innúmeros y antes vencidos enemigos, y ahogan a sus guerreros en su sangre, y sujetan al pueblo subygado, a largo cautiverio . . . ¡Cuanta Sangre y que vitalidad para soportar las terribles, constantes hecatombres!" "¡Que Epoca la de nuestras guerras! ¡Los batallones que combaten y sus restos que son vencidos o que triunfan, los escuadrones arrebatados por el vertigo de la carga, que caen destrozados; los cañones que truenan é iluminan siniestramente; los estandartes flotando, corriendo como llamas encendedoras, el los amigos y enemigos campos, tropas chorreando sangre, que se miran entre el fuego y el humo; brillo de armas, fragor de bronces, toques de cornetas, y tambores, flamear de banderas vencedoras o vencidas tal fue el cuadro epocalíptico de nuestras luchas intestinas!" (Biografía de Bernardo Reyes, FMGR, Tomo 13, pp. 54–55, 1901).

70. Lomnitz, *Death and the Idea of Mexico*, 54.

71. Ibid.

72. Ibid.

73. Cook-Lynne, *New Indians, Old Wars*, 60.

74. See Mufti, "The Aura of Authenticity."

75. Brooks, *Captives and Cousins*; Barr, *Peace Came in the Form of a Woman*; Brady, *Extinct Lands, Temporal Geographies*; and E. Perez, *The Decolonial Imaginary*, are all texts that complicate the histories of Anglos, Mexicans, and Indians in the U.S.–Mexico borderlands.

76. Brooks, *Captives and Cousins*, 15.

77. Hämäläinen, *Comanche Empire*, 25.

78. Acuña's now foundational text *Occupied America* (1988) is a perfect example of how early Chicano nationalist texts traced a history of colonialism to claim subaltern status. Other examples include *500 Años del pueblo Chicano/500 Years of Chicano History in Pictures* (1990) and, more recently, Aldama's "Millennial Anxieties" (2002). Both texts, one pictorial and the other critical, function like catalogues of violence to support a narrative of resistance to hegemony.

79. Gupta, "The Song of the Nonaligned World," 63.

80. Spivak, *Critique of Postcolonial Reason*, 304.

81. Mohanty, *Feminism without Borders*, 113.

82. See Donaldson, "The Breasts of Columbus" (2002); and Spivak, *A Critique of Postcolonial Reason* (2003) for excellent analyses of epistemic violence in the production of colonial history.

83. A tremendously helpful body of scholarship looks at violence topically, especially regarding lynching, rape, incest, and genocide. See Hartman, *Scenes of Subjection*; Goldsby, *A Spectacular Secret*; Scarry, *The Body in Pain*; Castañeda, "Sexual Violence in the Politics and Policies of Conquest"; A. Smith, *Conquest*; Foucault, *Discipline and Punish*; and Jacobs, *Victimized Daughters*, for exemplary studies on these topics.

84. Kazanjian, *The Colonizing Trick*, 7.

85. I use *Papago* rather than *Tohono O'odham* (Desert People) to label this southern Arizona/northern Mexico Indian group in this chapter because that is how the nineteenth-century documents refer to them. The term *Papago* (Bean-eaters) originated with the Spanish. The Papago were not a unified tribe at this time but bands of villagers connected by kinship networks. Tribal group identification was actually imposed by the U.S. government.

86. A more localized example of this kind of work is Cynthia Radding's scholarship on Opata service to the Spanish and Mexican governments in Sonora from the seventeenth century through the nineteenth as they were enlisted to police the Apache and Yaqui. See *Wandering Peoples* (1997).

87. Briggs, "Body Snatchers and Homeless Waifs," 25.

88. Grewal and Kaplan, "Transnational Practices and Interdisciplinary Feminist Scholarship," 12.

1. A WOMAN WITH NO NAMES

1. Weller would later become governor of California. He stopped in Downieville to sway voters in the upcoming election. Weller also witnessed the lynching and did nothing to stop it.

2. Seacrest, *Juanita of Downieville*, 9. Another source claims that when Cannon entered her home for the first time, he tried to bury his face in her heavy hair (Older, *Love Stories of Old California*, 222).

3. Josefa/Juanita testified that a young Mexican boy had told her that some of the boys wanted to get in her room and sleep with her. She said she was so frightened that she took a knife to defend herself (Mirandé and Enríquez, *La Chicana*, 70). In addition, she said she told the deceased not to call her bad names and invited him into the house, where she stabbed him (Seacrest, *Juanita of Downieville*, 22). Seacrest's (1967) and Aldama's ("The Time of Violence," 2003) accounts are the only ones that suggest

the threat of rape or that a rape occurred. Seacrest's account contains no footnotes indicating his source for this information.

4. "Woman Hung at Downieville."
5. Hurtado, *Intimate Frontiers*, 134.
6. Pierce-Barstow, "Statement of Recollections of 1849–51 in California," 7–8, 10.
7. Hurtado, *Intimate Frontiers*, 134.
8. Aiken's widow states that her husband lied about the pregnancy because "he would do anything to help a friend" (Older, *Love Stories of Old California*, 228).
9. Royce, *California, from the Conquest in 1846 to the Second Vigilance Committee*, 293; Older, *Love Stories of Old California*, 223.
10. Pierce-Barstow says she was given a half hour to prepare for her death (*Statement of Recollections of 1849–51 in California*, 8). Older states she was given three hours to live (*Love Stories of Old California*, 224). Seacrest states that she was given two hours to prepare for her death (*Juanita of Downieville*, 24).
11. "Woman Hung at Downieville."
12. Older, *Love Stories of Old California*, 226.
13. Pierce-Barstow, *Statement of Recollections of 1849–1 in California*, 9–10.
14. Based on this evidence, Older oddly claims that the story is one of unrequited love between two ill-fated lovers. Perhaps this is Older's way of reclassifying the violence of Josefa/Juanita's lynching as a romance; Older's twisted ending suggests that Cannon and Josefa/Juanita were united only in death through burial together, much like Romeo and Juliet (227). This is a narrative that centers seduction on multiple levels.
15. Spivak, "Can the Subaltern Speak?" 287; Viego, *Dead Subjects*, 4. I am exceedingly indebted to Viego's critique of the ethnic-racialized subject as a static invention of racist discourse that then gets reinscribed through ethnic studies claims of a whole, transparent subject that is not transformed into a subject by language (14).
16. The number of men who participated as spectators varies from account to account, ranging from as few as five hundred to as many as three thousand.
17. Brady, *Extinct Lands, Temporal Geographies*, 19.
18. Downie, *Hunting for Gold*, 146.
19. I elaborate one of Antonio Viego's main arguments, in which he stresses that ego and social psychology in the United States rely on racist constructions of a static ethnic-racialized subject that exists outside of language. The Lacanian psychoanalytic approach he advocates for centralizes the role of language as the thing that constructs subjects, not just power or social structures. For more on this point, see the introduction to *Dead Subjects*.
20. Viego, following Berguson, argues that language is encrusted upon the subject. It is overwritten and sometimes even injured by language, thus cutting the subject. *Dead Subjects*, 17.
21. Hartman, *Scenes of Subjection*, 88.
22. Alarcón, "Chicana Feminism," 378–79.
23. Van Haute, quoted in Viego, *Dead Subjects*, 14.
24. Seacrest, *Juanita of Downieville*, 7.
25. Ibid.

26. Incidentally, Older is a granddaughter of Gen. John C. Fremont, leader of the California Bear Flag revolt.
27. Older, *Love Stories of Old California*, 219.
28. Hurtado notes that the majority of women prostitutes in the gold camps were displaced California Indian women (*Intimate Frontiers*, 86–87).
29. It is also possible that the name Josefa is actually a reference to her as "José's woman."
30. See Martha Cotera, *Diosa y Hembra;* and Acuña, *Occupied America*, 119.
31. U.S. Congress, Senate, *On the Part of Citizens of the United States*. The actual text of the claim reads, "For the lynching of his wife and banishment of himself by a mob." The document says the event happened on July 2, 1852, not 1851, as most of the contemporary news reports indicate.
32. See Sturken, *The Vietnam War*, 13.
33. Royce, *California, from the Conquest in 1846 to the Second Vigilance Committee*, 291.
34. Older, *Love Stories of Old California*, 223. Josefa/Juanita's identification as a "greaser" anticipated the Greaser Act of 1855, which was an antivagrancy law directed more against racial groups (Mexicans, Chinese, and Indians in California) than against preventing undesirable behavior (see Gonzales-Day, *Lynching in the West*, 24–25).
35. Guidotti-Hernández, "Gender, Epistemology and Cooking"; see also Kaplan, *Erotics of Talk*.
36. Arteaga's foreword to *Violence and the Body: Race, Gender, and the State* describes the material effects of violence on the flesh (the blood that results from physical pain and violence), pointing to the importance of language, represented by black ink, as a way to make the violence against the sufferer known. Language—more specifically, language printed on the page—is what allows us to recall, theorize, and remember violence. Thus, we can extend the analysis of violence and the body to feminist theory and thereby address the gendered, racialized body as a "center of political action and theoretical production" (Grosz, "Time of Violence," 14–15).
37. Johnson's *Roaring Camp* discusses the southern mines (which did not include Downieville). She problematizes the assumption of racial homogeneity by discussing the roles of Chileans, Chinese, French, black, and Mexican men and women in the mines. However, the census of 1850 for Yuba County, where Downieville was located, shows it was predominately Anglo-American. Out of 4,982 total inhabitants, only 56 blacks and mulattoes were counted on the census for that year.
38. Spivak discusses this problem of excavation. She argues that the "nineteenth-century European historiography had designated the archives as a repository of 'facts.' . . . The Colonizer constructs himself as he constructs the colony. The relationship is intimate, an open secret that cannot be a part of official knowledge" (*Critique of Postcolonial Reason*, 203). As she questions how a colonizing historian constitutes an official history, Spivak marks the ways in which colonial epistemologies prevent the historical record from representing the voices of colonized women with accuracy. Josefa/Juanita emerges as one of those minimally documented individuals in frontier history, and we are left to interpret the questions of subjectivity from official fragments.
39. Bancroft, *Popular Tribunals*, 582.

40. "The violent proceedings of an indignant and excited mob, led by the enemies of the unfortunate woman, are a blot upon the history of the state. Had she committed a crime of really heinous character, a real American would have revolted at such a course as was pursued towards this friendless and unprotected *foreigner*. We had hoped that the story was fabricated. As it is the perpetrators of the deed have shamed themselves and their race." "The Hanging at Downieville" (emphasis added).

41. "The Hanging at Downieville."

42. The claim filed by her husband, José Maria Loiza, with the U.S. and Mexico Claims Commission further puts Josefa/Juanita's citizenship into question. José filed the claim in Mexico, and it is unclear whether he and his wife were naturalized U.S. citizens at the time of the lynching and José repatriated to Mexico after the fact, or whether they were Mexican migrants who came to California after the Treaty of Guadalupe Hidalgo was signed.

43. "The Hanging at Downieville."

44. In "The Metalanguage of Race," Evelyn Brooks-Higginbotham argues that the question of what constituted a lady was the basis for segregating railroad cars, in that *lady* signified white womanhood and not black womanhood, and the class dimensions held weight in the definition as well, excluding white working-class women and prostitutes from the privileges and protections due a lady. Josefa/Juanita's status is contradictory, straddling the line between whiteness and blackness in terms of race. Her class status ultimately denies her the privilege of being a lady because she is viewed as working class and a possible prostitute.

45. Griswold del Castillo, *The Treaty of Guadalupe Hidalgo*, 62.

46. Hispanic, as a nonwhite designation, did not appear on the U.S. census until 1960.

47. Menchaca, *The Mexican Outsiders*, 62–63.

48. John O'Sullivan coined the term "manifest destiny" in 1845 to signify the mission of the nation at that time. With religious overtones, the Puritans reinterpreted the doctrine of the Promised Land and God's chosen people during the Reformation. The term expressed the national mood toward the politics of expansion. As an ideology, it implied that the United States was destined by the will of God to become a country of political and territorial eminence. Stephanson argues that it "became a catchword for the idea of a providentially or historically sanctioned right to continental expansionism" (xii). The doctrine called for a renewed nationalism and vigor founded upon a particularly masculinist rhetoric of domination. It assigned to American citizens a sense of obligation to extend freedom to their less fortunate neighbors, but only those trained for self-governance. There was a popular sentiment that land was linked with opportunity and that territorial expansion of the Republic would guarantee humanity's future.

49. Ibid., 73. In 1851 the government passed the Land Claim Act that created a commission to check the land titles for their validity.

50. For more on the history of these stereotypes, miscegenation, and the *leyendas negras*, see De Leon, *They Called Them Greasers*, esp. 63–74.

51. Seacrest, *Juanita of Downieville*, 6.

52. Older, *Love Stories of Old California*, 219.

53. *Illustrated History of Plumas, Lassen, and Sierra Counties*, 458.

54. The actual designations for racial identity in the census were "W" for white, "B" for black, and "M" for mulatto.

55. Because Mexicans, Chileans, or Peruvians did not constitute a distinct category in the census, they are particularly hard to find in these already unreliable, inconsistent records.

56. Seacrest suggests that she was a saloon girl (*Juanita of Downieville*, 7). Older suggests that she was a homemaker: "In the sparkling morning air Juanita baked bread in the outdoor oven built by José. Her blithe fingers spun out flat tortillas for him. Afternoons she made fine embroidery and Mexican drawn work, or sang to her guitar" (*Love Stories of Old California*, 220). Although it is unclear what Josefa's occupation was, Susan Johnson (*Roaring Camp*, 30–31) states that Mexican women commonly sold food, worked as laundresses, and sold their gendered labor to miners, as such services were in great demand because of the lack of women in the gold camps. These shortages of women also bent gender boundaries, as Chinese men were often forced into gendered labor, such as cooking and laundering, further perpetuating a discourse of their femininity and racial inferiority.

57. *Illustrated History of Plumas, Lassen, and Sierra Counties*, 457.

58. Brady, *Extinct Lands, Temporal Geographies*, 135.

59. Downie, *Hunting for Gold*, 145.

60. The text says Wells but most likely that was a typo and referred to Sen. John B. Weller.

61. Pierce-Barstow, *Statement of Recollections of 1849–51 in California*, 8.

62. *Steamer Pacific Star*, July 15, 1851, 1.

63. Ibid.

64. Ibid.

65. Ibid.

66. Ibid. (emphasis added.)

67. Ibid.

68. Ibid.

69. Ibid.

70. U.S. Congress, Senate, "On the Part of Citizens of the United States," 94–95.

71. Ibid., 79–83.

72. A great majority of the claims were filed by Mexicans residing in both the United States and Mexico and related to injuries and property losses caused by the U.S. military, American Indians, or U.S. civilians in what the claimants asserted were unwarranted attacks. The dates of the alleged events ranged from as early as 1847, during the Mexican-American War, to as late as 1869. Among the claimants were men, women (eighty), Mexican state governors (of Chihuahua and Sonora), and entire towns (such as the towns of Lampazos and San Nicolás de las Garzas). There are occasional claims similar to the one filed by José María Loiza over his wife's lynching. M. and Josefa Chávez made a claim for $60,370.00 "for the murder of their father, Antonio José Chávez and the robbery of his property by a party of Americans" in the state of Kansas in February 1845. Their case was dismissed on July 6, 1870. Ibid., 74–75.

73. *Steamer Pacific Star*, July 15, 1851, 1.

74. The *Steamer Pacific Star* reporter writes "Jasefa's Testimony," again adulterating her name and showing the lack of desire to fix her as a historical subject.

75. *Steamer Pacific Star*, July 15, 1851, 1.

76. Pierce-Barstow, *Statement of Recollections of 1849–51 in California*, 10.

77. Downie, *Hunting for Gold*, 146–47.

78. Castañeda, "Political Economy of Nineteenth-Century Stereotypes of Californianas," 216.

79. Leonard Pitt states that she was a Mexican prostitute (*Decline of the Californios*, 73).

80. Bancroft, *Popular Tribunals*, 581.

81. Lomnitz, *Death and the Idea of Mexico*, 38.

82. See Pérez, *Decolonial Imaginary*.

83. Pitt, *Decline of the Californios*, 73.

84. Blea, *Chicanas in a U.S. Global Context*, 90.

85. Cott, *Public Vows*, 137.

86. Pierce-Barstow, *Statement of Recollections of 1849–51 in California*, 8–9.

87. Gilfoyle, "Prostitutes in History," 120, 121.

88. Ibid., 122.

89. Seacrest, *Juanita of Downieville*, 8.

90. Bancroft, *Popular Tribunals*, 582.

91. Older, *Love Stories of Old California*, 222.

92. Nathaniel Hawthorne defines *romance* as an attempt to connect with a bygone time in a present moment that is flitting away. He suggests that the wrongdoing of one generation lives into the lives of successive ones. Perhaps this is why Older classifies this narrative about a lynching as a romance (*House of the Seven Gables*, vii).

93. See Hartman, *Scenes of Subjection*, 88.

94. Buck, *A Yankee Trader in the Gold Rush*, 234.

95. Pierce-Barstow, *Statement of Recollections of 1849–51 in California*, 10.

96. Jensen, "No Irish Need Apply."

97. Brundage, *Lynching and the New South*, 17.

98. Pierce-Barstow, *Statement of Recollections of 1849–51 in California*, 10.

99. The census listed two miners by the name of José whose place of birth was given as Mexico. All of the narratives about Josefa/Juanita state that José was forced out of mining and into gambling. More specifically, the Foreign Miners Tax of 1850 was one example of laws that prevented Mexicans and Chinese immigrants from staking claims in gold rush mines. See Johnson, *Roaring Camp*, for more details about nativist agitation against people of color during the gold rush. Johnson argues that such agitation took three forms: individual instances of harassment; mining-district laws that prevented people of color from mining in particular areas; and a twenty-dollar-a-month tax assessed against foreign nationals who worked in the mines (31–32). Perhaps José was the target of one of these strategies.

100. Coronil and Skurski, *States of Violence*, 84.

101. Aldama, "Millennial Anxieties," 22.

102. Acuña, *Occupied America*, 111, 113, 118.

103. Ibid., 119.

104. Cited in ibid., but the quotation originally comes from the Los Angeles–based Spanish-language newspaper *El Clamor Público* (April 4 and 16, 1857).
105. Acuña, *Occupied America*, 119.
106. Aldama, "Millennial Anxieties," 22.
107. Pierce-Barstow wrote, "Some one states that the woman was with child, and the question was raised whether the execution should be defended. An examination was held and that statement pronounced false"; he makes no mention of rape (*Statement of Recollections of 1849–51 in California*, 8). However, such acts of sexual violence would likely not be spoken of explicitly but would be cloaked in euphemisms (see Hartman, *Scenes of Subjection*, 88).
108. See Fregoso, *MeXicana Encounters*, chap. 4.
109. Aldama, "Millennial Anxieties," 55.
110. I realize that this account is not transparent either in its meaning or the actual facts it presents. What I am proposing here is that contemporary theoretical and nationalist utterances about resistance and victimization sometimes elide the utterances of the past that problematize the neonationalist, familial present.
111. *The Steamer Pacific Star*, July 15, 1851, 1.
112. Murguía, *Medicine of Memory*, 38.
113. Spivak, *Critique of Postcolonial Reason*, 310.
114. Murguía, *Medicine of Memory*, 47.
115. Ibid., 51.
116. Mexica is another name to describe the Aztecs but particularly those from the Valley of Mexico. It is a word often used in Chicano nationalism to signal indigenismo.
117. Ibid., 57.
118. Rojas, "Re-membering Josefa," 129.
119. Numerous articles and books triangulate the relationship between the Virgin of Guadalupe (the patron saint of Mexico and Indigenous virgin of the Americas), La Llorona (a folklore figure who drowns her children to spurn her lover, her story is one of haunting children and policing the behavior of women), and La Malinche (or Doña Marina, the translator and eventual lover of Hernan Cortes who is considered the mother of the mestizo race and responsible for the fall of the Aztec empire) because they are the three most well-known models of Mexican womanhood on both sides of the U.S.–Mexico border.
120. Ibid., 136.
121. Green cited in ibid., 136.
122. D. Scott, *Conscripts of Modernity*, 76.
123. Rojas, "Re-membering Josefa," 141.
124. J. J. McClosky, "First Woman Hanged in California."
125. Ibid.
126. D. Scott, *Conscripts of Modernity*, 83.
127. "California History rewritten by CSULB Literary Scholar."
128. Ibid.
129. See hooks, *Killing Rage*, 11. hooks's explanation of how a series of incidents of discrimination based upon race and gender fuel "killing rage" provides a way to theorize the rage of racialized, gendered subjects.

130. Ibid., 15.

131. Ibid., 11.

132. Ibid., 12, 13.

133. Wald, *Constituting Americans*, 2.

134. Bancroft, *Popular Tribunals*, 583.

135. In *Criminal Law*, Rollin M. Perkins and Ronald N. Boyce elaborate the constraints of the term *crime of passion:* "To constitute the *heat of passion*, included in this requirement it is not necessary for the passion to be so extreme that the slayer does not know what he is doing at the time; but it must be so extreme that for the moment, his action is being directed by passion rather than by reason," 377.

136. Black, *Black's Law Dictionary*, 377.

137. Ibid., 726.

138. hooks, *Killing Rage*, 12.

139. Pierce-Barstow, *Statement of Recollections of 1849–51 in California*, 9.

140. Sneirson, "Black Rage and Criminal Law," 2252, 2253.

141. Ibid., 2253.

142. Ibid.

143. Gutiérrez, "Honor Ideology, Marriage Negotiation," 86.

144. Even if some would read the code of honor in Spanish America as oppressive and patriarchic, the code nonetheless reflects a desire to be virtuous by practicing discretion.

145. Alonso, *Thread of Blood*, 88.

146. Ibid., 89.

147. "Woman Hung at Downieville."

148. *Daily Alta*, "A Woman Hung at Downieville," July 9, 1851.

149. Mirandé and Enríquez suggest that José refused to fight Cannon because of his large size (*La Chicana*, 70).

150. Alonso, *Thread of Blood*, 165

151. *Steamer Pacific Star.*

152. The larger historical context of the moment, the foreign miners' tax passed in 1850, and the vigilante tactics that drove many Sonoran Mexicans from the mines and land claims support the supposition that José was a Mexican gambler and not a miner. See Johnson, *Roaring Camp*, esp. 32–33; and Pierce-Barstow, *Statement of Recollections of 1849–51 in California*, 7.

153. Bancroft, *Popular Tribunals*, 585.

154. Ibid., 585–86.

155. Hurtado, *Intimate Frontiers*, 134.

156. Pierce-Barstow, *Recollections of 1849–51 in California*, 8–9.

157. See Donaldson and Pui-lan, *Postcolonialism, Feminism and Religious Discourse*, 29.

158. Older, *Love Stories of Old California*, 226.

159. See Allen, *Without Sanctuary*, for detailed visual evidence of the fetishization of lynching and the objects collected after a lynching.

160. "Woman Hung at Downieville."

161. Scarry, *The Body in Pain*, 51.

162. See Donaldson, "The Breasts of Columbus," 54.

163. Scarry, *The Body in Pain*, 51.

164. Ibid.

165. Many of the photographs in Allen, *Without Sanctuary*, attest to this point.

166. Eiser, "Violence and Transcultural Values."

167. José María Loiza had to go through the Mexican government to make any kind of legal claim for his losses. For a second time, his losses (his wife's life and perhaps monetary losses plus interest) were denied, but this time officially by the U.S. government and the transnational claims commission. The repudiation of his claim had to have caused him a second injury, for he had already been denied his rights by the lynch mob and suffered the loss of his wife at the hands of state-sanctioned violence. Whether they were naturalized U.S. citizens through the Treaty of Guadalupe Hidalgo or Mexican migrants, they were treated as having no rights under either national governing body. This time, the psychological wounds were compounded and officially inscribed in law through the denial of his claim. Even though José sought reparation through this transnational judicial body, it was clear that Mexicanos who were not either part of the elite or part of a group of individuals filing a joint claim against the United States did not have sufficient rights or cultural capital to receive compensation. Further, the claim resembles a civil lawsuit, in that money is sought from the offender or a third party for causing physical or emotional injuries. Since José most likely did not have access to the California courts to file a criminal complaint, this was the only option he had that approximated direct legal action. Given that Josefa/Juanita, technically, was criminally prosecuted, this claim is also similar to a civil lawsuit in that a crime victim can file a civil suit against offenders and other responsible parties.

2. WEBS OF VIOLENCE

1. Sheridan, *Los Tucsonenses*, 69.

2. Oury, "Article on Camp Grant Massacre," 8.

3. Sidney DeLong Papers, Arizona Historical Society, MS 0216, F4, p. 10.

4. The records do not state if the small children killed were both male and female; they do state that the only men among the group were the older man and a 14-year-old boy.

5. The correct spelling of Chief Hashké Bahnzin's name is used by both Karl Jacoby in *Shadows at Dawn* (New York: Penguin, 2009) and Ian Record in *Big Sycamore Stands Alone* (Norman: University of Oklahoma Press, 2010). The spelling I rely upon throughout this chapter comes from the documents written from the time period. While for some this might seem like an effacement of Chief Hashké Bahnzin's subjectivity, I use the spelling from the documents to reflect the ways in which historical production, more often than not, was about failing to get the names of such people in the first place. BIA, *Report of the Commissioner of Indian Affairs*, 1871, 470.

6. Ibid.

7. Grenville Goodwin Papers, MS 17, folder 32, 17.

8. Ibid., 18–19.

9. I use *Papago* because this is the name used in the source material. The current official, federally recognized name of these Indians is Tohono O'odham.

10. Barr, *Peace Came in the Form of a Woman*, 179.

11. Brooks, *Captives and Cousins*; Hämäläinen, *Comanche Empire*, 7.

12. Jacoby, *Shadows at Dawn*, 276.

13. Hernández, "El México perdido," 23.

14. Brooks, *Captives and Cousins*; Gutiérrez, *When Jesus Came, the Corn Mothers Went Away*; and Jacoby, *Shadows at Dawn* are exceptions to this statement. Jacoby's exceptional work on the Tucsonense vecinos and their self-constructed identity as Indian fighters shows that Mexicans were doing everything in their power to disassociate themselves from anything Indian, and from the Apache in particular, using their own brutal forms of violence. While these texts are not overtly situated in Chicano history, they represent the most solid engagement with the types of questions that guide this chapter.

15. See Anzaldúa, *Borderlands/La Frontera*; Moraga, *The Last Generation*; Murguía, *Medicine of Memory*; Valdez, "Tale of La Raza"; Ech,"Mujeres con palabra"; and J. González, *Dew on the Thorn*.

16. DeLong, *History of Arizona*, 5.

17. Brooks, *Captives and Cousins*, 174.

18. Scarry, *The Body in Pain*, 165.

19. Sidney De Long Papers, MS 3, 16.

20. Scarry, *The Body in Pain*, 50.

21. Ibid., 279.

22. Sidney De Long Papers, Arizona Historical Society, MS 0216, folder 4, 6.

23. Radding, *Wandering Peoples*, 43–45.

24. *The United States vs. Sidney R. De Long*, December 6, 1871, 104. Testimony of Jose María Yesques.

25. "The Papagos."

26. Ibid.

27. Hämäläinen, *Comanche Empire*, 15.

28. "Who Is Right Again."

29. Oury, "Article on Camp Grant Massacre," 9.

30. "Gloomy Prospects in Arizona."

31. Higgs, *Transformation of the American Economy*, 8.

32. In *Los Tucsonenses* Thomas Sheridan states that these alliances split drastically after the arrival of the railroad, 45.

33. "Letter from Florence."

34. *The Revolutionary Imagination in the Age of Development*, 127.

35. Hernández, "El México perdido," 29.

36. Ibid., 30.

37. Higgs, *Transformation of the American Economy*, 27.

38. "Mining in Arizona."

39. Ibid.

40. *Daily Alta Californian*, January 22, 1871.

41. Truett, *Fugitive Landscapes*, 57.

42. "These Indians are not wholly well-disposed, but the rail road is more likely to be the means of taming them than the agents of obstructing or harming the road" (BIA, *Report to the Commissioner*, 1872, 469).

43. "Our Railroad Prospects."

44. Ibid.

45. Bonfil Batalla, *Mexico Profundo*, 76.

46. "Sensible Proceedings."

47. "The Committee on Safety."

48. BIA, *Report of the Commissioner*, 1872, 467.

49. "An Insane Idea." *Weekly Arizonan*, March 11, 1881.

50. Ibid.

51. Truett, *Fugitive Landscapes*, 43.

52. "An Insane Idea."

53. *Weekly Arizonan*, February 18, 1871.

54. Grosz, "The Time of Violence," 134.

55. Reid, "Relation of the Apache Indians to the Development of Arizona," 43.

56. Colwell-Chanthophonh, "Western Apache Oral Histories," 641–42.

57. The Pima were a part of the same kin group as the Papago and spoke a similar language, but the two are considered different tribes.

58. Arnold, *Camp Grant Massacre*; Kitt, "Mrs. Atanacia Hughes."

59. Kitt, "Mrs. Atanacia Hughes." Santa Cruz de Hughes is of particular importance to Chicana and Mexicana histories of Tucson because she is one of the few native Tucsonense women who has oral testimonies preserved in historical archives at the Arizona Historical Society. The lives of the Santa Cruz sisters and questions of power and intermarriage are documented in an article in progress.

60. Ibid., 5.

61. Ibid., 4.

62. Even today a high cultural premium is placed upon Tucsonenses who can trace their ancestry back to the presidio.

63. The Treaty of Mesilla, or Gadsen Purchase, encompassed the lands south of the Gila River and west of the Rio Grande that were purchased by the United States from Mexico for ten million dollars to build a southern route for the transcontinental railroad.

64. Siu, "Diasporic Cultural Citizenship," 12.

65. Child (1802–1880) was an abolitionist and women's rights and Indian rights activist most known for her 1868 pamphlet *An Appeal for the Indians*. Helen Hunt Jackson (1830–1885) wrote two influential books focusing on Indian reform (*A Century of Dishonor* and *Ramona*). Both represent a crucial generation of upper- and middle-class white women whose work was influenced by their abolitionist ties. Their racial politics contrast greatly with Mexican women such as Santa Cruz de Hughes, who was of the same generation. Geography and distinct racial formations informed this difference.

66. Smith and Watson, *De/colonizing the Subject*, xix.

67. Schellie, *Vast Domain of Blood*, 33; Sheridan, *Los Tucsonenses*, 41–46.

68. *United States vs. Sidney R. De Long*, 130.
69. Supposedly, the Papago participants were not issued guns because it was illegal to give an Indian firearms. However, Andrew Cargill suggests that Hughes issued guns to the Papago and that the governor gave him his blessing. "The Camp Grant Massacre," *Arizona Historical Review* 7, no. 3 (1936), 67.
70. Ibid.
71. "Indians! Indians!"
72. Ibid.
73. Higgs, *Transformation of the American Economy*, 15
74. "Outgoing Correspondence to Lola Oury Smith." Oury Family Papers, UASC, AZ 016.
75. Ibid.
76. In the chapter "Los Vecinos" in *Shadows at Dawn*, Jacoby maps the emergence of the Indian fighter identity for the Elías brothers as a project that protected their property but at the same time showed that Mexicans completely disidentified with indigenous communities in the state.
77. "Local Matters."
78. "Our Railroad Prospects."
79. Erickson, *Sharing the Desert*, 40.
80. Ibid., 13.
81. This description appears on the first page of the report for 1872, suggesting the vast contrast between government support of the Papago and frustration with the Apache.
82. Ibid. 391–92, 445.
83. "Article on Camp Grant Massacre," 4.
84. *United States vs. Sidney R. De Long*, 41.
85. Cremony, *Life among the Apaches*, 100–101.
86. Underhill, *Singing for Power*, 92. Underhill's work is problematic in terms of modern understandings of the practice of anthropology, but it is one of the major sources of information about Papago cultural practices in the late nineteenth century and early twentieth.
87. Underhill, *Papago Woman*, 49.
88. Underhill, *Papago Indians of Arizona*, 32.
89. Erickson, *Sharing the Desert*, 81.
90. Andrew Cargill, who was appointed secretary of the grand jury that sought indictment of the massacre participants, stated that for the case "the evidence was perfect. We knew who the five white men and twenty Mexicans were, but we had to guess concerning the Papagos." But the evidence was not so perfect, as they could not identify or failed to identify the Papago participants. They ended up getting the jury to indict but only to prevent the declaration of martial law in Arizona, with the charges naming "five white men and twenty Mexicans whose names he knew, and seventy-five Papagos by fictitious names." "The Camp Grant Massacre," *Arizona Historical Review* 7, no. 3 (1936), 66–67.
91. *United States vs. Sidney R. De Long*, 121–22.
92. Reid, "Relation of the Apache Indians to the Development of Arizona," 26.

93. Brooks, *Captives and Cousins*, 182.

94. In *Life among the Apaches* (1868), Capt. John Cremony asked, "Must we forever continue to accept the wild and impracticable theories of parlor readers on Indian character? Can we continue to pay millions annually for the shortsighted and pernicious policy which has heretofore regulated our Indian affairs? The American savage is no idiot" (268). After eight years of service he, among other members of the military serving in Arizona, called for troop withdrawal and a reformation of BIA policy. He argued, "Nor can this evil be remedied so long as the Indian Bureau continues to be a political machine . . . [it] should be abolished as a costly and unnecessary adjunct to a Government already overburdened with political patronage . . . and merging the Indian Bureau into the War department, a regular systematic policy would be pursued, upon which our savage tribes could place reliance" (314).

95. BIA *Report of the Commissioner of Indian Affairs*, 1872, 471.

96. Ibid.

97. Legislature of the Territory of Arizona, *Memorial and Affidavits*, 2.

98. Ibid., 4.

99. Colwell-Chanthophonh, *Massacre at Camp Grant*, 72.

100. Legislature of the Territory of Arizona, *Memorial and Affidavits* 10.

101. Ibid., 26.

102. This painting hung in the Cosmopolitan Hotel in Tucson until 1893, when it was, ironically, sold at auction to Sam Hughes, one of the main economic supporters of the Camp Grant massacre, for $5.50.

103. The word "roasting" is from the Arizona Historical Society's catalog description.

104. "Indian Outrages," *Weekly Arizonan*, May 15, 1869.

105. Ibid., 8.

106. Ibid., 10.

107. De Long, *History of Arizona*, 32.

108. Ibid., 1, 2.

109. Ibid., 5. This represents a large discrepancy from the 108 casualties cited earlier, suggesting that the numbers vary depending upon the politics of the individual reporting the evidence.

110. Brooks, *Captives and Cousins*, 9.

111. Interview with Daniel Jones, O'odham tribal member, April 2007.

112. Brooks, *Captives and Cousins*, 195.

113. BIA, *Report of the Commissioner of Indian Affairs*, 1872, 540, 541.

114. Ibid., 537.

115. Carrillo, originally from Sonora, became one of Tucson's Mexican elite. He is best known for creating, on land he owned, the Carrillo Gardens, a desert oasis with rose gardens and an artificial lake (see Sheridan, *Los Tucsonenses*, 50–52).

116. Hartman, *Scenes of Subjection*, 88.

117. Ibid., 89.

118. "Trial Transcript for Camp Grant," *Alta California*, February 3, 1872.

119. Ibid.

120. Bio file, Alvina Resenda Elías, as told to Mrs. Kitt 1865–1959. Arizona Historical Society, 1.

121. Ibid. 2.

122. Ibid 3–4.

123. At this point, in the early 1870s the former Civil War general and former director of the Freedman's Bureau was sent by President Ulysses S. Grant as part of a detachment to make a treaty with the Cochise and oversee peace agreements with various Indian tribes in New Mexico and Arizona.

124. The list of children is as follows: "Lola, a girl aged about ten years, in care of Leopoldo Carrillo with whom she had been living; Vicente, a boy about five years old, in the care of Samuel Martinez; Vicente, a boy about nine years of age, in the care of Simon Sanchez with whom he had been living; Juan, a boy about five years old, in the care of Samuel Martines, with whom he had been living; Luisa a girl about four years of age in the care of Jose Luis with whom she had been living; Lucia, a girl aged about three years old, in the care of Francisco Romero with whom she had been living; and Maria, a girl aged about twenty months in the care of Nicholas Martines with whom she had been living." Letter to Hon. R. C. McCormick, Delegate for Congress. May, 28, 1872, from J. E. McCaffery. Arizona Historical Society. Indians of North America-Apache-Camp Grant Massacre-Ephemera file.

125. Ibid.

126. Ibid. 3.

127. Alonso, "Intervention, Mobilization and Ideology," 213–14.

128. Koreck, "Space and Revolution in Chihuahua," 153; see also Jacoby, *Shadows at Dawn*.

129. Cremony, *Life among the Apaches*, 85, 95.

130. Lombroso and Ferrero, *Criminal Woman, the Prostitute, and the Normal Woman*, 65.

131. *United States v. Sidney R. De Long*, 103.

132. See oral history of Sherman Curley, Aravaipa tribal member, in Grenville Goodwin Papers, MS 17, folder 32, 17–18.

133. Andrew Cargill, "The Camp Grant Massacre," *Arizona Historical Review* 7, no. 3 (1936), 65

134. Lombroso and Ferrero, *Criminal Woman, the Prostitute, and the Normal Woman*, 71.

135. C. Smith, *William Sanders Oury*, 194.

136. See oral history of Sherman Curley in Grenville Goodwin Papers, 15–28.

137. See the testimony of the army scout John Rope in Goodwin, *Apache Raiding and Warfare*. He states that the first person to talk to them before war was an old woman who knew about war medicine: "You boys are like close relatives to me. I want you to look out for yourselves and do things the right way. If you see the Warm Springs people, follow them and don't let them get away" (118). While it was accepted that Apaches like John Rope allied themselves with the government of the United States in corralling other Apaches, it is not commonly mentioned that women often provided the historiographic and familial context that motivated young warriors entering into battle.

138. BIA, *Report of the Commissioner of Indian Affairs*, 1871, 488.

139. Royal Whitman Papers. Arizona Historical Society.

140. *United States v. Sidney R. De Long*, 7–9.

141. Ibid., 8.

142. Feldman, "Memory Theaters, Virtual Witnessing, and the Trauma-Aesthetic," 165.

143. Scarry, *The Body in Pain*, 148.

144. Blackhawk, *Violence over the Land*, 40

145. *United States vs. Sidney R. De Long*, 140. Testimony of Mr. Rowell.

146. Payne, *Unsettling Account*, 124–25.

147. Ibid., 125.

148. C. Smith, *William Sanders Oury*, 194.

149. Grenville Goodwin Papers, MS 17, folder 32, 17.

150. Barr, *Peace Came in the Form of a Woman*, 168.

151. BIA *Report of the Commissioner of Indian Affairs*, 1871, 53.

152. Grenville Goodwin Papers, MS 17, folder 32, 17–18.

153. Rooks and Gaskins, "Wearing Your Race Wrong," 280.

154. See Underhill, *Papago Indians of Arizona* (33–35), for a detailed description of taking scalps as war trophies, the communal value of scalps, and the sixteen-day purification process required of enemy killers. Also see Underhill, *Papago Woman*.

155. Underhill, *Papago Woman*, 44.

156. Shanley, "The Indian America Loves to Love and Read."

157. Arnold, *Camp Grant Massacre*, 413.

158. Ibid., 413–14.

159. Grosz, *Volatile Bodies*, 81.

160. Camacho-Schmidt, "Cuidadana X," 267

161. Arnold, *The Camp Grant Massacre*, 405.

162. Schellie, *Vast Domain of Blood*, 149

163. A. Smith, *Conquest*, 139.

164. The Papago committed violent acts with their traditional implements of war—small leather shields and clubs of hard wood—but there was still a colonial logic of violence operating in this moment. Underhill describes these clubs as "very good for cracking enemy heads" (*Papago Indians of Arizona*, 32), and they also required that the men come into close physical proximity of the enemy. While proximity to the enemy was seen as a public duty, not as an act of honor and sometimes not even as the warrior's choice, the reward for the warrior was that he had helped his village and would gain power and respect, not because of the killings but through the long purification process that the community engaged in afterward (ibid., 34–35). Warriors were isolated for sixteen nights and had to sing and smoke over the scalps they had taken. Finally, they were to take the scalps home wrapped in eagle feathers, talk to them, and care for them as if they were part of their family. These acts suggest that Papago attitudes toward war and bravery are steeped in humility not the sexual violence they are blamed for (ibid., 58).

165. Schellie, *Vast Domain of Blood*, 150.

166. Scarry, *The Body in Pain*, 198.

167. Underhill, *Papago Woman*, 42.

168. Erickson, *Sharing the Desert*, 81.

169. For examples of these exchange practices steeped in violence, see Brooks, *Captives and Cousins*; and Blackhawk, *Violence over the Land*.

170. Blackhawk, *Violence over the Land*, 36.

171. Cremony, *Life among the Apaches*, 245.

172. Mohanty, *Feminism without Borders*, 24.

173. "Who Is Right Again."

174. "Antiquity of the Apache."

175. Connell, "The Big Picture," 599.

176. Goodwin Papers, MS 17, folder 32, pp. 34, 37.

177. Goodwin, *Apache Raiding and Warfare*, 267.

178. Zacharias, "Trial by Fire," 28

179. Alarcón, "Theoretical Subjects of *This Bridge Called My Back*."

180. Bhabha, "DissemiNation," 300.

181. Oury "Article on Camp Grant Massacre," 5–6.

182. BIA, *Report of the Commissioner of Indian Affairs*, 1872, 398.

183. In *Los Tucsonenses* Sheridan argues that only the arrival of the railroad forever changed these racial alliances and social positioning of Mexicans in Tucson.

3. SPACES OF DEATH

1. The term *archive* has been loosely used by cultural studies scholars in the past several years to describe *any* body of material a critic works with. I want to tighten the definition of *archive* in relation to knowledge production as an act of power by regarding Jovita González's published and unpublished anthropological, fictional, and folkloric archives as the enactment of historical anthropological practices. As Johannes Fabian has noted, anthropological conventions "have allowed authors of ethnographies to boost their authority by keeping large parts of their work (such as the steps of a learning process, trial and error in interpretations, humbling evidence of limited linguistic competence, and justification of selectiveness) hidden from the reader and unavailable for public discussion. Leaving aside whatever the implications may be, such practices have been a legitimate target of epistemological critique" ("Presence and Representation," 779). What is different about González's archive is that its being kept from public consumption seemingly has not reinforced her authority as an anthropologist but, in fact, until recently has erased it. Her archive covers the period from Spanish conquest in the 1700s up to the 1950s. I look specifically at her work covering roughly the period from 1850 to 1930.

2. Now her papers are in various archives in Texas, including the University of Texas, Austin, Texas A&M, Corpus Christi, and Texas State University, San Marcos. González's work includes her MA thesis from the University of Texas, her long-unpublished novel *Caballero*, published by Texas A&M University Press in 1997, the recently released *Dew on the Thorn* (Arte Público Press, 1997), *The Woman Who Lost Her Soul* (Arte Público Press, 2000), and her personal papers. Her corpus suggests that historically a Tejana regional-spatial identity is bound to the memory of and values of the Mexican nation. By ideologically maintaining the Mexican national space upon what eventually became U.S. soil in Texas, González establishes a counternarrative of the nation that evokes and erases its totalizing boundaries.

3. One could cite Américo Paredes and Gloria Anzaldúa, among others, as having sparked interest in border theory from the 1980s onward.

4. Massey, *For Space*, 95.

5. González, "Social Life in Cameron, Starr, and Zapata Counties," 10.

6. Cotera, *Native Speakers*, 3.

7. Ibid., 10.

8. Ibid.

9. Ibid., 15.

10. Ibid., 16.

11. Mendoza, *Historia*, 41, 43.

12. Ibid., 46.

13. In "On Ethnographic Authority" Clifford states that "the new field worker theorist [of the 1920s] brought to completion a new scientific and literary genre, the ethnography, a synthetic cultural description based on participant observation" (119; also see 123).

14. In her book *Gente Decente*, Leticia Garza-Falcón argues that González combats "the myths of Texas history that continue to be perpetuated while the Texas-Mexican's history and perspective are never really taught" (18). I would argue that González attempts to create an alternative knowledge structure where the Tejana/o border people are subjects who can tell their own stories. José Limón understands González's work as follows: "There is clearly a dominant line to González's ethnographic rendering and to her discursive statements. She articulated a class/race paternalism, and colonialist attitude consistent with her padrino, Dobie, thereby reinforcing Anglo-American dominance in Texas as a whole" (69). I agree with Limón that many of her texts are concerned with preserving the stories of the *gente decente* (the mostly male descendants of the Spanish conquistadors) and the *peones* and vaqueros who work for them (Introduction, *Dew on the Thorn*). In her dissertation "Native Speakers" (2001), María Cotera argues that González's work is reflective of a U.S.–Third World feminist discourse.

15. In *Culture and Truth*, Renato Rosaldo argues that imperialist nostalgia emanates from the ways in which agents of colonialism "long for the very forms of life they intentionally altered or destroyed" (67). I use this term to clarify that González's nostalgia is not for the Indians who were lost through colonization, but rather is a lament for the power and superiority that the conquistadors gained by colonizing Indians.

16. Young, "Red Men, Princess Pocahontas and George Washington," 50.

17. Fabian, "Presence and Representation," 771.

18. Holland, *Raising the Dead*, 4.

19. Butler, *Psychic Life of Power*, 2.

20. Ibid., 3.

21. Holland, *Raising the Dead*, 4.

22. The Great Spirit and the Spirit of the Plains appear in another narrative in *Dew on the Thorn* about the male cardinal who is given a voice through his wife's sacrifice of her beautiful red color. Once the male cardinal can sing, he pecks his wife because of her ugliness. Again, the Great Spirit makes the partners equal through this moral: "So now, whenever the male begins to fuss and scold, she, knowing the vanity of his sex, tosses her little head and flies off laughing at the stupidity of husbands, who like hers, are all woman-made and yet are of what they think is their own achievement"

(49–50). I cannot include all of these stories of gender inequity and the ways in which Gods and spirits intervene to equalize them. However, this is another syncretic cultural story that recognizes the haunting presence of Plains Indians even if they are invisible in the larger narrative itself.

23. *Dew on the Thorn*, 48. Some would argue this story recalls the legends of both La Malinche and La Llorona, indigenous women who were spurned by their lovers. See Alarcón, "Chicana Feminist Literature: A Re-vision through Malintzin/or Malintzin: Putting Flesh Back on the Object"; Saldívar-Hull's chapter, "I Hear the Woman's Wails and Know Them to Be My Own" from *Feminism on the Border*; and Rebolledo's chapter, "From Coautlique to La Llorona: Literary Myths and Archetypes" from *Women Singing in the Snow*, for examples of Chicana scholarship on La Llorona and La Malinche.

24. *Dew on the Thorn*, 48.

25. Ibid., 59.

26. Ibid., 123.

27. Ibid.

28. Ibid., 123.

29. As BIA records indicate, the 1870s were a period of intensive efforts by the Kiowa and Comanche to lay claim to territory in what had become their Texas homelands. "The depredating Kiowas and the Quahada Comanches are utterly without excuse. They are compelled to go back as far as 1847 to find a single substantial grievance of which to complain. Since that time the United States have given them a noble reservation, and have provided amply for all their wants . . . yet they have persisted in leaving their reservation and marauding in Texas" (BIA, *Report of the Commissioner of Indian Affairs*, 1872, 396).

30. Ibid., 429.

31. See 50th Congress, 1st sess., Executive Document No. 219.

32. Lamar, *Report of the Secretary of the Interior*.

33. Brooks, "Served Well by Plunder," 26.

34. U.S. House of Representatives, Executive Document no. 219, March 15, 1888.

35. González, "Social Life in Cameron, Starr, and Zapata Counties," 23.

36. Ibid., 16–20.

37. The Karankawa were originally coastal Indians settled around Galveston, but they were eventually pushed up into the Rio Grande Valley.

38. Momaday, *The Man Made of Words*, 39.

39. In chapter 4 of her thesis González discusses at length the role of education in preserving Texas-Mexican cultural values (69–82).

40. *Dew on the Thorn*, 147.

41. Ibid., 145–46.

42. Vasconcelos, *La raza cósmica*.

43. "España quería colonizar la tierra entre el Rio Grande y el Río Nueces. Esta tierra estaba infestada por los indios bárbaros, algunos de los cuales eran caníbales. Aunque muchos españoles vivían en el Nuevo mundo ninguna quería venir a la tierra de los Texas, como llamaban Texas en aquel entonces. España estaba ansiosa por colonizar esta tierra, por temor que los franceses en la Luisiana adquirirían esta tierra."

("Quienes Somos," Jovita González de Mireles Papers, folder 1, Manuscripts, Short Stories, and Essays).

44. See Barr, *Peace Came in the Form of a Woman*, for a detailed account of how these nations eventually made alliances with the Spanish, although later in the Mexican period the Karankawa were exterminated by the Tejano Juan Cortina.

45. Gloria Anzaldúa subverts Vasconcelos's conception in *Borderlands/La Frontera* (1987), where *la raza cósmica* marks liberation for mestiza/os.

46. See the epilogue to Saldaña Portillo's *The Revolutionary Imagination in the Americas and the Age of Development* for a critique of how "living Indians" get erased from Chicana/o and Mexican narratives of culture and history through the biologically based discourses of mestizaje.

47. Brooks, "Served Well by Plunder," 43.

48. González, "Social Life in Cameron, Starr, and Zapata Counties," 28. González dates the riot to 1900, but the *New York Times* and *San Antonio Express* reported the date as November 19, 1899.

49. "Citizens Fire on Troops" *Chicago Tribune*, 1.

50. G. Christian, *Black Soldiers in Jim Crow Texas*, 40. This is an excellent detailed survey of racism and the conflicts African Americans experienced during their military service in Texas.

51. *Dew on the Thorn*, 77.

52. Menchaca, *Recovering History, Constructing Race*, 165. According to Menchaca, those born in Texas after 1827 were declared free people and those who came to Texas as slaves were to be emancipated within six months of their arrival (165).

53. James Brooks further notes, "Mexico attempted to stem the tide of American colonization [in Texas]—first by abolishing slavery in 1829, then by inviting free blacks and displaced southeastern Indian groups like the Texas Cherokees, Kickapoos, Seminoles, and black Seminole Maroons to settle on the frontier as military colonists," suggesting Texas had a more multiracial history than González's work acknowledges. "Served Well By Plunder," 67.

54. In *From Savage to Negro*, Baker states that in the paradigm of scientific racism, there was a "hierarchy of races beginning with the inferior savage and culminating with the civilized citizen" (29). In the case of blacks he traces this argument back to the social Darwinism that emerged in American ethnology and anthropology in the late nineteenth century. I argue that Pedro imagines himself to be above the Negro in the racial hierarchy and somewhat closer to being a civilized citizen.

55. Holland, *Raising the Dead*, 4.

56. Menchaca, *Recovering History, Constructing Race*, 1.

57. Kristeva, "The Powers of Horror," 234.

58. The law of the father is the first basis of the Oedipal complex, according to Freudian thought, where the father forbids the mother from being swept up in the child's desire for her. From this primary trauma of separation, many argue, secondary and third levels of abjection originate from that original scene of trauma based on the law of the father.

59. Ibid., 239.

60. González, *Dew on the Thorn*, 33.

61. González states that there was a yellow fever epidemic in the Rio Grande Valley in 1872, so the jaundice-like symptoms were probably not reflective of madness or melancholia (see "Social Life in Cameron, Starr and Zapata Counties").

62. González, *Dew on the Thorn*, 33.

63. Brodhead, *Cultures of Letters*, 18.

64. González, *Dew on the Thorn*, 33–34.

65. Herman, *Trauma and Recovery*, 33.

66. Ibid., 1.

67. Caminero-Santangelo, *The Madwoman Can't Speak*, 159.

68. Butler, *The Psychic Life of Power*, 25.

69. González, *Dew on the Thorn*, 32.

70. I use the term *queered* following Gil Z. Hochberg, where he describes the term as "stand[ing] as both an adjective—marking bodies, issues, desires, and so forth as queer—and as a verb, questioning normative articulations of the political and the very processes by which we determine the scope of what counts as political." "Introduction: Israelis, Palestinians, Queers: Points of Departure, 496." GLQ: *A Journal of Lesbian and Gay Studies*. Volume 16, Number 4, 2010.

71. Ibid.

72. Butler, *The Psychic Life of Power*, 23.

73. González, *Dew on the Thorn*, 32.

74. Ibid., 51.

75. Herman, *Trauma and Recovery*, 98.

76. González, *Dew on the Thorn*, 57–58.

77. Ibid., 58.

78. See Foucault, *Discipline and Punish*, 200–202.

79. González, "Social Life in Cameron, Starr and Zapata Counties," 75, 76.

80. Ibid., 69.

81. González, *Dew on the Thorn*, 112 (emphasis added).

82. González, *Dew on the Thorn*, 112; Anzaldúa, *Borderlands/La Frontera*, 54.

83. González, *Dew on the Thorn*, 112.

84. Anzaldúa, *Borderlands/La Frontera*, 42.

85. González, *Dew on the Thorn*, 112

86. For more on the shadow-beast, see Alarcón's reading of Anzaldúa in "Chicana Feminism," 373–75. Alarcón talks about the relationship between race and identity as refractory in Anzaldúa's work. This layering of names, having simultaneously no names and many names, identifies the multiple subject positions one occupies.

87. González, *Dew on the Thorn*, 112.

88. Ibid., 112–13 (emphasis added).

89. Holland, *Raising the Dead*, 65.

90. Ibid., 66.

91. González, *Dew on the Thorn*, 113.

92. As part of the Recovering the U.S. Hispanic Literary Heritage series, an edited collection of Jovita González's stories has been published under the title *The Woman Who Lost Her Soul and Other Stories*, with an introduction by Sergio Reyna. The same

narrative is also a separate chapter in *Dew on the Thorn*. Reyna does not address why he chose this particular "story" as the title of the collection.

93. González, *Dew on the Thorn*, 157.

94. Ibid., 157–58.

95. Kristeva, "The Powers of Horror," 232.

96. González, *Dew on the Thorn*, 158.

97. Alarcón, Kaplan, and Moallem, *Between Woman and Nation*, 6.

98. See Alarcón's discussion of Chicana identity as both reflective and refractory in "Chicana Feminism" (373).

99. González, *Dew on the Thorn*, 158 (all quotations).

100. Ibid., 159.

101. Ibid., 158.

102. Butler, *Psychic Life of Power*, 86–87.

103. González, *Dew on the Thorn*, 159–60.

104. Anzaldúa, *Borderlands/La Frontera*, 37–38.

105. González, *Dew on the Thorn*, 160.

106. See Saldívar-Hull, *Feminism on the Border*, especially the introduction.

107. González, *Dew on the Thorn*, 160.

108. Gupta, "Reincarnation of Souls and the Rebirth of Commodities," 190, 206.

109. González, *Dew on the Thorn*, 160.

110. Ibid.

111. Brady, *Extinct Lands, Temporal Geographies*, 6.

112. Cheng, *The Melancholy of Race*, 15.

113. Herman, *Trauma and Recovery*, 93.

114. González, *Dew on the Thorn*, 161.

115. Ibid., 164.

116. González, "Social Life in Cameron, Starr and Zapata Counties," 113.

117. I borrow this term from Doris Sommer's book *Foundational Fictions*, which casts the romance in Latin America as the novel of national consolidation through love plots and women's bodies. Also see Homi Bhabha's essay "DissemiNation," especially page 300, for a broader discussion of how exiles and displaced citizens contest seamless narratives of unity and progress.

PART TWO INTRODUCTION

1. Porfirio Díaz to Gen. Angel Martínez, Fondo Manuel González Ramírez, AGN, vol. 6, 135–36.

2. Drawing upon Foucault, Emma Pérez provides a useful definition of genealogies that I deploy in this chapter: "Genealogy as a method thematizes the body, power and social institutions where fictive truths and values are enacted upon the body" (*The Decolonial Imaginary*, 101).

3. Ibid., 7.

4. I use the term *Porfiriato* more as a time designation than as an expression of the political motives and policies of Porfirio Díaz.

5. Troncoso, *Las guerras con las tribus yaqui y mayo*, xii, quoting General Carrillo in a

dispatch to the secretary of war in 1882. Also used to describe hierarchies within the Mexican government, *subalterno* in this military context signals "subordinate" or "auxiliary." See "Sobre que los aministradores subalternos de rentas del estado," AGN, San Luis Potosí, Descretos y Circulares, C:561 E.8, Exp. 3, 1871.

6. In *Las guerras con las tribus yaqui y mayo*, Troncoso argues that wars with the Yaqui had been a consistent feature of Sonoran life from the 1740s onward.

7. Fontes's own research revealed a Yaqui woman warrior who defied Western gendered notions of what it means to be a soldier.

4. TRANSNATIONAL HISTORIES OF VIOLENCE

1. A fascinating feature of the archival materials is that the bulk comes from the Porfirio Díaz Papers and Secretaría de Relaciones Exteriores (Exterior Relations Secretariat) archives. If the Yaqui conflict was a problem internal to the Mexican nation, why was the department of external relations so invested in it? One could infer that Mexico treated the Yaqui as a foreign nation, simultaneously recognizing them and trying to squash their autonomy.

2. Perhaps Yaqui involvement in the campaigns against the French helped them solidify an abstract sense of nationalism apart from the Mexican nation, albeit in military service to the Mexican nation.

3. As late as 1905 the American secretary of commerce and labor forwarded letters to the secretary of exterior relations stating, "The Yaqui are now willing to make peace. They wish only assurance of immunity from arrest and permission to work un-molested. American interests in Sonora are large and increasing, and the Yaqui, who are the only good laborers in the country, are in demand. If the Mexican government is forced to carry out the policy of extermination which it professes, it will be a great blow to the development of the country" (SRE, L.E. 2250, vol. 1), 169–70.

4. Troncoso, *Las guerras con las tribus yaqui y mayo*, 64–65, citing the report of General Reyes in a government order dated May 29, 1881.

5. Reyes, May 29, 1881, quoted in ibid., 65.

6. See Ross and Smith, "American Studies without America," 310; and Ross, *Inventing the Savage*, 15.

7. The *New York Daily Tribune* for September 2, 1880, stated, "President Díaz has made a bold effort to satisfy three American companies which are seeking Mexican railroad grants, by tendering important privileges to each. Should his offers be ratified by the Mexican Congress and turned to account by the grantees, there will be, within a few years, a railroad company from the Mexican capital to the Pacific Coast and trunk lines to Texas and Arizona that will connect to the American System. Such facilities would add largely to our trade with Mexico, while they would increase the wealth and promote the tranquility of that country." (This article was found in the Mexican Secretaría de Relaciones Exteriores archives.) Also, a dinner held in New York City in 1905 in honor of the Mexican Minister to the United States, Matías Romero, entitled "A Mexican Night," featured a number of speeches declaring the Yaqui wars over and Sonora open for colonization and business development.

8. *Las Novedades*, "Construcción de ferrocarriles en México."

9. Concessions to the Southern Pacific: Concession of April 27, 1905.

10. Trennert, "The Southern Pacific Railroad of Mexico," 269.

11. On April 27, 1883, Romero wrote to Díaz in reference to the conflict: "It took place in the states of Sonora and Chihuahua, motivated by Apache invasions and Yaqui rebellion. It seemed convenient to transmit to this secretariat the partial publications here" (tenido lugar en los Estados de Sonora y Chihuahua, con motives de invasiones de Apaches y sublevación de Yaqui, me parece conveniente transmitir a esa Secretaría los partes publicados aquí). Archivo de Secretaría de Relaciones Exteriores.

12. Payne, *Unsettling Accounts*, 16.

13. Letter from Francisco Torres, AGN, vol. 1, Archivo Histórico Biblioteca y Museo de Sonora, Exp. 214.1, October 29, 1832, p. 134.

14. Written by Amuel E. Arvizo, vice governor of the state, ibid., March 31, 1833, p. 180.

15. General José Otero to Porfirio Díaz, CPD Leg. 10, 002991, May 3, 1885.

16. For more on the translation of langue on state-sponsored violence, see Frank Granziano, *Divine Violence*, esp. 33–35, where he argues that international and national relations require the transposition of mythological or mystifying discourses that justify violence into politically acceptable registers.

17. See CPD Leg. 10, 002386, attacks on March 15–17, 1885. Such attacks also prompted conspiracy theories about the next battles: "The latest news proves that they have invaded all the coast of this district [Guaymas] until they intercepted the road from Alamos to Fuerte, state of Sinaloa." (Las últimas noticias aseguran que han invadido toda la costa de aquel Distrito [Guaymas] hasta interceptar el camino de Álamos al Fuerte, Estado de Sinaloa.) Document after document goes into detail about these attacks on Guaymas.

18. See Lessie Jo Frazier's *Salt in the Sand: Memory, Violence and the Nation-state in Chile, 1890 to the Present*, esp. 85–90, for more on this point.

19. Pedro Hinojosa to Jose Carbó, CPD, Leg. 10, 12884, SRE, March 17, 1885.

20. Erickson, "Ethnic Places, Gendered Spaces," 6.

21. Alonso, *Thread of Blood*, 130.

22. In 1878 Carbó was named the military head of Sonora. In 1881, after ousting the governor of Sonora, Mariscal, he became the *jefe militar* of the first zone, which included Sonora, Sinaloa, and Baja California. Carbó fought mostly against Cajeme in the 1880s and was named jefe militar in Sonora from 1878 to 1885.

23. CPD, Leg. 10, 002385.

24. See Corral, *Obras históricas*, esp. 149–61.

25. The author of one of the most detailed military chronicles of the Yaqui Indian wars, Troncoso was a general in the Mexican army who also served as *jefe militar* for the first zone in the border region of Sonora and Arizona. Troncoso, *Las guerras con las tribus Yaqui y Mayo*, 61.

26. Scarry, *The Body in Pain*, 112.

27. Eng and Kazanjian, *Loss*, 2.

28. Many Yaquis considered Cajeme a traitor because he slaughtered his own people while serving in the Mexican military. His position in tribal history is a complex one.

29. Governor Coronel Luis E. Torres, November 1880, quoted in Troncoso, *Las guerras con las tribus Yaqui y Mayo*, 67–68.

30. When Cajeme's nephew was taken captive in 1885, along with his sister and other

family members, the documents gloss over what was done with the prisoners. See Capitán Celso Vega, AGS, May 30, 1885, pp. 276–78.

31. CPD, Leg. 12, 003111. April 12, 1887.

32. "Cajeme Was Shot." Governor Torres reported that he was shot, not executed, after a brief trial. For all intents and purposes, it was an execution by firing squad. This is one instance in which Torres used the U.S. press to diminish the barbarous image of Mexico.

33. Ángel Martínez to Porfirio Díaz, CPD, 003112–3113, April 21, 1887.

34. Eng and Kazanjian, Loss, 3.

35. Ángel Martínez to Porfirio Díaz, CPD, 004081, April 30, 1887.

36. Eng and Kazanjian, Loss, 4.

37. Carbó, quoted in Troncoso, Las guerras con las tribus Yaqui y Mayo, 121.

38. Cajeme was not the only figure of Yaqui leadership or autonomy, and to argue so would be misleading. Cajeme's case and his connection to the Mexican nation-state serve as a useful example of how fraught with complications the relationships between indigenous peoples and the government were.

39. CPD, Leg. 10, 002991.

40. Even Americans argued that the Yaqui had their own primitive form of nation that preexisted the Spanish colonization of Mexico. See the program for "A Mexican Night."

41. AGN, Fondo Manuel González Ramírez, January 16, 1827, p. 60; taken from Archivo Histórico Biblioteca y Museo de Sonora, Exp. 2 "214.1."

42. Roach, Cities of the Dead, 4.

43. Luis Emeterio Torres was a Mexican general who fought against the French and later became governor of Sonora from 1879 to 1911, the entire period of heightened military campaigns against the Yaqui. His rise to power was a direct result of his relationship to Porfirio Díaz, and through these ties to power he and his brother, Gen. Lorenzo Torres, appropriated Yaqui lands as their own. His family "annexed" extensive property in the conservative town of Torim, building a large house there. He and his brother worked together in trying to exterminate the Yaqui, push them off their land, and encourge the investement of multinational corporations in mining and farming in the Rio Yaqui. CPD, Leg. 10, 001164, February 26, 1885.

44. CPD Leg. 10, 00098.

45. CPD, Leg. 10, 000041.

46. Chato was one of Cochise's twelve captains. After he and his band were apprehended when they fled to Mexico in 1883, he aided General Crook in bringing his people to subjugation by commanding two hundred Indian scouts for the U.S. Cavalry.

47. Ambassador Matías Romero sent word from Washington, D.C., suggesting connections between the Yaqui and the Apache: "Telegrama: hayan guerra apaches intitularon curlandia y yaquis veneraron frugales festivales." This telegram doesn't make sense in translation, which makes one believe it is written in code. Curlandia refers to two places: the territory which is now Latvia and the Spanish word for Tobago. The translations would state "there will be Apache war that they are entitled to, and the Yaquis come in a thrifty celebration." It seems to indicate a quick and dirty war party

coming from far away. Matías Romero to Secretary of Foreign Relations, Archive of Mexican Foreign Relations, May 1, 1885.

48. "Report for the Month of April 1885," in Troncoso, *Las guerras con las tribus Yaqui y Mayo*, 115.

49. "Report for the Month of May 1885," in ibid., 115–16.

50. Ibid., 116–17.

51. Coronel Lorenzo García, in Troncoso, *Las guerras con las tribus Yaqui y Mayo*, 121.

52. SRE, May 1, 1885.

53. In this context, indigenismo represents a state ideology about Indians that advocates their oppression and even ethnocide that serves the nation.

54. Carbó to Díaz, CPD, Leg. 10, 003888, April 1, 1885.

55. CPD, Leg. 10, 003820, April 27, 1885.

56. Haas, "Fear in Colonial California," 3.

57. CPD, Leg. 10, 4639, May 22, 1885.

58. CPD, Leg. 10, 1164, February 26, 1885.

59. Logan was a principal stockholder in the Treadwell Mining Company. He was later discovered to be connected with many other mining propositions and was named in a Supreme Court lawsuit by John J. Gibbons, for embezzling $500,000 from the San Luis Mining Company. He was also found to be involved in multiple scams, including the conversion of the Forward Reduction Company, which was converted into a rice plantation scheme; the Sonora and Sinaloa Dvelopment Company; the Yaqui Land Company, an irrigation enterprise that capitalized $1½ in profits; the Santa Juliana Silver Mining Company; and the Deering Land and Water Company, which built reservoirs that did not hold water. "Mining Co. Looted, Director Declares," *New York Times*, May 28, 1907. Romero started his political career under Benito Juarez, serving as the secretary of treasury from 1876–1880 and again from 1892–1893. He later became the Mexican Minister to the United States in the mid 1880s.

60. "A Mexican Night," 51. Democratic Club of New York City. December 16, 1891. SRE holdings.

61. Cheng, *The Melancholia of Race*, 104.

62. A. E. Garcia, Mexican army coronel. FMGR Tomo 13.

63. Delay, *War of a Thousand Deserts*, xviii.

64. *Washington Post*, Febrary 20, 1885.

65. "Insurrectionary Yaqui Indians." *Washington Post*, February 23, 1885.

66. Guha, "The Prose of Counter-Insurgency," 343.

67. Brian Delay's chapter "The Politics of Vengance" in *War of a Thousand Deserts* nicely details the motives for Kiowa and Comanche raids in the 1830s and 1840s, suggesting that the laws of retaliation were about a politics of hurting Mexicans (135).

68. Ibid.

69. CPD, Leg. 003010, March 19, 1885.

70. Ibid. "Mi hermano Agustín reside en el Distrito de Álamos, en donde tiene a su cargo parte de los negocios de nuestra casa, y respecto de cual caísten sobrados motivos para tener que se intente en su contra." "My brother Agustín lives in the Alamos district, where he is in part in charge of the business of our house, with respect to everything that happens with motive against his person."

71. "El Sr. Aguilar fue diputada la Legislatura del Estado durante mi administra hecho sentir actos de encono y de venganza por parte de las autoridades de Sonora. El Sr. Muñoz desempeño la Prefectura del Distrito de Hermosillo en donde reside actualmente lo mismo que el Sr. Aguilar y se encuentra en idénticas condiciones que este Sr. habiéndose visto ambos repetidas veces muy seriamente amagados y obligados a abandonar a sus negocios y sus familias" (CPD, Leg. 10, 003010, March 19, 1885). "Mr Aguilar was deputy to the State Legislature during my administration and was made to feel anger and desire acts of retribution from the authorities of Sonora. Mr. Muñoz's performance as Prefect for the Hermosillo District where he currently resides as well as Mr. Aguilar is in the same conditions as this gentleman, having seen both several times very seriously threatened and forced to abandon their businesses and their families."

72. CPD, Leg. 10, 004393.

73. Ibid.

74. During this year there was an economic crisis in Sonora, making the number of troops occupying the region unstable: "Escasez de recursos que sufre el erario de [Sonora] que pone en la necesidad de manifestar . . . que el gobierno . . . dar de baja las fuerzas de Guardia nacional que están en campaña sobre los indios sublevados en los ríos Yaqui y Mayo, que exceden de los seincuentos hombres que paga la Federación en calidad de Agularidad" (L. and C. Herm, FMGR, AGN, vol. 5, July 23, 1885, p. 69). The campaign was actually suspended by Governor Ramón Corral on September 21, 1885, for lack of money (see FMGR, AGN, vol. 5, p. 145).

75. Ibid.

76. Ortiz is not the only one to accuse military officials in Sonora of using the Yaqui situation for their personal gain. See the letter to Ornelas from Capt. L. L. Goodrich, SRE, L.E. 2250, vol. 1, pp. 104–5: "I have never been convinced that President Díaz is, or has ever been, cognizant of the actual state of affairs as they exist, and the opinion I formed while observing the construction of malice in Sonora confirmed my previously formed opinion that a certain element was managing matters for personal gain. I was not alone in this belief, but found it to be so regarded by a great many of the better element of citizens."

77. Carbó was not the only military commander accused of back-door dealings during the Yaqui Indian wars. In a letter to Porfirio Díaz Luis Curiel states that a letter was sent to Juan A. Hernández, one of the people who pursued the Yaqui campaign in Sonora, to complain that Generals Ángel Martínez and Francisco Leyva y Carrillo "no hacen nada de aprovechar para sofocar el levantamiento de los indios. Advierte su ingerencia de Díaz es indispensable entre Corona, Galván y Tolentino en el asunto electoral" (CPD, Leg. 11, 8975–8977, August 4, 1886).

78. CPD Leg. 10, 003026, March 25, 1885.

79. SRE., L.E. 2250, vol. 1, 1906, p. 102,

80. "Letter from Mexican Consulate in San Francisco," SRE, L.E. 2250, vol. 1, July 25, 1905, 93–94; translated article from the *San Francisco Chronicle*. Spanish version: "Ha emprendido varias guerras de exterminio en las cuales mujeres y niños han entrado en la general carnicería. Esta política no ha hecho más que intensificar el odio de los Yaqui hacía los mexicanos, odio, que, los que han sobrevivido á esas guerras

sucesivas, han trasmitido á su progenie. Es bien claro que los Yaqui están tan lejos de ser disminuados hoy como nunca y que el problema de ponerlos bajo sujeción y de desarrollar los recursos del territorio que ocupan no está, al parecer, mas próximas á una solución hoy lo que estaba cuando la República declaró sobre su derecho y soberanía."

81. The Mexican anthropologist Guillermo Bonfil-Batalla calls such a practice ethnocide, not genocide, signaling the de-Indianization of Mexican populations that blocks the cultural continuity of a people as a historically differentiated group. I would argue that the violence evoked by the *carnicería* metaphor is an enactment of cultural and physical destruction of a historically differentiated racial and cultural group and that the Yaqui case is not ethnocide but genocide (*Mexico Profundo*, 17).

82. "Mexican Policy on Indian Issues," FMGR, AGN, vol. 3, pp. 49–52.

83. Ibid.

84. "La indole del pueblo y de la prensa americana" goes to great lengths to undermine credibility of the U.S. press by calling it "el pueblo de más novedades y más sensacionalista de la tierra" (SRE, L.E. 2250, vol. 2, years 1905–10, May 4, 1906, p. 168).

85. In 1906 (the year these photographs were published), sixty-two African Americans were lynched in the United States (see Tolnay and Beck, *Festival of Violence*, 115).

86. Kelly, "Red Raiders of Sonora's Hills."

87. The brothers, Enrique and Ricardo Flores Magón, were journalists and leaders of the Mexican Liberal Party (PLM) who advocated anarchy and the overthrow of the Díaz dictatorship. They are well known for their newspapers *Regeración* and *El Hijo de el Ahuizote*. From the offices of *El Hijo*, they hung a sign that said "the Constitution is Dead," which prompted the start of their many conflicts with the Porfiriato and their eventual exile to the United States.

88. This shift in punishment marked how "one no longer touched the body, or at least as little as possible, and only to reach something other than the body itself. It might be objected that imprisonment, confinement, forced labor, penal servitude, prohibition from certain areas, deportation—which have occupied so important a place in modern penal systems—are 'physical' penalties: unlike fines, for example, they directly affect the body" (Foucault, *Discipline and Punish*, 11).

89. SRE, L.E. 2250, vol. 3, document 296, May 19, 1906.

90. SRE, L.E. 2250, vol. 3, document 231, May 20, 1906 (newspaper unknown).

91. For an excellent treatment of how confessional accounts of state-sponsored violence unsettle truths put forth in national histories, see Payne, *Unsettling Accounts*, 7.

92. SRE, L.E. 2250, vol. 1, p. 94.

93. Archivo General del Gobierno del Estado de Sonora, vol. 2138, year 1906, Exp. No. 2, Reclamaciones de extranjeros.

94. For more on the Mexican government's preoccupation with the John Dwyer conspiracy theory, see SRE L.E. 2250, pp. 1–21.

95. SRE, L.E. 1038, Correspondence of Matías Romero, 1889–1899, 78. From the program for "A Mexican Night" in honor of Matías Romero, p. 53.

96. CPD, L12, 000382, January 22, 1887.

97. Even though there was a decisive battle at the Yaqui stronghold of Butachive on

May 11, 1886, in which roughly four thousand Yaqui were defeated, most of them were elderly, women, and children, and the peace lasted for only a few years. Cajeme and other leaders were not captured, signaling that the battles would continue without a peace treaty (see CPD, Leg. 11, 04638 and 04891).

98. SRE, L.E. 1038, Correspondence of Matías Romero, 1889—1899, 78. From the program for "A Mexican Night" in honor of Matías Romero, 54–55.

99. See CPD, Leg. 11, 004595, May 6, 1886, in which Porfirio Díaz wrote the following to Gen. Ángel Martínez in Baroyeca: "Explica que se verá la cantidad de terreno que corresponde a cado indio jefe de familia, tomando en cuenta los hijos que tenga capaces de trabajar."

100. CPD, Leg. 11, 007857, July 1, 1887.

101. AGN, FMGR, vol. 16, 1903, p. 234.

102. AGN, FMGR, vol., 19, March 4, 1905, p. 207: "Seguimos recogiendo a los Yaqui gran cantidad de armas y municiones de guerra, y con esta sola medida creímos fundada nuestras esperanzas de que muy pronto terminar a tan ingrata campaña; pero sucede que en las poblaciones del territorio de Arizona mas inmediatas a Sonora, los referidos indios se proveen de armas y parque y se vuelvan de nuevo para cometer sus depredaciones nadie ignora la gran cantidad de indios que hay en la poblaciones fronterizas a que me refiero, y todos saben que no van por falta de trabajo de aquí pues, lo tienen con mucha demanda por ende bien retribuido. . . . Antes del último periodo de la campaña, los Yaqui criminales se ocultaban confundiéndose con los Yaqui trabajadores de las Haciendas; pero ahora que se les persigue allí mismo emigran del Estado y se van al territorio de Arizona no solo a proveerse de armas y municiones como digje antes, sino a buscar allí un refugio, dejando burlada de ese modo de la persecución." 1906 was the year when telephonic communication was used. See FMGR, vol. 22, esp. pp. 123, 164.

103. Telegram from Prefect Jesús Cano to the Sonoran secretary of state, Altar, May 15, 1906. FMGR, vol. 22, p. 153.

104. Letter from the Phoenix consulate to the secretary of foreign relations, SRE L.E. 2250, vol. 1, October 3, 1905, 118.

105. See AGN, FMGR, vol. 18, p. 45, in which a telegram from Mina Dos Naciones warned the Sonoran government that twenty Yaqui were circulating in the area in search of water. Jesús Romero also reports from Rancho Viejo in Zubiate that he has discovered the tracks of about one hundred Yaqui near the rancho and thought it is the same group of Yaqui that fought Governor Izabál a month earlier (AGN, FMGR, vol. 18, p. 74).

106. Letter from Florencia Robles, municipal president of Rayón, to the Sonoran secretary of state, AGN, FMGR, vol. 18, p. 74. In correspondence from June 7, 1904, the secretary of state requested that the same Yaqui from Hacienda La Galera be apprehended, remitted to the capital, and treated like the others (AGN, FMGR, vol. 18, p. 81).

107. See AGN, FMGR, vol. 18, p. 91.

108. See AGN, FMGR, vol. 14, esp. pp. 66, 98, and 190 (as 1902 was a major year where municipal police departments in Sonora began to increase the apprehension of Yaqui) and AGN, FMGR, vol. 22, p. 55, introducing the Arizona Rangers as part of the means of "vigilen aquella frontera."

109. This was around the time when the U.S. Immigration Service was formed in Arizona. See documents from SRE stating that from 1905 to 1910 Yaqui caught buying guns in Arizona were deported to Hermosillo and then to Yucatán to work in the henequen plantations.

110. SRE, L.E. 2250, vol. 1, p. 207.

111. AGN, FMGR, vol. 22, Dispatch 23, April 7. 1906, p. 45.

112. AGN, FMGR, vol. 25, November 3, 1906, p. 20.

113. Ibid., 22.

114. During this time, roughly 1880–1910, photo documentation of Indians in Mexico is quite ambiguous as well. C. B. Waite's series of photographs of Indians in Mexico entitled "Retrato Étnico" spans the period from 1901 to 1910 but labels only Indians from Oaxaca, Amatecas, and the Tarahumaras of Chihuahua by their tribal affiliations (see photos 1, 8, 11, 30, and 87, among others). The majority of the photos are labeled generically "Tipos Mexicanos, nativas" or "ciquilla indígena" (137). Photo 31 is labeled "Belleza Indígena," and shows a woman who could be mestiza, Mexican, or Indian seated in portrait position. Thus, the Waite collection reflects a similar ambiguity about phenotype and the ability to visually distinguish Indians and Mexicans in the late nineteenth century and early twentieth. "Native" in this particular photo archive signals indigenous, much like the U.S. designation Native American. Photo 79 from 1908 of "Nativa de Nuevo México, con pequeño cargado en la espalda," proves this point, making the question of indigenous identity quite ambiguous in the Mexican context (AGN, Fototeca: Instrucción Pública y Bellas Artes, Serie Propiedad Artística y Literaria).

115. SRE, L.E. 2250, vol. 1, 207.5.

116. The U.S. Border Patrol (founded as a government agency in 1924) was informally organized in 1904. It consisted of mounted patrols that unevenly regulated supposedly illegal crossings and coincided with the problems that arose from organized illegal Chinese immigration after the restriction laws of 1888 and the extension in 1904 of the Chinese Exclusion Act (Lytle-Hernández, "Entangling Bodies and Borders," 19–20). These mounted anti-Chinese patrols in addition to the Yaqui Indian wars and smuggling of arms from Arizona into Sonora form the basis of early border patrol history in the Immigration Services Agency. For a detailed study of this history, see ibid.

117. SRE, L.E. 2250, vol. 2, April 10, 1906, 52.

118. See document 218, L.E. 2250, January 15, 1906.

119. SRE, L.E. 2250, 260, March 8, 1906.

120. SRE, L.E. 2250, January 15, 1906, 233.

121. On February 25, 1905, the *San Francisco Call* reported that minor depredations had been consistently reported in the area for six months, and on February 24, the Sonoran government began punishing Yaqui for murdering prominent Americans. In the same article, the lynching of six Yaqui chiefs is reported.

122. SRE, L.E. 2250, vol. 1, 250, February 10, 1905.

123. Ibid.

124. A report of March 8, 1906, from the Tucson consulate suggests further racial or ethnic conspiracy around the selling of arms: "Having acquired reports that the

Chinese shops were selling arms and ammunition to the Indians, violating the provisions of the District Attorney, the detective went to Meyer street of this city, where the Chinese market was located; but could not find any sales among the 11th and the 20th, as well of records of what was previously sold" (Arturo Elías to the SRE, SRE, L.E. 2250, vol. 1). Given the racist assumptions in Tucson about the inferiority of Chinese immigrants (which in some respects mirrored attitudes toward American Indians), their social and economic isolation as merchants, and their somewhat liminal sense of citizenship, it is not surprising the Chinese were believed to be selling arms to Indians. See Delgado, "In the Age of Exclusion: Race, Region, Identity and the Making of the Arizona/Sonora Borderlands, 1863–1943," which complicates this idea by showing how Tucsonense Chinese married into and created alliances not with Indians but with Tucson Hispanos. People who were at the edges of the social and economic circles, like Indians and other Asian immigrants, were engaging in commerce because no one else would. In order to turn a profit during this period, many found it simple and almost necessary to economic survival to sell and trade with Indians, even if such activities brought charges of a racial conspiracy. Arizona Mexicans engaged in this commerce as well. On the other side of Mexican American relations with Yaqui Indians were those who engaged in state-sponsored violence in alliance with Mexico. The governor of Sonora named a Mexican American man named Lorenzo Biodio, an American citizen born in Tucson but a vecino in Guaymas, as leader of an auxiliary force of Pima Indians and Mexican soldiers "a la persecución y castigo de los bandoleros yaquis." AGN, FMGR, vol. 22, 100–101, May 29, 1906.

125. CPD, Leg. 12, 001276. October 29, 1886.

126. "En el estado de Colima existen algunos fincas de campo que tienen infinidad de ranchos casi despoblados y sin explotación, alguna por falta de brazos . . . son personas que llevan conmigo muy buenos relaciones de amistad" (CPD, Leg. 12, 001276, October 29, 1886.

127. Hu-DeHart, *Yaqui Resistance and Survival*, 181, citing INAH reports by Governor Izabál from 1903 to 1907, 181. An account from 1905 says that at the beginning of the wars in 1885 there were twelve thousand Yaqui, a number which had been reduced by half in 1905 (AGN, Gobernación, Exp. 12, Foja 2, April 6, 1905).

128. AGN FMGR, vol. 4, p. 212.

129. Troncoso, *Las guerras con las tribus yaqui y mayo*, 84.

130. AGS. Tomo 2130, 1906, Exp. 7.

131. Beck, "Developing a Voice," 118. Beck argues that urban migration of Indians is not a twentieth-century phenomenon. He describes a series of U.S. policies that created the boom in urban Indian populations, using Chicago as a case study.

132. For an excellent example of urban Mexican Indian elites, see Lomnitz, *Death and the Idea of Mexico*, which outlines how elite Indian families in Mexico City participated in Spanish and Mexican constructions of death in ritual public culture.

133. CPD, Leg. 11, 009130, July 22, 1896.

134. AGN, FMGR, vol. 15, December 1902, Documents 215—20, show a distribution of the prisoners by age, gender, and passive or rebellious status, illustrating the state's need to identify who was being sent to Yucatán and why. "Lista de Yaqui prisioneros" is

document 215; 216 is "Lista de muchachos que se van a deportar"; 217 is "Lista de Yaqui mujeres que se van a deportar"; 218 is "Lista de Yaqui rebeldes que se van a deportar"; 219 is "Lista de Yaqui rebeldes"; 220 is "Lista de niños Yaqui"; 221 is "Lista de familias Yaqui. Se investiga si tienen maridos en la cárcel pública."

135. AGN, FMGR, vol. 15, pp. 158–59, 161.

136. Ibid., pp. 162–69.

137. AGN, FMGR, vol. 14, 1902, p. 18.

138. Prefect of Guaymas A. E. García, AGN, FMGR, vol. 22, pp. 64–65, October 21, 1904.

139. "Micronutrient Intervention in Brazil," clinical study retrieved from http://clinical trials.gov/ (accessed November 2, 2008).

140. DeJong, " 'Unless They Are Kept Alive,' " 263.

141. Quoted in DeJong, ibid.

142. AGN, FMGR, vol. 22, pp. 83–84, 90–92.

143. Archivo General del Gobierno del Estado de Sonora, vol. 2138, Year 1906, Exp. 2, p. 5.

144. Ibid.

145. Ibid.

146. AGN, FMGR, vol. 15, p. 214, shows a new category: *niños de pecho*, or babies who were still being breast-fed. Of the ten women who were accounted for in this particular list, six were breast-feeding infants. The Mexican government did not separate these women from their infants, perhaps because they were being taken away from their cultural land base in Sonora.

147. AGN, FMGR, vol. 12, p. 215.

148. One could, however, argue that these were pseudonyms intended to deflect attention away from insurgent family members. AGN, FMGR vol. 15, p. 216.

149. AGN, FMGR, vol. 15, p. 217.

150. AGN, FMGR, vol. 15, p. 215.

151. AGN, FMGR, vol. 15, pp. 217–19, 226, 228.

152. AGN, FMGR, vol. 15, p. 230.

153. Butler, *Psychic Life of Power*, 7.

154. AGN, FMGR, vol. 22, March 24, 1906, p. 18. Ayuntamiento de Río Chico Número 133. Concentración Río Chico, March 24, 1906, El Presidente Municipal C. Tona al Prefecto del Distrito Álamos.

155. Scarry, *The Body in Pain*, 112.

156. AGN, FMGR, vol. 22, March 24, 1906, pp. 18–19. Ayuntamiento de Río Chico Número 133. Concentración Río Chico, March 24, 1906, El Presidente Municipal C. Tona al Prefecto del Distrito Álamos.

157. Graziano, *Divine Violence*, 96.

158. Ibid., 97.

159. Ibid.

160. Hu-DeHart (*Yaqui Resistance and Survival*, 181) argues that women and children were spared deportation until 1907, but the documents cited herein suggest that deportation of women and children occurred as early as 1902, when the state policy of mass deportations began.

161. Archivo General del Gobierno de Sonora, vol. 2138, Year 1906, Exp. No 2.

162. Ibid., p. 2.

163. Ibid., 3. My professional translator refused to translate this passage about torture. This refusal to engage with the language and actual practice of torture is something I take up in the postscript, which addresses the unspeakable nature of violence.

164. Soto, "Seeing Photographs through Borderlands (Dis)order," 429.

165. Ibid., 430.

166. AGN, FMGR, vol. 15, p. 171.

167. "En completo estado de descomposición, adviertióle que fueron cruelmente martirizados y muertos a puñaladas y palos; que para poder traer sus restos fue necesario cremaros de acuerdo" (AGN, FMGR, vol. 25, October 12, 1904, pp. 62–63).

168. AGN, FMGR, vol. 25, October 15, 1904, pp. 63–64.

169. AGN, FMGR, vol. 25, December 27, 1904, pp. 68–69.

170. Brooks, *Captives and Cousins*, 214.

171. For more on the ideas of costs and profits in the undertaking of violence, see Chafee, *The Economics of Violence in Latin America*, esp. chap. 7.

172. CPD, Leg. 10, 000098, June 1884.

173. AGN, FMGR, telegram February 20, 1906, pp. 289–90.

174. Interestingly, most of the government documents cite the rounding up of women and children from the haciendas. See figure 1 in AGN, FMGR, vol. 15, pp. 140–41.

175. The language of Yaqui enslavement, a terminology coined by the Magonista-aligned U.S. journalist Kenneth Turner, is a huge point of contention in Raquel Padilla Ramos's book *Progreso y libertad*. She goes to great lengths to problematize how the Yaqui situation was not necessarily slavery but a combination of peonage, prisoner-of-war status, and a status as victims of progress and order.

176. For a history of the Yaqui deportation, see Turner, *Barbarous Mexico*.

177. Hu-DeHart, *Yaqui Resistance and Survival*, 180.

5. STRIPPING THE BODY OF FLESH

1. Spivak, *Critique of Postcolonial Reason*, 116; see also Althusser, "Ideology and Ideological State Apparatuses."

2. Spivak, *Critique of Postcolonial Reason*, 117.

3. Interview with Montserrat Fontes, June 23, 2001, Glendale, Calif. Fontes explained that the Yaqui elders allowed her to peruse their records for a few hours only and to use one piece of paper and a pencil. Their skepticism and guarding of history are no doubt influenced by their historically hostile relationship with mestizo Mexicans and outsiders trying to take their resources.

4. These individuals aren't referred to as prisoners of war until 1902, when the number of prisoners increased exponentially. See correspondence between Gen. Luis E. Torres and Governor Izabal (AGN, FMGR, P 139–1, November 1902), in which Torres calls women and children detained in a Guaymas hospital and holding house "prisioneros de guerra."

5. *Cultural Critique* 12 (Fall 1989): 57–87.

6. Scarry, *The Body in Pain*, 50–51.

7. The corrido is a folk song form of popular ballad that originated in the 1700s in Mexico. It usually describes some kind of conflict and reslolution, most often commemorating battles, violence, and family history. In a Chicana/o studies context,

corridos are often studied for their oral historical preservation of experiences of Mexicana/os living on the U.S.–Mexico border. A new form of corrido has emerged in the last ten years, the narcocorrido, which details the pitfalls and violence of narcotrafficking across the U.S.–Mexico border. McDowell, *Poetry and Violence*.

8. Fontes, *Dreams of the Centaur*, 17–18. (Hereafter cited by page number in the text.)

9. Interview, June 23, 2001.

10. Brady, *Extinct Lands, Scarred Bodies*, 174.

11. Pérez, *Decolonial Imaginary*, xvi.

12. Pérez draws on Joan Scott's *Gender and the Politics of History*. Scott suggests that processes be studied over origins, and Pérez takes up that thread to expand her thesis about archeology based on Foucault's work. The pairing of the two concepts allows Pérez to propose, "Archeology asks that disciplines be exploded, opened up, confronted, inverted, and subverted; genealogy recognizes how history has been written upon the body" (*Decolonial Imaginary*, xv–xvi).

13. It was common practice to separate male and female Yaqui prisoners and deportees. According to one source, prisoners were sorted by gender, age, and degree of hostility toward the Mexican government (see AGN Fondo Manuel González Ramírez, vol. 14, December 1902, pp. 215–21).

14. "Los auxiliares Francisco Campillo y Adelaido Mundo que condujeron a esa Capital algunas indias yaquis prisoneras," AGN, FMGR, vol. 13: Guaymas, June 9, 1901; R. F. Nieto to Secretary of State, p. 20; and *Buffalo Express*, January 19, 1900: "Yes, the Yaquis have demonstrated that they are unconquerable. . . . The revolution of the Yaqui Indian nation in the state of Sonora has had various months of progress, and we assume proportions that will determine the resolution that the Yaqui will not submit any longer to the Mexican government. . . . The Yaquis can't tolerate more time with Mexican army in Sonora. The said regiment is all criminals. The Mexican government, in their hatred of the United States, has not been helping the Yaquis and since then a number of them have fallen with injuries and calamities" (AGN FMGR vol. 9, p. 146).

15. *Bartolina* soldiers were prisoners who, in exchange for entering the service of the army, had their prison sentences commmuted. President Díaz instituted this program in the 1880s to increase the size of the army for the specific purpose of fighting the Yaqui and patrolling the frontier states.

16. Fontes, 203.

17. See Del Castillo, "Malintzín Tenepal," and D. González, "Malinche Triangulated, Historically Speaking," both of which address the male nationalist interpretations the figure of the indigenous La Malinche as a whore, passive mother, and race traitor.

18. Fontes, 204.

19. Troncoso, *Las guerras con las tribus Yaqui y Mayo*, 36.

20. Fontes, 203.

21. Ibid., 204.

22. Ibid., 204.

23. CPD 002385, Carbó to Díaz, March 19, 1885.

24. Fontes, 204.

25. *Harper's Weekly*, May 2, 1908.

26. Their loan resulted in pay of $.75 pesos. AHGES Tomo 1983, Expediente 3. "Municipio de Banamichi, Distrito de Arizpe. Septeiembre 18, 1905.

27. Hartman, *Scenes of Subjection*, 50.

28. Fontes, 205.

29. Scarry, *The Body in Pain*, 21.

30. The archetype of "the" maligned indigenous woman that Norma Alarcón and Gloria Anzaldúa describe is remembered, according to Alarcón, "by invoking the 'dark Beast' within and without, which many have forced us to deny, the cultural and psychic dismemberment that is linked to imperialist racist and sexist practices are brought into focus" ("Chicana Feminism," 251). See also *Borderlands/La Frontera*. Following Alarcón, I put "the" in quotation marks here both to signal a plurality and to question the universal figure of a singular indigenous female subject. Although this archetype has a useful theoretical currency for reading Chicana literature and understanding how these tropes reinforce particular ideas about indigenous women more broadly, the same tropes have been appropriated by the uncritical, ahistorical neo-nationalism of lo indio/la india discussed in the introduction.

31. "En todos los Distritos del Estado se están llevando á cabo los atentados mas escandalosos y por desgracia la campaña contra los Yaquis, . . . a quien todo Sonora lo juzca, por sus hechos, capaz de cometer las mas infames atrocidades" (CPD 003023, May 25, 1885).

32. AHS, tomo 1899, 1904: "Exhortos relativos á la aprehensión de criminals dirijidos por los Jueces de Distrito."

33. Essentially, they were "patrimonial troops, . . . [who] were under direct control of Díaz: most of them were volunteers, recruited from the peasant and artisan classes of Central Mexico. Initially used to subject regional caudillos to central authority, the Rurales were subsequently deployed to make Mexico 'safe' for capitalism" (Alonso, *Thread of Blood*, 130).

34. Ibid.

35. *Harper's Weekly*, May 2, 1908.

36. SRE 15–8–113, January 1900.

37. Puar, *Terrorist Assemblages*, 80.

38. Fontes, 161.

39. Scarry, *The Body in Pain*, 27.

40. Fontes, 161.

41. See FMGR correspondence, vols. 20–25, which contains numerous accounts of Governor Izabal leaving his office as governor for weeks at a time to chase Yaquis in the Sierra Madre. According to Raquel Padilla Ramos, he, along with the Torres brothers, in particular, Luis, the Mexican vice president and former governor of Sonora Ramón Corral, and the Yucatecan governor and hacendado Olegarario Molina, formed a triangle of power that increased the wealth and power of the elite through the exploitation of hunted and deported Yaquis (Padilla, *Fin del sueño yaqui*, iii, 63–64).

42. "Finalmente supe que le había llegado su turno en la tortura a Luis Pérez, que se le habían atado los manos a un poste, y que había sido tenido boca abajo al rayo del sol, atando una cuerda alrededor de sus pies, cuyos extremos fueron ligados dos veces al

poste, y los soldados, por orden del Gobernador, trataban la cuerda por los extremos, quedando Pérez de esta manera ceñido, en horrible agonía y mómetro y observé que marcaba 100 grados a la sombra; durante más de dos horas pudieron escucharse sus gritos de dolor por toda la ciudad de San Mariscal, pues la tortura tenía lugar en el centro de la cuidad. . . . Se me informó que Perez había perdido la razón, a juzgar por sus actos, y que la tortura había terminado. . . . Uno por uno de los peones reunidos, supe, sufrió igual tortura, la que se prolongó hasta que se les puso en condiciones de decir todo lo que se quisiera de ellos . . . El Gobernador que ordenara se les fusilara, para que terminaran sus sufrimientos, y aun suplicaba a los soldados que estaban inmediatos que los mataran pidiéndoles que tuvieran piedad y les ahorraran aquel padecimiento" ("Informe Extrañjero," Consulado de Los Estados Unidos, Nogales, Sonora, Mexico, FMGR, vol. 18, September 22, 1904, p. 185).

43. Foucault, *Discipline and Punish*, 153.

44. In the data set I collected from two Mexican archives, AGS and AGN, the eighteen hundred deportation and incarceration cases of Yaqui men, women, and children between 1902 and 1907 represents just over 10 percent of the population that was removed, eliminated, and most likely killed en route to henequen plantations in Yucatán, laboring in Yucatán, or trying to escape.

45. "De cuyo momento quiso aprovechar al prisionero para buscar con la fuga su libertad; pero Alferez Co. Pablo Murillo le dió alcance tenido que quitarle la vida—por repelar la resistencia que hizo." ("Campana contra los yaquis y los mayos. Un sello con el Escudo Nacional que dice: Rimera Zona Militar General en Gefe de Coronel F. Miranda y Castro," Fondo Manuel González Ramírez, vol. 5, Archivo General del Gobierno del Estado de Sonora, 1885, p. 36).

46. Fontes, 151.

47. Ibid., 165.

48. Scarry, *The Body in Pain*, 109.

49. Hu-DeHart, *Yaqui Resistance and Survival*, 133–34, 35–36.

50. Tetibiate was identified as the Yaqui leader by Mexican officials and blamed for breaking the peace, but in reality the Yaqui ways of warfare and tribal structure had several bands of warriors and families with communal leadership, a fact the Spanish or Mexicans never completely understood.

51. "Díganos ahora: lo que queremos es que salgan los blancos y las tropas. Sí salen por las buenas, entonces hay paz; sino entonces declaramos la guerra. Porqué la paz que firmamos en Ortiz, fue con la condición de que se fueran tropas y blancos, y eso todavía no lo cumplen, al contrario, en lugar de cumplir fueron a quitar las armas. De suerte que ahora son Ustedes del todo negocia y nosotros tendrémos la culpa de toda la desgracia que haya" ("Carta enviada por los yaquis al General Luis Torres," FMGR, vol. 9, p. 81).

52. SRE 2250, vol. 3, p. 2.

53. But what gave rise to the three-second water cure was not the animosities expressed in the Spanish-American War itself but the fact that Filipino and American ideas of what should happen to the country were at odds. Initially, the Filipinos welcomed U.S. military officials but later became suspicious of them, to the point where in 1889, just days before the U.S. Senate was to ratify the treaty with Spain that would have

secured the Philippines as a U.S. colony, U.S. soldiers fired on Filipino soldiers. To "liberate" the island's population from the military regime established by the former general Emilio Aguinaldo, U.S. forces began a counterinsurgency campaign against suspect Filipinos that included torture. A letter by A. F. Miller, of the Thirty-Second Volunteer Infantry Regiment, published in the *Omaha World-Herald* in May 1900, describes subjecting a prisoner to the "water cure": "Now, this is the way we give them the water cure," he explained. "Lay them on their backs, a man standing on each hand and each foot, then put a round stick in the mouth and pour a pail of water in the mouth and nose, and if they don't give up pour in another pail. They swell up like toads. I'll tell you it is a terrible torture" (Kramer "The Water Cure: Debating Torture and Counterinsurgency—A Century Ago," *New Yorker*, February 25, 2008). Another soldier described a similar process, but the throat was held closed so that water could not pass into the stomach, then the water was forced out of the victim, either by hand or foot (ibid.).

54. Fontes, 223–24.

55. Ibid., 172.

56. Hartman, *Scenes of Subjection*, 76.

57. Fontes, 177.

58. Ibid., 178.

59. Ruiz, "Teki Lenguas del Yolotzin," 357.

60. Ibid., 360.

61. Foucault, *Discipline and Punish*, 138.

62. Fontes, 179.

63. Ibid., 181.

64. Momaday, *The Man Made of Words*, 114.

65. Fontes, 182.

66. AGS Tomo 1983, Expediente 3. "Municipio de Banámichi, Policia Rural," September 24, 1905.

67. Foucault, *Discipline and Punish*, 135.

68. Brown, *Trauma: Explorations in Memory*, 101.

69. Ibid., 102–3.

70. Fontes, 189, emphasis added.

71. Caruth, *Trauma: Explorations in Memory*, 10.

72. Ibid., 5.

73. In his essay on racial memory "An American Land Ethic" Momaday writes, "There was no distinction between the individual and racial experience, even as there was none between the mythical and historical. Both were realized in one memory, and that was of the land" (211). Momaday's recollections of his grandmother's relationship to the landscape and collective memory lend themselves to the discussion of collective memory as it is linked to both land and flesh. Stripping away flesh is like taking away one's individual humanity. However, Momaday argues, these larger connections to collective memory, to racial memory, to the landscape, to something bigger than individual experience allow memory to imbue the trauma or everyday stories of living with a significance that can distance the individual from his own body and connect the self and memory to a larger collective body.

74. Cantu, "Hybrid Resolutions," 144.

75. See FMGR, vol. 6, January 1886, pp. 10–25, and vol. 11, April, May, June 1900, p. 75.

76. Fontes, 189.

77. Ibid., 185.

78. In "Women and the Mafia: The Power of Silence and Memory," Renate Siebert makes several compelling arguments about masculinity, femininity, memory, and mob violence that are embedded in unspoken social codes. The wall of silent complicity is the ultimate social contract, where people are expected under any and all circumstances to maintain silence about violence and death.

79. Fontes, 193.

80. Foucault, *Discipline and Punish*, 144.

81. Fontes, 199.

82. "Hay dos inditos uno de 3 meses y otro de 4 años y dos inditas de 3 años" ("niños Yaquis prisoneros," AGN, FMGR, vol. 13, p. 80). A few days earlier three Yaqui women and four children were picked up and brought to the prefect of Hermosillo, A. G. Hernández, and "estan a disposicion de Ud. [Governor Luis Torres]" (AGN, FMGR, vol. 13, October 8, 1901, p. 78.

83. Fontes, 195.

84. Troncoso argues in a dispatch to the secretary of navy and war that "ever since the boy can understand the mother, she turns him against the Yori (the white), telling him 'The Yori will eat you.'" ("Desde que el niño puede comprender a la madre, esta lo amenaza con el Yori (el blanco) diciéndole": "te come el Yori"; p. 36). This directive is part of a larger government discourse of social pathology that justifies state-sponsored violence. Also see Hu-DeHart, *Yaqui Resistance and Survival*, 151.

85. Ibid., 152.

86. Foucault, *Discipline and Punish*, 143.

87. Fontes, 265.

88. McMillen, "The Red Man and the White Plague," 608.

89. DeJong, " 'Unless They Are Kept Alive,' " 256.

90. Ibid., 261.

91. I draw this point from James H. Jones, *Bad Blood: The Tuskegee Syphilis Experiment*. Jones argues that the denial of medication to African American male syphilis patients for the purpose of scientific study was part of a larger social effort to isolate these patients in the prison of their sickness and thus to make the ill stand in for the entire race, which in turn took away any possibility of an urgent response to change their conditions (see 25–28).

92. Both Turner and Fontes use the term *slaves* to describe the deported Yaquis. Padilla Ramos is a bit more cautious and avoids the term because she found evidence of Yaquis who were in fact compensated for their labor on the henequen plantations (Padilla Ramos. *Fin del Sueño Yaqui*).

93. "Algunos de los indios llegaron aquí en pésimas condiciones de salud, al grado que había unos que apenas podían dar paso" (quoted in Ramos Padilla, *Fin del Sueño Yaqui*, 84–85).

94. Ibid., 85.

95. "Es preciso hacerlo así porque no se logra reprimir a esos rebeldes ni tenerlos en

quietud, sufriendo la población pacífica asesinatos, robos y vejámenes de todas clases. Es duro pero necesario lo que se hace con los yaquis, desalojándolos de us terreno y confinándolos donde no pueden hacer mal, antes que fusilarlos en monton" (*El Diario Popular*, March 24, 1908, quoted in Ramos Padilla, *Fin del sueño yaqui*, 85).

96. Gustavo Vega y Gil Rojas a secretario, April 30, 1908 (quoted ibid., 97–98).

97. Fontes, 232.

98. Ibid., 217.

99. Ramos Padilla, *Fin del sueño yaqui*, 99–100.

100. Fontes, 219.

101. Dumond, "Talking Crosses of Yucatan," 291.

102. Francisco Bulues says that even in 1899, when the Yucatecan henequen industry was starting to peak, Mayans could be part of the "well paid pueblos but often don't want to work this war [and not working] will not allow them to defend their land" (AGN, Fondo Francisco Bulues, Caja 12, Exp. 11, p. 13).

103. Colección Lourdes Martínez Guzman, AGN, Colección de Archivos Incorporados, Colección Fotografico Hacienda Henequera de Yucatán, has twenty-nine photos (dating ca. 1900–1910) of Hacienda Konchen, a typical hacienda owned by Martínez Paredes, which show the expansive, contained, and isolated nature of that plantation. Most henequen plantations had a *casa de máquinas* (photo 1), a chapel, a park, and a main house where the owners of the plantation worshipped, spent their leisure time, and lived (photo 2). They also had extensive train tracks for transporting the henequen within the hacienda and the rigid leaves of henequen (photos 4 and 6) and for *el tranvía*, a trolley to transport the hacendado and his guests around the expansive property (photo 21). All the photos of leisure activities are of "light-skinned" Mexicans or Yucatecos with their clearly Mayan servants, as these photos were taken before the arrival of the Yaquis (photos 9, 10, 16, 17, 18, 19). Overall, the photo collection shows a vast distribution and monitoring of space that made it almost impossible for workers to escape the surveillance of the henequen plantations. Conspicuously absent from these photos, which constitute a small selection from the large Martínez Guzmán collection housed in Yucatán, are any images of Yaqui workers. All the workers in these photos appear to be Mayan.

104. Fontes, 227–28.

105. AGN, Fondo Francisco Bulues, Caja 12, Exp. 11, p. 5.

106. AGN, Fondo Francisco Bulues, Caja 12, Exp. 11, p. 17.

107. AGN, Fondo Francisco Bulues, Caja 12, Exp. 11, pp. 14, 9.

108. "El Articulo de Sr. Consul de EE.UU. en Yucatan," December 3, 1921.

109. "Los Límites de nuestro progreso," AGN, Fondo Francisco Bulues, Caja 12, Exp. 11, p. 18.

110. AGN, Fondo Francisco Bulues, Caja 12, Exp. 11, p. 19. Bulues actually uses the word "libre cambio" to describe the free trade market he desires, which is fascinating because most people think of free trade as an issue of the late twentieth century, not the nineteenth. But even Bulues realizes its limits: "El libre cambio no es posible sobre todo productos y razones politicas, sucesos de los ricos proprietarias del territorio encima," because power can be ceded in such an agreement.

111. Fontes, 228.

112. Ibid., 228.
113. Taylor, "Double Bind," 714.
114. Fontes, 239.
115. Butler, *Psychic Life of Power*, 9.
116. Ibid.
117. Fontes, 238.
118. Taylor, "Double Bind," 720.
119. Fontes, 239–40.
120. SRE 15–8–113, p. 9.
121. SRE 15–8–113, p. 9.
122. SRE 15–8–113, pp. 9, 12.
123. Hu-DeHart, *Yaqui Resistance and Survival*, 143.
124. Fontes interview, June 26, 2001.
125. Troncoso, *Las guerras con las tribus Yaqui y Mayo*, 286.
126. "Los indios rebeldes reconocían como Jefe supreme y que fué sin duda, el alma de la rebelión. Además, se les hicieron como 1000 prisioneros, mujeres y niños en gran parte, de los cuales, unos murieron en el camino de Mazacoba al Tetacombiate" (287).
127. In the FMGR source, the article is a translated copy in Spanish of an article originally published in the *Saint Louis Democrat* in English. I did not seek out the original English version of the article because I did not want to have the Spanish intent of the translation influenced by the English. "Cuenta de un plan proyectado para soprender algunos de los secretos de los indios yaquis, consistiendo este en la apprehensión de un sacerdote de apellido Beltran y de cuatro monjas josefinas que habían residido por varios años entre los indios yaquis, siendo muy partidario de ellos. Al ser examinados, declararon que sabían de una reunión que los yaquis habían para llevar a cabo un plan diabólico—de ataque simultáneo contra Potam, Torin, Mediano y Cocorit con mil hombres para cada población en determinado día y ahora esta noticia ha causado gran sensación entre las tropas mexicanas y se hace todo lo posible para destruir este projecto. . . . Se dice que muchos soldados se están haciendo ricos por esta guerra y que mucho del ejército nacional voluntaries ha pedido su relevo. El Dia 22, 4000 soldados mexicanos salieron con rumbo del bacatete y se espera tengan un combate formal con los indios. Gran excitaioón reina en Mexico y sobre todo Sonora, con el reciente tratado entre Mexico y China, pues este tratado es completamente desfavorable para los Estados Unidos, debido a que los chinos que han obtenido documentos de la ciudadanía Mexicana pueden impunemente ser admitidos en los Estados Unidos. Los Generales Luis y Lorenzo Torres han ordenado la construcción de barracas y diques en la vecindad de Potam y Torrin, para que sirvan de trincheras a las tropas y hay la intención de establecer allí el cuartel general. El General Luis Torres posee una faja de terreno cerca de Potam, y el General Lorenzo Torres posee terreno cerca de Torrin asi como Gobernador interino Ortiz; antes de que empezara la guerra contra los yaquis encontraron dificultad para utilizar estos terrenos debido a la carencia de aguas para su irrigación, pues entre sus terrenos y el lugar donde se encuentra el agua necesaria para su irrigación se halla el terreno perteneciente a los indios yaquis, no pudiéndose obtener que dichos indios concediesen permiso para proveer de agua a esos terrenos. Se creía que un individuo

llamado Nacho González que vivía en el rancho de José Dracamonte, estaba suministrando informes con respeto a la posición de las fuerzas nacionales y se le mandó aprehenderlo asaltaron a la esposa é hija de este quemando despues su jacal. A todos los hombres de Torin, Potam, Cocorit y Medano se les obliga a portar armas, pues se espera un ataque por los yaqus, de un momento a otro" (FMGR, March 3, 1900).

128. Fontes interview, June 26, 2001.

129. Halberstam, *Female Masculinity*, 2.

130. Ibid., 4 and Fontes, 273.

131. In my interview with Fontes, she said that Pilar is a not just a fictional character but a historical one that appears in both oral and written histories of the Yaqui and the Mexican government. "At one point," states Fontes, "the bounty on her head exceeded 5,000 pesos," a huge amount in the late nineteenth century. This bounty underscores the value of Pilar's dead body and the threat this woman posed to the government's desire to suppress Yaqui guerrilla warfare.

132. Halberstam. *Female Masculinity*, 1.

133. Fontes, 273.

134. Ibid., 283.

135. Ibid., 283

136. Ibid., 283.

137. Said, *Culture of Imperialism*, 78.

138. Fontes, 283.

139. See Catriona Rueda Esquibel, "Velvet Malinche," for a complete reading of the glorification of the dead Indian woman's body as a means of venerating indigenous masculinity in national mythologies.

140. Fontes, 283.

141. Ibid., 279.

142. Ibid., 283.

143. Ibid., 286.

144. Ibid., 285.

145. Ibid., 287, emphasis added.

146. Ibid., 287.

147. Saldaña-Portillo, *Revolutionary Imagination in the Americas and the Age of Development* 67.

148. Ibid., 68.

149. Fontes, 301.

150. Ibid., 290.

151. Ibid., 292.

152. Ibid., 293.

153. Hu-DeHart, *Yaqui Resistance and Survival*, esp. 56–117, describes these uprisings in detail.

POSTSCRIPT

1. María de la Luz González, (March 25, 2009). "Suman 10 mil 475 ejecuciones en esta administración: PGR." *El Universal.* http://www.eluniversal.com.mx. Retrieved on April 18, 2009.

2. Hutchinson, ASA, Director Drug Enforcement Administration, and Kathryn and Shelby Cullom Davis. "Narco-Terror: The International Connection between Drugs And Terror." April 2, 2002. http://www.usdoj.gov. Retrieved April 13, 2009.

3. Glenn E. Curtis, "A Report Prepared by the Federal Research Division, Library of Congress under an Interagency Agreement with the United States Government," Washington: Federal Research Division, Library of Congress, 3.

4. See Marisa Belausteguigoitia (coordinadora), *Fronteras, violencia, justicia: nuevos discursos* (Mexico City: Editorial PUEG UNAM: 2008); Marisa Belausteguigoitia, "Descaradas y deslenguadas: el cuerpo y la lengua india en los umbrales de la nación," *Debate Feminista.* Year 18, vol. 36, 2007; *Debate Feminista: Cuerpos Sufrientes.* Year 19, vol. 17, April 2008. Patricia Ravelo Blancas and Hector Domínguez Ruvalcaba (coordinadores), *Entre las Duras Aristas de las Armas: Violencia y Victimmización en Ciudad Juárez* (Mexico City: CIESAS, 2006); and Alliet Bautista, Valentina Batres, Maricela Contreras, and Sonia Ibarra (coordinadoras), *Contradicciones y retractaciones sobre la verdad histórica de los hechos Caso: Ernestina Ascención Rosario* (Mexico City: PRD, 2008).

5. "Historic Femicide Trial Gets Underway." FSN News Special Report. May 4, 2009.

✳ Bibliography

ARCHIVES ABBREVIATIONS

AGN   Archivo General de la Nación, Mexico City
AGS   Archivo General de Sonora, Hermosillo, Sonora, Mexico
AHS   Arizona Historical Society, Tucson
BANC   Bancroft Library, University of California, Berkeley
CPD   Catalogo de Porfirio Díaz, Universidad Iberoamericana, Mexico City
CSA   California State Archives
FMGR   Fondo Manuel González Ramírez, AGN, Mexico City
INAH   Instituto Nacional de Antropología e Historia
SRE   Secretaria de Relaciones Exteriores, Mexico City
TAMUCC   Archives of Texas A&M University, Corpus Christi
TSU   Archives at Texas State University, San Marcos
UASC   University of Arizona Special Collections
UTAB   Nettie Lee Benson Collection, University of Texas, Austin

PUBLICATIONS AND DOCUMENTS

Acuña, Rodolfo. *Occupied America: A History of Chicanos*. Cambridge, Mass.: Harper Collins, 1988.

Alarcón, Norma. "Anzaldúa's Frontera: Inscribing Gynetics." *Displacement, Diaspora, and Geographies of Identity*, ed. Smadar Lavie and Ted Swedenbug. Durham: Duke University Press, 1996.

———. "Chicana Feminism: In the Tracks of the Native Woman." *Living Chicana Theory*, ed. Carla Trujillo. Berkeley: Third Woman Press, 1998.

———. "Chicana Feminist Literature: A Re-vision through Malintzin/or Malintzin: Putting Flesh Back on the Object." *This Bridge Called My Back: Writings by Radical Women of Color*, ed. Gloria Anzaldúa and Cheeríe Moraga. New York: Kitchen Table Press, 1983.

———. "Conjugating Subjects: The Heteroglossia of Essence and Resistance." *An Other Tongue: Nation and Ethnicity in the Linguistic Borderlands*, ed. Alfred Arteaga. Durham: Duke University Press, 1994.

———."Theoretical Subjects of *This Bridge Called My Back*." *Criticism in the Borderlands: Studies in Chicano Literature, Culture and Ideology*, ed. H. Calderón and J. D. Saldívar. Durham: Duke University Press, 1991.

Alarcón, Norma, Caren Kaplan, and Minoo Moallem, eds. *Between Woman and Nation:*

Nationalisms, Transnational Feminisms, and the State. Durham: Duke University Press, 1999.

Aldama, Arturo. "Millennial Anxieties: Borders, Violence, and the Struggle for Chicana and Chicano Subjectivities." *Decolonial Voices: Chicana and Chicano Cultural Studies in the Twenty-First Century*, ed. Arturo Aldama and Naomi Quiñónez. Bloomington: Indiana University Press, 2002.

——, ed. *Violence and the Body: Race, Gender and the State*. Bloomington: Indiana University Press, 2003.

Allen, James, et al. *Without Sanctuary: Lynching Photography in America*. Santa Fe: Twin Palms, 2000.

Almaguer, Tomás. *Racial Faultlines: A History of White Supremacy in California*. Berkeley: University of California Press, 1994.

Alonso, Ana Maria. "Intervention, Mobilization and Ideology." *Rural Revolt in Mexico*, ed. Daniel Nugent. Durham: Duke University Press, 1998.

——. *Thread of Blood: Colonialism, Revolution and Gender on Mexico's Northern Frontier*. Tucson: University of Arizona Press, 1997.

Alonzo, Armando. *Tejano Legacy: Rancheros and Settlers in South Texas, 1734–1900*. Albuquerque: University of New Mexico Press, 1998.

Althusser, Louis. "Ideology and Ideological State Apparatuses." *Lenin and Philosophy*. New York: Monthly Review Press, 1971.

Anderson, Benedict. *Imagined Communities*. New York: Verso, 1991.

"Antiquity of the Apache." *Weekly Arizonan*, April 15, 1871.

Anzaldúa, Gloria. *Borderlands/La Frontera*. San Francisco: Ante Lute Press, 1987.

Anzaldúa, Gloria, and Cherríe Moraga, eds. *This Bridge Called My Back*. New York: Kitchen Table Press, 1983.

"Apache Outrages." *Daily Alta California*, February 7, 1871.

Aranda, José. *When We Arrive: A New Literary History of Mexican America*. Tucson: University of Arizona Press, 2003.

Arnold, Elliott. *The Camp Grant Massacre*. New York: Simon and Schuster, 1976.

Arteaga, Alfred, ed. "Introduction: The Here, the Now." *An Other Tongue: Nation and Ethnicity in the Linguistic Borderlands*. Durham: Duke University Press, 1994.

——. "The Red and the Black." Foreword to *Violence and the Body: Race, Gender and the State*, ed. Arturo Aldama. Bloomington: Indiana University Press, 2003.

Baker, Lee D. *From Savage to Negro: Anthropology and the Construction of Race, 1896–1954*. Berkeley: University of California Press, 1998.

Balibar, Etienne. "Citizen Subject." *Who Comes After the Subject?*, ed. Eduardo Cadava, Peter Connor, and Jean-Luc Nancy. New York: Routledge, 1991.

Bancroft, Hubert Howe. *Popular Tribunals*. San Francisco: History Company, 1887.

Barr, Juliana. *Peace Came in the Form of a Woman: Indians and Spaniards in the Texas Borderlands*. Chapel Hill: University of North Carolina Press, 2007.

Bass, Thomas. "Counterinsurgency and Torture." *American Quarterly* 60, no. 2 (2008): 233.

Beck, David R. M. "Developing a Voice: The Evolution of Self-Determination in an Urban Indian Community." *Wicazo Sa Review* 17, no. 2 (2002).

Berger, Alan and Naomi Berger. *Second Generation Voices: Reflections by Children of Holocaust Survivors and Perpetrators*. Syracuse: Syracuse University Press, 2001.

Bhabha, Homi K. "DissemiNation: Time, Narrative and the Margins of the Modern Nation." *Nation and Narration*, ed. Homi K. Bhabha. New York: Routledge, 1990.

Black, Henry Campbell. *Black's Law Dictionary*, ed. Brian Garner. 7th edn. St. Paul: West Group, 1999.

Blackhawk, Ned. *Violence over the Land: Indians and Empires in the Early American West.* Cambridge: Harvard University Press, 2006.

Blea, Irene. *Chicanas in a U.S. Global Context.* New York: Praeger/Greenwood Press, 1997.

Bonfil-Batalla, Guillermo. *Mexico Profundo: Reclaiming a Civilization.* Austin: University of Texas Press, 1996.

Bordo, Susan. "The Body and the Reproduction of Femininity." *Writing on the Body: Female Embodiment and Feminist Theory*, ed. Katie Conboy, Nadia Medina, and Sarah Stanbury. New York: Columbia University Press, 1997.

Bourdieu, Pierre. *Language and Symbolic Power.* Cambridge: Harvard University Press, 1999.

Brady, Mary Patricia. "Extinct Lands, Scarred Bodies: Chicana Literature and the Reinvention of Space." Ph.D. diss. UCLA, 1992. Ann Arbor: UMI, 1992.

——. *Extinct Lands, Temporal Geographies: Chicana Literature and the Urgency of Space.* Durham: Duke University Press, 2002.

Briggs, Laura. "Body Snatchers and Homeless Waifs: Contesting Reproduction and Negotiating U.S. Foreign Policy in Transnational Adoption." Manuscript.

Briggs, Laura, Gladys McCormick, and J. T. Way. "Transnationalism: A Category of Analysis." *American Quarterly* 60, no. 3 (2008): 503–21.

Brodhead, Richard. *Cultures of Letters: Scenes of Reading and Writing in Nineteenth-Century America.* Chicago: University of Chicago Press, 1993.

Brogan, Kathleen. *Cultural Hauntings: Ghosts and Ethnicity in Recent American Literature.* Charlottesville: University of Virginia Press, 1998.

Brooks, James. *Captives and Cousins: Slavery, Kinship, and Community in the Southwest Borderlands.* Chapel Hill: University of North Carolina Press, 2002.

——. "Served Well by Plunder: La Gran Ladronería and Producers of dHistory Astride the Río Grande." *American Quarterly* 52, no. 1 (2000): 23–58.

Brooks-Higginbotham, Evelyn. "The Metalanguage of Race." *Signs* 17, no. 2 (1992): 251–74.

Brown, Laura S. "Not Outside the Range: One Feminist Perspective on Psychic Trauma." *Trauma: Explorations in Memory*, ed. Cathy Caruth, 119–33. Baltimore: Johns Hopkins University Press, 1995.

Brundage, W. F. *Lynching and the New South.* Urbana: University of Illinois Press, 1993.

Buck, Franklin S. *A Yankee Trader in the Gold Rush: The Letters of Franklin S. Buck.* New York: Houghton Mifflin, 1930.

Bureau of the Census. Executive Document. November 6, 1889.

Bureau of Indian Affairs [BIA]. *Report of the Commissioner of Indian Affairs.* Washington: Government Printing Office, 1870.

——. *Report of the Commissioner of Indian Affairs.* Washington: Government Printing Office, 1871.

——. *Report of the Commissioner of Indian Affairs.* Washington: Government Printing Office, 1872.

Burke, Kenneth. *Barbarous Mexico.* Chicago: Charles Kerr, 1910.

Butler, Judith. *The Psychic Life of Power: Theories in Subjection.* Stanford: Stanford University Press, 1997.

"Cajeme Was Shot," *New York Times,* May 9, 1887.

"California History rewritten by CSULB Literary Scholar." *Signal Tribune* 27, no. 30, January 4, 2007.

Caminero-Santangelo, Marta. *The Madwoman Can't Speak: Or Why Insanity Is Not Subversive.* Ithaca: Cornell University Press, 1998.

Cantú, Roberto. "Hybrid Resolutions: Liberal Democracy and Ethnic Identity in Montserrat Fontes's *Dreams of the Centaur.*" *Arizona Journal of Hispanic Cultural Studies* 4 (2000): 141–58.

Cargill, Andrew Hayes. Cargill Papers, 1864–1908. Arizona Historical Society.

"A Carnival of Blood." *Daily Alta California,* February 4, 1871.

Carr, Helen. *Inventing the American Primitive: Politics, Gender and the Representations of Native American Literary Traditions, 1789–1936.* New York: New York University Press, 1996.

Caruth, Cathy. Introduction to *Explorations in Memory.* Baltimore: Johns Hopkins University Press, 1995.

——. *Unclaimed Experience: Trauma, Narrative and History.* Baltimore: Johns Hopkins University Press, 1996.

Castañeda, Antonia I. "History and Politics of Violence Against Women." *Living Chicana Theory,* ed. Carla Trujillo. Berkeley: Third Woman Press, 1998.

——. "The Political Economy of Nineteenth-Century Stereotypes of Californianas." *Between Borders: Essays on Mexicana/Chicana History,* ed. Adelaida Del Castillo. Encino, Calif.: Flor y Canto Press, 1990.

——. "Sexual Violence in the Politics and Policies of Conquest: Amerindian Women and the Spanish Conquest of Alta California." *Building with Our Hands: New Directions in Chicana Studies,* ed. Adela de la Torre and Beatríz Pesqueira. Berkeley: University of California Press, 1993.

Chabram-Dernersesian, Angie. "Chicana! Rican? No, 'Chicana, Riqueña!' " *Between Woman and Nation: Nationalisms, Transnational Feminisms, and the State,* ed. Norma Alarcón, Caren Kaplan, and Minoo Moallem. Durham: Duke University Press, 1999.

——. "I Throw Punches for My Race but That Doesn't Mean I Want to Be a Man: Writing Us—Chica-nos (Girl, Us)/Chicanas into the Movement Script." *The Chicana/o Cultural Studies Reader,* ed. Angie Chabram-Dernersesian. New York: Routledge, 2006.

——. "The Spanish Colón-ialista Narrative: Their Prospectus for Us in 1992." *Mapping Multiculturalism,* ed. A. Gordon and C. Newfield. Minneapolis: University of Minnesota Press, 1996.

Chambers, Ross. *Story and Situation: Narrative Seduction and the Power of Fiction.* Minneapolis: University of Minnesota Press, 1984.

Chapman, Mary, and Glenn Hendler. *Sentimental Men: Masculinity and the Politics of Affect in American Culture.* Berkeley: University of California Press, 1999.

Cheng, Anne. *The Melancholy of Race: Psychoanalysis, Assimilation, and Hidden Grief.* Oxford: Oxford University Press, 2001.

Cheung, Floyd. "Performing Exclusion and Resistance: Anti-Chinese League and Chee Kong Tung Parades in Territorial Arizona." *The Drama Review* 46, no. 1 (2002): 39–59.

Christian, Barbara. "The Race for Theory." *Within the Circle: An Anthology of African American Literary Criticism from the Harlem Renaissance to the Present*, ed. Angelyn Mitchell. Durham: Duke University Press, 1994.

Christian, Garna L. *Black Soldiers in Jim Crow Texas, 1899–1917*. College Station: Texas A&M University Press, 1995.

"Citizens Fire on Troops." *Chicago Tribune*, November 22, 1899, p. 1.

Clifford, James. "On Ethnographic Authority." *Representations* 2 (spring 1983): 118–46.

Colwell-Chanthophonh, Chip. *Massacre at Camp Grant: Forgetting and Remembering Apache History*. Tucson: University of Arizona Press, 2007.

——. "Western Apache Oral Histories and Traditions of the Camp Grant Massacre." *American Indian Quarterly* 27, no. 3 (2003): 639–66.

"The Committee on Safety." *Weekly Arizonan*, April 1, 1871.

Concessions to the Southern Pacific: Concession of April 27, 1905

Connell, R. W. "The Big Picture: Masculinities in Recent World History." *Theory and Society* 22, no. 5. Special Issue: Masculinities (October 1993): 597–623.

Cook-Lynne, Elizabeth. *New Indians, Old Wars*. Urbana: University of Illinois Press, 2007.

Coronil, Fernando, and Julie Skurski. "Dismembering and Remembering the Nation: The Semantics of Political Violence in Venezuela." *States of Violence*. Ann Arbor: University of Michigan Press, 2006.

——, eds. *States of Violence*. Ann Arbor: University of Michigan Press, 2006.

Corral, Ramón. *Obras historicas: reseña del estado de Sonora, 1856–1877. Biografía de José María Leyva Cajeme y las razas indígenas de Sonora*. Hermosillo: Biblioteca Sonorense de Geografía e Historia, 1959.

Cotera, María. "Native Speakers: Locating Early Expressions of U.S.–Third World Feminist Discourse; A Comparative Analysis of the Ethnographic Writing and Literary Writing of Ella Cara Deloria and Jovita Gonzalez." Ph.D. diss., Stanford University, 2001. Ann Arbor: UMI, 2001.

——. *Native Speakers: Ella Deloria, Zora Neale Hurston, Jovita Gonzalez, and the Poetics of Culture*. Austin: University of Texas Press, 2008.

Cotera, Martha. *Diosa y Hembra: The History and Heritage of Chicanas in the U.S.* Austin: Information Systems Development, 1976.

Cott, Nancy. *Public Vows*. Cambridge: Harvard University Press, 2000.

Coulter, Charles Caruthers. "The Last of the Yaqui." *Collier's Weekly*, March 11, 1905.

Cremony, John C. *Life among the Apaches*. San Francisco: A. Roman, 1868.

DeJong, David. " 'Unless They Are Kept Alive': Federal Indian Schools and Student Health, 1878–1918." *American Indian Quarterly* 31, no. 2 (2007).

Delay, Brian. *War of a Thousand Deserts: Indian Raids and the U.S.-Mexican War*. New Haven: Yale University Press, 2008.

Del Castillo, Adelaida. "Malintzín Tenepal: A Preliminary Look into a New Perspective." *Chicana Feminist Thought: The Basic Historical Writings*, ed. Alma García. New York: Routledge, 1997.

De Leon, Arnoldo. *They Called Them Greasers: Anglo Attitudes Towards Mexicans in Texas, 1821–1900*. Austin: University of Texas Press, 1983.

———, ed. *Between Borders: Essays on Mexicana/Chicana History*. Encino, Calif.: Flor y Canto Press, 1990.

Delgado, Grace. "In the Age of Exclusion: Race, Region, Identity and the Making of the Arizona/Sonora Borderlands, 1863–1943." Ph.D. diss, University of California, Los Angeles, 2000.

De Long, Sidney R. *The History of Arizona*. San Francisco: Witaker and Ray, 1905.

———. Manuscript. MS 0216, Sidney R. DeLong Papers, Arizona Historical Society.

De Vries, Hent, and Samuel Weber, eds. Introduction to *Violence, Identity and Self Determination*. Stanford: Stanford University Press, 1997.

El Diario Popular, March 24, 1908.

Díaz, Porfirio. Catálogo y Papeles de Porfirio Díaz. Universidad Iberoamericana, Mexico City.

Dobie, Frank. *Texas and Southwestern Lore*. Austin: Texas Folklore Society, 1927.

Donaldson, Laura. "The Breasts of Columbus: A Political Anatomy of Postcolonialism and Feminist Religious Discourse." *Postcolonialism, Feminism, and Religious Discourse*, ed. Laura E. Donaldson and Kwok Pui-lan. New York: Routledge, 2000.

Donaldson, Laura E., and Kwok Pui-lan, eds. *Postcolonialism, Feminism, and Religious Discourse*. New York: Routledge, 2000.

Downie, William. *Hunting for Gold*. Palo Alto: American West Publishing, 1971.

Duffy-Turner, Ethel. Ethel Duffy Turner Collection. INAH.

Dumond, Don E. "The Talking Crosses of Yucatan: A New Look at Their History." *Ethnohistory* 32, no. 4 (1985): 291–308.

Ech, En Lak. "Mujeres con palabra." Email correspondence from the National Association for Chicana and Chicano Studies—Southern California Foco list serve. ⟨naccs -scal-naccsonline.org⟩. August 12, 2008.

Eiser, Arnold R. "Violence and Transcultural Values." *Violence against Women: Philosophical Perspectives*, ed. Stanley French, Laura Purdy, and Wanda Teays. Ithaca: Cornell University Press, 1998.

"El Articulo de Sr. Consul de EE.UU. en Yucatan." 3 deciembre 1921, y sin subvención. *La Revista de Mérida*.

Eng, David L., and David Kazanjian. *Loss: The Politics of Mourning*. Berkeley: University of California Press, 2003.

Erickson, Kirsten Christenson. "Ethnic Places, Gendered Spaces: The Expressive Constitution of Yaqui Identities." Ph.D. diss., University of Wisconsin, Madison, 2003. Ann Arbor: UMI, 2003.

Erickson, Winston. *Sharing the Desert: The Tohono O'odham in History*. Tucson: University of Arizona Press, 1994.

Escobar, Edward J. *Race, Police, and the Making of a Political Identity: Mexican Americans and the Los Angeles Police Department, 1900–1945*. Berkeley: University of California Press, 1999.

"Expenses Occurred in Suppressing Indian Hostilities." 50th Congress of the United States, sess. 1, Ex. Doc. no. 219. 1888.

Fabian, Johannes. "Presence and Representation: The Other and Anthropological Writing." *Critical Inquiry* 16 (1990): 753–72.

Feldman, Alan. "Memory Theaters, Virtual Witnessing, and the Trauma-Aesthetic." *Biography* 27, no. 1 (2004): 163–202.

———. "Virtual Archives and Ethnographic Writing." *Current Anthropology* 43, no. 5 (2002): 775–86.

"First Woman Hanged in California." *San Jose Pioneer*, November 12, 1881.

Flores, Richard. *Remembering the Alamo: Memory, Modernity and the Master Symbol.* Austin: University of Texas Press, 2002.

Fontes, Montserrat. *Dreams of the Centaur.* New York: W. W. Norton, 1996.

———. Unpublished personal interview, June 23, 2001.

Foucault, Michel. *Discipline and Punish: The Birth of the Prison.* New York: Vintage, 1975.

———. *The History of Sexuality.* Vol. 2, *The Use of Pleasure.* New York: Vintage, 1980.

———. *Power/Knowledge; Selected Interviews and Other Writings, 1972–1977.* Edited by Colin Gordon. New York: Pantheon, 1980.

Frazier, Lessie Jo. *Salt in the Sand: Memory, Violence and the Nation-State in Chicle, 1890 to the Present.* Durham: Duke University Press, 2007.

Fregoso, Rosa Linda. *MeXicana Encounters: The Making of Social Identities on the Borderlands.* Berkeley: University of California Press, 2003.

Gamez Chavez, Javier. *Lucha Social y Formación Histórica de la Autonomía Yaqui-Yoreme, 1884–1939.* Tesis Licenciado en Estudios Latinoamericanos. UNAM, 2004.

Galtung, Johan. "Cultural Violence." *Journal of Peace Research* 27, no. 3 (1990): 291–305.

Garcia, Alma. *Chicana Feminist Thought: The Basic Historical Writings.* New York: Routledge, 1997.

Garner, Bryan A., ed. *Black's Law Dictionary.* 7th edn. St. Paul: West Group, 1999.

Garza-Falcón, Leticia. *Gente Decente: A Borderlands Response to the Rhetoric of Dominance.* Austin: University of Texas Press, 1998.

Gaspar de Alba, Alicia. "Book Review of *Brown Gumshoes: Detective Fiction and the Search for Chicana/o Identity.*" *Latino Studies* 5 (2007): 144–45.

Gilfoyle, Timothy. "Prostitutes in History: From Parables of Pornography to Metaphors of Modernity." *American Historical Review* 104, no. 1. (1999): 117–41.

Glenn, Evelyn Nakano. "Citizenship and Inequality: Historical and Global Perspectives." *Social Problems* 47, no. 1 (2000): 1–20.

———. *Unequal Freedom: How Race and Gender Shaped American Citizenship and Labor.* Cambridge: Harvard University Press, 2002.

"Gloomy Prospects in Arizona." *Weekly Arizonan*, February 4, 1871.

Goldsby, Jacqueline Denise. "After Great Pain: The Cultural Logic of Lynching and the Problem of Realist Representation in America, 1882–1922." Ph.D. diss., Yale University, 1998. Ann Arbor: UMI, 1998.

———. *A Spectacular Secret: Lynching in American Life and Literature.* Chicago: University of Chicago Press, 2006.

Gomez-Quiñonez, Juan. "Questions Within Women's Historiography." *Between Borders: Essays on Mexicana/Chicana History*, ed. Adelaida Del Castillo. Encino, Calif.: Flor y Canto Press, 1990.

González, Deena. "Malinche Triangulated, Historically Speaking." *Feminism, Nation, and Myth: La Malinche*, ed. Rolando Romero and Amanda Nolacea Harris. Houston: Arte Público Press, 2005.

———. *Refusing the Favor: The Spanish Mexican Women of Santa Fe 1840–1880.* London: Oxford University Press, 1999.

——. "Speaking Secrets: Living Chicana Theory." *Living Chicana Theory*. Ed. Carla Trujillo. Berkeley: Third Woman Press, 1998.

González, Jovita [de Mireles]. *Dew on the Thorn*. Houston: Arte Público Press, 1997.

——. Jovita González de Mireles Papers. Nettie Lee Benson Collection, University of Texas, Austin.

——. "Social Life in Cameron, Starr and Zapata Counties." MA thesis, University of Texas, Austin, 1930.

——. *The Woman Who Lost Her Soul and Other Stories*. Houston: Arte Público Press, 2000.

Gonzales-Day, Ken. *Lynching in the West, 1850–1935*. Durham: Duke University Press, 2006.

González de Mireles, Jovita, and Eve Raleigh. *Caballero: A Historical Novel*. Edited by José Limón and María Cotera. College Station: Texas A&M University Press, 1996.

Goodwin, Grenville. Grenville Goodwin Papers. MS 17, folders 32, 34, 37. Arizona State Museum.

——. *Western Apache Raiding and Warfare*. Tucson: University of Arizona Press, 1971.

Granziano, Frank. *Divine Violence: Spectacle, Psychosexuality, and Radical Christianity in the Argentine Dirty War*. Boulder: Westview Press, 1992.

Grewal, Inderpal, and Karen Kaplan. "Transnational Practices and Interdisciplinary Feminist Scholarship: Refiguring Women's and Gender Studies." *Women's Studies on Its Own: A Next Wave Reader in Institutional Change*, ed. Robin Weigman. Durham: Duke University Press, 2002.

Griswold del Castillo, Richard. *The Treaty of Guadalupe Hidalgo: A Legacy of Conflict*. Norman: University of Oklahoma Press, 1990.

Grosz, Elizabeth. "The Time of Violence." *Violence and the Body: Race, Gender, and the State*, ed. Arturo Aldama. Bloomington: Indiana University Press, 2003.

——. *Volatile Bodies: Toward a Corporeal Feminism*. Bloomington: Indiana University Press, 1994.

Guha, Ranajeet. "The Prose of Counter-Insurgency." *Culture/Power/History: A Reader in Contemporary Social Theory*, ed. Nicholas Dirks, Geoff Eley, and Sherry Ortner. Princeton: Princeton University Press, 1994.

Guidotti-Hernández, Nicole. "Gender, Epistemology and Cooking: Rethinking Encarnación Piñedo's *El Cocinero Español*." *Women's Studies International Forum* 31 (2008): 6, 449–56.

Gunning, Sandra. *Race, Rape and Lynching: The Red Record of American Literature, 1890–1912*. Oxford: Oxford University Press, 1996.

Gupta, Akhil. "The Reincarnation of Souls and the Rebirth of Commodities: Representations of Time in 'East' and 'West.'" *Cultural Critique* 22 (fall 1992): 187–211.

——. "The Song of the Nonaligned World: Transnational Identities and the Reinscription of Space in Late Capitalism." *Cultural Anthropology* 7, no. 1 (1992): 63–79.

Gupta, Akhil, and James Ferguson. "Beyond 'Culture': Space, Identity and the Politics of Difference." *Cultural Anthropology* 7, no. 1 (1992): 6–23.

Gutiérrez, Ramón A. "Honor Ideology, Marriage Negotiation, and Class-Gender Domination in New Mexico, 1690–1846." *Latin American Perspectives* 12, no. 1 (1985): 81–104.

——. *When Jesus Came, the Corn Mothers Went Away*. Stanford: Stanford University Press, 1990.

Gutiérrez-Jones, Carl. *Rethinking the Borderlands: Between Chicano Culture and Legal Discourse*. Berkeley: University of California Press, 1995.

Haas, Lisbeth. *Conquests and Historical Identities in California, 1769–1936*. Berkeley: University of California Press, 1995.

——. "Fear in Colonial California: Native Writers vs. the Spanish Archive." Manuscript.

Halberstam, Judith. *Female Masculinity*. Durham: Duke University Press, 1998.

Hall, Christopher. "Downieville: A Former Mining Town in the Sierra Revels in Its Golden Years." *Via Magazine for the California Automobile Association*, 2007.

Hämäläinen, Pekka. *The Comanche Empire*. New Haven: Yale University Press, 2008.

"The Hanging at Downieville." *Daily Alta California*, July 14, 1851.

Harper, Phillip Brian. *Framing the Margins: The Social Logic of Postmodern Culture*. New York: Oxford University Press, 1994.

Harris, Cheryl. "Whiteness as Property." *Critical Race Theory: The Key Writings That Formed the Movement*, ed. Kimberlee Crenshaw et al. New York: New Press, 1995.

Hartman, Saidya. *Scenes of Subjection: Terror, Slavery, and Self-Making in Nineteenth-Century America*. New York: Oxford University Press, 1997.

Herman, Judith. *Trauma and Recovery: The Aftermath of Violence—From Domestic Abuse to Political Terror*. New York: Basic Books, 1992.

Hernández, Jose Angel. "El México perdido, el México olvidado, y el México de afuera." Ph.D. diss, University of Chicago, 2008.

Higgs, Robert. *The Transformation of the American Economy, 1865–1914*. New York: John Wiley and Sons, 1971.

Hochberg, Gil. "Introduction: Israelis, Palestinians, Queers: Points of Departure." GLQ: A Journal of Lesbian and Gay Studies 16, no. 4 (2010): 493–516.

Hodes, Martha. "Interconnecting and Diverging Narratives." *Sex, Love, Race: Crossing Boundaries in North American History*. New York: New York University Press, 1999.

Holland, Sharon Patricia. *Raising the Dead: Readings of Death and (Black) Subjectivity*. Durham: Duke University Press, 2000.

Holloway, Karla F. C. *Passed On: African American Mourning Stories*. Durham: Duke University Press, 2002.

hooks, bell. *Killing Rage: Ending Racism*. New York: Henry Holt, 1995.

——. "Selling Hot Pussy: Representations of Black Female Sexuality in the Cultural Marketplace." *Writing on the Body: Female Embodiment and Feminist Theory*, ed. Katie Conboy, Nadia Medina, and Sarah Stanbury. New York: Columbia University Press, 1997.

Horsman, Reginald. *Race and Manifest Destiny: The Origins of American Racial Anglo-Saxonism*. Cambridge: Harvard University Press, 1981.

Hu-DeHart, Evelyn. *Yaqui Resistance and Survival*. Madison: University of Wisconsin Press, 1984.

Hughes, Samuel. Samuel Hughes Papers. Arizona Historical Society.

Hurtado, Alberto. *Intimate Frontiers: Sex, Gender, and Culture in Old California*. Albuquerque: University of New Mexico Press, 1999.

Illustrated History of Plumas, Lassen, and Sierra Counties. San Francisco: Farriss and Smith, 1882.

"Indian Outrages." *Weekly Arizonan*, May 15, 1869.

"The Indian Question." *Daily Alta California*, January 18, 1871.

"Indians! Indians!" *Weekly Arizonan*, March 25, 1871.

"An Insane Idea." *Weekly Arizonan*, January 28, 1871.

Jacobs, Janet Liebman. *Victimized Daughters: Incest and the Development of the Female Self*. New York: Routledge, 1994.

Jacoby, Carl. *Shadows at Dawn: A Borderlands Massacre and the Violence of History*. New York: Penguin, 2008.

Jensen, Richard. "No Irish Need Apply: A Myth of Victimization." *Journal of Social History* 36, no. 2 (2002): 406.

Johnson, Susan Lee. *Roaring Camp: The Social World of the California Gold Rush*. New York: W. W. Norton, 2000.

Jones, James H. *Bad Blood: The Tuskegee Syphilis Experiment*. New York: Free Press, 1981.

Kaplan, Carla. *The Erotics of Talk: Women's Writing and Feminist Paradigms*. New York: Oxford University Press, 1996.

Kaup, Monica. *Rewriting North American Borders in Chicano and Chicana Narrative*. New York: Lang, 2001.

Kazanjian, David. *The Colonizing Trick: National Cultural and Imperial Citizenship in Early America*. Minneapolis: University of Minnesota Press, 2003.

Kelly, Allen. "Red Raiders of Sonora's Hills: Guerrilla Operations of Bronco Yaquis in the Mining Districts." *Los Angeles Times*, June 12, 1906.

Kitt, Edith. "Mrs. Atanacia Hughes." Hughes Family Papers. Arizona Historical Society, 1926.

Klor de Alva, Jorge. J. "Chicana History and Historical Significance." *Between Borders: Essays on Mexicana/Chicana History*, ed. Adelaida Del Castillo. Encino, Calif.: Flor y Canto Press, 1990.

Koreck, Maria Teresa. "Space and Revolution in Chihuahua." *Rural Revolt in Mexico*, ed. Daniel Nugent. Durham: Duke University Press, 1998.

Kramer, Paul. "The Water Cure: Debating Torture and Counterinsurgency—A Century Ago." *New Yorker*, February 25, 2008, 1–3. Available online at www.newyorker.com.

Kristeva, Julia. "The Powers of Horror: Approaching Abjection." *The Portable Kristeva*, ed. Kelly Oliver. New York: Columbia University Press, 1997.

Lamar, Lucius Quintus Cincinnatus. *Report of the Secretary of the Interior*. Vol. 2. Washington: Government Printing Office, 1885.

Laplantine, François, and Alexis Nouss. *Mestizajes: De Arcimbolod a Zombi*. Mexico City: Fondo de Cultura Económica, 2007.

Las Novedades. "Construcción de ferrocarriles en México, con capital americano, sin monopolio." Mayo 1907.

Lee, Rachel. "Notes from a non-field: Teaching and Theorizing Women of Color." *Meridians* 1, no. 1(fall 2000): 85–109.

Legislature of the Territory of Arizona. *Memorial and Affidavits Showing Outrages Perpetrated by the Apache Indians in the Territory of Arizona, during the Years 1869 and 1870*. San Francisco: Francis and Valentine, 1871.

"Letter from Florence." *Weekly Arizonan*, February 11, 1871.

Limón, José. "Introduction." *Dew on the Thorn*. Houston: Arte Publico Press, 1997.

"Local Matters." *Weekly Arizonan*, January 29, 1871.

Lockwood, Frank. *Life in Old Tucson 1854–1864 As Remembered by the Little Maid Atanacia Santa Cruz*. Tucson: Tucson Civic Committee, 1943.

Lombroso, Cesare, and Gugllelmo Ferrero. *Criminal Woman, the Prostitute, and the Normal Woman*. Reprint, Durham: Duke University Press, 2004.

Lomnitz, Claudio. *Death and the Idea of Mexico*. Brooklyn: Zone Books, 2005.

Lytle Hernández, Kathleen. "Entangling Bodies and Borders: Racial Profiling and the U.S. Border Patrol, 1924–1955." Ph.D. diss, University of California, Los Angeles, 2002.

MacKinnon, Catharine A. "Rape: On Coercion and Consent." *Writing on the Body: Female Embodiment and Feminist Theory*, ed. Katie Conboy, Nadia Medina, and Sarah Stanbury. New York: Columbia University Press, 1997.

Madriz, Esther. *Nothing Bad Happens to Good Girls: Fear of Crime in Women's Lives*. Berkeley: University of California Press, 1997.

Massey, Doreen. *For Space*. Thousand Oaks, Calif.: Sage, 2005.

Matroy, J. Lorand. *Black Atlantic Region: Tradition, Transnationalism and Matriarchy in the Afro-Brazilian Candomblé*. Princeton: Princeton University Press, 2005.

McClosky, J. J. "First Woman Hanged in California." *San Jose Pioneer*, November 12, 1881.

McDowell, John. H. *Poetry and Violence: The Ballad Tradition of Mexico's Costa Chica*. Urbana: University of Illinois Press, 2008.

Menchaca, Martha. "The Anti-miscegenation History of the American Southwest, 1830 to 1970: Transforming Racial Ideology into Law." Paper presented at the Transnational Exchanges in the Texas-Mexico Borderlands conference, April 7–8, 2005.

——. *Recovering History, Constructing Race: The Indian, Black and White Roots of Mexican Americans*. Austin: University of Texas Press, 2001.

Mariscal, George. "The Role of Spain in Contemporary Race Theory." *Arizona Journal of Hispanic Cultural Studies* 2 (1998): 7–22.

Martínez, Elizabeth. *500 Años del pueblo Chicano/500 Years of Chicano History in Pictures*. Albuquerque: Southwest Organizing Project, 1990.

——." 'Chingón Politics,' Die Hard: Reflections on the First Chicano Activist Reunion." *Living Chicana Theory*, ed. Carla Trujullo. Berkeley: Third Woman Press, 1998.

McMillen, Christian W. "The Red Man and the White Plague: Rethinking Race, Tuberculosis, and American Indians, ca. 1890–1950." *Bulletin on the History of Medicine*. 82, no. 3 (2008): 608–45.

Memorial and Affidavits Showing Outrages Perpetrated by the Apache Indians in the Territory of Arizona during the Years of 1869 and 1870. San Francisco: Francis and Valentine Printers, 1871.

Mendoza, Louis Gerard. *Historia: The Literary Making of Chicana and Chicano History*. College Station: Texas A&M University Press, 2001.

Methvin, J. J., ed. *Andale, or The Mexican-Kiowa Captive: A Story of Real Life among Indians*. Albuquerque: University of New Mexico Press, 1996.

Miller, Toby. "Introducing . . . Cultural Citizenship." *Social Text* 19, no. 4 (2001): 1–5.

"Mining in Arizona." *Daily Alta California*, January 18, 1871.

Mirandé, Alfredo, and Evangelina Enríquez. *La Chicana: The Mexican-American Woman*. Chicago: University of Chicago Press, 1979.

Mohanty, Chandra Talpade. *Feminism without Borders: Decolonizing Theory, Practicing Solidarity*. Durham: Duke University Press, 2004.

Momaday, N. Scott. "An American Land Ethic." *The Man Made of Words*. New York: St. Martin's, 1997.

Montejano, David. *Anglos and Mexicans in the Making of Texas*. Austin: University of Texas Press, 1987.

Moraga, Cherríe. *The Last Generation: Prose and Poetry*. Boston: South End Press, 1993.

———. *Loving in the War Years: Lo Que Nunca Pasó Por Sus Labios*. Boston: South End Press, 1983.

Mufti, Aamir. "The Aura of Authenticity." *Social Text* 18, no. 3 (2000): 87–103.

Mulvey, Laura. "Narrative Pleasure in Cinema." *Contemporary Literary Criticism: Literary and Cultural Studies*, ed. Robert Con Davis and Ronald Schleifer. New York: Longman, 1998.

Murguía, Alejandro. *The Medicine of Memory: A Mexica Clan in California*. Austin: University of Texas Press, 2002.

New York Daily Tribune. "Mexico Advices." September 2, 1880.

O'Brien, Gail Williams. "Lynching Revisited." *Reviews on American History* 27, no. 3 (1999): 462–69.

Older, Cora Miranda Baggerly. *Love Stories of Old California*. Bedford, Mass.: Applewood Press, 1995.

Omi, Michael, and Howard Winant. *Racial Formation in the United States: From the 1960s to the 1980s*. New York: Routledge and Kegan Paul, 1986.

"Our Railroad Prospects." *Weekly Arizonan*, February 4, 1871.

Oury, William S. William S. Oury Papers. Special Collections, University of Arizona Library.

———. William S. Oury Papers. Arizona Historical Society.

———. "Article on Camp Grant Massacre Read before the Society of Arizona Pioneers," April 6, 1885. Manuscript on file, Arizona Historical Society.

Padilla, Genaro. *My History, Not Yours: The Formation of Mexican-American Autobiography*. Madison: University of Wisconsin Press, 1993.

Padilla, Yolanda. "Indian Mexico: The Changing Face of Indigeneity in Mexican American Literature, 1910–1984." Ph.D. diss., University of Chicago, 2004.

Padilla Ramos, Raquel. *Yucatán: Fin del sueño Yaqui*. Hermosillo, Sonora, México: Gobierno del Estado de Sonora, Secretaría de Educación y Cultura, Instituto Sonorense de Cultura, 1995.

———. *Progreso y libertad: los yaquis en la víspera de la repatriación*. Hermosillo, Sonora: Instituto Sonorense de Cultura, 2005.

"The Papagos." *Weekly Arizonan*, April 22, 1871.

Paredes, Américo. *George Washington Gómez*. Houston: Arte Público Press, 1990.

———. *"With His Pistol in His Hand": A Border Ballad and Its Hero*. Austin: University of Texas Press, 1958.

Parker, Andrew, and Eve Kosofsky Sedgwick. *Performativity and Performance*. New York: Routledge, 1995.

Pascoe, Peggy. "Miscegenation Law, Court Cases and Ideologies of 'Race' in Twentieth-Century America." *Journal of American History* 83, no. 1 (1996): 44–69.

Payne, Leigh, *Unsettling Accounts: Neither Truth nor Reconciliation in Confessions of State Violence*. Durham: Duke University Press, 2008.

Pérez, Domino Renee. "Caminando Con La Llorona: Traditional and Contemporary Narratives." *Chicana Traditions: Continuity and Change*, ed. Norma E. Cantú and Olga Nájera-Ramírez. Urbana: University of Illinois Press, 2002.

Pérez, Emma. *The Decolonial Imaginary: Writing Chicanas into History*. Bloomington: Indiana University Press, 1999.

Pérez-Torres, Rafael. *Mestizaje: Critical Uses of Race in Chicano Culture*. Minneapolis: University of Minnesota Press, 2006.

——. "Miscegenation Now!" *American Literary History* 17, no. 2 (2005): 369–80.

——. *Movements in Chicano Poetry: Against Myths, against Margins*. Cambridge: Cambridge University Press, 1995.

——. "Refiguring Aztlán." *The Chicano Studies Reader: An Anthology of Aztlán, 1970–2000*, ed. Chon A. Noriega et al. Los Angeles : UCLA Chicano Studies Research Center, 2001.

Perkins, Rollin M., and Ronald N. Boyce. *Criminal Law*. 3d. edn. Mineola, N.Y.: Foundation Press, 1982.

Pierce-Barstow, David. "Statement of Recollections of 1849–51 in California." Bancroft Archives, University of California, Berkeley, 1878.

Pitt, Leonard. *The Decline of the Californios*. Berkeley: University of California Press, 1999.

Pratt, Mary Louise. "Women, Literature, and National Brotherhood." *Nineteenth-Century Contexts* 18, no. 1 (1994): 27–47.

Puar, Jasbir. *Terrorist Assemblages: Homonationalism in Queer Times*. Durham: Duke University Press, 2008.

Radding, Cynthia. *Wandering Peoples: Colonialism, Ethnic Spaces and Ecological Frontiers in Northwestern Mexico, 1700–1850*. Durham: Duke University Press, 1997.

Rebolledo, Tey Diana. *Women Singing in the Snow: A Cultural Analysis of Chicana Literature*. Tucson: University of Arizona Press, 1995.

Record, Ian. *Big Sycamore Stands Alone: The Western Apache, Aravaipa and the Struggle for Place*. Norman: University of Oklahoma Press, 2008.

Regan, Margaret. "A Short History of the Stevens House." *Tucson Weekly*, April 5, 2001.

Reid, Ida C. "The Relation of the Apache Indians to the Development of Arizona." Ph.D. diss., University of Chicago, 1910.

Reyna, Sergio. Introduction to *The Woman Who Lost Her Soul and Other Stories*, by Jovita González. Houston: Arte Público Press, 2000.

Rios, Kathryn. "Silence as a Discourse: Resistance in the Writing of Women of Color." Ph.D. diss., Cornell University, 1994. Ann Arbor: UMI, 1994.

Roach, Joseph. *Cities of the Dead: Circum-Atlantic Performance*. New York: Columbia University Press, 1996.

Rodriguez, Jeanette. *Our Lady of Guadalupe; Faith and Empowerment among Mexican American Women*. Austin: University of Texas Press, 1994.

Rodriguez, Ralph. *Brown Gumshoes: Detective Fiction and the Search for Chicana/o Identity*. Austin: University of Texas Press, 2005.

Rojas, Maythee. "Re-membering Josefa: Reading the Mexican Female Body in California Gold Rush Chronicles." *Women's Studies Quarterly* 35 (2007): 126–48.

Rooks, Noliwe, and Bill Gaskins. "Wearing Your Race Wrong: Hair Drama, and a Politics of Representation for African American Women at Play on the Battlefield." *Recovering the Black Female Body: Self-Representations by African American Women*, ed. Muchale Bennett and Vanessa Dickerson. New Brunswick: Rutgers University Press, 2001.

Rosaldo, Renato. "Cultural Citizenship, Inequality, and Multiculturalism." *Latino Cultural Citizenship: Claiming Identity, Space, and Rights*, ed. William V. Flores and Rina Benmayor. Boston: Beacon Press, 1997.

———. *Culture and Truth: The Remaking of Social Analysis*. Boston: Beacon Press, 1993.

Rosales, Francisco A. *Pobre Raza: Violence, Justice, and Mobilization among México Lindo Immigrants, 1900–1936*. Austin: University of Texas Press, 1999.

Ross, Luana. *Inventing the Savage: The Social Construction of Native American Criminality*. Austin: University of Texas Press, 1998.

Ross, Luana, and Andrea Smith. "American Studies without America: Native Feminisms and the Nation-State." *American Quarterly* 60, no. 2 (2008): 309–15.

Royce, Josiah. *California, from the Conquest in 1846 to the Second Vigilance Committee in San Francisco*. Boston: Houghton Mifflin, 1886.

Rueda Esquibel, Catriona. "Velvet Malinche." In *Velvet Barrios: Popular Culture and Chicana/o Sexualities*, ed. Alicia Gaspar de Alba. New York: Palgrave/St. Martins, 2003.

Ruiz, Delberto Dario. "Teki Lenguas del Yolotzin" (cut tongues from the heart). *Decolonial Voices: Chicana and Chicano Cultural Studies in the 21st Century*, ed. Arturo J. Aldama and Naomi Quinonez. Bloomington: Indiana University Press, 2002.

Said, Edward. *Culture of Imperialism*. New York: Vintage Books, 1994.

Saldaña-Portillo, María Josefina. *The Revolutionary Imagination in the Americas and the Age of Development*. Durham: Duke University Press, 2003.

———. "Who's the Indian in Aztlán?" *The Latin American Subaltern Studies Reader*. Durham: Duke University Press, 2001.

Saldívar, José David. *Border Matters: Remapping American Cultural Studies*. Berkeley: University of California Press, 2000.

Saldívar, Ramón. *Chicano Narrative: The Dialectics of Difference*. Madison: University of Wisconsin Press, 1990.

Saldívar-Hull, Sonia. *Feminism on the Border: Chicana Gender Politics and Literature*. Berkeley: University of California Press, 2000.

———. "Feminism on the Border: From Gender Politics to Geopolitics." *Criticism in the Borderlands: Studies in Chicano Literature Culture and Ideology*, ed. Calderón et al. Durham: Duke University Press, 1994.

———. "Woman Hollering Transfronteriza Feminisms." *Cultural Studies* 13, no. 2 (1999): 251–62.

Sánchez, Rosaura. *Telling Identities: The Californio Testimonios*. Minnesota: University of Minnesota Press, 1995.

San Francisco Call. Untitled article. February 25, 1905. SRE Clipping File, LE 2250, Vol. 2.

Scarry, Elaine. *The Body in Pain: The Making and Unmaking of the World*. New York: Oxford University Press, 1985.

Schellie, Donald. *Vast Domain of Blood*. Los Angeles: Westernlore Press, 1968.

Schmidt-Camacho, Alicia. "Cuidadana X: Gender Violence and the Denationalization of Women's Rights in Ciudad Juárez, Mexico." CR: The New Centennial Review 5, no. 1 (spring 2005): 255–92.

Scott, David. Conscripts of Modernity: The Tragedy of Colonial Enlightenment. Durham: Duke University Press, 2004.

Scott, Joan. Gender and the Politics of History. New York: Columbia University Press, 1999.

Seacrest, William. Juanita of Downieville. Fresno, Calif.: Saga-West, 1967.

Segura, Denise. "Chicanas and Triple Oppression in the Labor Force." Chicana Voices: Intersections of Class, Race and Gender. Albuquerque: University of New Mexico Press, 1990.

"Sensible Proceedings." Weekly Arizonan, April 15, 1871.

Shanley, Kathryn W. "The Indian America Loves to Love and Read: American Indian Identity and Cultural Appropriation." Native American Representations: First Encounters, Distorted Images, and Literary Appropriations, ed. Gretchen M. Bataille. Lincoln: University of Nebraska Press, 2001.

Sheridan, Thomas. Los Tucsonenses: The Mexican American Community in Tucson. 1854–1941. Tucson: University of Arizona Press, 1986.

Siebert, Renate. "Women and the Mafia: The Power of Silence and Memory." Gender and Memory, ed. Selma Leydesdorff, Luisa Passerini, and Paul Thompson. New Brunswick: Transaction Publishers, 2005.

Siu, Lok. "Diasporic Cultural Citizenship: Chineseness and Belonging in Central America and Panama." Social Text 19, no. 4 (2001): 7–28.

Smith, Andrea. Conquest: Sexual Violence and American Indian Genocide. Boston: South End Press, 2005.

——. "Not an Indian Tradition: The Sexual Colonization of Native Peoples." Hypatia 18, no. 2 (2003): 70–85.

Smith, Cornelius. William Sanders Oury: History-Maker of the Southwest. Tucson: University of Arizona Press, 1967.

Smith, Sidonie, and Julia Watson. De/colonizing the Subject: The Politics of Gender in Women's Autobiography. Minneapolis: University of Minnesota Press, 1992.

Sneirson, Judd. "Black Rage and the Criminal Law: A Principled Approach to a Polarized Debate." University of Pennsylvania Law Review 143, no. 6. (1995): 2251–88.

Soja, Edward. Postmodern Geographies: The Reassertion of Space in Critical Social Theory. London: Verso, 1989.

Sommer, Doris. Foundational Fictions: The National Romances of Latin America. Berkeley: University of California Press, 1991.

Soto, Sandra. "Seeing Photographs through Borderlands (Dis)order." Latino Studies 5, no. 4 (2007): 418–38.

Spicer, Edward. The Yaquis: A Cultural History. Tucson: University of Arizona Press, 1980.

Spivak, Gayatri Chakravorty. "Can the Subaltern Speak?" Marxism and Interpretation of Culture, ed. Cary Nelson and Lawrence Grossberg. Urbana: University of Illinois Press, 1988.

——. A Critique of Postcolonial Reason: Toward a History of the Vanishing Present. Cambridge: Harvard University Press, 1999.

——. "Subaltern Studies: Deconstructing Historiography." *The Spivak Reader: Selected Works of Gayatri Chakravorty Spivak*, ed. Donna Landry and Gerald MacLean. New York: Routledge, 1996.

The Steamer Pacific Star. "Tremendous Excitement at Downieville—A Man Murdered by a Woman—the Murderess Hung by Populace—Proceedings in the Court of Judge Lynch." July 15, 1851.

Stephanson, Anders. *Manifest Destiny: American Expansionism and the Empire of Right.* New York: Hill and Wang, 1995.

Stevens, Hiram Stanford. Stevens Papers, 1856–1909. MS 0764. Arizona Historical Society.

——. Probate Records for the Estate of Hiram Stevens. Pima County Courts, December 26, 1893.

Stevens, Petra Santa Cruz. Last Will and Testament. December 15, 1909.

Sturken, Marita. *The Vietnam War, the AIDS Epidemic, and the Politics of Remembering.* Berkeley: University of California Press, 1997.

"A Suggestion to the People." *Weekly Arizonan* editorial, January 21, 1871.

Taylor, Diana. *The Archive and the Repertoire: Performing Cultural Memory in the Americas.* Durham: Duke University Press, 2003.

——. "Double Bind: The Torture Case." *Critical Inquiry* (summer 2007): 715–20.

Terdiman, Richard. *Discourse/Counter-Discourse: The Theory and Practice of Symbolic Resistance in Nineteenth-Century France.* Ithaca: Cornell University Press, 1985.

Thompson, Stith. *Motif-Index of Folk-Literature: A Classification of Narrative Elements in Folktales, Ballads, Myths, Fables, Mediaeval Romances, Exempla, Fabliaux, Jest-books, and Local legends.* Bloomington, Indiana University Press [1955–58].

Tinker Salas, Miguel. *In the Shadow of Eagles: Sonora and the Transformation of the Border During the Porfiriato.* Berkeley: University of California Press, 1997.

Tolnay, Stewart Emory, and E. M. Beck. *A Festival of Violence: An Analysis of Southern Lynchings, 1882–1930.* Urbana: University of Illinois Press, 1995.

Trennert, Robert, Jr. "The Southern Pacific Railroad of Mexico." *Pacific Historical Review* 35, no. 3 (August 1966): 265–84.

Troncoso, Francisco P. *Las guerras con las tribus yaqui y mayo.* Mexico City: Instituto Nacional Indigenista, 1977.

Truett, Samuel. *Fugitive Landscapes: The Forgotten History of the U.S.–Mexico Borderlands.* New Haven: Yale University Press, 2006.

Turner, John Kenneth. *Barbarous Mexico.* Chicago: C. H. Kerr, 1911.

Underhill, Ruth. *The Papago Indians of Arizona.* Sherman Pamphlets No. 3. Washington: Education Division of the U.S. Office of Indian Affairs, 1940.

——. *Papago Woman: Case Studies in Anthropology.* New York: Holt, Rinehart and Winston, 1979.

——. *Singing for Power: The Song Magic of the Papago Indians of Southern Arizona.* Berkeley: University of California Press, 1968.

U.S. Congress. Senate. *On the Part of Citizens of the United States and Mexico under the Convention of July 4, 1868, between the United States and Mexico.* Senate Executive Document no. 31, 44th Cong., 2nd sess., 94–95.

United States. Treaties, etc. 1845–1849 (Polk). *Guadalupe Hidalgo, Treaty of Peace, 1848; and the Gads[d]en treaty with Mexico, 1853*. Truchas, N.M.: Tate Gallery, 1967.

United States Bureau of the Census. California, Yuba County, 1850.

United States House of Representatives Executive Document no. 219, March 15, 1888.

Valdez, Luis. "Tale of La Raza." *Bronze* 1, no. 1 (1968): 27.

Vasconcelos, José. *La raza cósmica*. Los Angeles: Centro de Publicaciones, Dept. of Chicano Studies, CSULA, 1979.

Viego, Antonio. *Dead Subjects: Towards a Politics of Loss in Latino Studies*. Durham: Duke University Press, 2007.

Villarreal, José Antonio. *Pocho*. Garden City: Doubleday, 1959.

Wald, Priscilla. *Constituting Americans: Cultural Anxiety and Narrative Form*. Durham: Duke University Press, 1995.

Weber, David J. *The Mexican Frontier, 1821–1846: The American Southwest under Mexico*. Albuquerque: University of New Mexico Press, 1982.

Royal Whitman Papers. Royal Whitman Biofile. Arizona Historical Society.

——. Cargill Papers. MS 0134. Arizona Historical Society.

"Who Is Right Again." *Weekly Arizonan*, March 11, 1871.

Wilcox, Camdus. *History of the Mexican War*. Washington, D.C.: Church News, 1892.

"Woman Hung at Downieville." *Daily Alta California*, July 9, 1851.

Young, Elliott. "Red Men, Princess Pocahontas, and George Washington: Harmonizing Race Relations in Laredo at the Turn of the Century." *Western Historical Quarterly* 29, no. 1 (1998): 48–85.

Zacharias, Usha. "Trial by Fire: Gender, Power and Citizenship in Narratives of the Nation." *Social Text* 19, no. 4 (2001): 29–51.

Arizona–Sonora borderlands (*cont.*)
173, 176, 178 (map), 329–30 n.124; arms
trading in, 189–90, 210–16, 223–24, 231,
247, 255, 264, 278, 329 n.109 and n.116;
Yaqui Indian Wars, 288, 322 n.7, 323 n.25,
328 n.102, 328 n.108
Arnold, Elliot, *The Camp Grant Massacre*,
124–26

Bacasehua, Juan José, confession of, 225–27
Bacatete, Sonora, 21–22, 277, 283, 339 n.127;
Sierra, 237, 276; Tetabiate and, 21, 254, 282
Bacum, Sonora, 206, 217
Bahnzin, Hashké. *See* Eskeminzin, Chief
Bancroft, Hubert Howe, 35, 44, 56; Josefa/
Juanita and, 71, 74–75, 77
Banderas, Juan, 181, 184
Bennett, D. A., 94
Blackhawk, Ned, 8, 25, 26
blackness, 294; Afro-mestizo and, 148–50,
169–70; black rage and, 69–72; blacks
and, 31, 47, 71, 138–40, 149, 151–52, 169,
295, 303 n.37, 304 n.44, 305 n.54, 319
nn.53–54
Blea, Irene, 57
borderlands, 3, 10, 12, 17; Anzaldúa and, 18–
19, 133; of Arizona–Sonora, 87, 116, 173;
capitalist development in, 91–92, 94, 144,
231; Chicana/o studies and, 26, 176;
indigenous identity and culture in, 21,
25, 148; race in, 29, 140; of South Texas,
142, 143, 150; subject formation and, 8, 9,
80; subjectivity and, 78, 185; Texas–
Mexican, 144; U.S.–Mexican, 6, 9, 18, 121,
175–77, 236, 266, 289, 300 n.75; violence
in, 4, 5, 27, 83, 105, 110, 170, 290
Bourke, John C., 109
Brady, Mary Pat, 8, 25, 48, 168, 243
Briesley, Conant B., 118–21
Briggs, Laura, 31
Brooks, James, 25–26, 83, 105, 110, 144, 231,
300 n.75, 319 n.53
Brown, Laura, 260–61
brownness, 66, 72, 78–79, 113, 151, 176, 213,
257, 290–91; brown rage and, 70

Buck, Franklin S., 60
Buitimea, Basilo, 226
Buitimea, Miguel, confession of, 225–26
Burke, Kenneth, 177, 270
Bureau of Indian Affairs (bia), 87, 95, 103,
105, 111, 121, 131, 220, 309 n.5, 311 n.42, 313,
n.94, 318 n.29
Butler, Judith, 140, 156, 165, 224–25, 275

Cajeme, 174, 182–89, 192–95, 207, 278, 323
n.22, 323 n.28, 323n.30, 324 n.32, 324 n.38,
327–28 n.97
Calderón, Felipe, 292
California, 1, 3, 36, 45; annexation of, 297
n.3; citizenship and, 46, 78; colonial, 10;
courts in, 309 n.167; gold rush and, 43,
52, 62; Mexicans in, 304 n.42; Spanish in,
50, 191; statehood of, 35; tourism and
Juanita/Josefa in, 2; women in, 47, 303
n.28
Camp Grant, 81–83, 87–88, 94, 107, 110, 120
Camp Grant Indian massacre (1871), 30, 81,
83–84, 94, 98–99, 103–5, 109–10; Apache
and, 88–89, 92, 100; captives and, 111–16;
economic threat of, 86, 92, 97, 101–2;
gender and, 120–21; interracial alliances
and, 85–86, 131; masculinity and, 128–29;
Papago and, 88, 127, 312 n.69, 312 n.90;
scalping and, 122–24, 146, 315 n.154, 315
n.164; sexual violence at, 116–18, 125–28;
Tucson and, 93; Tucsonenses and, 91; of
women and children, 87, 130; Zinns's
painting of, 107–8, 313 n.102
Cañada del Oro, 82, 107–8
Cananea, Sonora, 215; Copper Company,
211
Cannon, John, 30, 37–38, 53, 57, 69, 72, 73,
79; grave of, 302 n.14; José and, 52, 308
n.149; Josefa/Juanita and, 56; Josefa/
Juanita's body and, 58–60, 63; sensationalism and, 40; stabbing of, 49–50,
70–71, 75; trespass of, 46, 57, 74, 301 n.2
capitalism, 11, 15, 21, 30, 84, 90, 92–94, 97, 98,
101, 107–8, 118, 125, 130, 131, 210, 222, 231,
286, 296; Camp Grant Indian massacre

and, 96–97, 100, 106, 109, 112–13; Chi-
cana/o studies and, 16; Conant and, 207–
8; in *Dreams of the Centaur*, 244; family
and, 86, 229–30; gender and, 13, 243, 279;
Josefa/Juanita and, 30; Mexican modernity and, 237, 249, 268, 273; Mexico and, 31,
91, 97, 131, 147, 198–200, 203, 334 n.33; race
and, 151; racial alliances and, 29, 126;
Saldaña-Portillo on, 16, 91; space and, 144,
244, 285; transnational, 10, 27, 202, 291–93,
295; violence, 29; Yaqui and, 147, 173, 180,
192–95, 203, 206, 208, 237, 285; Yaqui arms
trade and, 215; Yaqui deportation and, 216,
218–19, 228, 232–33
Carbó, General José, 182–83, 186, 188, 190–
92, 195–98, 246, 278, 323 n.22, 326 n.77
Cargill, Andrew, 81, 100, 109, 110, 312 n.69,
312 n.90
Carrillo, Francisco, 103
Carrillo, Leopoldo, 112–14, 314 n.124
Carrillo, Óscar, 214
Castañeda, Antonia, 11, 55–56
Castañeda-García, Carmen, 13
Chabram-Dernersesian, Angie, 14, 17
Chan Santa Cruz, 271
Chato, 188, 324 n.46
Cheng, Anne, 168, 192
Chicana feminism, 8, 18, 42, 137–39, 239,
299 n.55. *See* also Chicana/o studies;
feminism
Chicana/o studies, 10, 13–14, 17–19, 24, 27,
68–69, 84, 135, 136, 148, 334 n.40; Chi-
cana/o and, xi; family romance and, 162;
González and, 31, 170; *indigenismo* and,
67, 104; Josefa/Juanita and, 39, 62; mes-
tizaje and, 85, 319 n.46; nationalism and,
16, 73, 148; resistance and, 26, 39, 40, 72,
138, 170; transnational, 179, 298 n.29. *See*
also Chicana feminism
Child, Lydia Maria, 100
Chinese immigrants: in California, 303
n.34, 303 n.37, 305 n.56; Chinese Exclusion Act (1904) and, 329–30 n.116; foreign miner's tax and, 62, 306 n.99; in
Mexico, 277–78

Chona, María, 103, 124
citizenship, 1–10, 13, 15, 20, 29–32, 42, 70,
130, 177, 288, 291; Camp Grant Indian
massacre and, 81, 84–86, 88, 91–93, 98;
capitalism and, 100, 109, 129, 219; Chinese and, 277, 329–30 n.124; cultural,
164; gender and, 147; Josefa/Juanita and,
44, 47, 74, 75, 79, 80, 304 n.42; of Texas–
Mexicans, 163; of U.S. Mexicanas/os, 78;
Yaqui Indians and, 191, 196, 213, 253
citizen-subject, 7, 29 43, 56, 69, 74, 86, 115,
130, 139, 145, 152, 167, 183, 191, 291
Civil War, 91; economies of, 93, 101; recon-
struction after, 90, 96; slavery and, 148
Coatlicue, 298 n.37; Anzaldúa and, 161
Cócorit, Sonora, 185, 217, 277–78, 339 n.127
Colomé, Francisco, 268
colonial systems: Indians and, 25, 126; over-
lapping of, 8, 29
Colwell-Chanthophonh, Chip, 97
Conant, Carlos, 207–10
Contreras, Alvina Rosenda Elías, 114
Coronil, Fernando, 4–5
Corral, Ramón, 184, 276, 278, 326 n.74, 334
n.41
Cortina, Juan, 144, 319 n.44
Cotera, María, 135–39, 142, 317 n.14
Cotera, Marta, 41–42
Cott, Nancy, 57
counterinsurgency, 4, 21, 195, 210, 228, 335–
36 n.53
Cremony, John C., 128, 313 n.94
Cumuripa, Sonora, 217
Curley, Sherman, 83, 122–23, 314 n.132

DeJong, David, 220, 266
Delay, Brian, 193, 325 n.67
Del Castillo, Adelaida R., 10–11, 13, 333 n.17
De Long, Sidney R., 82, 87–88, 104
Díaz, Porfirio, 21; correspondence of, 20,
185, 187; dictatorship of, 327 n.87; military regime of, 247, 249–51, 321 n.4, 333
n.15, 335 n.33; nation building of, 145–47,
180, 219; railroad and, 322 n.7; Yaqui and,
173–74, 183, 190–92, 195–98, 206–9, 217,

Díaz, Porfirio (*cont.*)
231–32, 237, 244, 323 n.11, 324 n.43, 326
nn.76–77. *See also* Porfiriato
Downie, William, 38, 48, 55–56
Downieville, California, 1–2, 35–46; census
of, 303 n.37; Weller and, 301 n.1; women
in, 47, 58–59
Dreams of the Centaur. See Fontes,
Montserrat, *Dreams of the Centaur*
Dwyer, Long, 206–7, 327 n.94

Elías, Arturo, 200, 329–30 n.124
Elías, Jesús María, 81, 96, 101–2, 104, 114,
131, 201, 312 n.76
Elías, José, 114
Elías, Juan María, 96, 101–4, 312 n.76
Eng, David, 9, 185
Erickson, Kirsten, 177, 182
Eskeminzin, Chief, 82–83, 94, 123, 130, 309
n.5
ethnic studies, 23–24, 28, 39, 289, 304 n.14;
resistance and, 30

family, families, 157, 265; Camp Grant
Indian massacre and, 98–99, 111, 113–14;
Chicana/o, 63–66, 68, 92, 155; destruction of, 83; honor of, 162; of Indians, 115,
222, 228–30, 264; Texas–Mexican, 137;
violence against, 155, 158. *See also* kinship
feminism, 8, 10–14, 31, 69, 136–39; black,
70; Chicana, 17–19, 41–42, 57, 62, 66–68,
135, 148, 164, 239, 244, 298 n.37, 299 n.55,
299 n.61, 318 n.23, 320 n.86, 334 n.30;
methodology of, 24–30, 141, 161, 239,
289–90; Mexican, 295; Native American,
124, 179–80; theory of, 128, 303 n.36; torture and, 250; transnational, 24–30, 79,
292, 296; trauma and, 261; U.S. third
world, 317 n.14; women of color and, 70,
307 n.129
First Military Zone, 182, 187, 195–96, 205,
217, 246, 323 n.22, 323 n.25
Flores Magon, Enrique, 327 n.87
Flores Magon, Ricardo, 327 n.87
Fontes, Monserrat, *Dreams of the Centaur,*

174, 233, 236, 241–42, 244–51, 253–54,
256, 257, 259, 260–63, 270, 279, 280–81,
284, 285, 287, 288; corrido in, 332–33 n.7;
deportation in, 265–66; female masculinity in, 278, 322 n.7, 340 n.131; henequen plantations in, 271–75; literary representation and, 239; masculinity in, 260;
Mazacoba Massacre (1900) and, 176, 276,
278; mestizaje in, 235; racialized violence
in, 255; research for, 332 n.3; sexual violence in, 243, 264; silence and, 282; slavery (Yaqui) in, 337 n.92; solidarity in,
283; subjectivity (radical) in, 238, 240;
torture in, 258, 273; trauma in, 61
Fort Ringgold, 148–50
Foucault, Michel: on discipline and
punishment, 158, 204, 226, 260, 264, 327
n.88; on docile bodies, 173; on torture,
252
Fregoso, Rosa Linda, 63–64

Galerita, Chief Francisco, 102, 104, 130
Gámez-Chávez, Javier, 177
García, General Lorenzo, 190, 196, 208
García-Peña, Angel, 217
Gaspar de Alba, Alicia, 18
gender, 3–4, 6, 13, 19, 43, 44, 53, 85, 117, 118,
120, 129, 245, 278, 290, 305 n.56; analytic
framework for, 12, 28, 31; Camp Grant
Indian massacre and, 85, 99, 102, 111–12,
116, 123, 128; capitalism and, 30; Chi-
cana/o studies and, 24; deportation and,
218, 222–23, 244, 265; female masculinity
and, 176, 279–82, 284, 322 n.7; femicidios
and, 291–92, 295; femininity and, 41, 47,
123, 130, 137, 141, 228, 248, 280, 337 n.78;
genocide and, 18; González and, 135, 139–
40, 152, 156, 164, 169; heteronormativity
and, 68–69, 229, 243; hierarchies of, 29,
78, 118, 137, 142, 282; honor and, 69, 72–
74; inequality of, 12, 18, 79, 138, 167, 170,
317–18 n.22; of Josefa/Juanita, 38, 48, 50–
52, 57, 64, 67, 79; lynching and, 63; masculinist and masculinity and, 10, 15, 38,
55, 66, 74, 102, 104, 117, 125, 128–29, 137,

Indians (*cont.*)

10, 14, 16–20, 23–24, 67, 299 n.61, 319 n.46; as "civilized," 92, 99, 103, 115, 126–27, 146, 182–83, 222; colonial project and, 3–4, 28, 91, 131; Comanche, 3, 25, 28, 109, 138, 318 n.29, 325 n.67; complicity of, in violence, 30, 32, 90, 98, 103, 305 n.72; cultural reproduction of, 115; as economic threat, 52, 90, 92–94, 98, 102, 106, 108, 131; extermination of, 92, 99, 101, 114, 173, 175, 182, 199, 204–5, 257, 322 n.3; government policy for, 20–21, 94, 131, 202, 215; "Indian Question" and, 99–100; Indian Territory and, 143; *indigena* and, xi, 14, 329 n.114; as indigenous, xi, 6, 16–17, 20–21, 23–25, 31, 312 n.76, 324 n.38, 329 n.114, 334 n.30, 340 n.139; *indios bárbaros* and, 88, 100–101, 105, 112, 116, 121, 131–32, 318 n.43; *indios rebeldes* and, 193–94, 339 n.126; *lo indio/the Indian* and, 14, 18, 21, 23, 334 n.30; intraethnic violence and, 124; Karankawa, 28, 147, 318 n.37, 319 n.44; Kickapoo, 28, 319 n.53; Kiowa, 28, 138, 318 n.29, 325 n.67; Maya, 233, 267, 271–72, 338 n.102; mestizaje and, 20; Mexican, xi, 8, 14, 21, 30, 92, 108, 148, 170, 214, 330 n.132; as Native, xii, 17, 126, 281; as non-citizen, 90; North American, xii, 8, 89–90, 130, 140, 170; Plains, 317–18 n.22; raids and, 87, 91, 101–2, 109, 173, 180, 188, 194, 196, 200, 202, 211, 231, 325 n.67; removal of, 117, 122, 173, 218, 221, 240, 242, 250, 266, 286; reproduction and, 115–17, 199, 243; reservations of, 93–94, 174, 189, 214, 216–17, 318 n.29; as savages, 20, 22, 92, 105, 113, 116–18, 126, 129, 179, 181, 183, 188, 195, 216, 230, 313 n.94; scalping and, 122, 315 n.154, 315 n.164; as universal subject, 16. *See also* Apache; Mayo Indians; Papago; Yaqui Indians

Izabál, General Ignacio, 278

Izabál, Rafael, 220, 230, 232, 251, 277–78, 328 n.105, 330 n.127, 332 n.4, 334 n.41

Jackson, Andrew, 21

Jackson, Helen Hunt, 100, 312 n.65

Jacoby, Karl, 83–84, 102, 309 n.5, 310 n.12, 310 n.14, 312 n.76, 314 n.128

Josefa/Juanita: 2–3, 5, 37, 38, 42–47, 53, 55, 56, 62–79, 169, 239, 244, 297 n.6, 301 n.3, 304 n.44, 305 n.56; body of, 9, 54, 58; Cannon and, 30, 57–58, 245; Chicana/o nationalism and, 80; Chicana/o studies and, 10, 39–40; citizenship and, 80; gendered labor and, 58; in kangaroo court, 48–49; Loiza and, 50–51, 59, 304 n.42, 305 n.72, 309 n.167; lynching of, 6, 10, 48, 52, 61, 290, 297 n.8, 302 n.14; naming of, 40–41, 303 n.29, 305 n.72; prostitution and, 56–60; race and, 38, 50, 61, 303 n.34; rape and, 52, 58; representational violence and, 39, 303 n.38; womanhood and, 54, 61

Kanzanjian, David, 9, 29, 185

Kaup, Monika, 18

kinship, 98; Camp Grant Indian massacre and, 98, 115; of captives, 25, 110–14; Chicana/o, 66; Papago, 102, 104, 301 n.85, 311 n.57; violence and, 83, 296; Yaqui, 221, 279. *See also* family, families

Klor de Alva, J. Jorge, 12–13

Knowles (John Cannon's mining partner), 49–48

Kristeva, Julia, 9, 150, 152, 163, 298 n.26, 319 n.57, 321 n.95

Latina/o studies, 12, 15, 30, 174; Latina/o and, xi

La Llorona, 67, 163–64, 307 n.119, 318 n.23

Logan, Walter S., 192–93, 207–8, 325 n.59

Loiza, José María, 37–38, 50, 53, 306 n.99, 308 n.152; Cannon and, 52, 79, 308 n.149; guilt of, 51; Josefa/Juanita and, 58–59, 70, 76, 303 n.29; masculinity and, 74; racialization and, 61; testimony of, 49, 60; U.S. and Mexico Claims Commission and, 42, 52, 58, 304 n.42, 305 n.72, 309 n.167

Lomnitz, Claudio, 22–23, 330 n.132

López, José María, 223

loss, 8–9, 32, 156, 191, 289; in Chicana/o

national imaginaries (*cont.*)
289; erasure and, 162; Mexican, 23, 29,
140; Texas–Mexican, 30, 140, 147, 150,
156, 169–70; U.S., 29, 136, 138–40, 238,
291; Yaqui, 181, 237
nationalism, 4, 5–6, 9, 18, 19, 22, 24, 27, 29,
32, 69, 73, 78, 174, 235, 236, 239, 284, 289–
90, 296; black, 68; Chicana/o, 8–10, 16,
23, 42, 43, 67, 73, 80, 130, 132, 138, 146, 148,
288, 307 n.116; Mexican, xii, 181, 196, 235;
neo-, 20, 334 n.30; revolutionary, 15;
Texas–Mexican, 139, 147, 169; U.S.
(Anglo), 8, 43, 169, 181, 287, 304 n.48;
Yaqui, 280, 322 n.2
nation-state formation, 6, 27; Camp Grant
Indian massacre and, 81, 90, 99, 106,
130–31; citizenship and, 92; González
and, 164; Josefa/Juanita and, 39; mestizaje and, 236; in Mexico, 146, 205;
Texas–Mexican, 140; transnationalism
and, 28; violence and, 31, 125
Nava, Gregory, 63–64
Navojoa, 197
Nickerson, Tomas, 180
North American Free Trade Agreement
(NAFTA), 291–93

Obama, Barack, 292–94
Older, Cora, 41, 47, 60, 76–77, 301 n.2, 302
n.8, 302 n.10, 302 n.14, 303 n.6, 303 n.34,
305 n.56, 306 n.92
Opata Indians, 181, 184, 213, 301 n.86
Opodope, 282
Ord, E. O. C., 95
Ortiz, Carlos, 196–99, 233, 326 n.76, 339
n.127
Ortiz Peace Treaty (1897), 254–55, 335 n.51
Otero, General José, 187
Oury, William S., 81, 88, 90, 91, 98, 101–4,
118, 122, 131

Padilla Ramos, Raquel, 177, 267, 270, 332
n.175, 334 n.41, 337 n.92, 337 n.95
pain, 6–7, 40, 64, 70, 77–78, 87–88, 111, 121,
141, 153–55, 170, 175–77, 203–4, 236–37,

239–40, 246, 248, 252, 258–59, 262–64,
270, 273–75, 287, 291, 303 n.36; Yaqui
body in, 204, 207, 238, 241, 288
Papago (San Xavier and Pan Tak), 83, 85,
92, 102–3, 104, 118, 122–24, 127; arms and
ammunition of, 215, 312 n.69, Camp
Grant Indian massacre and, 30, 82, 98,
311 n.57, 312 n.90; capitalist relations of,
90, 96–97, 107; as captives, 117; as "civilized," 121; gender and, 118, 126–30; as
historical subjects, 104, 126, 130, 132;
interracial alliances of, 85–86, 88–89;
intraethnic violence and, 105, 107, 315
n.164; as legal subjects, 312 n.90; revenge
of, on Apache, 86, 91, 105, 127, 312 n.81;
scalping and, 146, 315 n.154, 315 n.164;
sexual violence and, 126; Tohono
O'odham and, 84, 86, 301 n.85, 310 n.9
Parker, Chief Quanah, 146
Payne, Leigh, 8, 122, 181, 327 n.91
people of color, 6; lynching and, 297 n.8;
political racism and, 138, 306 n.99, 309
n.5; rage and, 72; solidarity of, 151;
trauma and, 261; violence and, 26, 140,
175, 295
Pérez, Emma, 25, 244, 300 n.75, 321 n.2, 333
n.12
Pérez, Luis, 252–53, 259, 334–35 n.42
Pérez-Torres, Rafael, 17
Pierce Barstow, David, 44, 54, 57, 61, 71, 302
n.10, 307 n.107, 308 n.152
Pima Indians, 95, 98, 102, 181, 184, 213, 311
n.57, 330 n.124
Pitahya, Sonora, 189
Pitt, Leonard, 56–57, 306 n.79
Pochote, Sonora, 189
Porfiriato, 31, 147, 173–75, 179, 183, 186, 188,
217, 257, 262, 271, 286, 288, 321 n.4, 327
n.87
Potam, Sonora, 189, 217, 277–78, 339 n.127
Puar, Jasbir, 250

race, 24, 26, 65, 95, 105, 251; analytic framework for, 12, 31; Aztec as, 22, 145; Cajeme
and, 186; Camp Grant Indian massacre

and, 85, 90, 123, 126; criminality and, 55, 244; discourse of, 15; economic relations and, 30, 130, 297 n.3; feminism and, 136, 307 n.129; gender and, 140, 150–51, 169–70, 196, 246, 304 n.44; González and, 137, 139–40, 146, 148, 317 n.14; hegemony and, 10, 61; hierarchies of, 29, 137, 141–42, 152, 190, 226, 282, 319 n.54; Josefa/Juanita and, 38, 41, 45, 60–61, 63, 70, 74–75, 304 n.44; masculinity and, 150, 198; nation and, 29; pathology and, 267, 270; power and, 41, 79, 85; racism and, 215, 292, 295, 319 n.54; sexuality and, 246; social construction of, 6, 17, 213; subjectivity and, 28; transnational, 292, 294; transnational feminism and, 28, 136; Vasconcelos and, 148; violence and, 35, 47, 140, 174, 253, 275; Yaqui Indians and, 186–87, 204, 215, 244–45, 267, 270, 282. *See also* blackness; brownness; whiteness

racialization, 6, 258; abjection and, 152, 156, 162, 170; Apache and, 121; body and, 43, 85; citizenship and, 47; difference and, 123, 295; economic relations and, 84, 99, 132, 237; femininity and, 41, 47, 246; gender and, 55; González and, 31; Indianness and, 255; justice and, 54; masculinity and, 125, 141, 148, 226, 257; passing and, 212, 214, 222; as pathology, 270, 292; policing of, 29; positioning and, 3–4; of punishment, 259; representation and, 30; of savagery, 118; of sexuality, 57–58, 61, 67; Spanish and, 46, 50; of *subalternos*, 175; subjectivity and, 176, 247, 288; subjects and, 8, 28, 38, 40, 78–79, 174; transnational, 32, victims and, 26; of violence, 2–3, 7, 29, 124, 130, 133, 140, 170, 173, 249

rage, 69; criminality of, 71–72; gendered, 35, 40, 46, 53, 73, 245–46, 307 n.129; of Josefa/Juanita, 37, 51, 56; lynching and, 61, 63, 75, 79; racialized, 30, 70–71, 76, 142, 275, 307 n.129

railroads, 180; construction of, 91, 93, 174; in Mexico, 180, 267, 311 n.63, 322 n.7; segregation on, 304 n.44; Sonora Railway,

202; Southern Pacific Railroad, 94; Tucson and, 131, 310 n.32, 316 n.183; Yaqui and, 210, 285

rape: at Camp Grant Indian massacre, 118–26, 128, 130; of Josefa/Juanita, 52, 55, 58, 63–65, 301–2 n.3, 307 n.107; representation of, 7; Yaqui and, 228, 242–48, 250, 264, 284

Rayón, Sonora, 220, 328 n.106

reservation, reservations, 189; Apache, 95, 114; Camp Grant reservation, 94; containment on, 174, 318 n.29; extermination vs., 93; public support for, 94; removal to, 143, 148; San Carlos Apache Reservation, 83, 188; Yaqui and, 214, 216–17

resistance, 24, 80, 258; assimilation vs., 39, 289, 296; Camp Grant Indian massacre and, 85, 108, 120; Chicana feminism and, 67, 136–37; Chicana/o nationalism and, 63–66, 139; Chicana/o studies and, 10, 17–18, 20, 23, 92, 132, 135, 301 n.78; to erasure of indigenous people, 147–48; ethnic studies and, 30; González and, 135, 138, 144, 170; Josefa/Juanita and, 69, 72, 78, 303 n.38; narrative of, 3–4, 26, 39; victimization and, 26, 40, 69, 307 n.110; violence and, 260, 262; of Yaqui, 23, 197, 204, 207, 209–10, 214, 251, 253, 256, 265, 270, 278

Reyes, General Bernardo, 21–22, 278

Río Yaqui. *See* Yaqui River Valley

Rivera, Javier, 224

Roach, Joseph, 5, 187

Rojas, Maythee, 62, 67–69, 307 n.118

Romero, Matias, 180, 190, 192, 207, 209, 322 n.7, 323 n.11, 324 n.47, 325 n.59

Ruiz, Pablo. *See* Opodepe

Safford, A. K. P., 90, 112, 312 n.69

Saldaña-Portillo, María Josefina, 14–16, 25, 91, 284, 319 n.46

Saldívar-Hull, Sonia, 17, 167

San Carlos Apache Reservation. *See* reservation, reservations

Sánchez, Rosaura, 11–12
Santa Cruz de Hughes, Atanacia, 98–100, 104, 311 n.59, 311 n.65
Scarry, Elaine: nation and, 184; pain and, 6, 87, 121, 254; radical subjectivity and, 88, 240; representation and, 126; torture and, 177
Schellie, Don, *Vast Domain of Blood*, 99, 126
Schmidt-Camacho, Alicia, 125
Scott, David, 68, 300 n.63
Seacrest, William, and Josefa/Juanita, 41, 47, 56, 59, 62, 301 n.2, 301–2 n.3, 302 n.10, 305 n.56
sensationalism, 39, 40, 201; lynching as, 67; seduction as, 60; silence and, 63; violence as, 49; yellow journalism and, 270
sexuality, 6, 30, 44, 86, 118, 243–44; analytic framework for, 26, 28; capitalist relations and, 132; defense of, 248, 251; genocide and, 18; heterosexual, 160, 279; Josefa/Juanita and, 40, 43, 53, 55–61, 65, 67, 71; lynching and, 77–78; masculinity and, 129; nation building and, 290, 292; patriarchy and, 248; politics of reproduction and, 115–17, 199; queer, 279; sexual agency and, 125, 128; sexual desire and, 59, 166–67, 247, 264; sexual difference and, 4, 42, 121; sexual excess and, 250; sexual identities and, 3; sexualized bodies and, 43; sexual violation and violence and, 2, 6, 7, 24, 28–30, 32, 38, 40, 55, 85, 87, 116, 119–22, 124–28, 130, 173, 227, 237–38, 242, 246, 249, 250, 264, 286–87, 295, 307 n.107, 315 n164; social death, 139, 170; space and, 168; subjects, 3, 7–8, 29, 175; Texas–Mexican, 152–53, 169; women and womanhood and, 29, 128, 130
slavery, 111; African, 40, 139, 148, 150–51, 294, 319 n.52, 319 n.53; of Apache, 83, 110, 123, 127; Indian slave trade and, 113; social death and, 170; of Yaqui, 202, 233, 237, 243, 262, 267, 271, 275, 332 n.175, 337 n.92
Smith, Andrea, 124, 126, 179–80, 298 n.19
Smith, Cornelius, 118, 122, 124
Smith, Lola Oury, 101

Smith, Sidonie, 100
Sneirson, Judd, 71–72
solidarity: economic alliances and, 175; indigenous movements and, 16, 283–85; lack of recognition and, 151; violence and, 32, 61
Sonora–Arizona borderlands. *See* Arizona–Sonora borderlands
Soto, Sandra, 229–30
southern Arizona. *See* Arizona
space, 48, 87, 144, 168; body and, 47; capitalist, 92–93, 98, 100–101, 106, 112, 118, 125, 147, 180, 193, 208, 219, 233, 291; of death, 140, 151; gendered, 99, 160, 278–81; memory, 54, 145, 259, 316 n.2; modern, 130–31; physical, 145, 242; private, 99, 168; production of, 133, 135; psychic, 169; public, 70, 99, 168, 246, 253; regulation of, 48; representation of, 28; sacred, 259; subjectivity and, 8; time and, 251
Spanish America: Spanish American War and, 150, 335 n.53; women in, 43, 72–74, 308 n.144
Spears, William, 48
Spicer, Edward, 177, 270
Spivak, Gayatri Chakravorty, 28, 66, 237–38, 301 n.82, 303 n.38
Stevens, Hiram Stanford, 90–91, 94, 98
Stoneman, George, 90, 96
Suaqui, Sonora, 227
subaltern, 175, 238, 249; history of, 235; production of, 15, 260, 301 n.78, 321–22 n.5; rebellion and, 190, 192; speaking, 182, 243; *subalterno* and, 175, 190
subject, 9, 26–28, 29–30, 38, 42, 43, 78, 79, 115, 145, 224, 237, 288; abjection and, 163; Althusser on, 238; borderlands and, 80; Butler on, 225; citizen-subjects and, 7–8, 56, 69, 74, 86, 130, 139, 142, 152, 167, 183, 291; Chicana/o, 10, 18–19, 24, 62–63, 320 n.86, 334 n.30; death and, 77, 151, 168; in *Dew on the Thorn*, 151–57, 161–62, 317 n.14; differentiation and, 3; dissident and, 161, 183, 189, 191, 244, 247, 259, 287; in *Dreams of the Centaur*, 261–62, 273,

Tucsonenses (*cont.*)
and, 90; Indians and, 99, 116, 118; railroad and, 310 n.32, 316 n.183; violence and, 85
Tully, Ochoa, and DeLong Freighting Company, 90, 106–8
Turner, Kenneth, 202, 332 n.175

Underhill, Ruth, 103–4, 312 n.86, 315 n.154, n.164
United States v. Sidney R. De Long, 103–4, 119
unspeakable, the, 2, 5, 6, 29, 71, 81, 121, 235, 238, 249, 287; Apache body and, 127; body and, 7; *Dreams of the Centaur* and, 176; González and, 153, 165; history and, 4, 79, 125, 209; Josefa/Juanita and, 1, 51, 53, 79; national imaginary and, 8, 165, 205, 289, 296; rape and, 120, 125; resistance and, 18, 23; subject formation and, 32, 151; violence and, 4, 32, 295–96, 332 n.163; Yaqui Indian Wars and, 185, 187, 205, 223–24, 236–37
Urés, Sonora, 204, 213
U.S. exceptionalism, 202, 250
utterance, 2–3, 5–6, 9, 16, 39, 51, 53, 57, 60, 74, 77–79, 155, 258, 307 n.110

Valle Carrero, 222
Vasconcelos, José, xii; Anzaldúa and, 19, 319 n.45; González and, 146, 148; *la raza cósmica* and, 19, 146–47
violence: abjection and, 9–10, 152; acts of, 6, 24, 32, 38, 70–73, 194; aftereffects of, 9; body and, 45, 57, 60–61, 78–79, 85, 124, 141, 161, 186, 202, 239, 248, 258, 285, 287, 303 n.36; in borderlands, 4, 5, 6, 10, 121, 140, 170, 231, 241; citizenship and, 2, 7, 29, 32, 45, 47, 54, 79, 92; colonialism and, 17, 24, 29, 315 n.164; complicity and, 88, 294; cultural politics of, 8, 26, 201; denial and, 4–5, 19, 182–83, 288; discursive, 8, 10, 29, 31, 39, 51, 135, 169, 223, 251, 286, 294; empire and, 25, 144, 257; epistemic, 10, 25–27, 29, 43, 62, 66, 79, 85, 132, 135, 176,

301 n.82; euphemization of, 40, 60–61, 111–12; excessive, 87, 98, 105, 120, 124, 127, 157, 181, 199, 229, 231, 241, 253, 289–90; forgetting and, 8, 19, 27, 29, 124, 144, 203, 205, 241, 286; gendered, 7, 28, 48, 102, 116, 118, 123–25, 129, 133, 174, 177, 228, 237, 285, 290; genocide and, 18, 32, 97, 175, 204, 236, 239, 285, 286; histories of, 5, 16, 23, 29, 33, 66, 83, 97, 104, 124, 127–28, 139, 170, 176, 202, 210, 241, 242, 265, 286, 289, 292; impunity and, 32, 295; interracial, 24, 84; intrafamilial, 155; intraracial, 24, 84, 88, 124, 185; material, 5, 43; memory and, 8, 155, 239; mourning and, 7, 229, 296; narratives of, 2, 5, 174; nationalism and, 8, 16, 18, 20, 23, 27, 78, 125, 286, 290; national imaginaries (national histories) and, 2, 4, 5, 8, 23, 125, 127, 135, 174, 202, 228, 241, 286, 291, 296; nation-state formation and, 186–87, 202, 276; pain and, 6, 87, 141, 155; physical, 6, 8–10, 26, 27, 28, 32, 47, 53, 55, 58, 79, 86, 87, 88–89, 93, 125, 127–28, 152, 154, 158, 175, 185, 194, 223, 238, 253, 259, 287; power and, 85, 105, 125, 155, 179, 196, 224, 240, 251, 275–76; process of differentiation and, 3, 9, 45, 61, 92, 141, 294, 295, 327 n.81; psychic, 8, 10, 26, 28, 76–77, 152, 154, 158, 238, 240, 243, 262; quotidian, 2, 127, 186, 195, 237, 239, 270; racialized, 2, 3, 7, 26, 28–29, 38, 79, 130, 133, 140, 173, 177, 202, 237, 246, 248–49, 286, 290; radical subjectivity and, 244, 253; "real," 7; representation and, 5, 7–8; resistance and, 24, 26, 92, 301 n.78; retaliation and, 25–26, 68, 83, 89, 104, 116, 188, 230–31, 250, 310 n.14; ritualized, 87, 176, 224, 271; seduction and, 39–40, 54, 56–57, 60, 69, 112, 289–90, 302 n.14; sensationalism of, 78, 246, 249, 283; sexual, 24, 30, 38, 53, 86, 87, 116, 118, 122, 124–28, 238, 244, 246, 249, 250, 264, 307 n.107; sexualized, 2, 3, 28, 38, 54, 119, 121, 132, 248, 250; silence and, 4, 39, 51, 79, 174–75, 227, 289, 337 n.78; as social practice, 5, 6, 8–9, 25, 39, 61, 63, 66, 78, 127,

135, 175, 186, 243, 270 289; as social transformation, 3; state-sanctioned, 31, 78, 83,
86, 92, 97, 98, 121–22, 127, 173–76, 179–83,
196–201, 205, 224, 228, 229, 235–40, 260,
265, 286, 288, 290, 292, 309 n.167, 323
n.16, 327 n.91, 330 n.124, 337 n.84; structural, 173, 295; subject formation and, 38,
41, 63, 79, 170, 240–41, 248, 288; subjectivity and, 5, 7, 102, 139, 175, 238, 244, 251,
253, 276; symbolic meaning of, 121; systematic, 3, 29, 61, 67, 99, 244; technologies of, 224, 256, 263, 290; torture as,
156, 235, 238, 249, 253, 287; trauma and, 7,
155, 237, 296 n.19; unspeakable, 4–5, 7, 18,
29–30, 79, 125, 153, 185, 205, 235, 332 n.163;
war and, 99, 181, 183, 184, 210, 238, 246,
248; vigilante, 20, 61, 77; witness to, 155,
246; Yaqui and, 174, 194–96, 212, 231–32,
235–38, 248
La Virgen de Guadalupe, 67, 146, 307 n.119

Wald, Priscilla, 70
Watson, Julia, 100
Weller, John B., 37, 54, 301 n.1, 305 n.60
Wells, John. *See* Weller, John B.
whiteness, 46, 56; Americanness and, 150–
51; Indians and, 99, 213, 262; Irish, 61;
masculinity and, 279, 282; mestizaje and,
xii; Mexicans and, 45, 84, 116, 219, 254;
rage and, 69–70, 72; Vasconcelos and,
148; womanhood and, 40, 47–48, 55, 66,
128, 304 n.44, 311 n.65; Yori and, 245–46,
251, 254–55, 259, 265, 279–80, 282–83, 337
n.84. *See* Anglo Americans
Whitman, Royal, 82–83, 94, 110, 118–20,
124–25
womanhood: Mexicana, 54, 61, 161–62, 307
n.119; Victorian, 44–45, 47, 128; western,
118, 160; white, 128, 304 n.44

Yaqui Indians: citizenship and, 31, 177, 191,
213, 233, 253, 288; confessions and, 174,
223–28, 251, 256; criminality and, 181,
223, 264; cultural genocide of, 216, 218,
264, 327 n.81; cultural practices of, 181,

187, 191, 218, 240, 247, 265, 279–80, 283,
287; families of, 176, 189, 199, 209, 219–
22, 227–30, 240, 262–65, 279, 283, 285,
326 n.71, 328 n.99, 330–31 n.134, 331 n.146,
331 n.160; gender and, 174, 187, 204, 218–
27, 237–38, 243–46, 248, 257, 265, 278–83,
330–31 n.134, 333 n.13; genocide and, 31,
147, 173, 175, 177, 180, 183, 199–200, 209,
214, 216, 235–37, 239, 241, 245, 247, 261–
62, 278–79, 285, 287–88, 327 n.83; as
industrious, 200; interrogations of, 227–
28; modernity and, 31, 173–76, 179–80,
182–83, 186, 198–99, 204–5, 212, 222, 232,
235–39, 249, 266, 268, 272–73, 286, 288;
pain and, 176, 185, 203–4, 207, 236–38,
240–41, 246, 248, 250, 252, 258–59, 262–
64, 270, 273–75, 285, 287–88; race and,
186–87, 198, 204, 213, 215, 244–46, 251,
253, 261–62, 267, 270; radical subjectivity
and, 230, 240, 244, 248, 253; as "savages"
and *barbaros*, 179, 181, 183; self-making
and, 288; social disorder and, 173, 181;
social pathology and, 31, 238, 245–46,
266–70, 337 n.84; surnames of, 223; violence and, 186; U.S. media and, 192
Yaqui Indian Wars (1880–1910), 21, 323 n.25;
arms of, 189–90, 210–16, 223–24, 231,
247, 255, 264, 278, 329 n.109, n.116;
cabecillos and, 186, 227, 253; deportation
and, 31, 174–75, 187, 200, 203, 209–19,
221–24, 226, 228, 230–33, 237–42, 244,
256–57, 265–70, 272, 283, 285–86, 327
n.88, 329 n.109, 331 n.160, 333 n.13, 334
n.41, 335 n.44, 337 n.92; historical
amnesia and, 287; labor force and, 179,
219, 233, 267; lynching and, 175, 201–7,
228, 230, 240, 286, 290; masculinity and,
179, 191, 197, 226, 228, 253, 257, 278–80;
Mazacoba Massacre (1900) and, 176,
210–11, 217, 237, 264, 276–78, 281–83, 285,
288; Mexican military, 179, 184–86, 189,
191, 200, 206, 209, 247, 249, 251, 253, 257,
260, 262, 270, 279, 280, 323 n.25, 326 n.77,
333 n.14; pain and, 240; rebellion and,
180–81, 186–96, 202, 204, 206–7, 208,

Nicole M. Guidotti-Hernández is associate professor of
gender and women's studies at the University of Arizona.

Library of Congress Cataloging-in-Publication Data
Guidotti-Hernández, Nicole Marie.
Unspeakable violence : remapping U.S. and Mexican
national imaginaries / Nicole M. Guidotti-Hernández.
p. cm. — (Latin America otherwise : languages, empires,
nations)
Includes bibliographical references and index.
ISBN 978-0-8223-5057-6 (cloth : alk. paper)
ISBN 978-0-8223-5075-0 (pbk. : alk. paper)
1. Violence—Mexican-American Border Region—
History—19th century. 2. Violence—Mexican-
American Border Region—History—20th century. 3.
Nationalism—United States. 4. Nationalism—Mexico. 5.
Mexican Americans—Ethnic identity. I. Title. II. Series:
Latin America otherwise.
HN79.A165G85 2011
305.89′68720730721—dc23   2011021951